Report of the Irish Boundary Commission
1925

Report of the
Irish Boundary Commission
1925

Introduction by
Geoffrey J. Hand

IRISH UNIVERSITY PRESS
Shannon · Ireland

327.41
I 68r

MN

Introduction © 1969
Geoffrey J. Hand

The list of items in the Class-list Cabinet 61 and the text of the Report
of the Irish Boundary Commission (Ref. Cab. 61/161) are reproduced
from Crown copyright records in the Public Record Office, London,
by permission of the Controller of Her Britannic Majesty's Stationery
Office.

SBN 7165 0997 0

Irish University Press Shannon Ireland
DUBLIN CORK BELFAST LONDON NEW YORK
T M MacGlinchey Publisher

FILMSET AND PRINTED IN THE REPUBLIC OF IRELAND
BY ROBERT HOGG, PRINTER TO THE IRISH UNIVERSITY PRESS SHANNON

CONTENTS

INTRODUCTION

The introductory remarks which follow are not intended to be a general survey of the history of the Boundary Commission. A study of the Commission's history in greater detail is forthcoming and readers who may find the argument and documentation of this Introduction thin are referred to it.[1] Attention is here concentrated on the following topics:

    1   The Origins and Political Background of the Commission

    2   The Commissioners

    3   The Problem of Interpretation

    4   The Procedure of the Commission

    5   The Failure of the Commission

1   THE ORIGINS AND POLITICAL BACKGROUND OF THE COMMISSION

An Irish Boundary Commission was an obvious device to be used in connection with any scheme for solving the Irish problem by partition of the island. The idea was aired when the last Home Rule Bill was under discussion in the British House of Commons in 1912[2] and the Cabinet toyed with the idea in preparing the actual 'Partition Act'—the Government of

---

   1 G. J. Hand, 'Eoin MacNeill and the Boundary Commission', in *The Scholar Revolutionary: Eoin MacNeill, 1867–1945, and the Making of the New Ireland*, ed. F. X. Martin and F. J. Byrne (Irish University Press: forthcoming). I should wish once more to thank Dr. and Mrs. Michael Tierney for the freedom of access which I enjoyed to the MacNeill Papers; and my thanks are again due to those whose kind help is acknowledged in Appendix I to that paper. Appendix II to 'Eoin MacNeill and the Boundary Commission' contains relevant extracts from the unpublished 'Memoirs' of Eóin MacNeill. The sources and authorities for the subject are discussed ibid., Appendix I. The best account hitherto in print has been that of D. Gwynn, *The History of Partition* (Dublin 1950); mention may also be made of W. Alison Phillips, *The Revolution in Ireland, 1906–1923* (2nd ed., London 1926) and (for the Ulster Unionist standpoint) St. John Ervine, *Craigavon: Ulsterman* (London 1949). In his edition of Thomas Jones, *Whitehall Diary; I: 1916–1925* (London 1969), R. K. Middlemas indicates the substantial material which is to be included in vol. iii of the Jones diaries.

   2 39 H.C. Deb. ser. 5, col. 809 (Dr. W. A. Chapple: 11 June 1912).

Ireland Act, 1920.[3] Nothing came of it, however, and the existing county boundaries of the six counties were instead followed. Boundary commissions were very much in the international air after the Treaty of Versailles and it is not surprising that such a commission should have been suggested in the negotiations leading to the Anglo-Irish Treaty of 1921. The problem of interpretation to which the relevant clause, Article XII, gave rise is discussed in a separate section of this Introduction. Here it may be noted that the Commission was to consist of a chairman appointed by the British government and two other members, appointed respectively by the governments of the Irish Free State and of Northern Ireland.

Events greatly delayed the implementation of the Article. In the Irish Free State there was the Civil War of 1922 and the task of reconstruction. In Britain—a point which has tended to be ignored by Irish commentators—there was a period of exceptional political instability, with the collapse of the Lloyd George coalition and the uneasy three-party system which followed. Neither in Dublin nor in London, therefore, was there at first much opportunity to press ahead. The government of Northern Ireland refused to concede that it was bound by the Article to which it had not expressly been a party. Before 1922 was out, however, the Free State government established an agency, the North-East Boundary Bureau, to deal with the problem in general.[4] The Dublin government had three forces to contend with at home. As the months and years went by the defeated Republican party naturally seized on the boundary question, even though the matter had not been to the fore in the initial division of opinion in the Irish Dáil.[5] The constitutional opposition formed by the Labour Party often joined the Republicans in criticism of apparent inactivity on the issue. And there was of course great strength of feeling, both among the government's supporters and its opponents, reflecting the anger of the Catholic areas adjacent to the existing six-county boundary at continued exclusion from the Free State. In July 1923 the Free State government firmly put the onus of further

3   P.R.O., London, Cab. 23/18, no. 16 of 1919.
4   The most valuable source for the history of the North-East Boundary Bureau is the E. M. Stephens papers, Boxes V–VII, now in the Library of Trinity College, Dublin (Stephens was the Secretary of the Bureau). They include the Final Report to the I.F.S. Government, 26 Feb. 1926 (Box VI, file 7) and an Index to Dates (Box VII, file 1). There is also substantial material in the MacNeill papers, though there is considerable duplication between these collections.
5   The celebrated 'Document No. 2' did not provide an alternative formula for the Boundary Commission, and the issue was little mentioned in the 'Treaty Debates'.

action on the British government by appointing its commissioner, Eóin MacNeill.

On its part, the London government was nervous of further Irish troubles and puzzled as to how to handle the firmly unco-operative attitude of Sir James Craig and his ministers in Belfast. After various fruitless conferences and negotiations, the British government, then led by Ramsay MacDonald, formally requested the government of Northern Ireland to appoint a commissioner; a formal refusal was sent in reply on 10 May 1924.[6] For an interlude, much of the problem of the Commission was passed from the politicians to the lawyers. Could the British government act instead of that of Northern Ireland? The question, and other legal matters, went to the Judicial Committee of the Privy Council, which reported at the end of July that the royal prerogative did not extend to such an appointment in the circumstances and that some new arrangement was necessary.[7] Both in Dublin and in London ministers feared the fall of their governments on the issue.[8] A supplemental agreement was reached between Britain and the Irish Free State, however. Legislation was brought in to empower the British government to appoint the third member of the Commission (as well as the chairman, whom in fact Britain had already appointed) and, after its enactment by both parliaments, the appointment was made in October. The Boundary Commission met for the first time on 6 November 1924.[9] A summary of the immediate political background to it might be: intransigence on the part of Northern Ireland; eagerness to secure the Catholic areas of the six counties, coupled with nervousness at any threat to internal security, on the part of the Irish Free State; and timidity at the thought of further involvement in Ireland on the part of British politicians, especially those in the minority Labour government of 1924. These factors had contributed to the delay of almost three years between the Treaty and the first meeting of the Commission.

6 Many of the formal exchanges are collected in *Correspondence between the Government of the Irish Free State and His Majesty's Government relating to Article 12 of the Treaty . . . from 19th July, 1923, to 17th June, 1924* (Dublin, Stationery Office, 1924). But there is important unpublished material in the Cabinet and Home Office Papers in the P.R.O., London (references in article cited in note 1, above). Cf. Jones, *Whitehall Diary*, ed. Middlemas, i, 277–9.

7 Cmd. 2214 (1924).

8 For the mutual confiding of fears by Cosgrave and MacDonald, see P.R.O., London, Cab. 23/48, no. 46 of 1924.

9 The Minute-Book of the Commission is now in P.R.O., London, Cab. 61/1. A list of the items in the class Cab. 61 follows this Introduction.

Undoubtedly, both in theory and in fact, the most important member of the Irish Boundary Commission was its chairman, Mr. Justice Richard Feetham, a judge of the Supreme Court of the then Union of South Africa. He had not been the British government's first choice. They had sought the services of a better-known figure, Sir Robert Borden, a former Prime Minister of Canada; but the Irish Free State, at least, should have been relieved that Borden refused in the light of the fact that his reason for refusing was that he would not proceed without the co-operation of Northern Ireland.[10] Feetham was an Englishman, born in 1874, and had been one of the group associated with 'Milner's kindergarten' and especially with Lionel Curtis. His earlier career, his contribution to the Boundary Commission and its *Report*[11] and his later opposition to the apartheid régime in South Africa (he died as recently as 1965) suggest a conscientious lawyer with a keen analytical mind, courageous in standing for Christian and liberal ideas. He could, however, leave on those who knew him—and respected him—the impression of a somewhat humourless and unimaginative man.[12] An obituarist wrote of 'his extraordinary industry and conscientiousness',[13] and no one who has seriously studied his approach to the Irish Boundary Commission is likely to question that tribute.

Yet Mr. Justice Feetham was criticized with great vigour, not to say venom, in Ireland when the broad lines of his Award became known, and a generation later he was still reviled.[14] In the present writer's view, no evidence has yet been brought forward (not that it is likely to be) which throws doubt on his integrity of conduct. The reasons for the onslaught on his reputation lay chiefly in the feeling that his interpretation of the terms of reference was responsible for the (to the Irish Free State) disappointing outcome of the Commission. There are in fact criticisms that can be made with some plausibility, but they are more subtle than a crude defamation of his character. Feetham's approach to his extremely difficult task was marked by a legalism and remoteness from political realities, perhaps the other side of his conscientious precision. That the Commission had no power to carry out a plebiscite, for example,

10   Material on the negotiations with Borden is to be found in P.R.O., London, H.O. 45/12296, files 12, 18.
11   Cf. especially pp. 32–68, below.
12   Private information.
13   *The Times*, 8 Nov. 1965, p. 12, col. 4.
14   So in F. Gallagher, *The Indivisible Island* (London 1957), pp. 175–6.

was a conclusion hardly open to question; that the absence of a provision to confer such a power implied, not only an absence of any intention to make use of a plebiscite, but also a rejection of 'verdicts of bare majorities', was a refinement of argument far removed from the hectic negotiation of the 'peace by ordeal'.[15] A man like Borden—politician as well as lawyer—might have, marginally at any rate, brought a greater width of approach. Feetham did his job most conscientiously; it is just possible that he was not the right kind of man for it.

The same doubt exists with regard to his colleague, the member of the Commission nominated by the Irish Free State, Eóin MacNeill. This is not the place in which to assess that remarkable 'scholar revolutionary'.[16] His obvious merits and qualifications for the task were great. But his post as Minister for Education at Dublin made it difficult for him to afford all the time for the Commission that might have been desirable and may in part explain the somewhat passive role he played— the pace was set by Feetham. And unfortunately his weak points in the conduct of the Commission—a certain dilatoriness in administrative affairs, for example—coincided with Feetham's points of strength.

Feetham and MacNeill had more in common than their integrity. The course of the Commission was to prove damaging to both—perhaps tragic, indeed, would be a better word in MacNeill's case. The public career of both had reached an apex: curiously enough, the remaining distinctions of both were in the academic world—MacNeill's do not need itemization, while Feetham was a notable Chancellor of the University of the Witwatersrand. Their colleague, J. R. Fisher, appointed by the British government as representative of Northern Ireland, was much their senior, born in 1855, and his career was obviously behind him. He was a staunch Ulster Unionist who had been for many years editor of the *Northern Whig*. He is a shadowy figure in the story of the Commission, and yet he may have been more important than appears at first sight. One thing is unquestionably clear, and it is not to his credit. At their very first meeting the Commissioners, very properly, decided on strict secrecy.[17] It was not an obligation that Fisher

15 Cf. Feetham's memorandum on interpretation, p. 59, below. *Peace by Ordeal* is the title of the classical study of the negotiation of the Anglo-Irish Treaty of 1921 (by Frank Pakenham, now Earl of Longford: London 1935).

16 The volume with that title cited in note 1, above, is a collection of studies of MacNeill's life and achievement.

17 P.R.O., London, Cab. 61/1, meeting of 6 Nov. 1924.

respected.[18] This must naturally make him, in the light of his journalistic connections, the main suspect in any investigation into the 'leak' which set in motion the events leading to the crisis of the Commission's failure.

3 THE PROBLEM OF INTERPRETATION

The greatest problem which faced the members of the Commission, that which provoked the heaviest pressures upon them and the sharpest reactions to their suspected conclusions, was the problem of interpretation. The only words available to them for guidance were those of Article XII:

> . . . shall determine in accordance with the wishes of the inhabitants, so far as may be compatible with economic and geographic conditions, the boundaries between Northern Ireland and the rest of Ireland . . .

As Feetham stressed, these brief phrases were in sharp contrast to the elaborate language of comparable clauses in the Treaty of Versailles.[19] The Article, as a high legal authority put it within less than six months of the conclusion of the Treaty, was 'full of grave and dangerous ambiguity'.[20] A phrase of Feetham's during one of the hearings of counsel representing the Irish Free State, 'it was something preparatory', probably goes near to the historical truth.[21] But the preparations were never followed by a more detailed document and so Feetham, without formal dissent on MacNeill's part but without his support, produced his own elaboration of the clause by legal interpretation. Historians have differed as to whether, granted that Feetham's interpretation was correct, the words of the Article had been deliberately so framed to deceive the Irish delegation in 1921 or whether the full legal implications were not realized by either side.[22] It is beyond argument, however, that the Irish delegation thought the Article would give very substantial

18 Fisher's letters to Mrs. (later Lady) Reid on the course of the Commission have been extensively quoted by St. John Ervine, *Craigavon*, pp. 498–500. It is fair to say that the present writer knows of no hard evidence to show how much further the information in them may have gone.

19 *Report*, p. 48.

20 Lord Buckmaster: 49 H.L. Deb. ser. 2, col. 757 (22 Mar. 1922).

21 Appendix 1, p. 25.

22 The former view seems to have been Lord Longford's in *Peace by Ordeal*, pp. 386–7; the latter is that of A. J. P. Taylor, in a very brief but valuable note, *English History, 1914–1945* (Oxford 1965), p. 162. Cf. Jones, *Whitehall Diary*, ed. Middlemas, i, 176, which accords better with the latter view.

areas of Northern Ireland to the Free State and that Conservative spokesmen, in particular, in Britain soon began to press a restrictive interpretation.[23]

It was a commonplace of Free State criticism of Feetham that he had been swayed by the pressure for a restrictive interpretation.[24] Readers of his elaborate discussion of the interpretation problem must decide for themselves. One reader must, however, go on record as saying that he has found the evidence for Feetham's independence of mind and legal acumen too overwhelming to make this criticism plausible.[25] But there is a much more refined criticism, based on the view that Feetham was too narrowly a common lawyer accustomed to the restricted principles of interpretation of instruments that have tended to prevail in English law and excessively conservative in his approach to an international document. In this respect, the arguments of Serjeant (later Mr. Justice) Hanna for the Irish Free State deserve to be read as a preliminary to Feetham's own writing.[26]

A short introduction cannot hope to survey the wealth of meaning Feetham drew from the maddeningly few words he was left by the Treaty-makers. Instead, some brief comments follow on some of his answers to the particular questions he discussed in chapter three of the *Report*.[27]

(2) (*b*) Does the Article enable the Commission . . . to shift the existing boundary in either direction . . . ?

Both Northern Ireland and the Irish Free State had advanced

23   Every book that has dealt with the Boundary Commission in any detail has assembled materials on these points: e.g., W. A. Phillips, *Revolution in Ireland* (2nd ed.), pp. 326–30; Gallagher, *The Indivisible Island*, pp. 155–65; Gwynn, *History of Partition*, pp. 212–18.

24   One of the most important attacks on these lines came from Cosgrave himself on 22 Nov. 1925: *The Times*, 23 Nov. 1925, p. 13.

25   In March 1924, however, an agent of the North-East Boundary Bureau reported at second-hand that Lionel Curtis, whose influence over Feetham was unquestionably great, held views that in certain respects foreshadow Feetham's interpretation of his terms of reference: MacNeill Papers, Boundary, 5/22. There is no point in pursuing the question of this evidence (which has some difficulties) here, as this has been done in the paper mentioned in note 1, above. But certainly there is a possibility that informal discussions with Curtis may have shaped Feetham's views to some extent.

26   Appendix 1, pp. 13–22. Unfortunately, a memorandum by Hanna on the international law question is not in print (MacNeill Papers, Boundary, 3/6). In the present writer's view, Hanna was the ablest of the counsel retained by the Irish Free State; it is curious that he was an Ulster Presbyterian. The 'high legal authority' mentioned in the explanatory note to the Chairman's Memorandum on Article XII (*Report*, p. 32) has not been identified with absolute certainty, but was very possibly Hugh Kennedy, Chief Justice of the Irish Free State: the point is discussed in detail in the paper mentioned in note 1, above.

27   *Report*, pp. 26–32, with which should be taken relevant material in the Chairman's Memorandum, pp. 32–68.

arguments to confine transfers to a single direction. The argument of Northern Ireland was lacking in legal force, though there was something to be said in favour of the Free State view.[28] But there was not really a very great deal to be said for it, and the Free State in practice accepted the idea of a two-way transfer and was prepared to make administrative plans to cope with its implementation.[29]

(2) (c) Can the Commission make changes in the existing boundary which involve the transfer of large areas and populations to one side or the other, or is its scope restricted to the making of minor modifications in the existing boundary?

Feetham insisted that the terms of the Article made it necessary that Northern Ireland should remain as 'the same provincial entity' and that there was consequently a scale of changes which could not be recommended.[30] Logically, this is not a wholly satisfactory answer to the question he himself put; it may be that in the form of this question, if not elsewhere, he showed the effect of the prolonged public argument between wide and restrictive interpretations—between 're-drawing' and 'adjustment'. At the same time, Feetham rejected the view that the scope of the Commission was limited to 'a mere correction of irregularities'.[31]

(3) What is the relation between the three different factors . . .
—wishes of inhabitants and economic and geographic conditions?

In practice, this was the most vital of all the questions. It was on the answer to it, for example, that the hopes of the Free State for Newry and South Down were wrecked, for, as the *Report* put it, the factors were there 'definitely in conflict'.[32] Again, readers of the *Report* have to consider for themselves the wording 'so far as may be compatible with'. The writer believes that Feetham was broadly right in his view and that, as Feetham put it in his decisive meeting with Cosgrave, Craig, Baldwin

28   The Northern Ireland argument was based on the Colonial Boundaries Act 1895 and the Government of Ireland Act 1920, but, all other considerations apart, the applicability of the Colonial Boundaries Act was extremely questionable (cf. the comments on the Colonial Laws Validity Act 1865, which is of some analogous importance, in H. Calvert, *Constitutional Law in Northern Ireland* [London and Belfast 1968], p. 160). The I.F.S. argument was based on the general tenor of the Treaty.

29   The story of the civil service negotiations in the late summer and early autumn of 1925 is told at some length in the paper cited in note 1, above, and there are extensive materials in the MacNeill Papers and in P.R.O., London, H.O. 45/12296. But the matter is worthy of a short study on its own.

30   *Report*, p. 29, and cf. especially p. 49.

31   *Report*, p. 29.

32   *Report*, pp. 135–7.

and Churchill, 'Article 12 has not been expressed so as to bear the interpretation put on it by the Free State.'[33]

(4) and (5) What qualifications entitle persons to rank as "inhabitants" . . . and by what procedure are the wishes of inhabitants to be ascertained? . . .

. . . Is unanimity to be required, or is a bare majority one way or the other to be sufficient?

Feetham's answers to these questions do arouse misgivings. His stress on 'permanent' inhabitants seems to have had underlying it a class distinction.[34] While his rejection of the plebiscite, in the absence of any steps by the governments concerned to make one possible, may have been fully justified,[35] his rejection of decision by bare majority is another matter. Combined with his view—in itself plausible—that the onus of proof rested on those demanding changes in the boundary, it operated against the Free State. It can be argued that this is perhaps, legally and logically, the weakest point in the whole scheme of interpretation.

(6) On what principle should units of area be chosen or defined for the purpose of ascertaining the wishes of inhabitants?

'Wishes of the inhabitants' is the language of democracy, not of nationalism, and on democratic principles it was surely right of Feetham to take the smallest possible units of area. Criticisms based on ideas of national or community identity are criticisms that go straight to the terms of reference, not to Feetham's interpretation of them.

One matter of great importance was scarcely in the contemplation of any of the parties to the Treaty of 1921—the prolonged delay before the Boundary Commission began its deliberations. The Commission took the view—it seems that it may have been MacNeill's as well as Feetham's,[36] and one may take for granted it was Fisher's—that they must take things as they found them and not endeavour to go back to 1921. The practical difficulties of finding out in 1925 what

33   The record of this conference is in P.R.O., London, Cab. 61/1, Annex A to Minutes, 5 Dec. 1925, and in Cab. 24/176, no. 503; brief notes by the Commission's secretary are in Cab. 61/16. It is interesting that the idea of economic factors being decisive in marginal situations was imported into the award in the Turco-Armenian arbitration of 1920: cited in A. O. Cukwurah. *The Settlement of Boundary Disputes in International Law* (Manchester 1967), p. 166.

34   *Report*, pp. 52–3, 58–9, 60–1. It is curious that on this point Feetham cited an authority *in extenso*—Dicey's *Conflict of Laws*—yet the relevance and force of the references are not as clear as one might wish.

35   There was an illuminating discussion with counsel on the plebiscite matter: Appendix 1, pp. 22–4.

36   I suggest this on the, admittedly flimsy, basis of MacNeill's interventions in the argument of counsel: Appendix 1, pp. 28, 30. But I may well be wrong.

would have been the wishes of the inhabitants in 1921 were obvious, and counsel for the Irish Free State had a difficult brief in combining argument for a plebiscite with argument for reference to the situation in 1921.[37] On the other hand, the Commission ended by using census figures for 1911 so that where the wishes of the inhabitants were concerned the argument about the relevant date was somewhat unreal. But where economic conditions were in question the view taken was of considerable importance, especially with regard to the development of waterworks in South Down.[38]

There is a measure of disproportion about any study of the meaning of the Article when it is placed beside the short phrases of the original. One may put a last question. If the opportunity for a detailed study of the Article had been presented to Feetham before, rather than after, he had accepted the chairmanship, would he (or any other prudent lawyer) ever have undertaken the task?

4 THE PROCEDURE OF THE COMMISSION

In chapters one and two of the *Report* the procedure followed by the Boundary Commission is set out in considerable detail. Three elements may be found in the manner by which the Commissioners reached their conclusions. The figures of the religious census of 1911 were accepted by them as the fundamental guide to the wishes of the inhabitants, on the traditional equations of Protestant=Unionist and Catholic=Nationalist. Their own study of the question was aided by a permanent staff in the Commission's offices in Clements Inn. (It is to be remembered that Feetham and Fisher were full-time, unlike MacNeill, and that the Irish Free State did not contribute anyone to the Staff of the Commission.[39]) Lastly, there were the representations of interested parties—public bodies, *ad hoc* committees and individuals. The Belfast government at first attempted to obstruct the taking of evidence in Ireland itself, but their attempts were defeated and the Commission held both

37 Appendix 1, pp. 26–7, 30–1: the Attorney-General (later Mr. Justice O'Byrne) was plainly having an awkward time.

38 *Report*, p. 133; cf. the discussion in Appendix 2, pp. 55–65. The waterworks development had caused concern in Dublin from an early stage.

39 The British government paid salaries to Feeham and Fisher, while the running expenses were shared: P.R.O., London, H.O. 45/12296, files 55, 59, 60, 61, 103, 107, 108. The failure to secure Irish representation on the staff is one of the minor mysteries of the Commission's history.

an informal preliminary tour and a series of formal sittings for the taking of evidence.[40]

Inevitably, the representations made to the Commission (other, perhaps, than those of a few public-spirited individuals) tended to have been carefully concerted. On the Free State side, the North-East Boundary Bureau sent its secretary, E. M. Stephens (not himself a Roman Catholic), north to organize meetings and the preparation of evidence.[41] The present writer has not had access to comparable information concerning the Unionist side, but it may be assumed that broadly similar preliminary work was done. The *Report* is of course silent on these aspects, and in any event it may be suspected that the role of the various rival local submissions was in securing the feeling and impression of justice being done, rather than in greatly swaying the minds of the Commissioners. At the end of its labours the Commission had certain items removed from the evidence received; for the convenience of those interested the list of documents surviving in the present Public Record Office class has been appended to this Introduction.

5   THE FAILURE OF THE COMMISSION

In the early autumn of 1925 the Commission appeared to be approaching the presentation of its Award. The shape of the new boundary was decided upon in a series of meetings from 13 to 17 October. The staff were able to get down to the final stages of their technical work, which was estimated to take six weeks.[42] It would seem, however, that Feetham and Fisher had not fully understood the serious misgivings in MacNeill's mind and assumed that they were more truly unanimous than was in fact the case. The secrets of the decisions taken seem at first to have been well kept. The British cabinet was concerned at the problems of implementation of the *Report* but had apparently an impression that it was likely to be much more unfavourable to Northern Ireland than was in fact the case. Contrary to the advice of their civil service advisers and to the trend of thought of the Prime Minister, Baldwin, and his adviser, Thomas Jones, the Home Secretary and the Dominions

---

40   For the attempted obstruction, P.R.O., London, H.O. 45/12296, file 55A; a semi-official diary of the preliminary tour survives in the MacNeill Papers, though not in the P.R.O.

41   MacNeill Papers, Boundary, 5/23, is a file of reports from Stephens.

42   *Report*, p. 14.

Secretary, both of them imperialists on the right wing (Joynson-Hicks and Amery), pressed for prior consultation with Belfast.[43] A conference with Free State ministers on 29 October showed that the Dublin government was also in the dark; both cabinets were concerned at the dilemma—to force through implementation the moment the Award was published, with the administrative chaos that would temporarily follow, or to secure a breathing-space, which very possibly would allow the forces of violence to gather on both sides.[44]

On 5 November the Commissioners approved a first draft of the actual terms of the Award and agreed to call the Governments into consultation.[45] On 7 November the ultra-Tory *Morning Post* published a substantially accurate 'forecast' accompanied by a map.[46] This 'unfortunate and unaccountable mischance', this 'premature and unauthorised publication', by making MacNeill's position 'impossible' was to destroy the work of the Commission.[47]

Who was responsible for the *Morning Post* 'leak'? Was it deliberately calculated and, if so, what was the object? Perhaps, as the years go by and tongues are loosened and desks unlocked, these questions will be confidently answered. As things stand, only suspicions can be offered. If only on the principle of economy of hypothesis, it is reasonable to put Fisher's name at the head of the suspects, for it is known that the obligations of secrecy did not weigh too heavily upon him.[48] But there is always the possibility that someone of lesser rank than Commissioner was indiscreet. Whether Fisher or someone else was guilty, it is not easy to set up a plausible motive, though whatever it was it can be assumed to have been related to the interests of Northern Ireland (or, possibly, so far as those interests were distinct, those of the right wing of the British Conservative Party)—the choice of the *Morning Post* is evidence to point to that. In the present state of our knowledge, the best guess may be that Fisher talked too much to Tory journalist contacts,

43 P.R.O., London, Cab. 24/175, no. 445; Cab. 23/51, no. 51 of 1925; Jones, *Whitehall Diary*, ed. Middlemas, i, 330–1.

44 P.R.O., London, Cab. 24/175, nos. 467, 470.

45 *Report*, p. 14.

46 *Morning Post*, 7 Nov. 1925, p. 13; cf. *Truth*, 18 Nov. 1925, p. 929. The *Morning Post* map is printed at p. xix of the present volume, to allow readers to compare it with the authorized map of the Award.

47 These phrases are from a letter drafted for Baldwin to send to General Hertzog, the South African Prime Minister, in January 1926: P.R.O., London, H.O. 45/12296, file 106.

48 Note 18, above. Other circumstantial points are discussed in the paper mentioned in note 1, above.

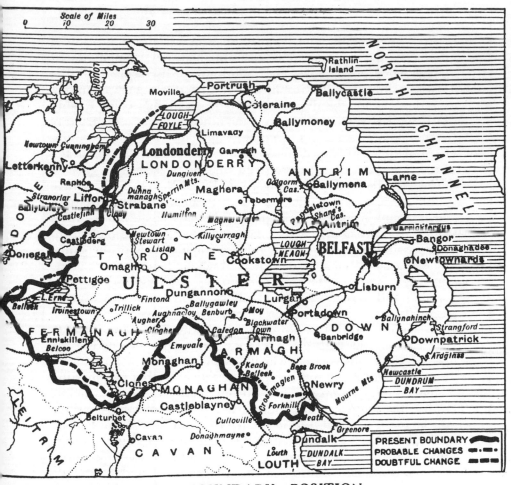

THE BOUNDARY POSITION

The Boundary Position. Map printed in the *Morning Post*, 7 November 1925.

who, deeper calculations apart, knew a good story when they got one.[49]

At all events, the question whether an advance indication of the terms of the Award was desirable had now been answered in the worst possible way by unauthorized disclosure (and it is just possible that the resolution of that dilemma was among the motives for the disclosure). If the news had come freshly to Craig his reaction may well have been relief, and certainly at this stage Craig and his ministers appear to have been willing to implement an Award on some such lines.[50] But opinion in the Free State was quite unprepared for an Award which gave so little and even took something away. By 16 November Cosgrave could write to MacNeill, 'As far as I can learn the movement against any portion of our territory being transferred is growing.'[51] Emphasis in the Free State, in fact, was being put on the possibility of loss, rather than the inadequacy of the gains. The quasi-judicial attitude which MacNeill had taken throughout the history of the Commission was coming under severe strain, and circumstantial evidence suggests that Cosgrave strongly urged him to resign from the Commission.

Resignation, however, presented no way out in law. In 1924 the British and Irish governments had been concerned at the capacity for obstruction which a commissioner acceptable to Belfast might have, and Feetham had insisted that the question whether the Commission should operate by majority principle or by unanimity should be submitted to the Judicial Committee of the Privy Council.[52] In its advice the Judicial Committee had affirmed what has been called the Rule in *Grindley* v. *Barker*, that in such arbitrations on matters of public concern majority rule prevails and that, once the Commission had been duly constituted, the resignation of one member would not invalidate decision by the other two.[53] But, whatever about the

49 It would be fascinating if even it could be known whether the map in the *Morning Post* was composed from the verbal information received or followed a sketch-map 'leaked'.

50 P.R.O., London, Cab. 23/51, no. 52 of 1925; H.O. 45/12296, file 88 (Tallents to Markbreiter, 17 Nov. 1925).

51 MacNeill Papers, Boundary, 3/8, no. 19 (Cosgrave to MacNeill, 16 Nov. 1925). A useful study of public opinion as manifested in the newspapers has been carried out as a B.A. dissertation (U.C.D., 1969) by Mr. J. E. Maddock, 'The Political Storm of the Boundary Commission, with particular reference to public reaction to it, in the period November-December, 1925'. At p. 19 he cites the *Irish Independent* (18 Nov.): 'Not since Partition was introduced has feeling run so high.'

52 P.R.O., London, Cab. 24/167, no. 398.

53 On the law of the matter, see G. J. Hand, 'The Development of the Common Law Principle of Majority Rule in the "Arbitration" of Matters of Public Concern', in 4 *Irish Jurist* (n.s., 1969), pp. 74-90.

law, the political reality was that the resignation of one member of the Commission would make the Award unenforceable. On 20 November MacNeill attended a meeting of the Commission at Clements Inn and immediately after the minutes announced his resignation.[54]

There followed a fortnight of frantic negotiation between the three governments. The result was the agreement reached on 3 December by which the boundary remained unchanged and certain financial and other adjustments were made, largely in favour of the Irish Free State. The story of these events has been told more than once[55] and in the present context it seems preferable to say something of the strange twilight of the Commission's existence after MacNeill's resignation. Feetham and Fisher continued to meet almost daily and acted as an independent force, for Feetham stuck to the strictly legal position that they had authority from the governments that could not be revoked. The chairman's determination to proceed as if nothing had happened was acutely embarrassing to the British government, which alone was now in effective contact with him. Thus, when Feetham arranged a preliminary inspection of the new map on 26 November, the decision was taken by the British cabinet not to send representatives unless the Irish Free State also did so.[56] One product of Feetham's attitude which has survived is in fact the *Report* in its present form, which was hastily produced in vindication of the Award.[57] While Feetham was ignoring political realities in an almost comical way, his conduct showed a determination which it is difficult not to admire, as well, perhaps, as an anger with which it is difficult not to sympathize. Before the governments could conclude their agreement they had to be confident that Feetham's independent line would not wreck it.

The last scene in the history of the Irish Boundary Commission took place at the House of Commons on 3 December 1925.[58] Baldwin, Churchill, Cosgrave and Craig met Feetham

54 *Report*, p. 152. The circumstances in which MacNeill came to his decision are extensively discussed in the paper mentioned in note 1, above.

55 The fullest account is perhaps that in Ervine, *Craigavon*, pp. 500–8; cf. D. O'Sullivan, *The Irish Free State and its Senate* (London 1940), pp. 178–81. It may be necessary to repeat the correction slip in Ervine to the legend that Feetham came down to Chequers and was kept in isolation from the rest of those in attendance (cf. K. Middlemas and J. Barnes, *Baldwin* [London 1969], p. 364). So far as the story has worth, it relates to F. B. Bourdillon, the Commission's secretary (and now the last surviving actor).

56 P.R.O., London, Cab. 23/51, no. 54 of 1925.

57 *Report*, p. 153.

58 The final form of the record of this conference is in P.R.O., London, Cab. 61/1, Annex A to Minutes, 5 Dec. 1925, and in Cab. 24/176, no. 503. But the informal notes taken by Bourdillon should be consulted also: Cab. 61/16.

and Fisher in an endeavour to secure the suppression of the *Report*. Feetham attempted to obtain a justification of the Commission's approach through publication of the chapter on interpretation, but finally Churchill found an acceptable compromise—that Feetham should send Baldwin a public letter explaining the principles on which he had acted.[59] On those terms, he agreed to withdraw publication. Twenty copies of the *Report* were run off and remained in obscurity until the generous policy of the British government towards historical research opened the text to the public on 1 January 1968.[60]

The present edition has been reproduced from Crown copyright records in the Public Record Office, London (Ref. Cab.61/161), by permission of the Controller of Her Britannic Majesty's Stationery Office. The original bears at some points signs of the haste with which it was prepared and printed. Careful readers may detect slight errors: e.g., p. 114, line 18, 'follow' for 'follows'. In Appendix 4, p. 63, line 37, the rendering of the Attorney-General's remarks is obviously corrupt.

59 Feetham's request for publication of the chapter on interpretation is not mentioned in the final record (prepared by the Cabinet Office) but was noted by Bourdillon. His letter to Baldwin was duly published in *The Times*, 18 Dec. 1925, p. 19.
60 Three copies of the general matter, omitting the Award, were run off as souvenirs for Feetham, Fisher and Bourdillon: P.R.O., London, Cab. 61/1, minutes, 9 Dec. 1925.

LIST OF DOCUMENTS RELATING
TO THE
IRISH BOUNDARY COMMISSION
1924-1925

ITEMS IN THE CLASS-LIST CABINET 61,
PUBLIC RECORD OFFICE, LONDON[1]

This class consists of the minutes, papers, correspondence and Report of the Irish Boundary Commission and records of oral and written evidences submitted to the Commission.

Pieces 19–158 include (in some cases) printed material such as press cuttings, copies of old Acts and local or commercial publications either of a general nature or peculiar to the authority giving evidence. Where this occurs the date on which the material was exhibited, rather than the date of publication, has been indicated.

---

1   This transcript of Crown copyright records in the Public Record Office appears by permission of the Controller of H. M. Stationery Office.

Microfilms of the Class Cab. 61 have been made available in the National Library of Ireland (references: P.6509–6532). Closely related material from the Home Office papers (H.O. 45/12296) is similarly available (P.6532–6534).

Reference Cab. 61	Date	Description
I	1924 Nov.— 1925 Dec.	Minute Book (*see also* Cab. 61/163)

MAPS

2 [MPI 378]	—	Tracings showing the boundary line to be fixed between the Irish Free State and Northern Ireland as detailed in the 24th Minute of the Commission
3 [MPI 379]	—	Further tracings containing figures showing religious complexion of townlands
4 [MPI 380]	—	Map of North East Ireland showing religious majority in district electoral divisions according to 1911 Census figures
5 [MPI 381]	—	Map of Northern Ireland showing religious majority in district electoral divisions according to particulars submitted to the Commission concerning electoral registers 1924/1925

MAJOR BOGER'S NOTES AND MEMORANDA*

6	1925 Sept. 9	Schemes relating to Armagh and Newry, Castlederg, Londonderry and East Donegal, South-East and West Fermanagh
7	1925 Sept. 9	Procedure
8	1925 Sept. 9	Geographic and economic considerations
9	1925 Sept. 9	Precedents for boundary settlements on waterways
10	1925 Oct. 13	Modifications to previous schemes [*see* Cab. 61/6 above]
11	1925 Oct. 14	Report on maps inspected in Dublin and inspection of the ground in the neighbourhood of Belleek
12	1925 Nov. 4	Suggestions relating to the line described at the meeting of 17 October 1925
13	1925 Sept. 9	Secretary's memoranda on Bessbrook, Fermanagh, Keady and Newtown Hamilton, Londonderry and Strabane, Lough Erne, Newtown Butler and Newry
14	1925 Oct. 14	Statistical notes on prepared schemes
15	1925 Dec. 11	Extracts from published statistics showing the religious persuasions of the inhabitants of the townlands in certain electoral divisions of Counties Armagh, Cavan, Donegal, Down, Fermanagh, Londonderry and Monaghan

*R. A. Boger, R.E., Chief Technical Assistant to the Commission.

Submissions, Evidences and Exhibits—*contd.*

Reference	Date	Description	File No.
Cab. 61			
33	1925 April 29	Burke H. S., Chairman, Lough-erne Drainage Board	R.F.128
34	1925 Dec. 17	Cagney J.B.	R.G.79
35	1924 Dec. 30—1925 Feb. 24	Camlough Waterworks Trustees	R.N.23B
36	1925 April 23—June 12	Castlederg, Protestant Churches	R.T.133
37	1925 Feb. 28—June 12	Castlederg Rural District Council	R.T.131
38	1925 Feb. 5—May 28	Clarke, Trevisa	R.D.10
39	1924 Dec. 20—1925 May 4	Clogh Parish, Unionist inhabitants	R.F.63
40	1925 Mar. 14—June 23	Clogher Rural District Council	R.T.140
41	1925 Mar. 9	Clogher Rural District, Nationalist inhabitants	R.T.111
42	1924 Dec. 22—1925 May 6	Clones Urban District Council	R.F.40
43	1924 Dec. 26—1925 Feb. 11	Cooke, D.	R.F.56
44	1925 June 6—June 22	Cookstown Union, Unionist inhabitants	R.F.118
45	1924 Dec. 10—1925 Sept. 17	Copeland Trimble, W.	R.F.11
46	1924 Dec. 3—1925 April 25	Coyle, Rev. E. (*see also* Cab. 61/67)	R.F.3
47	1925 Feb. 27	Devine J. (*see also* Cab. 61/145)	R.D.55
48	1924 Dec. 29—1925 Feb. 14	Dickson J.	R.D.61
49	1924 Dec. 30	Donaldson R. J. (*see also* Cab. 61/125)	
50	1924 Dec. 15—1925 May 29	Donegal County, group of business men	R.D.2
51	1924 Dec. 3—1925 June 12	Donegal County, Protestant Registration Association	R.D.6 (Vol.1)
[52]	WANTING	Donegal County, Protestant Registration Association	R.D.6 (Vol.2)

Submissions, Evidences and Exhibits—*contd.*

Reference	Date	Description	File No.
Cab. 61			
53	1925 May 25— May 28	Donegal County, Protestant Registration Association	R.D.6 (Vol.3)
54	1924 Dec. 29— 1925 Mar. 10	Doris, John	R.T.57
55	1924 Dec. 24— 1925 Mar. 18	Down, East; Committee of Nationalist inhabitants	R.N.65
56	1925 Jan. 17— May 4	Drummully Parish, Unionist inhabitants	R.F.101
57	1924 Dec. 18	Dundalk Chamber of Commerce	R.N.73
58	1925 Mar. 13— Mar. 20	Dungannon Board of Guardians (*see also* Cab. 61/60)	R.T.139
59	1925 Mar. 20	Dungannon Union, inhabitants (*see also* Cab. 61/60, 164 and 165)	R.T.137
60	1925 Mar. 18— June 24	Dungannon Urban District Council	R.T.136
61	1924 Dec. 27— 1925 April 30	Elliott E. and Ross C. W.	R.F.60
62	1924 Dec. 15	Enniskillen Urban District Council	R.F.100
63	1925 June 12	Fearn Townland	R.T.134
64	1924 Dec. 20— 1925 May 18	Fermanagh County Council	R.F.29 (Vol.1)
65	1925 April 27— May 15	Fermanagh County Council	R.F.29 (Vol.2)
66	1925 April 27— April 30	Fermanagh County Council	R.F.29 (Vol.3)
67	1924 Dec. 29— 1925 July 2	Fermanagh Nationalist Committee	R.F.36 (Vol. 1)
68	1925 April 22— April 24	Fermanagh Nationalist Committee	R.F.36 (Vol.2)
69	Undated	Fleming R. J. (*see also* Cab. 61/51)	R.D.95
70	1924 Dec. 29— 1925 May 8	Glasslough and adjoining District, group of inhabitants	R.A.59
71	1925 April 3— May 6	Glasslough and District, Nationalist inhabitants	R.A.115
72	1925 Feb. 27— Mar. 5	Granemore Area, group of inhabitants	R.A.33A

Submissions, Evidences and Exhibits—*contd.*

Reference	Date	Description	File No.
Cab. 61			
73	1925 June 11 — June 30	Green H. D.	R.T.113
74	1924 Dec. 23 — 1925 Feb. 11	Henry J. M.	R.A.50
75	1924 Dec. 17	Herdmans Ltd.	R.D.83
76	1925 June 11 — June 19	Irish Free State Customs Service	R.G.117
77	1925 July 2	Irish Free State, Government	R.G.1
78	1924 Dec. 8 — 1925 Dec. 30	Irish Society, The Hon.	R.D.91
79	1925 June 13 — July 1	Irvine, Colonel H., C.B.	R.D.142
80	1925 Jan. 13 — May 2	Judge, J. M.	R.F.99
81	1924 Dec. 15 — 1925 Mar. 23	Keady, Committee of inhabitants of the Town End	R.A.33B
82	1924 Dec. 15 — 1925 Feb. 25	Keady Urban District Council	R.A.71
83	1924 Dec. 21	Kennedy, C. J.	R.G.28
84	1925 Feb. 15 — Mar. 18	Killoo Parish, Nationalist inhabitants	R.N.106
85	1924 Dec. 22 — 1925 Mar. 18	Kilkeel Board of Guardians	R.N.20
86	1924 Dec. 22 — 1925 Mar. 17	Kilkeel Rural District Council (*see also* Cab. 61/85)	R.N.19
87	1925 June 2 — June 15	King, W. Ashe (Portal Supervisor, Londonderry)	R.D.123
88	1925 May 26 — June 22	Large, T. J. D. (Collector of Customs, Belfast)	R.G.124
89	1924 Dec. 2	Larkin, W. J.	R.G.94
90	1924 Dec. 23 — July 28	Liddy, G. B.	R.G.51
91	1925 Mar. 16 — June 2	Londonderry City Corporation	R.D.112
92	1924 Dec. 30 — 1925 May 27	Londonderry, members of Shirt Manufacturers Federation (Ireland)	R.D.27
93	1924 Dec. 29 — 1925 Nov. 14	Londonderry Nationalist Registration Association	R.D.34 (Vol.1)

Reference	Date	Description	File No.
Cab. 61			
94	1925 May 14— May 20	Londonderry Nationalist Registration Association	R.D.34 (Vol.2)
95	1922 Nov. 4— 1925 May 20	Londonderry Nationalist Registration Association	R.D.34 (Vol.3)
96	1925 Jan. 28— Sept. 28	Londonderry Port and Harbour Commissioners *see also* King, W. Ashe	R.D.109
97	1925 Jan. 14— May 19	Londonderry Union, Nationalist inhabitants	R.D.34A
		Lougherne Drainage Board *see* Burke H. S.	
98	1924 Dec. 29	Lynch M (*see also* Cab. 61/145)	R.T.77
99	1924 Dec. 11	McArthur J (*see also* Cab. 61/51)	R.D.87
100	1925 June 3— June 7	McCarter W.	R.D.122
101	1924 Dec. 23	MacDermott, Rev. J.	R.G.49
102	1924 Dec. 27— 1925 Feb. 5	McGuire, Rev. M.	R.T.62
103	1925 Jan. 21— May 4	Madden, Col. J. C. W.	R.F.103
104	1924 Dec. 29— 1925 June 19	Magherafelt Rural District, Committee of Nationalist inhabitants	R.T.41
105	[1924 Dec. 16]	Melley, H.	R.D.14
106	1924 Dec. 29— 1925 Mar. 24	Middletown, Committee of inhabitants	R.A.33
107	1924 Dec. 27— 1925 April 24	Milroy, S.	R.G.76
108	1925 April 6— June 10	Monaghan County Council	R.F.130
109	1924 Dec. 30	Moore, Major R. L. (*see also* Cab. 61/125)	R.F.44
110	1925 Mar. 20— April 3	Mullen Mills, Ltd. (*see also* Cab. 61/71)	R.A.114
111	1925 Feb. 5— Mar. 27	Mullyash District, Committee of inhabitants	R.A.70
112	1924 Dec. 29— 1925 July 21	Newry and Kilkeel Unions, inhabitants	R.N.25 (Vol.1)

Submissions, Evidences and Exhibits—*contd.*

Reference	Date	Description	File No.
Cab. 61			
113	1925 Mar. 16	Newry and Kilkeel Unions, inhabitants	R.N.25 (Vol.2)
114	1925 Mar. 13—Mar. 21	Newry and Kilkeel Unions, inhabitants	R.N.25 (Vol.3)
115	1925 Jan. 2—Nov. 9	Newry Chamber of Commerce	R.N.74B
116	1924 Dec. 30	Newry Port and Harbour Trust (*see also* Cab. 61/119)	R.N.35
117	1925 Mar. 14	Newry No. 1 Rural District Council	R.N.74
118	1925 Feb. 12—April 28	Newry No. 2 Rural District	R.N.74A
119	1924 Dec. 27—1925 Feb. 20	Newry Urban District Council	R.N.31 (Vol.1)
120	1925 Feb. 4—Mar. 10	Newry Urban District Council	R.N.31 (Vol.2)
121	1925 Feb. 6—June 10	Northern Ireland, various groups of Nationalist residents	R.G.75
		North of Ireland Shipbuilding Co. *See* Clarke, Trevisa	
		O'Golain, P. *See* Irish Free State Customs Service	
122	1924 Dec. 28—1925 Feb. 28	Omagh Nationalist Ex-Service-men (*see also* Cab. 61/145)	R.T.64
123	1925 Jan. 5—Feb. 23	Omagh Urban District Council (*see also* Cab. 61/145)	R.T.8
124	1924 Dec. 31	O'Neill, C. L. (*see also* Cab. 61/93)	R.D.93
125	1924 Dec. 26—1925 May 1	Pettigo Unionist inhabitants (*see also* Cab. 61/51)	R.F.66
126	1924 Dec. 3—1925 Feb. 4	Phillips, J.	R.G.7
127	1924 Dec. 22—1925 Mar. 14	Portadown and Banbridge Joint Waterworks Board	R.G.39
128	1924 Dec. 9—Dec. 29	Raphoe Presbytery	R.D.85
129	1924 Dec. 26	Redmond, S. A.	R.G.48

Submissions, Evidences and Exhibits—*contd.*

Reference	Date	Description	File No.
Cab. 61			
130	1924 Dec. 29— 1925 Sept. 25	Riordan J. F.	R.G.54
		Ross, C. W., *see* Cab. 61/61	
131	1925 April 30	Saunderson, E. A.	R.F.127
132	1924 Dec. 12	Smith, R. J.	R.G.82
133	1925 April 24— May 5	Smith, T.	R.F.129
134	1924 Dec. 12	Smyth, Dr. W. J.	R.A.86
135	1924 Dec. 15	Stack, Rev. T. F. L.	R.T.81
136	1924 Dec. 30— 1925 June 26	Strabane Presbyterian Church Congregational Committee	R.D.67
137	1924 Dec. 27— 1925 Feb. 27	Strabane Trader's Association (*see also* Cab. 61/136)	R.D.46
138	1925 Feb. 27— June 25	Strabane Urban District Council	R.D.30
139	1925 Feb. 28	Tempo Parish Nationalist inhabitants	R.F.110
140	1925 Feb. 19— June 24	Thompson, Dr. E.	R.T.78
141	1925 Jan. 27— Feb. 18	Tirconnaill County Council	R.D.47
142	1924 Dec. 6	Torrens, Rev. F.	R.D.88
143	1925 June 11— 30	Tyrone County Boundary Defence Association	R.T.132 (Vol.1)
[144]	WANTING	Tyrone County Boundary Defence Association	R.T.132 (Vol.2)
145	1925 Jan.— Aug. 1	Tyrone County Committee of Nationalist inhabitants	R.T.42 (Vol.1)
146	1925 June	Tyrone County Committee of Nationalist inhabitants	R.T.42 (Vol.2)
147	1925 June 6— June 19	Tyrone County Committee of Nationalist inhabitants	R.T.42 (Vol.3)
148	1925 June 6— June 19	Tyrone County Committee of Nationalist inhabitants	R.T.42 (Vol.4)
149	1925 June	Tyrone East, Committee of Nationalist inhabitants	R.T.43 (Vol.1)
150	1925 June 17— June 22	Tyrone East, Committee of Nationalist inhabitants	R.T.43 (Vol.2)

Submissions, Evidences and Exhibits—*contd.*

Reference	Date	Description	File No.
Cab. 61			
151	1925 June 17— June 22	Tyrone East, Committee of Nationalist inhabitants	R.T.43 (Vol.3)
152	1925 Mar. 2— June 25	Tyrone North West Boundary Defence Association	R.T.107
153	1925 June 15— June 26	Urney Parish, Unionist inhabitants	R.T.116
154	1924 Dec. 30	Waller, B. C.	R.G.92
155	1924 Dec.	Warburton, Lt. Col. F. T	R.G.18
156	1924 Dec. 29— 1925 Mar. 14	Warrenpoint Harbour Authority	R.N.21
157	1924 Dec. 30— 1925 Oct. 19	Warrenpoint, principal property owners	R.N.22
158	1923 Jan. 23— 1925 Mar. 12	Warrenpoint Urban District Council	R.N.24
159	1925 Sept. 9	Summaries of cases in support of claims	
160	1924 Dec. 3— 1925 Dec. 7	Statements issued to the Press	
161	1925 Dec. 9	Report of the Commission *Printed*	
162	1925 Dec. 9	Report of the Commission (duplicate) *Printed*	
163	1924 Nov.— 1925 Dec.	Duplicate (loose-leaf) set of Minutes of Meetings of the Commission	

NUMERICAL CENSUS GIVING NAMES OF HEADS OF HOUSEHOLD AND
TOTALS OF CATHOLIC AND NON-CATHOLIC PERSONS WITHIN
EACH HOUSEHOLD

164	[1925]	Dungannon Union Vol. I*†
165	[1925]	Dungannon Union Vol. II†
166	[1925]	Castlederg Union†
167	[1925]	Clogher Union†
168	[1925]	Omagh Urban District‡

*Index to Registration Units in Vol. I *and* II at front.
†Townlands within Registration Units, a list of townlands appears at the front of each unit.
‡Wards within the District, streets within wards.

REPORT

of the

IRISH BOUNDARY

COMMISSION

REPORT

of the

Irish Boundary Commission

In view of events which have supervened since the date when the Draft of this Report was prepared, the Commission's Award,* to which the Report refers, has not been signed, and the whole Report must now be read in the light of the "Concluding Statement" which will be found on page 154.

The decision of the Commission is contained in its Award, which sets out in legal and operative form the Commission's determination of the boundaries between Northern Ireland and the rest of Ireland; but we have thought it right, in addition to delivering the Award, to present the following Report for the information of the Governments concerned. This Report forms no part of the Award and is to be read as subject to the terms of the Award, which is in all respects the final and governing document, and is complete in itself.

The Report is divided into Parts and Chapters, with Appendices, as specified below.

---

* For Draft Award, see Appendix V.

(13849)

Contents.

Volume I.

PART I.—GENERAL.

PART II.—AREAS CONSIDERED.

PART III.—SKETCH OF PROPOSED NEW BOUNDARY AND ITS EFFECTS.

PART IV.—CONCLUSION.

Volume II.

APPENDICES.

PART I.—GENERAL.

CHAPTER I.

INTRODUCTORY.

PROCEEDINGS OF THE COMMISSION.

AGREEMENTS UNDER WHICH THE COMMISSION WAS APPOINTED.

The Irish Boundary Commission was appointed under Article XII of the Articles of Agreement for a Treaty between Great Britain and Ireland, dated the 6th December, 1921, and the supplementary Agreement dated the 4th August, 1924.

These Agreements were confirmed by the Parliament of the United Kingdom and the Parliament of the Irish Free State. [See the "Irish Free State (Agreement) Act, 1922" (12 Geo. 5, Ch. 4), the "Irish Free State (Constitution) Act, 1922" (13 Geo. 5, Ch. 1), and the "Irish Free State (Confirmation of Agreement) Act, 1924" (14 & 15 Geo. 5, Ch. 41), the "Constitution of the Irish Free State Act, 1922," and the "Treaty (Confirmation of Supplemental Agreement) Act, 1924."]

Article XII of the Articles of Agreement reads as follows :—

"If before the expiration of the said month an address is presented to His Majesty by both Houses of Parliament of Northern Ireland to that effect, the powers of the Parliament and Government of the Irish Free State shall no longer extend to Northern Ireland, and the provisions of the Government of Ireland Act, 1920, (including those relating to the Council of Ireland) shall so far as they relate to Northern Ireland, continue to be of full force and effect, and this instrument shall have effect subject to the necessary modifications.

Provided that if such an address is so presented a Commission consisting of three persons, one to be appointed by the Government of the Irish Free State, one to be appointed by the Government of Northern Ireland, and one who shall be Chairman to be appointed by the British Government, shall determine in accordance with the wishes of the inhabitants, so far as may be compatible with economic and geographic conditions, the boundaries between Northern Ireland and the rest of Ireland, and for the purposes of the Government of Ireland Act, 1920, and of this instrument, the boundary of Northern Ireland shall be such as may be determined by such Commission."

[13849]

The Supplementary Agreement of the 4th August, 1921, reads as follows :—

"*Agreement supplementing Article Twelve of the Articles of Agreement for a Treaty between Great Britain and Ireland to which the force of law was given by The Irish Free State (Agreement) Act, 1922, and by The Constitution of the Irish Free State (Saorstat Eireann) Act, 1922.*

WHEREAS the Commissioners to be appointed under the said Article Twelve by the Government of the Irish Free State and by the British Government respectively have been duly appointed by those respective Governments, but the Government of Northern Ireland has declined to appoint the Commissioner to be so appointed by that Government, and no provision is made by the said Articles for such a contingency :

Now it is hereby agreed, subject to the confirmation of this Agreement by the British Parliament and the Oireachtas of the Irish Free State, that if the Government of Northern Ireland does not before the date of the passing of the Act of the British Parliament or of the Act of the Oireachtas of the Irish Free State confirming this Agreement, whichever is the later date, appoint the Commissioner to be so appointed by that Government, the power of the Government of Northern Ireland to appoint such Commissioner shall thereupon be transferred to and exercised by the British Government, and that for the purposes of the said Article any Commissioner so appointed by the British Government shall be deemed to be a Commissioner appointed by the Government of Northern Ireland, and that the said Articles of Agreement for a Treaty shall have effect accordingly.

Signed on behalf of the British   Signed on behalf of the Govern-
Government :   ment of the Irish Free State :
J. RAMSAY MacDONALD.   LIAM T. MacCOSGAIR."

August 4, 1924.

CONSTITUTION OF COMMISSION.

The constitution of the Commission was announced in the London Gazette of the 31st October, 1924, in the following terms :—

"10, *Downing Street,*
October 31, 1924.
Irish Boundary Commission.

Consequent upon the passing into law of the Treaty (Confirmation of Supplemental Agreement) Act, to which the King's Assent was signified by the Governor-General of the Irish Free State on the 25th October, His Majesty's Government have, in virtue of the Irish Free State (Confirmation of Agreement) Act, 1924, appointed Joseph R. Fisher, Esq., to be the Commissioner deemed to be a Commissioner appointed by the Government of Northern Ireland for the purposes of Article XII of the Articles of Agreement for a Treaty between Great Britain and Ireland signed on the 6th December, 1921.

The Commission contemplated by that Article is accordingly constituted as follows :—

The Honourable Mr. Justice Feetham, C.M.G., *Chairman.*
Professor Eoin McNeill.
Joseph R. Fisher, Esq.''

The Commission held its first meeting on Thursday, the 6th November, 1924, at No. 6, Clement's Inn, London, where offices had already been engaged for it.   Mr. F. B. Bourdillon was appointed Secretary of the Commission, and it was decided that in the first instance at any rate the sittings of the Commission should be held in private.

ENQUIRIES DIRECTED TO GOVERNMENTS AND THEIR REPLIES.

On the 7th November, 1924, the Commission addressed identical enquiries to the Governments of the Irish Free State, to Northern Ireland and the United Kingdom.   The text of the letter addressed to the Government of the United Kingdom was as follows :—

6, *Clement's Inn,*
'' Sir, *London, November 7, 1924.*
The Irish Boundary Commission, appointed under Article XII of the Articles of Agreement for a Treaty between Great Britain and Ireland and the Agreement supplementing that Article, directs me to enquire whether His Majesty's Government wishes to submit to the Commission any statement with reference to the work with which the Commission is charged.

If His Majesty's Government proposes to submit such a statement the Commission will be glad to receive its statement with any supporting documents as soon as possible.

I am further directed to enquire whether His Majesty's Government wishes to appear before the Commission by Counsel, or by other accredited representatives, for the purpose of supplementing any written statement by fuller oral exposition, or discussing with the Commission any points which may arise with regard to it.   If so, the Commission will be glad to have an indication as to the date on which such representatives will be ready to appear.

The Commission would also be glad to know whether His Majesty's Government desires to submit to the Commission any evidence, and, if so, to be informed of the nature of the evidence to be submitted.

The Commission hopes to visit Ireland at an early date, and thinks that it will probably be convenient that sittings for the purpose of hearing evidence should be held in Ireland.

I am addressing a similar communication to the Government of the Irish Free State and to the Government of Northern Ireland.

I have the honour to be,
Sir,
Your obedient Servant,
F. B. BOURDILLON, <i>Secretary.</i>

The Right Hon. Stanley Baldwin, P.C. M.P.,
10, Downing Street, London, S.W. 1.''

The following replies were received :—

10, <i>Downing Street, Whitehall, S.W.</i> 1,

'' Sir, <i>November</i> 18, 1924.

I am directed by the Prime Minister to say, in reply to your letter of the 7th instant, that His Majesty's Government do not desire to submit to the Irish Boundary Commission any statement with reference to the work with which the Commission is charged, nor to appear before the Commission by Counsel or other representative, nor to submit any evidence to the Commission.

His Majesty's Government will of course be happy to afford to the Commission any information which the Commission may desire and which it is within the power of His Majesty's Government to afford.

I have the honour to be,
Sir,
Your obedient Servant,
(Signed)   RONALD WATERHOUSE.

The Secretary, Irish Boundary Commission.''

'' SAORSTAT EIREANN.
OIFIG AN UACHTARAIN
(The President's Office),

Ref. No.
S. 4150.

SRAID MHUIRBHTHEAN UACH
(Upper Merrion Street),
BAILE ATHA CLIATH
(Dublin).

'' The Secretary,
   Irish Boundary Commission,
      6, Clement's Inn, London, W.C. 2.

Sir, <i>November</i> 20, 1924.

I am directed by President Cosgrave to asknowledge receipt of your letter of the 7th inst. and in reply thereto to submit for the consideration of the Irish Boundary Commission the accompanying statement* which sets forth the views of the Government of the Irish Free State in regard to the work with which the Commission are charged. This statement is not intended to be comprehensive, and my Government propose

---

* Printed as Appendix II.

from time to time, as the occasion arises and as the operations of the Commission proceed, to supplement it by further statements covering any considerations which, in their opinion, call for the attention of the Commission.

My Government desire to appear before the Commission by Counsel for the purpose of supplementing by oral exposition the statement now submitted, and they will be glad to be informed as to the procedure which the Commission propose to adopt at their sittings for the hearing of Counsel and the examination of witnesses. They will be represented by Messrs. John O'Byrne, K.C., Attorney General of the Irish Free State, Sergeant Hanna, K.C., Patrick Lynch, K.C., and Cecil Lavery, B.L., and these gentlemen will be ready to appear before the Commission at any date not earlier than the 2nd proximo which will suit the convenience of the Commission.

In regard to the submission of evidence to the Commission my Government find it difficult, in the absence of definite information as to the Commission's intended procedure, to decide at what stage and on what aspects of the matter it may be necessary or desirable for them to produce witnesses in support of their contentions.

I have the honour to be,

Sir,

Your obedient Servant,

(Signed)   DIARMUID ÓHÉIGCEARTUIGH,

Secretary to the Executive Council."

Stormont Castle, Strandtown,

" Sir,   *Belfast, Ulster, November* 13, 1924.

I am directed by the Government of Northern Ireland to acknowledge receipt of your letter dated 7th November, addressed to the Prime Minister of Northern Ireland. I am instructed to inform you that the Government of Northern Ireland does not wish to submit to the Commission any statement with reference to the work with which the Commission is charged, nor to appear before the Commission by Counsel, or by other accredited representatives, nor to submit to the Commission any evidence dealing with the question.

I am, Sir, Your obedient Servant,

(Signed)   W. B. SPENDER,

Lieut.-Colonel, Secretary to the Cabinet,

Northern Ireland.

The Secretary, Irish Boundary Commission,

6, Clement's Inn, W.C. 2."

The Government of the Irish Free State in the Memorandum accompanying its letter of the 20th November, 1924, which is attached as an appendix, give an account of the historical circumstances which led up to the signing of the Articles of Agreement for a Treaty.

In the final paragraphs of the Memorandum the Government of the Irish Free State put forward the following view :—

"The presentation of the address mentioned in Article 12 of the Treaty had the effect of staying for the moment, and pending the operations of the Boundary Commission, the powers of the Parliament and Government of the Irish Free State in 'Northern Ireland'; but it was not contemplated by the Treaty that any area within 'Northern Ireland' should have the right to withdraw permanently from the jurisdiction of the Irish Free State, unless the majority of the inhabitants of such area were in favour of this course.

This Government considers that it is in the position of a trustee for such of the inhabitants of 'Northern Ireland' as wish to remain within the jurisdiction of the Irish Free State. It submits that the work of the Commission consists in ascertaining the wishes of the inhabitants of 'Northern Ireland,' with a view to determining, in accordance with such wishes, so far as may be compatible with economic and geographic conditions, what portions of that area are entitled to withdraw permanently from the jurisdiction of the Irish Free State."

HEARING OF COUNSEL ON BEHALF OF THE GOVERNMENT OF THE IRISH FREE STATE.

In accordance with the wish expressed by the Government of the Irish Free State arrangements were made for the hearing of Counsel on their behalf, and the hearing took place at the Commission's offices in London on the 4th and 5th December, 1924.

A verbatim report of the proceedings at this hearing is printed as Appendix I.

INVITATION OF REPRESENTATIONS.

On the 28th November the Commission decided to issue the following advertisement in the Irish Press :—

"Irish Boundary Commission

THE IRISH BOUNDARY COMMISSION is now willing to receive written representations from Public Bodies, Associations, or individuals resident in Ireland with reference to the work with which the Commission is charged. Such representations should be addressed to *Secretary of the Commission, at 6, Clement's Inn, London, W.C. 2, and should reach the Commission not later than the 31st December, 1924.*

Senders of written representations who may desire subsequently to submit evidence in support of their representations should give intimation to this effect at the time of sending in their communications, mentioning the nature of the evidence which it is proposed to submit, and in the case of Public Bodies and Associations the names and status of the witnesses whom they propose to appoint for this purpose.

The Commission contemplates arranging to hold Sittings in Ireland for the purpose of receiving evidence.

The dates and places of such Sittings will be announced subsequently.

The work with which the Commission is charged under the terms of Article XII of the Articles of Agreement for a Treaty between Great Britain and Ireland is to 'determine in accordance with the wishes of the inhabitants, so far as may be compatible with economic and geographic conditions, the boundaries between Northern Ireland and the rest of Ireland.'

F. B. BOURDILLON,
Secretary to the Commission."

PRELIMINARY VISIT TO IRELAND.

The Commission announced through the Press, on the 9th December, that it proposed to pay a preliminary visit to Ireland for the purpose of seeing portions of the country, acquainting itself with economic and geographic conditions, and ascertaining what sources of information were likely to be available for the purposes of its work. It was stated in the announcement that the Commissioners did not propose during this visit to hold formal sittings, but looked forward to coming into contact with some of those persons who might be prepared to assist the Commission by contributing their views on the subject with which it had to deal.

The Commissioners arrived at Armagh on the 9th December, and spent three nights at each of four centres, namely, Armagh, Enniskillen, Newtown Stewart and Londonderry. A considerable area was traversed during the fortnight, the principal points of interest in the border were visited, and the Commissioners met in an informal way representatives of various public bodies, deputations representing different interests, and prominent citizens.

Among the groups and individuals whose acquaintance the Commissioners made on this tour were: The Chairmen and some members of the County Councils of Armagh, Monaghan, Fermanagh, Tyrone and Londonderry, and of the Town Councils of Armagh, Monaghan, Newry, Enniskillen, Omagh, Strabane, and Londonderry; a number of H.M. Lieutenants and of the members of Parliament for Northern Ireland for the districts visited; a number of the principal ecclesiastical dignitaries whose seats lay in the border counties; the principal officers of Police in Armagh, Down, Monaghan, Fermanagh, Tyrone, Londonderry and Donegal; and the principal representatives of local political organisations in the counties visited.

REPRESENTATIONS RECEIVED IN ANSWER TO THE COMMISSION'S
INVITATION.

The Commissioners met on the 29th January, 1925, to consider
the Representations which had been received in response to their
advertisement.

The number of communications received by this date was 103.
Of this number a certain proportion dealt with questions which
required a reply defining to some extent the attitude of the
Commission with regard to the receipt of Representations. The
Secretary of the Fermanagh County Council forwarded on the
20th December, 1924, a copy of a Resolution passed by his Council
to the following effect :—

" Proposed by Sir Basil Brooke, Bart.,
Seconded by Mr. H. Kirkpatrick, J.P.,

and Resolved—That if an assurance is given by the Boundary
Commissioners that their duties are confined to mere rectification of anomalies on both sides of the existing border only, the
Fermanagh County Council will prepare a case and submit
evidence. That the Council adjourn consideration of this matter
pending a reply from the Commission."

An enquiry dated the 20th December, 1924, was also received
from residents in County Monaghan asking whether any land on
the Free State side of the existing border would be transferred.

The Commission replied to the effect that it did not propose
at that stage of its enquiry to make any pronouncement on the
questions raised by the County Council's resolution. The letter
which was sent in reply to that received from the Secretary of the
Council continued :—

" The Commission has already heard argument on behalf of
the Government of the Irish Free State as to the interpretation
to be placed on Article XII of the Articles of Agreement for a
Treaty under which the Commission is appointed, and has
received a number of written representations from various
parties which bear on the same subject. During its forthcoming
visit to Ireland, opportunities will be afforded to the parties
concerned to urge their views before the Commission. If your
Council desires to supplement its letter by putting forward
considerations in support of the interpretation of the Article
suggested by the terms of its resolution, the Commission will
be glad to hear representatives appointed for the purpose.

With reference to one of the points raised by the terms of
your Council's resolution, I may add for your information that
the Commission, while reserving its decision on the relevant
questions raised as to the interpretation of Article XII, has
intimated to parties putting forward claims with regard to the
determination of the boundary its willingness to hear and to
receive evidence in support of such claims, both in cases where
the claims involve inclusion in the Free State of territory situate

on the Northern Ireland side of the existing border and in cases where they involve inclusion in Northern Ireland of territory situate on the Free State side of that border.''

Résumé of Representations submitted.

In addition to representations received by the 31st December, 1924, the date by which it had been requested they should be sent in, further representations were received in the course of the next two months, and during the hearing of evidence.

Altogether 130 separate Representations were received, of which—

23 Representations were submitted by local authorities;
13　　　　,,　　　　by other public bodies.
44　　　　,,　　　　by local political groups; and
50　　　　,,　　　　by private persons and business firms.

Sittings held in Ireland for the Hearing of Evidence.

In February 1925, after a preliminary examination of the Representations received, the Commission proceeded to arrange for sittings in Ireland for the purpose of hearing evidence on behalf of those groups, associations or individuals, who, in submitting representations, had expressed a desire to submit evidence or bring forward witnesses in support of the contentions which they put forward.

In February the services of Major R. A. Boger, R.E., who had been British member of the German-Polish Boundary Commission set up under the Treaty of Versailles, were obtained as Chief Technical Assistant to the Commission. A staff of shorthand writers and other clerical assistance was also engaged.

The sittings were announced beforehand through the Press in the following statement :—

'' The Irish Boundary Commission held further meetings on the 28th and 29th January. Sittings are to be held in Ireland for the purpose of hearing evidence in support of representations which have been received by the Commission. These sittings will begin as soon as the necessary arrangements can be made, probably in about a month's time.

'' The Commission will continue, as hitherto, to sit in private. Where conflicting proposals concerning a particular region have been made in the representations received, and where it appears to the Commission that the progress of its enquiry would be facilitated if the bodies or groups submitting proposals in one sense were placed in a position to offer observations on the proposals offered in an opposing sense, the Commission will forward to the different bodies or groups concerned copies of the relevant representations.

'' Sittings will be held in different centres in order, so far as possible, to meet the convenience of the parties concerned. It is proposed in the first instance to deal with questions relating to the eastern section of the boundary.

"Due notice will be given as to the places and dates at which witnesses will be heard. The Commission is in communication with the different bodies and groups concerned with regard to the arrangements for presentation of the evidence to be given on their behalf."

DATES AND PLACES OF SITTINGS.

Sittings for the purpose of hearing evidence were held at the Judges' Lodgings, Armagh, from the 3rd to 7th March, 1925, inclusive, and again on the 19th March. Sittings were held at the Great Northern Hotel, Rostrevor, County Down, from the 9th March, 1924, with the exception of one day when sittings were held at the Slieve Donard Hotel, Newcastle.

The hearing of evidence was then interrupted in view of the approaching elections for the Parliament of Northern Ireland; they were resumed after Easter.

Sittings were held at Killyhevlin, Enniskillen, from the 22nd April to the 6th May; at the Irish Society's House, 1, St. Columb's Court, Londonderry, from the 14th May to the 5th June, and at Knock-na-Moe, Omagh, from the 6th June to the 2nd July. Both morning and afternoon sittings were usually held; but time had also to be allowed in order that the Commissioners might be enabled to pay visits to places with which the enquiry was concerned.

In all 575 witnesses representing 58 groups and public bodies were heard, as well as 10 individuals who had also submitted representations.

OFFICIAL EVIDENCE.

In addition to hearing evidence in support of representations received, the Commission also arranged to hear evidence on the practice obtaining at the Customs frontier from representatives of the Board of Customs of the United Kingdom and of the Customs Service of the Irish Free State. The Portal Inspector of the Port of Londonderry, the Local Manager of the Cross Channel Steamship Services, and the Chairman of the Lough Erne Drainage Board also supplied information at the request of the Commission.

HEARING OF WITNESSES PUT FORWARD BY THE GOVERNMENT OF THE IRISH FREE STATE.

Before the close of the sittings, at which evidence was heard, a special sitting was arranged at which evidence was given on behalf of the Government of the Irish Free State on certain general questions affecting statistics, concerning which correspondence had passed between the Commission and that Government. At the hearing of Counsel on the 4th and 5th December, 1924, the desirability of hearing evidence on these points had been indicated,

and in a letter addressed to the Government of the Irish Free State
on the 2nd February the Commission enquired whether the Government desired to submit evidence relating to " the conclusions which
should be drawn from data such as are available in census figures
and election returns as to ' wishes of the inhabitants' referred to
in Article XII of the Articles of Agreement. for a Treaty." On
the 19th February the Government of the Free State expressed a
desire to offer evidence and requested that it might be supplied
with copies of such of the representations received by the
Commission as dealt with this subject. In its reply of the
24th March the Commission indicated the main points relating
to this subject dealt with in representations, and on the 2nd July
witnesses representing the Government of the Free State were
heard on these points.

RETURN OF THE COMMISSION TO LONDON.

On the 3rd July, on the conclusion of the sittings held in
Ireland for the purpose of hearing evidence, the staff of the
Commission returned to London.

During the next two months the transcription of the evidence
heard was completed, and the process of examining, arranging, and
analysing the evidence, oral and documentary, was carried out.

FURTHER HEARING OF COUNSEL ON BEHALF OF THE GOVERNMENT OF THE IRISH FREE STATE.

On the 6th April the Government of the Irish Free State had
written asking that they might be supplied with particulars of
certain representations received by the Commission which raised
" considerations other than such as could be adequately dealt with
by local groups and associations," so that the Government "might
be in a position to make submissions to the Commission on matters
arising out of the considerations thus put forward." On the
7th May the Secretary to the Commission wrote forwarding extracts
from a number of representations dealing with such general
considerations. On the 11th July the Secretary to the Executive
Council of the Free State forwarded a memorandum containing
submissions on the points raised in these representations, and
stating that Counsel would be prepared to appear before the
Commission to supplement these submissions by oral exposition.

After further correspondence a hearing of Counsel was held in
London on the 25th August, at which certain points raised in the
memorandum were dealt with. Copies of the memorandum and
of the correspondence relating thereto, together with a verbatim
note of the proceedings at the hearing on the 25th August, are
printed as Appendix IV.

SITTINGS OF THE COMMISSION IN LONDON.

On the 9th September the Commissioners reassembled in
London and held further sittings during the latter part of September
and in October.

After a very full examination of the position in different areas in the light of the evidence obtained, and consideration of various possible alternative lines, the Commission was able, on Saturday, the 17th October, at the conclusion of a series of meetings held during that week, to record a decision approving in its general features a line showing the whole of the new boundary to be adopted, and instructions were given for the preparation of a full detailed description of this line with the necessary maps. It was considered necessary to show the whole line on 6-inch Ordnance sheets, and to prepare three sets of such sheets so that one set could be attached to each copy of the Award, which the Commission decided to issue in triplicate. Major Boger, the Commission's Chief Technical Assistant, estimated that this work would occupy approximately six weeks.

The Commission held further meetings on the 4th and 5th November, at which certain points of minor local detail were dealt with, and a draft Award, and the drafts of other documents to be issued with the Award, were considered.

It was also decided at the meeting on the 5th November that letters should be sent to the Government of the United Kingdom and to the Government of the Irish Free State, stating that the proceedings of the Commission had reached a stage when it appeared desirable that the Commission should have an opportunity of conferring with representatives of the two Governments on the questions of the date on which the Commission's Award should be delivered, the procedure to be adopted with regard to the publication of the Award, and the publication and custody of documents other than the Award.

CHAPTER II.

PROCEDURE AND COURSE OF ENQUIRY.

1. Procedure in connection with hearing of Evidence.

In the case of public bodies and political groups a circular was issued outlining the course of procedure to be followed at sittings held for the purpose of receiving evidence. In this circular the Commission requested all bodies and groups who desired to bring forward witnesses to inform the Commission beforehand of their names and to submit a short statement in writing, signed by each witness, of the particular points on which he would give evidence. Individuals who desired to give evidence were asked to submit written statements. The Commission reserved the right to decide what witnesses it would be desirable to hear. It was intimated that in the case of public bodies or important groups at least the principal witnesses would be heard in every instance. In practice, with the exception of a few individuals who suggested giving evidence on points already covered by groups or public bodies, the Commissioners heard all the witnesses put forward and on several occasions stretched a point in favour of the admission of witnesses whose names had not been notified before the opening of the sitting concerned.

One question of importance, which was also covered by the circular, was the question of giving the representatives of each party opportunity to comment on the contentions put forward by the other. It was felt to be desirable that the proceedings should not be publicly reported. It was also felt that it would lead to an indefinite prolongation of the proceedings if each group were represented by Counsel, and particularly if Counsel representing one party were allowed to cross-examine witnesses put forward by the other party. The Commissioners themselves accordingly undertook the asking of the questions necessary for the purpose of eliciting the evidence of the witnesses. They also arranged in all cases which seemed to warrant such a course that the representations submitted by groups belonging to one party should be submitted for comment to groups of the other party which had made representations concerning the same areas. The comments thus obtained enabled the Commissioners to put to witnesses the principal questions which would have been raised in cross-examination. To facilitate the course of the proceedings, and to ensure that witnesses belonging to each group collectively covered the ground which it was intended to cover, it was arranged that the solicitor, or other person who acted as organising secretary of each group, should be present throughout the sitting or sittings devoted to hearing that group.

2. ANALYSIS OF REPRESENTATIONS RECEIVED.

Nature of the Claims, in support of which Evidence was heard.

Claims made to the Commission were either positive, *i.e.*, in favour of changes of jurisdiction, or negative, *i.e.*, opposed to such changes. The Positive claims received by the Commission ranged from a claim asking for the transfer of a single townland in either direction to one which suggested inclusion in the Irish Free State of the entire counties of Tyrone and Fermanagh, and portions of Londonderry, Armagh, and Down. In general, the Positive Claims fell into five groups :—

(*a.*) Claims dealing with small areas adjacent to the existing border where Census figures were alleged to show a majority, arrived at on the basis of religious denominations, indicating a wish for transfer.

(*b.*) Claims for the transfer of mixed areas, including groups and districts, representing divergent views, which were alleged to show a similar majority, indicating a wish for transfer for the areas considered as wholes.

(*c.*) Claims based on purely economic or geographic grounds, generally concerned with small areas.

(*d.*) Claims for the transfer of individual towns or parishes not adjacent to the existing border.

(*e.*) Claims for changes of a comprehensive character involving several counties.

The areas to which the claims related may be briefly summarised as follows :—

(A.) POSITIVE CLAIMS

(a.) Claims relating to small Border Areas.

Sixteen of these claims were concerned with areas of limited extent, adjoining the existing border, in which it was contended that the majority of the inhabitants desired to be transferred to the other side of the border on political grounds. These areas were :—

Districts claimed for transfer to Northern Ireland.

Pettigo and District;
A small area in Tirconaill adjoining Belleek;
The District Electoral Division of Castle Saunderson (Co. Cavan);
Part of Co. Monaghan in the neighbourhood of Clones;
Part of Co. Monaghan in the neighbourhood of Glasslough;
Part of Co. Monaghan in the neighbourhood of Mullyash;
The townland of Fearn, Tirconaill;
The District Electoral Division of St. Johnstown, Killea and Castleforward and adjoining areas in Tirconaill;
A district in Tirconaill extending to a distance of roughly 10 miles from the City of Londonderry.

Districts claimed for transfer to the Irish Free State.

The Urban district of Strabane;
The District Electoral Division of Middletown and Keady (Co. Armagh).

(b.) Claims relating to Mixed Areas.

Areas claimed for transfer to Northern Ireland.

(i.) Tirconaill (Co. Donegal), or alternatively, the former parliamentary division of East Donegal with an additional area in North Donegal; or, as a third alternative, the former rural districts of Strabane No. 2 and Londonderry No. 2, with part of those of Letterkenny and Stranorlar.

Areas claimed for transfer to the Irish Free State.

(i.) The City of Londonderry;
(ii.) The City and Rural District of Londonderry;
(iii.) The City of Londonderry, and the Rural Districts of Londonderry, Limavady, and Magherafelt;
(iv.) The County of Fermanagh;
(v.) The County of Tyrone;
(vi.) The Rural District of Clogher;
(vii.) The town and neighbourhood of Aughnacloy;

(viii.) The former parliamentary constituency of South Armagh;

(ix.) The former constituency of South Armagh, together with the City of Armagh and a great part of the rural district of Armagh;

(x.) The unions of Newry and Kilkeel;

(xi.) The unions of Newry and Kilkeel; together with that of Downpatrick.

(c.) *Claims based on economic or geographic grounds.*

In the majority of the claims made for the areas already mentioned it was urged that economic and geographic conditions supported the contentions advanced.

Other claims were also received for the transfer of certain areas on economic or geographic grounds alone. Such claims were put forward in respect of the following areas :—

For transfer to Northern Ireland.

(i.) The catchment areas of the Londonderry Corporation's reservoir at Killea;

(ii.) The works and buildings situated in Tirconaill belonging to the Londonderry Port and Harbour Commission;

(iii.) The two sluice gates at Belleek situated in Tirconaill;

(iv.) The bridge and fort at Belleek and the road connecting them with Co. Fermanagh on the south bank of the River Erne;

(v.) The District Electoral Division of Drummully, Co. Monaghan.

(d.) *Claims for transfer of individual towns or parishes not adjacent to the existing border.*

For transfer to the Irish Free State.

(i.) The town of Omagh;

(ii.) The city of Armagh;

(iii.) The parish of Ballymacnab, Co. Armagh;

(iv.) The parish of Kilskeery, Co. Tyrone;

(v.) The parish of Kilcoo, Co. Down;

(vi.) The parish of Tempo, Co. Fermanagh.

(e.) *Claims for changes of a comprehensive character involving several counties.*

Eighteen of the Representations made suggestions of this nature. Under this heading may be included—

(1.) Seven Representations which contended that the boundary should follow the former boundary of the Province of Ulster;

[13849]

(2.) The proposal that the Counties of Tyrone and Fermanagh with the greater part of the counties of Londonderry and Armagh, and the southern portion of County Down, should be transferred to the Irish Free State;

(3.) One Representation which suggested that Northern Ireland should be divided into two separate provinces, the eastern province to include part of County Monaghan, and the western province to include part of Tirconaill;

(4.) A number of Representations which argued that there should be no partition of Ireland.

(B.) NEGATIVE CLAIMS.

Forty claims were received contending that particular areas should not be transferred or that no transfer should be made except by mutual agreement.

Particular areas concerning which such claims were received were :—

> The City and Liberties of Londonderry;
> Belleek and neighbourhood;
> The Union of Kilkeel;
> The Urban District of Warrenpoint;
> Bessbrook;
> The Bessbrook and Newry Tramway;
> The Camlough Lake and Catchment Area;
> The area covered by the Reservoirs and Catchment Areas of the Belfast Water Commissioners situated in the Mourne Mountains;
> Portadown and Banbridge Joint Water Works and Catchment Area;
> Lough Island Reavey and Catchment Area of the Bann Reservoir Company;
> The Town and District of Strabane;
> The Union of Newry;
> The County of Armagh;
> The County of Fermanagh;
> Castlederg Rural District;
> Dungannon Urban and Rural Districts;
> Cookstown Urban and Rural Districts;
> Clogher Rural District;
> The town of Aughnacloy;
> Glasslough and the adjoining district of Co. Monaghan;
> The District Electoral Division of Drummully; and adjoining parts of Co. Monaghan.

3. List of Bodies, Groups, &c., whose Evidence was heard.

The following is a list of Local Authorities, Public Bodies, Groups and Associations, which gave evidence before the Commission in Ireland, in support of Representations submitted, and a summary showing the nature of their evidence.

Date.		Name.	Summary of Evidence.
1925. March	3	A Committee of inhabitants of the border district of Middletown, Co. Armagh.	Evidence in support of their claim for the inclusion of this area in the Irish Free State.
,,	4	A group of inhabitants of Glaslough and the adjoining district of Co. Monaghan which borders on Co. Armagh.	Evidence mainly directed to proving the inconvenience at various points of the existing boundary.
,,	5	A Committee appointed by inhabitants of the town and district of Keady, supported by the Keady Urban District Council.	Evidence in support of their claim for the inclusion of the district in the Irish Free State.
,,	6	The Armagh Urban District Council.	Evidence in support of their claim for the inclusion of the City of Armagh in the Irish Free State.
,,	6	A Committee appointed by a meeting of inhabitants of the City of Armagh.	Do. do.
,,	7	A Committee of the inhabitants of the district of Mullyash, Co. Monaghan.	Evidence in support of their claim for the inclusion of the district in Northern Ireland.
,,	9 and 10	Newry Urban District Council.	Evidence in support of their claim for the inclusion of the town of Newry and the adjoining districts in the Irish Free State.
,,	11	Newry Chamber of Commerce.	Evidence in opposition to claims made for the inclusion of the town of Newry and the adjoining districts in the Irish Free State.
,,	12	Warrenpoint Urban District Council.	Evidence in support of their claim for the inclusion of Warrenpoint in the Irish Free State.
,,	12	A group of property owners, traders and inhabitants of Warrenpoint.	Evidence in opposition to the claims made by the Warrenpoint Urban District Council for the inclusion of Warrenpoint in the Irish Free State.

[13849]

Date.		Name.	Summary of Evidence.
1925. March 13, 16 and 20		A group of inhabitants of the Union of Newry (including Crossmaglen) and the Union of Kilkeel.	Evidence in support of their claim for the inclusion of this area in the Irish Free State.
,,	14	Newry No. 1 Rural District Council.	Evidence in opposition to the claims made for the inclusion of that district in the Irish Free State.
,,	14	Portadown and Banbridge Waterworks Board.	Evidence in opposition to the claims made for the inclusion in the Irish Free State of the area in Co. Down in which the Board's waterworks and portions of its pipe line are situate.
,,	14	Messrs. John Kelly, Ltd. (in their capacity as owners of Warrenpoint Harbour).	Evidence in opposition to claims made for the inclusion of Warrenpoint in the Irish Free State.
,,	14	Belfast & County Down Railway Co., Ltd.	Evidence in opposition to claims made for the inclusion in the Irish Free State of any part of the area served by that railway.
,,	17	Kilkeel Rural District Council.	Evidence in opposition to the claims made for the inclusion of the Kilkeel Union in the Irish Free State.
,,	17	Kilkeel Board of Guardians.	Do. do.
,,	18	A Committee of Inhabitants of East Down.	Evidence in support of their claim for the inclusion in the Irish Free State of an area based on the former Parliamentary Division of East Down.
,,	19	Armagh County Council ...	Evidence in opposition to claims made for the inclusion in the Irish Free State of any portion of County Armagh.
,,	20	A group of inhabitants of Ballymacnab and adjoining townlands in the District Electoral Division of Lisnadill.	Evidence in support of their claim for the inclusion of that area in the Irish Free State.
,,	21	The Bessbrook Spinning Co., Ltd.	Evidence in opposition to the claims made for the inclusion in the Irish Free State of the areas in Co. Armagh in which their undertakings are situate.

Date.		Name.	Summary of Evidence.
1925. March	21	The Bessbrook & Newry Tramway Co.	Evidence in opposition to the claims made for the inclusion in the Irish Free State of the areas in Co. Armagh in which their undertakings are situate.
,,	21	The Camlough Waterworks Trustees.	Do. do.
,,	23	Newry No. 2 Rural District Council.	Evidence in opposition to the claims made for the inclusion of that district in the Irish Free State.
,,	24	Belfast City and District Water Commissioners.	Evidence in opposition to claims made for the inclusion in the Irish Free State of the area in the Mourne Mountains in which the Commissioners' Waterworks are situate, and the district adjoining that area.
Apr.	22, 23, 24 and 25	A Committee of Nationalist Inhabitants of Co. Fermanagh.	Evidence in support of their claim for the inclusion of Co. Fermanagh in the Irish Free State.
,,	27, 28 and 29	Fermanagh County Council...	Evidence in opposition to the claims made for the inclusion of any part of Co. Fermanagh in the Irish Free State.
,,	30	Certain Inhabitants of Belleek.	Evidence in opposition to claims made for the inclusion of Belleek in the Irish Free State.
May	1	Co. Donegal Protestant Registration Association, on behalf of certain inhabitants of the District concerned.	Evidence in support of claims made for the inclusion in Northern Ireland of Pettigoe and the adjoining district and certain townlands on either side of the River Erne in the neighbourhood of Belleek.
,,	2	Ballyshannon Harbour Commissioners.	Evidence in support of their claim for the inclusion in the Irish Free State of that portion of Co. Fermanagh which prior to 1922 formed Ballyshannon Rural District No. 2.
,,	4	Inhabitants of the parishes of Drummully and Clogh.	Evidence in support of their claim for the inclusion in Northern Ireland of the whole of the two parishes, including those portions which are situate in Co. Monaghan.

Date.	Name.	Summary of Evidence.
1925. May 6	Certain inhabitants of Glasslough and the adjoining district of Co. Monaghan.	Evidence in opposition to the claims made for the inclusion of this district in Northern Ireland.
„ 6	Urban District Council of Clones.	Evidence in support of claims for the inclusion in the Irish Free State of that portion of Co. Fermanagh which prior to 1922 formed Clones No. 2 Rural District.
„ 14, 15 16, 19 and 20	Derry Nationalist Registration Association.	Evidence in support of their claim for the inclusion in the Irish Free State of the City of Londonderry and of the North-West Liberties, i.e., the portion of the County of Londonderry adjoining the City on the west bank of the River Foyle.
„ 18 and 19	Certain Inhabitants of the Poor Law Union of Londonderry.	Evidence in support of their claim for the inclusion in the Irish Free State of the area of the Union which includes Londonderry Rural District in addition to the City of Londonderry.
„ 21	Londonderry members of the Shirt and Collar Manufacturers' Federation in Northern Ireland.	Evidence in opposition to claims made for the inclusion in City of Londonderry in the Irish Free State.
„ 22	Londonderry Port and Harbour Commissioners.	Evidence in support of their contention that the entire Port of Londonderry including the whole of Lough Foyle is included within the present limits of Northern Ireland; that the boundary should be defined to recognise this position and also so as to give the Commissioners uninterrupted right of access to the Pilot Station on Inishowen Head, the Warren Light, and the Piers at Moville and Carickarory over which they now exercise control.
„ 25, 26, 27 and 28	County Donegal Protestant Registration Association.	Evidence in support of their claim for the inclusion in Northern Ireland of the whole of Co. Donegal, or, alternatively, of certain portions of the County adjacent to the present boundary.

Date.		Name.	Summary of Evidence.
1925. May	29	A group of Co. Donegal Business Men.	Evidence in support of their claim for the inclusion in the Irish Free State of the Port and City of Londonderry, or, alternatively, of the Port of Londonderry and that portion of the City which is situate on the West bank of the Foyle. Evidence was also given on their behalf in opposition to the claims for the inclusion in Northern Ireland of any portion of Co. Donegal.
June	1 and 10	A group of Nationalist residents in various parts of Northern Ireland.	Evidence in support of their claim for inclusion in the Irish Free State of an area consisting of the Counties of Tyrone and Fermanagh, the City of Londonderry, and portions of the Counties of Londonderry, Armagh and Down.
,,	2	The Corporation of the City of Londonderry.	Evidence in opposition to claims made for the inclusion of the City of Londonderry in the Irish Free State, and in support of claims made by the Corporation for adjustments of the existing boundary so as to include in Northern Ireland certain portions of East Donegal bordering on the Liberties and on the River Foyle and the Lough.
,,	6, 8, 9, 16, 17, 18, 19 and 22	A Committee of Nationalist Inhabitants of Co. Tyrone.	Evidence in support of their claim for the inclusion of Co. Tyrone in the Irish Free State.
,,	11, 12, and 30	Tyrone Boundary Defence Association.	Evidence in opposition to claims made for the inclusion of any part of Co. Tyrone in the Irish Free State.
,,	19	A Committee of Nationalist Inhabitants of Magherafelt Rural District, Co. Londonderry.	Evidence in support of their claim for the inclusion of that area in the Irish Free State.
,,	22	A group of Unionist Inhabitants of the Urban and Rural Districts of Cookstown.	Evidence in opposition to claims made for the inclusion of those districts in the Irish Free State.
,,	23	Aughnacloy Town Commissioners.	Evidence in opposition to claims made for the inclusion of the town of Aughnacloy in the Irish Free State.

Date.		Name.	Summary of Evidence.
1925. June	23	Clogher Rural District Council.	Evidence in opposition to claims made for the inclusion of that Rural District in the Irish Free State, and in support of their claim for the inclusion in Northern Ireland of a portion of Co. Monaghan adjoining the town and district of Aughnacloy.
,,	24	Dungannon Urban District Council.	Evidence in opposition to claims made for the inclusion of their district in the Irish Free State.
,,	24	Dungannon Board of Guardians.	Do. do.
,,	24	A group of Unionist Inhabitants of Dungannon Urban and Rural Districts.	Do. do.
,,	25	Strabane Urban District Council.	Evidence on the position of the town of Strabane as affected by the present boundary between Northern Ireland and the Irish Free State.
,,	25	North-West Tyrone Boundary Defence Committee. Strabane Rural District Council.	Evidence in opposition to claims made for the inclusion in the Irish Free State of any portion of the Castlederg or Strabane Rural Districts, with the exception of such portions of Castlederg District as might be affected by a modification of the boundary at its western end, and in support of a claim for the inclusion in Northern Ireland of portions of East Donegal adjacent to Co. Tyrone.
,,	26	The Congregational Committee of the Strabane Presbyterian Church.	Evidence in opposition to claims made for the inclusion of Strabane in the Irish Free State and in support of a claim for the inclusion of portions of East Donegal in Northern Ireland.
,,	26	Strabane Traders' Association.	Do. do.
,,	26	A group of Unionist inhabitants of the Parish of Urney.	Do. do.

CHAPTER III.

ARTICLE XII.

INTERPRETATION AND PRINCIPLES OF APPLICATION.

Various contentions with regard to the interpretation of Article XII of the Articles of Agreement for a Treaty between Great Britain and Ireland, and the principles which should govern its application, have been put forward in representations submitted to the Commission, and in arguments heard and evidence received in support of such representations.

Article XII, in its opening sentence, refers to the provisions of the immediately preceding Article; it will therefore be convenient to give here the terms of the two Articles, which read as follows :—

Article XI :—

" Until the expiration of one month from the passing of the Act of Parliament for the ratification of this instrument, the powers of the Parliament and the Government of the Irish Free State shall not be exercisable as respects Northern Ireland, and the provisions of the Government of Ireland Act, 1920, shall, so far as they relate to Northern Ireland, remain of full force and effect, and no election shall be held for the return of members to serve in the Parliament of the Irish Free State for constituencies in Northern Ireland, unless a resolution is passed by both Houses of the Parliament of Northern Ireland in favour of the holding of such elections before the end of the said month."

Article XII :—

" If before the expiration of the said month, an address is presented to His Majesty by both Houses of the Parliament of Northern Ireland to that effect, the powers of the Parliament and Government of the Irish Free State shall no longer extend to Northern Ireland, and the provisions of the Government of Ireland Act, 1920 (including those relating to the Council of Ireland), shall so far as they relate to Northern Ireland, continue to be of full force and effect, and this instrument shall have effect subject to the necessary modifications.

" Provided that if such an address is so presented a Commission consisting of three persons, one to be appointed by the Government of the Irish Free State, one to be appointed by the Government of Northern Ireland, and one who shall be Chairman to be appointed by the British Government, shall determine in accordance with the wishes of the inhabitants, so far as may be compatible with economic and geographic conditions, the boundaries between Northern Ireland and the rest of Ireland, and for the purposes of the Government of Ireland Act, 1920, and of this instrument, the boundary of Northern Ireland shall be such as may be determined by such Commission."

The principal questions raised by the contentions put forward may be summarised as follows :—

(1.) What is the meaning and effect of Article XII as viewed in relation to the Articles of Agreement as a whole?

(2.) What is the scope of the powers and duties entrusted to and imposed upon the Commission by Article XII?

This second question includes the following more specific questions :—

(a.) In determining the future boundaries between Northern Ireland and the rest of Ireland, what regard is the Commission to pay to the existing boundary? Is it the duty of the Commission to make an entirely fresh determination of boundaries, and to lay down a new line of division without regard to the existing boundary, or is the Commission required to start its work on the basis of the existing boundary, and to treat that boundary as holding good except where considerations of which the Commission is entitled to take account justify its alteration?

(b.) Does the Article enable the Commission, in determining the boundaries between Northern Ireland and the rest of Ireland, to shift the existing boundary in either direction, that is, either so as to include in the Irish Free State territory at present forming part of Northern Ireland, or so as to include in Northern Ireland territory at present forming part of the Irish Free State, or is the power of the Commission confined to shifting the boundary in one direction only? In other words, is the Commission required, in carrying out its work, to respect the integrity either of Northern Ireland or of the "rest of Ireland" as defined by existing boundaries?

(c.) Can the Commission make changes in the existing boundary which involve the transfer of large areas and populations to one side or the other, or is its scope restricted to the making of minor modifications in the existing boundary?

(3.) What is the relation between the three different factors mentioned as affecting the determination of boundaries— wishes of inhabitants and economic and geographic conditions? In what sense is the reference to economic and geographic conditions to be understood, and what are the areas in relation to which such conditions are to be taken into account?

(4.) What qualifications entitle persons to rank as "inhabitants" whose wishes are to be considered, and by what procedure are the wishes of inhabitants to be ascertained?

(5.) In considering the wishes of inhabitants with regard to the determination of boundaries, what is the position with regard to majorities and minorities? Is unanimity to be required, or is a bare majority one way or the other to be sufficient?

(6.) On what principle should units of area be chosen or defined for the purpose of ascertaining the wishes of inhabitants?

These and certain related questions are discussed at length in the Memorandum by the Chairman of the Commission, which forms an Annex to this Chapter. This memorandum examines in detail the various arguments which have been advanced. We propose to state in this Chapter the general conclusions reached by the Commission as to the answers which should be given to these questions. For detailed examination of the various arguments advanced reference should be made to the Chairman's Memorandum.

It is necessary to make one or two general remarks by way of preface before coming to the questions themselves.

The answers to be given to the questions stated depend—

(i) on the actual terms of the proviso to Article XII, which provides for the setting up of the Commission;

(ii) on the proviso as considered in relation to the preceding clause of the Article to which it belongs; and

(iii) on the whole Article as considered in relation to the other provisions of the instrument of which it forms part.

Further, the Commission has been asked to take into account the historical circumstances which led up to the Articles of Agreement for a Treaty, and the conditions actually existing at the date when these Articles were signed, which, it is said, defined the nature of the problem which Article XII was intended to solve. It has been urged that such circumstances and conditions throw light on the question of the interpretation which should be given to Article XII, and evidence bearing on this aspect of the case has been received by the Commission.

In support of views advanced as to the interpretation of Article XII evidence has also been offered as to various statements made on the subject by signatories to the Articles of Agreement, both in the course of the negotiations and subsequent to the actual signing of the Articles, but the Commission has regarded such evidence as inadmissible and has declined to receive it.

The terms of the Proviso to Article XII which define the functions of the Commission are general and not specific. If this Proviso is compared with the provisions with regard to the settlement of boundaries contained in the Treaty of Versailles (Articles 88, 94/97 and 109) or in the Treaty of St. Germain-en-Laye (Articles 49/50), to which reference has been made in the course of arguments addressed to the Commission, a striking contrast is at once apparent. In the Articles referred to in those Treaties general terms are employed, corresponding to but not identical with those contained in the Proviso to Article XII, but they are supplemented by a series of specific detailed provisions which give in each case precise directions (1) as to the extent of the areas to be considered, *i.e.*, the regions or areas which are recognised as being within the range of boundary variations, (2) as to the means by which the wishes of the inhabitants of such areas are to be ascertained (the method specified being a plebiscite for the conduct of which full provision is made in each case), and (3) as to the units of area which are to be used for the purpose of such ascertainment. Article XII gives no specific directions on any of these points, but leaves to the Commission discretion to determine these points for itself subject to the general terms used, and in the light of such circumstances as the Commission's examination of the actual position in the territory on either side of the existing boundary may reveal.

Having made these general observations, we now proceed to state the answers which should in our opinion be given to the questions stated above.

Question 1.

The meaning of Article XII is that if the Address therein referred to is presented, Northern Ireland shall continue to exist as a province of the United Kingdom in accordance with the provisions of the Government of Ireland Act, 1920, subject to the "determination" of boundaries, for which machinery is set up under the proviso, and its terms require that once such an Address has been presented the several Articles of Agreement for a Treaty shall be modified, so far as necessary, to give effect to all the consequences which under the provisions of Article XII follow upon such presentation.

To the extent thus indicated Article XII necessarily becomes on the presentation of such Address a governing Article in the light of which the other Articles of the Treaty must be read, and to which in case of conflict their provisions must yield.

Question 2 (a).

The Commission is required by the proviso to Article XII to " determine the boundaries between Northern Ireland and the rest of Ireland." Until the boundaries have been altered by the Commission "Northern Ireland" is the region constituted as such by Section 1 (2) of the Government of Ireland Act, 1920; that is to say the region consisting "of the parliamentary counties of Antrim, Armagh, Down, Fermanagh, Londonderry and Tyrone, and the parliamentary boroughs of Belfast and Londonderry," and "the rest of Ireland" is the region constituted as "Southern Ireland" by the same section—that is to say, the region consisting of "so much of Ireland as is not comprised within the said parliamentary counties and boroughs." The Commission having to deal with these two ascertained territorial entities must start from the existing boundaries of those entities; that is, it must start its examination of the whole question on the basis of the division marked by the existing boundary, and must treat that boundary as holding good where no sufficient reason, based on considerations of which the Commission can properly take account, is shown for altering it.

Question 2 (*b*).

In determining the boundaries between Northern Ireland and the rest of Ireland under the terms of the proviso, the Commission has power to shift the existing boundary line in either direction,—it has no more and no less authority to take land from the Northern Ireland side of the existing boundary and give it to the Free State, than it has to take land from the Free State side and give it to Northern Ireland. It has the same authority and duty in each case, namely to make whatever transfer of territory is involved by a determination of the boundary in accordance with the terms of the Article.

Question 2 (*c*).

The fact that the wishes of the inhabitants are to be a determining factor shows that the scope of the Commission's work is not limited to a mere correction of irregularities in the present boundary; at the same time no wholesale reconstruction of the map is contemplated by the proviso—the Commission is not to reconstitute the two territories, but to settle the boundaries between them. Northern Ireland must, when the boundaries have been determined, still be recognisable as the same provincial entity; the changes made must not be so drastic as to destroy its identity or make it impossible for it to continue as a separate province of the United Kingdom with its own parliament and government for provincial affairs under the Government of Ireland Act. The same principle applies *mutatis mutandis* to the "rest of Ireland," which must, after the determination of the boundaries, retain its identity as the Irish Free State as constituted under the terms of the Treaty, and be in a position to function as a self-governing Dominion "in the Community of Nations known as the British Empire."

The Commission starting its examination of the question on the basis of the existing boundary must first consider the wishes of the inhabitants adjacent to that boundary, and where it finds an area of sufficient size and population to merit separate consideration which is at present on the right side of the boundary, that is on the side where its inhabitants wish to remain, the existence of that area will in itself be a reason against making an alteration which would involve its transfer to the wrong side, and help to indicate the point beyond which alterations intended to give effect to the wishes of the inhabitants should not extend.

No precise rule can be laid down as to the requirements which must be fulfilled in the case of individual areas in order to entitle the wishes of their inhabitants to prevail. The conditions of an individual area cannot be considered alone, but must be considered in relation to conditions in adjoining areas, and different factors, such as comparative numbers of population, and strength of majorities, must be taken into account.

Question 3.

Under the terms of the Article the wishes of the inhabitants are made the primary but not the paramount consideration. The first point for the Commission to consider in dealing with a particular area is the question of the wishes of the inhabitants of that area, but such wishes are only to prevail "so far as may be compatible with economic and geographic conditions." The intention of the Article as indicated by its reference to such conditions is that the Commission should take into account the economic and geographic relations between different areas, and should avoid drawing a boundary line which, by its defiance of economic or geographic conditions, would involve, as the result of its adoption, serious economic detriment, or geographic isolation, to communities on either side of it.

It is therefore the duty of the Commission to overrule the wishes of inhabitants, whether for or against transfer, where the result of giving effect to such wishes would be incompatible with economic or geographic conditions in the sense indicated. On the other hand economic or geographic considerations may give extra strength to a case for transfer which rests in part on the wishes of the inhabitants, but where the evidence available does not show the existence of a decisive majority in favour of transfer.

Questions 4 and 5.

"Inhabitants" in Article XII means persons having a permanent connection with any particular area concerned. Temporary or casual residence within an area cannot be regarded as qualifying a person to have his wishes considered on the question whether the permanent destiny of the area is to be in one country or another.

The Article contains no provision for ascertaining the wishes of inhabitants by a plebiscite taken for the purpose, which is the only means by which precise figures as to the wishes of the inhabitants could be ascertained. It is clearly impossible to conduct a plebiscite in the results of which any confidence could be placed except under the authority of special legal provisions of a comprehensive and stringent character.

The absence from the Article of any provision for a plebiscite affords ground for inferring (1) that it was not the intention of the parties to the Treaty that the Commission should ascertain the wishes of the inhabitants in that manner, and (2) that it was not intended that the Commission should, in seeking to give effect to the wishes of the inhabitants, rely on the verdicts of bare majorities as sufficient to justify alterations of the existing boundary.

As it has not been open to the Commission to ascertain the wishes of inhabitants by a direct vote, the Commission has necessarily had recourse to other sources of information, such as census returns, election results and evidence of persons claiming to speak on behalf of inhabitants in different areas or to have knowledge of their views.

The Commission has been invited by both parties to the boundary controversy to rely upon the census returns of 1911, showing the religious denominations to which inhabitants belong, as affording an indication of the wishes of the inhabitants,—the members of Protestant denominations being reckoned as wishing to be in Northern Ireland and Roman Catholics as wishing to be in the Irish Free State. The evidence heard from both sides, taken as a whole, strongly supports the view that in the areas to which it relates religious and political divisions do to-day, broadly speaking, correspond, and that apart from special circumstances affecting limited areas the 1911 Census returns may still be relied upon as showing with approximate accuracy the proportionate numbers of Catholics and Protestants in the different districts.

In examining these census returns for the purpose of ascertaining the wishes of inhabitants, allowance must however be made for many factors which cannot be determined with precision, *e.g.*, the extent to which the returns include temporary residents who are not entitled to be reckoned as inhabitants, or persons under age and therefore not qualified to vote.

The question of what majority of the inhabitants, estimated on the basis of census figures and the other information available, should be regarded as sufficient to justify an alteration in the existing boundary is a question to be determined by the Commission according to its discretion, with due regard to the above considerations, and to facts disclosed in the course of its enquiry as affecting particular areas.

With regard to the exercise of the Commission's discretion on this question, while unanimity is neither to be expected nor required, the Commission has adopted the principle that the case for a change on the basis of "the wishes of the inhabitants," apart from economic or geographic considerations one way or the other, is not made out unless the majority in favour of the change appears to be a substantial majority, *i.e.*, a majority representing a high proportion of the total number of persons entitled to rank as inhabitants of the district directly concerned.

Question 6.

The Commission, being required to determine the boundaries in accordance with the wishes of the inhabitants, should seek, in those areas which are recognised as falling within the range of boundary variations, to follow the wishes of inhabitants as closely as is reasonably possible, and should therefore be prepared to take as a unit of area in relation to which the wishes of inhabitants are to be ascertained the smallest area which can fairly be entitled, having regard to its size and situation, to be considered separately, and with regard to which separate data are available.

If the Commission were to adopt the suggestion that large areas such as the County or the Union should, on administrative grounds, be regarded as indivisible units, it would find itself compelled on such grounds to refuse to treat separately particular portions of a county or union where the inhabitants differed from the majority in the county or union as a whole, and therefore to override the wishes of the inhabitants of such portions. The Commission would thus in effect be setting up a new factor, administrative considerations, as superior to the wishes of the inhabitants.

The Commission, not being required to adopt any particular type of local division as the unit of area in reference to which the wishes of the inhabitants should be ascertained, is free to mark out, for the purpose of its work, as occasion requires, convenient units of area in the light of the three factors which it is required to take into account—wishes of inhabitants, economic and geographic conditions.

ANNEX TO CHAPTER III.

Chairman's Memorandum

ON ARTICLE XII OF ARTICLES OF AGREEMENT FOR A TREATY BETWEEN GREAT BRITAIN AND IRELAND.

[This Memorandum was prepared by the Chairman of the Commission, and submitted as a draft for consideration by his colleagues individually on September 11th, 1925, and subsequently formed the subject of private discussion with each of them. It was not at that stage treated as a document formally before the Commission. The Memorandum is printed without alteration in the form in which it was handed by the Chairman to his Colleagues, except that it was then marked as a draft.

Dr. MacNeill has requested that, in the event of the publication of this Memorandum among the Commission's documents, the following points should be recorded :—

(1.) That the Chairman when handing copies of the Memorandum to him and to Mr. Fisher stated that he did not wish to invite written replies, and suggested that they should abstain from furnishing written comments, at any rate at that stage, and that the subject should be dealt with by verbal discussion:

(2.) That Dr. MacNeill at a later stage furnished to the Chairman and to Mr. Fisher in a similar informal way copies, not signed, of an Opinion, stated to have been obtained from a high legal authority, in which the following question was discussed :—

" Can the Boundary Commission transfer any part of the area now within the jurisdiction of the Government of the Saorstat and add such part to the joint jurisdiction of the Government of Great Britain and the Government of Northern Ireland? "—

and a negative answer was given.]

Article XII reads as follows:—

" If, before the expiration of the said month, an address is presented to His Majesty by both Houses of Parliament of Northern Ireland to that effect, the powers of the Parliament and Government of the Irish Free State shall no longer extend to Northern Ireland, and the provisions of the Government of Ireland Act, 1920 (including those relating to the Council of Ireland), shall, so far as they relate to Northern Ireland, continue to be of full force and effect, and this instrument shall have effect subject to the necessary modifications.

" Provided that if such an address is so presented a Commission consisting of three persons, one to be appointed by the Government of the Irish Free State, one to be appointed by the Government of Northern Ireland and one, who shall be Chairman, to be appointed by the British Government, shall determine in accordance with the wishes of the inhabitants, so far as may be compatible with economic and geographic conditions, the boundaries between Northern Ireland and the rest of Ireland, and for the purposes of the Government of Ireland Act, 1920, and of this instrument, the boundary of Northern Ireland shall be such as may be determined by such Commission."

The Government of the Irish Free State have set forth their view as to the interpretation of this Article in the statement forwarded to the Commission with their letter of the 20th November, 1924. That view is summarised in the Government's submission :

" That the work of the Commission consists in ascertaining the wishes of the inhabitants of ' Northern Ireland,' with a view to determining in accordance with such wishes, so far as may be compatible with economic and geographic conditions, what portions of that area are entitled to withdraw permanently frcm the jurisdiction of the Irish Free State."

This submission must be read in conjunction with the view expressed in an earlier portion of the Statement that :

" It was not contemplated by the Treaty that any area within ' Northern Ireland ' should have the right to withdraw permanently from the jurisdiction of the Irish Free State, unless the majori y of the inhabitants of such area were in favour of this course."

In further explanation of the contention of the Government of the Irish Free State, the following passage may be quoted from the Proceedings before the Commission when the Attorney-General and Serjeant Hanna argued the case on behalf of that Government :

" *The Chairman.*—Do I understand that the position you take up is that the Proviso requires the Commission to exclude from Northern Ireland, as hitherto defined, such portions as may be selected for exclusion after ascertaining the wishes of the inhabitants?

The Attorney-General.—Yes.

The Chairman.—The difficulty which suggests itself is that the terms of the Article do not say ' exclude from Northern Ireland.' It says ' determine the boundaries '—which might mean either exclusion or inclusion.

The Attorney-General.—Your work consists in ascertaining, in accordance with the wishes of the inhabitants, what portions of the six counties are entitled to go permanently out of the jurisdiction of the Irish Free State. When once the work of the Commission is finished and that has been determined, the portions so determined shall constitute Northern Ireland for the purpose of the Government of Ireland Act, 1920, and of the Treaty.

The Chairman.—You say it should be ' what portions of Northern Ireland are to be permanently included in Northern Ireland.' Or you would say ' what territory included in the present limits of Northern Ireland is to constitute the permanent territory of Northern Ireland?'

The Attorney-General.—That is just it; the present arrangement is a purely temporary one."

The Attorney-General further said at a later stage :

" The question as to whether an area is to be under the jurisdiction of the Parliament of the Irish Free State or under the jurisdiction of the Parliament of Northern Ireland is to be determined by the wishes of the inhabitants of that area, subject in case of necessity to the qualification in connection with economic and geographic conditions. For that reason I suggest that though the word ' areas ' is not expressly referred to in Article 12, it is

[13849]

referred to by implication when you are directed to ascertain the wishes of the inhabitants, because that is clearly indicated in Article 12 as being the dominant factor in determining this boundary."

In dealing with the question of a plebiscite, the Attorney-General proposed to exclude from the area in which a vote should be taken the whole County of Antrim and the City of Belfast. With regard to this point, he said :

The Attorney-General.—" It is well known that in a portion of the County of Antrim there is a very considerable community who would be strongly in favour of being under the jurisdiction of the Irish Free State ; but I am afraid they are so much cut off by a population whose views are the other way that for geographical reasons it would be impossible for them to come in.

Prima facie, I would suggest that the vote should be taken over the entire of Northern Ireland ; but at the moment I do not ask you to take a vote over any portion of the County of Antrim or in the City of Belfast. That is of course without prejudice to any claim which may be made by local persons or local bodies."

Before proceeding further, one general remark may be made with regard to the contention of the Government of the Irish Free State as explained in the above extracts. Their contention as to the interpretation to be put on Article XII means that the effect of the proviso is not merely to provide for the determination of the boundaries of Northern Ireland, but to raise, as to every portion of the existing territory of Northern Ireland, the question whether that territory shall be retained within the limits of Northern Ireland, and thus to open up the fundamental question as to whether or not Northern Ireland itself shall continue to exist. Though the Attorney-General was prepared to concede, taking into account the actual facts as to the distribution of the population, that no purpose would be served by taking a vote in Antrim and Belfast, the logical effect of the contention of his Government is—that the question of remaining within the limits of Northern Ireland is, by the proviso to Article XII, made an open question for the inhabitants of the whole of Northern Ireland as defined by the Government of Ireland Act, 1920 ; so that the Commission, if it could so read the wishes of the inhabitants of Northern Ireland, would, under the terms of the proviso, be entitled to abolish Northern Ireland altogether and include the whole of its area within the territory of the Irish Free State. Even if it be conceded, as the Attorney-General did concede, that after full effect had been given to the proviso, interpreted in the sense for which he contended, certain areas would inevitably be left to " Northern Ireland," the total area and population so left might on this interpretation be so reduced as to make the continued existence of Northern Ireland as such, *i.e.,* as a province of the United Kingdom governed under the provisions of the Government of Ireland Act, impossible. Some of the advocates of this interpretation frankly acknowledged that this was, in fact, the object which they hoped to see achieved as the result of an application of the proviso interpreted in this sense.

For the purposes of comparison it may be as well to set side by side with the contention of the Irish Free State the contention as to the interpretation of Article XII put forward by the County Council of Fermanagh, in the Resolution forwarded with their letter of the 20th December, in which the Council in effect asks the Commission for an assurance that the duties of the Commission " are confined to the mere rectification of anomalies on both sides of the existing border only." The contention embodied in this formula may be taken as typical of the views of many of the supporters of the Northern Ireland point of view. The use of the words "rectification" and "anomalies," both of which themselves appear to require definition, make this suggested formula itself somewhat difficult to interpret; but the main points on which the interpretation, which it is intended to convey, differs from that put upon the proviso to Article XII by the Free State Government are:—

(1) that in determining the boundary under the terms of reference, the Commission has to treat the existing boundary as its starting point and to correct the defects in that boundary instead of setting out, as the Free State Government invite it to do, to make a new boundary without regard to the existing boundary save in so far as that existing boundary is to bar the addition of any territory to the present territory of Northern Ireland;

(2) that, in this suggested "rectification" of the existing boundary, that boundary may be shifted in either direction, that is either so as to include in the Irish Free State portions of territory at present forming part of Northern Ireland, or so as to include in Northern Ireland portions of territory at present forming part of the Irish Free State; and

(3) that the Commission is not entitled to make alterations of the boundary affecting large areas, but that its scope is restricted to the making of what may be described as minor modifications of the existing boundary.

In supporting the contention put forward by the Government of the Irish Free State, the Attorney-General and Serjeant Hanna based their arguments—

(1) on the construction of Article XII itself;

(2) on the relation between that Article and the other Articles of the Treaty; and

(3) on the circumstances leading up to the Treaty, and the nature of the problem existing at the date when the Treaty was signed, which, according to their contention, Article XII was intended to solve.

In arguing their case they took the third point first, but it will be convenient to take their arguments in the order above given, for the first duty of a Court interpreting any written instrument is to consider what is the meaning of the words taken in their grammatical and ordinary sense. I will begin therefore with the question of construction of Article XII.

The two main points of interpretation which arise in connection with the contention to which the greater part of the argument was devoted—that the Commission in "determining the boundaries" must confine its attention to the existing area of Northern Ireland, and is not authorised to shift the existing boundary so as to include in Northern Ireland any territory on the Irish Free State side of that boundary, are—

(1) the meaning of the phrase "determine the boundaries," and

(2) the words to be supplied after "inhabitants." The Commission is to determine the boundaries "in accordance with the wishes of the inhabitants," and the question is "the inhabitants of what?" What are the areas which the inhabitants, whose wishes must be taken into account, are to inhabit?

[13849]

These two questions are very closely linked together—if we can settle the point as to the meaning of the phrase '' determine the boundaries,'' that in itself will throw some light on the question as to the inhabitants whose wishes are to be regarded. On the other hand, if we can settle the point as to the areas where the wishes of the inhabitants are to be ascertained, we shall get light as to what is meant by '' determination of the boundaries.'' The two questions may therefore be fairly described as interdependent, neither can be satisfactorily solved without the other.

Primâ facie the words ' determine the boundaries '' do not appear in themselves to offer any difficulty so far as this point is concerned. Power to '' determine the boundaries '' between two already ascertained areas A. and B. clearly includes, in the absence of some indication in the context to the contrary, power to vary in either direction any existing boundary between such areas; that is, power to shift the boundary so as to give either to area A. portions of area B., or to area B. portions of area A.

The question as to the words to be supplied after '' the inhabitants '' is not one to which any obvious answer immediately suggests itself. The word '' inhabitants '' taken by itself is clearly incomplete. A person can only be an '' inhabitant '' in relation to some particular place or territory, and we must therefore ask ourselves what words should, on the natural reading of the clause, taking the words in their ordinary and natural sense, be supplied after '' the inhabitants.'' The Attorney-General says that the place which is being dealt with by the Article is Northern Ireland; that the words '' Northern Ireland '' are repeated right through the beginning of the Article, and that therefore the natural words to supply after '' the inhabitants '' are the words '' of Northern Ireland.'' It is quite true that Article XII deals with Northern Ireland, and that in the first portion of the Article, before we come to the proviso, the words '' Northern Ireland '' are three times repeated. The Parliament of the Irish Free State is, however, mentioned in this first portion of the article as well as the Parliament of Northern Ireland. When we come to the proviso we find three governments referred to as entitled to appoint members to the Commission—the Government of the Irish Free State, the Government of Northern Ireland and the British Government; and the duties of the Commission so appointed are stated in the words '' shall determine, in accordance with the wishes of the inhabitants, so far as may be compatible with economic and geographic conditions, the boundaries between Northern Ireland and the rest of Ireland.'' It appears to me that if the order of these words had been altered so as to make the object of the verb '' determine '' follow immediately the word itself—'' shall determine the boundaries between Northern Ireland and the rest of Ireland in accordance with the wishes of the inhabitants,'' it would have been quite impossible to contend that the words to be read in after '' inhabitants '' should be words which would exclude from the inhabitants to be taken into account any inhabitants other than the inhabitants of Northern Ireland, and I do not think that the mere fact that the object of the verb comes late in the clause is sufficient to make the construction contended for the natural construction. It appears to me that the natural reading of the clause is to take the words '' the inhabitants '' as meaning the inhabitants concerned— that is the inhabitants concerned in a determination of the boundaries between Northern Ireland and the rest of Ireland, and that according to ordinary grammatical construction no words can properly be read in after "inhabitants" so as to restrict the area in which the wishes of the inhabitants are to be taken into account to Northern Ireland. Who then are the inhabitants concerned? The inhabitants concerned are surely the inhabitants whose fate may be affected by the determination of the boundary; in other words, the inhabitants of boundary regions or areas. That, no doubt, is itself a vague term, and further consideration of the other terms of the clause is required in order to see what regions or areas should, for the purpose of the clause, be regarded as boundary regions or areas.

We come back then to the words "determine the boundaries," and, if there is nothing which compels us to modify the meaning of those words taken in their ordinary and natural sense, there can, I think, be no doubt at all that a Commission which is appointed to determine the boundaries between two areas is entitled to shift the existing boundary between such areas—if there is one—in either direction; that is, a Commission which is required to determine the boundaries between A and B may so shift an existing boundary as to take away from A and give to B, or to take away from B and give to A. There is an existing boundary of which this Commission appointed to determine the boundaries between Northern Ireland and the rest of Ireland is bound to take account. That boundary is the boundary established by Section *one* of the Government of Ireland Act, which by sub-section (2) provides that:

" for the purposes of this Act, Northern Ireland shall consist of the parliamentary counties of Antrim, Armagh, Down, Fermanagh, Londonderry, and Tyrone, and tho parliamentary boroughs of Belfast and Londonderry, and Southern Ireland shall consist of so much of Ireland as is not comprised within the said parliamentary counties and boroughs."

The term "Northern Ireland" as used in Article XII clearly means not some vague indefinite area in the north of Ireland, but the Northern Ireland established and defined by the Government of Ireland Act, 1920, and it is the boundary between this "Northern Ireland" and "the rest of Ireland" which is to be "determined," or in effect, as there is already an existing boundary, redetermined. But there is nothing in the Article to make this boundary a limit which can only be shifted to the advantage of the Irish Free State and to the disadvantage of Northern Ireland, or in other words, a limit which, while reserving to the Irish Free State its present territory as an inalienable and irreducible minimum, makes the present territory of Northern Ireland a maximum which is subject to reduction, but which is incapable of the slightest extension. Taking then the proviso to Article XII in the ordinary and natural sense of the words used, the Commission set up by that Article is authorised to shift the boundary in either direction as may be required on a proper assessment of the different factors which the proviso directs it to take into account.

To come back to the interpretation offered by the representatives of the Irish Free State, it is worthy of remark that the mere supplying of the words "of Northern Ireland" after "the inhabitants" would not give the clause the meaning for which they contend. If the clause were read with these words inserted, it would apparently mean that the boundaries of Northern Ireland were to be determined in accordance with the wishes of the inhabitants of Northern Ireland consulted *en bloc* as a single group; whereas what the Free State Government desire, and what they say the clause itself was intended to provide for, is the ascertainment of the wishes of the inhabitants of

Northern Ireland by areas, so that the inhabitants of each area may decide the destiny of that particular area. It is clear that in order to get this meaning into the clause other words would have to be read in, in addition to the words " of Northern Ireland." It is difficult to say exactly what such words should be. It would not do from the Free State point of view to say " the inhabitants concerned within Northern Ireland," because according to their contention every inhabitant of Northern Ireland may claim to have his wishes taken into account. By Northern Ireland therefore they mean the whole of Northern Ireland and not certain selected regions. The interpretation they contend for would apparently be expressed by supplying after the words " the inhabitants of Northern Ireland " the further words " as ascertained by selected areas."

So far I have, in examining Article XII, concentrated attention on the proviso, but the proviso must of course be examined in relation to the preceding provision of the Article to which it is attached. The opening words of the Article give to the two Houses of Parliament of Northern Ireland the power by presenting an Address to His Majesty to secure that " the powers of the Parliament and Government of the Irish Free State shall no longer extend to Northern Ireland," and that " the provisions of the Government of Ireland Act, 1920 (including those relating to the Council of Ireland), shall, so far as they relate to Northern Ireland, continue to be of full force and effect." If the proviso were given the effect for which the Government of the Irish Free State contend, its terms would be wide enough, as pointed out above, to destroy the effect of the clause which it purports to qualify. If, however, the object of the proviso is not to give all the inhabitants of Northern Ireland a second option with regard to their inclusion in, or exclusion from, the Irish Free State, but to provide for the revision of the boundaries of the excluded area, it falls into its natural place as a subordinate provision of the Article to which it is appended.

The proviso to Article XII was described by the Attorney-General as " a qualification upon the right of the six counties to go out of the jurisdiction of the Irish Free State." Serjeant Hanna put a similar point : —

" What I submit to your judgment is this :—that if the Northern Parliament present a petition that the Irish Free State powers should no longer extend to them, the position would then be that the Northern Parliament shall continue their powers under the Act of 1920, but they shall not necessarily have the territory of 1920. And why should they not have that territory? Because of the Treaty, and because on the Treaty basis of Ireland being a unit, there is a portion of that population who desire to secede from the Free State. The wishes of the ' inhabitants ' are to be ascertained. The word ' inhabitant ' implies territory; it connotes geographical habitation. Therefore you cannot deal with inhabitants in this connection save by dealing with an area of territory. When the word ' inhabitant ' is used it clearly shows that it is a question of the territory which those inhabitants inhabit. The Northern Government, if they put in the petition, were to continue to have the powers under the Act of 1920, but they were not to have the territory, unless it is determined under the Treaty that they are entitled to it. The only territory they are to have will be the territory determined by the Boundary Commission, under the Treaty."

This argument suggests that the proviso to Article XII should be read in effect as involving a penalty which the Government and Parliament of Northern Ireland were to suffer in the event of their deciding to remain outside the Irish Free State. It does not, however, appear to me that either the actual terms of the Article itself, or the general situation arising under the Treaty with which it was intended to deal, support this view. If under the first portion of Article XII the Northern Parliament decides for separation, the proviso says the boundaries of Northern Ireland are to be determined by a Commission. There is, as I have already remarked, nothing in the proviso itself which limits the determination of the boundaries to the exclusion from Northern Ireland of portions of the territory included within Northern Ireland by the Government of Ireland Act, 1920. The Article provides for the contingency of separation between two portions of Ireland. If there was to be a separation under Article XII, it was a separation of far greater importance than the separation provided for under the Government of Ireland Act, because the boundary between Northern Ireland and the Free State was to be a far more important boundary than the boundary between Northern Ireland and Southern Ireland. Under the Government of Ireland Act the boundary was a boundary between two provinces, both of which still remained portions of the United Kingdom and were represented in the Imperial Parliament at Westminster. Under the Treaty, in the contingency provided for in Article XII, the boundary was to become a boundary between a province of the United Kingdom and a Dominion, vested with all the powers of a self-governing Dominion, including powers to make its own customs tariff and thus to render necessary the erection of a customs barrier between the two countries. The boundary which had originated as a provincial boundary might under Article XII be converted into a national boundary. A provision, that in this event the boundary should be reconsidered, would appear to be a natural provision to insert in the Treaty in the interests of the inhabitants of both territories concerned. Similar reasons explain the distinction made between Article XII and Article XIV, by the insertion of the proviso as to boundaries in Article XII, and its omission from Article XIV. The boundary of Northern Ireland, if it remained outside the Free State under Article XII, was obviously destined to be a very much more important boundary than it would have been if Northern Ireland had become a provincial area forming part of the Free State under Article XIV.

Before leaving the question of the construction of Article XII considered by itself, I must also refer to the argument which was put forward by the Attorney-General and by Serjeant Hanna that the terms of the Article are not such as to cover any transfer to Northern Ireland of territory from the Irish Free State side of the existing border. I have had some difficulty in following this argument, except in so far as it depends on interpretation of those phrases in the proviso which have already been examined ; but the Attorney-General said:

" You will of course remember this; the Irish Free State is a self-governing power within the British Commonwealth of Nations with full and absolute powers of legislation . . . There are some express limitations to which the Free State has agreed. Subject to these, of course, it is a State with full powers; and may I suggest that I do not think this Commission or any other body will have power to come in or to interfere in any way with its territory."

The point was further dealt with by Serjeant Hanna, who said:

" If it had been intended that the Free State territory should be transferred to Northern Ireland—or in other words, to Great Britain—if it had been the intention that territory should be transferred from this new State (the 26 counties) to Great Britain, the people who provided that must be presumed to have understood that the Free State had plenary powers and that the reserved powers would have been introduced on the transfer of any portion of the Free State 26 counties; so that the plenary powers which had been transferred should be re-transferred."

The Chairman.—" Is not the reference to the Government of Ireland Act quite sufficient ? "

Serjeant Hanna.—" That would be a very inapt and inartistic and unprofessional way of re-transferring powers which were in the Irish Free State."

The Chairman.—" You say ' re-transferring.' "

Serjeant Hanna.—" If they had contemplated taking Free State territory into Great Britain, they would have had supplemental words to indicate that whatever was necessary to make it a legal adjustment would follow."

The Chairman.—" Would it be more difficult supposing such a change was made? The boundary fixed by the Government of Ireland Act is maintained, until the Commission has decided it, for the purpose of government and legislation for the time being. If the result of the Commission's award was to diminish the territory of Northern Ireland, that would mean that various laws which now apply to a portion of Northern Ireland would cease to apply and the Free State laws would apply instead. If the words of the Article are sufficient for that, are they not also sufficient for a transfer of the other kind ? "

Serjeant Hanna.—" I contend they are not; I think it is because there is a difference between the two. This topic arose by my submitting to you that this Commission had no powers to transfer to Great Britain the plenary powers over any portion of the Free State which they might determine to transfer back to Great Britain. This Commission has no power to transfer Free State powers back to the British Parliament."

I find it very difficult to follow the argument indicated in the above extracts. The proviso to Article XII concludes with the words, " and for the purposes of the Government of Ireland Act, 1920, and of this instrument, the boundary of Northern Ireland shall be such as may be determined by such Commission." It appears to me that these words are sufficient to cover any transfer of territory resulting from the determination of the boundaries by the Commission, whether the transfer is from Northern Ireland to the Irish Free State or from the Irish Free State to Northern Ireland. On the determination of the boundaries by the Commission all the necessary legal results will follow by virtue of the words just quoted. The representatives of the Irish Free State say that these words are sufficient to cover the transfer of territory from Northern Ireland to the Irish Free State, but not sufficient to cover the transfer from the Irish Free State to Northern Ireland. It appears to me that the two transfers stand exactly on the same footing—if the words are sufficient to cover the one then they are also sufficient to cover the other. In my opinion the words are clearly sufficient to cover any transfer of territory from one side or the other of the existing border which the Commission's determination of boundaries may involve.

I now come to the argument based on the relation between Article XII and the rest of the instrument of which it forms part. The contention of the representatives of the Irish Free State under this head was that Article XII must be read in the light of the other provisions of the Treaty, that the general intention of the Treaty must be taken into account in interpreting that Article, and that the actual terms of the Article itself must be given a liberal interpretation so as to bring it into accord with the intention of the Treaty as a whole. The intention of the Treaty as a whole was, they say, to recognise the unity of Ireland and to provide that the whole of Ireland should become the Irish Free State. "The Treaty," said the Attorney-General,

" was undoubtedly a Treaty for the whole of Ireland and not for any part of Ireland. It is only necessary to look at the first Article of the Treaty in order to see this. The document itself is called ' Articles of Agreement for a Treaty between Great Britain and Ireland,' and it provides in the first Article that ' Ireland shall have the same constitutional status in the Community of Nations known as the British Empire as the Dominion of Canada, the Commonwealth of Australia, the Dominion of New Zealand and the Union of South Africa, with a parliament having powers to make laws for the peace, order and good government of Ireland, and an Executive responsible to that Parliament, and shall be styled and known as the Irish Free State.' "

Serjeant Hanna dealing with the same point, said:

" I would ask the Commission to regard this from the standpoint of international law as a *secession* of a section of the inhabitants of the Irish Free State from the Free State, and that you should regard yourselves—as I submit you are—as a tribunal established to determine the extent and method of that secession. For the purpose of establishing that main issue it is necessary in the first place that you should be satisfied that the unit—the fundamental governing unit—the geographic unit—with which you are concerned is *Ireland*, with its existing territorial and geographical boundaries. That I think, and venture to submit, is almost demonstrated by the clauses of the Treaty. The more important clauses were referred to by the learned Attorney-General, more especially Clause I.

In almost every one of these sections of the Treaty the territory that was being dealt with from a geographical point of view was Ireland; and it is referred to sometimes as ' Ireland ' and sometimes as the ' Irish Free State,' the two terms being for the purpose of the Treaty geographically coterminous. Sec. 1 refers to ' Ireland ' and says that it shall have a certain status with a Parliament having powers to make laws ' for the good government of Ireland '—that is the geographical Ireland ; the island—and ' it (*i.e.*, Ireland) shall be known as the Irish Free State.' "

He then dealt with various Articles of the Treaty in detail down to Article VIII, and proceeded:

" This all shows, in the interpretation of this Treaty, the basic idea that the tribunal will seek for, what is the common thought that runs through the minds of the two parties who are making the Treaty ? No interpretation that may be sought to be put on it several years after the contract has been entered into can affect what was the common thought of the two parties when they entered into this Agreement. I respectfully submit that it becomes clearer and clearer that the British Government were dealing with the whole, and that the common thought in their mind was to make provision for the whole of Ireland and for the people who wish to secede from the Irish Free State."

For the purpose of dealing with the argument as to the relation between Article XII and the other Articles of the Treaty, I am separating it from the argument as to the circumstances leading up to the Treaty, which I shall take last, though the two arguments were put forward together. Excluding for the moment, therefore, the argument as to the circumstances leading up to the Treaty, and regarding the Treaty as speaking for itself, I understand the argument to be that in view of the title given to the instrument, and of the recognition of the unity of Ireland contained in its leading provisions, a restrictive interpretation must be given to the terms of Article XII so as to minimise the extent to which under that Article a breach can be made in the unity of Ireland, and the extent to which the territory assigned to the Free State by the opening Articles of the Treaty can under the terms of that Article be reduced. It does not appear to me that this argument can derive much support from a detailed examination of the terms of the Treaty. It is quite true that until we come to Article XII Ireland is treated as a single unit, and the terms "Irish Free State" and "Ireland" are treated as interchangeable, but Article XI introduces the question of separate treatment for Northern Ireland; and Article XII provides definitely for the exclusion of Northern Ireland from the Irish Free State and for the continued existence of Northern Ireland under the terms of the Government of Ireland Act, 1920. The Article provides that if the Address to which it refers is presented, the provisions of that Act shall, so far as they relate to Northern Ireland, continue to be of full force and effect, and that "this instrument (the Treaty) shall have effect subject to the necessary modifications." This means that all the modifications which necessarily follow from the provisions as to Northern Ireland contained in the first part of Article XII shall be made in the other Articles of the instrument. If full effect is given to these words in Article XII, it follows that, once the Address provided for in that Article has been presented, its provisions as to the future of Northern Ireland must be treated as governing the interpretation of the other Articles of the Treaty. It appears to me, therefore, that, once the Address has been presented, the other Articles of the Treaty must be interpreted in the light of Article XII rather than *vice versa*.

I come now to a subordinate argument as to the relations between Article XII and Article XV. Articles XIV and XV together provide what is to be the position of Northern Ireland in the event of no such Address as is mentioned in Article XII being presented. Article XIV says that in that event "the Parliament and Government of Northern Ireland shall continue to exercise, as respects Northern Ireland, the powers conferred on them by the Government of Ireland Act, 1920, but the Parliament and Government of the Irish Free State shall, in Northern Ireland, have, in relation to matters in respect of which the Parliament of Northern Ireland has not power to make laws under that Act (including matters which under the said Act are within the jurisdiction of the Council of Ireland), the same powers as in the rest of Ireland, subject to such other provisions as may be agreed in manner hereinafter appearing"—that is agreed under the terms of Article XV. Article XV provides that the Government of Northern Ireland and the provisional Government of Southern Ireland (which is to be constituted under Article XVII for the purpose of carrying on the administration of Southern Ireland pending the institution of a parliament and government of the Irish Free State) may meet for the purpose of discussing and agreeing upon the provisions subject to which Article XIV is to operate, and these provisions may include various safeguards in respect to Northern Ireland, including " (d) safeguards for minorities in Northern Ireland."

The Attorney-General's argument with regard to the bearing of this Article on Article XII was as follows:

" It was recognised that once the territory of the six counties was left intact, as set up by the Government of Ireland Act, some provision would have to be made with reference to these large minorities in Northern Ireland. It was done by Article 15, which contemplates safeguards in this way. The other alternative is Article 12, which contemplates the North going out. In that event there is no suggestion for any Convention of this kind, because, may I suggest, it was contemplated that in that event the work of this Commission would be to bring these minorities—those large minorities—within the jurisdiction of the Parliament and Government of the Irish Free State."

The contention therefore is, that the absence from the Treaty of any special provision for safeguarding minorities in Northern Ireland, in the event of Northern Ireland exercising the option, given to it under Article XII, to remain outside the Free State, shows that the intention of the proviso to Article XII was that, in the event of Northern Ireland remaining outside the Free State, the minorities in Northern Ireland which were in favour of the Free State should, by a rearrangement of the boundaries, be removed from Northern Ireland. There are several answers to this argument:—

(1) the provision made in Article XV is a provision enabling the two Governments to come to an agreement which, if arrived at, would govern the application of Article XIV; but, if the two Governments fail to arrive at an agreement, there is nothing in Article XV to compel the provision of such safeguards as might be provided by agreement; and if the two Governments fail to arrive at such an agreement as that article contemplates, the article becomes inoperative. It is clear, from an examination of the different sub-clauses of Article XV, that the idea of that Article was, that, in the event of Northern Ireland remaining within the Free State, both sections of the population in Northern Ireland might obtain protection for their respective interests by means of an agreement between the two Governments. If clause (d) is to be taken as referring only to the minorities in Northern Ireland, which were regarded as in close sympathy with the Free State, the other clauses of the Article are obviously intended to make provision for the protection of the interests of other sections of the population of Northern Ireland, which, in the event of Northern Ireland becoming a portion of the Free State, might be adversely affected by the action of the Free State Government and Parliament. In such a negotiation, therefore, as was contemplated by Article XV each Government might have something to gain and something to give. Article XV, though in itself inoperative until the agreement between the two Governments was reached, pointed the way to an arrangement which might be for the benefit of both sections of the population, and might thus facilitate the union of the whole of Ireland in the Irish Free State. If, however, Northern Ireland chose under Article XII to remain outside the Free State, a similar opportunity for negotiation would not arise, and therefore in that case there is no corresponding provision.

(2) Article XVI contains general provision for the protection of religious minorities both in the Irish Free State and in Northern Ireland. In effect it re-enacts Section *five* of the Government of Ireland Act, which prevents the passing of legislation which would adversely affect the interests of religious minorities. Provision for the protection of religious minorities in Northern Ireland is therefore made by Article XVI, and that provision operates whether Northern Ireland remains outside the Free State or becomes part of the Free State.

(3) Owing to the facts with regard to the distribution of population in Northern Ireland, it was inevitable that in any event a substantial Catholic minority should remain within the limits of Northern Ireland. This is recognised by the Attorney-General in his argument, when he accepts the position that no arrangement of boundaries could be made

under the proviso to Article XII which would not leave within the limits of Northern Ireland the Catholic population of Belfast and Antrim.

I now come to the argument based on the circumstances leading up to the Treaty, and the nature of the problem existing at the date when the Treaty was signed which Article XII was intended to solve. The Attorney-General contended that—

(1) all the circumstances leading up to the Treaty, and
(2) the "unquestioned and unquestionable fact" that the problem which Article XII was designed to solve was the problem existing in the six counties of Northern Ireland

showed that this Article must be considered solely with reference to the area included in Northern Ireland.

With regard to the circumstances leading up to the Treaty the Attorney-General's contention was that those circumstances showed that the Irish delegation which negotiated the Treaty was acting for the whole of Ireland. As I have already mentioned he contended that this fact appeared on the face of the Treaty itself. In dealing with the historical facts on which he relied for the purpose of reinforcing the argument based on the terms of the Treaty, he referred generally to the history of Ireland since the passing of the Act of Union, and traced the course of the agitation in favour of Home Rule, which ultimately resulted in the passing of the Government of Ireland Act, 1914, the operation of which was suspended by a suspensory act during the European war. Then, after touching on the history of the intervening years, he came to the events which immediately preceded the negotiations for the Treaty, and dealt with the position of the First and Second Dail. The delegates who negotiated the Treaty were appointed by the Second Dail—"that Second Dail, like the First Dail, proceeded to act as a Parliament for the whole of Ireland." "The Second Dail claimed to represent all Ireland; the plenipotentiaries appointed by it claimed to represent all Ireland, and were undoubtedly accepted on that basis by the representatives of the British Government. The Treaty which they arranged and signed was undoubtedly a Treaty for the whole of Ireland and not for any part of Ireland." Further the Attorney-General pointed out that of the "five plenipotentiaries" included in the Irish delegation two actually represented parliamentary seats in Northern Ireland. These historical facts, with regard to the authority and composition of the Irish delegation which negotiated the Treaty, were relied upon as showing that, as Ireland was represented as a nation in the negotiations for the Treaty, any provision for the exclusion from Ireland of a portion of the territory which that delegation claimed to represent should be restrictively interpreted, and should be limited in its operation so as to reduce to a minimum the portion of Ireland which might be taken out of the whole, and thereby infringe upon the principle of national unity.

For the purpose of dealing with this argument I assume all the facts to be as stated in the formal statement of the Irish Free State and the argument of the Attorney-General. Accepting the facts as thus stated, I am not satisfied that this argument, based on extrinsic circumstances, carries the case for a restrictive interpretation of Article XII further than the arguments, already referred to, based on the terms of the Treaty itself. The question is not what were the aspirations and efforts of the Irish people, or a majority of them, towards attainment of national unity and self-government during the period prior to the signature of the Treaty, but how far does the Treaty itself by its own terms go towards fulfilling such aspirations and crowning such efforts with success. We cannot be justified in starting with an *a priori* view that the intention of the Treaty was to fulfil completely aspirations towards national unity, and then set to work on that basis to minimise any qualifications on such fulfilment which the Treaty itself contains. The terms of the qualifications themselves must be examined in due relation to the Treaty as a whole. I must add that, on the question of the representative character of the Irish delegates, the provision made for ratification in Article XVIII of the Treaty cannot be left out of account. That Article provides that the instrument "shall be submitted forthwith by His Majesty's Government for the approval of Parliament and by the Irish signatories to a meeting summoned for the purpose of the members elected to sit in the House of Commons of Southern Ireland." It is noteworthy that though the Treaty itself is described as a "Treaty between Great Britain and Ireland" the authority to which the Irish signatories were to submit it for ratification was an authority representing only Southern Ireland.

I now come to the argument as to the nature of the problem with which Article XII was intended to deal. In order to show the nature of the argument on this point the following passage may be quoted from the Proceedings:

The Attorney General.—"What was the problem intended to be solved by these Articles? It was this; that you had an area of six counties with a mixed population; a Parliament and Government had been set up for these six Counties which had acted to a certain extent, but in a halting and maimed manner, because of the 52 elected representatives only 40 ever attended the Parliament. You had portions of that area in which the inhabitants were almost unanimously in favour of being under the jurisdiction and control of the Irish Free State : you had portions which were opposed to that. I start off with this proposition : that the problem which was intended to be solved by Article XII and Article XIV of the Treaty was the problem of a mixed population in these six counties."

The Chairman.—" So far as the question of mixed population is concerned, may there not be evidence that there is a mixed population on the other side of the border as well?"

The Attorney-General (continuing).—"Immediately after the Act of 1920 had been put into operation, or after an attempt had been made to put it into operation, of the persons elected to represent constituencies in Southern Ireland no one attended except the representatives for Dublin University. You cannot very well take Dublin University by itself. Not a single representative of the 26 counties attended. That was in June 1921. The Parliament was summoned for June 1921 (the 17th I think). Where is there any evidence there of any call by anybody in Southern Ireland to be taken out of the Free State or to have the 1920 Act put into operation? Please mark the sequence of events : the 17th June—abortive meeting of the House of Commons of Southern Ireland; early in July—negotiations for a truce which was arranged, and came into operation on the 11th July; correspondence between Mr. Lloyd George and Mr. de Valera up to September; plenipotentiaries appointed in September who came immediately to London; and the Treaty signed in December. I say—and I do not think I can be contradicted in this—that the sequence of events from June to December shows that the Treaty, or some arrangement of that kind, was necessitated by the events arising out of the Government of Ireland Act."

I may refer also to a portion of the Proceedings during Serjeant Hanna's argument:

Serjeant Hanna.—'' The history that has been put forward by the learned Attorney-General indicates, and the Treaty itself proclaims, that the dispute is a dispute as to the delimiting of Northern Ireland. Great Britain made no claim in connection with the Treaty or on the face of the Treaty for any of the 26 counties, and as to those in geographical Ulster prior to 1920, Great Britain had placed them outside the pale of the Northern Government in that year.''

The Chairman.—'' We have been asked to take into account historical circumstances. If we take those into account, this point should be considered by you and perhaps dealt with. The Attorney-General referred, and you refer, to certain historical circumstances bearing upon your argument. The Commission, I take it, is expected to keep its eyes open for any historical circumstances which could legitimately be taken into consideration. Can we therefore disregard the fact that there is a mixed population—to use the Attorney-General's phrase—on both sides of the existing border of Northern Ireland, and that the question as to the limit to be assigned to the jurisdiction of the Government and Parliament of Northern Ireland was a question which was a live one at the time that the Act of 1920 was dealt with, and had been a matter of very keen controversy before? If there was to be a division, the great point was as to where the dividing line should fall, and there were various claims. I want you to tell me what your contention is as to what the attitude of the Commission should be to that part of history.''

Serjeant Hanna.—'' There is no mandate in the Treaty or in Article 12 entitling you to take into consideration the wishes of the population anywhere in the Irish Free State, and I give you my reasons.''

The Chairman.—'' Are you basing this on the language of the Article or general circumstances?''

Serjeant Hanna.—'' As regards general circumstances, we have confined ourselves to what is contained in Acts of Parliament and international documents.''

The Chairman.—'' The statement covers other matters than Acts of Parliament; it indicates general history.''

Serjeant Hanna.—'' Our contention is that your minds should not be shut to our argument that the subject matter of the Treaty could not be to take territory from the Free State as well as from Northern Ireland, inasmuch as that would be going against the situation as depicted by the Treaty itself.''

The point put to the Attorney-General and to Serjeant Hanna with regard to the existence of a mixed population on the Irish Free State side of the Border, was not answered except by the contention that the Commission should confine its attention to the position which had developed subsequent to the enactment of the Government of Ireland Act, 1920. The argument, that the events which followed the passing of that Act showed that the question to be dealt with under Article XII was a question which concerned only the area of Northern Ireland as defined in the 1920 Act, is in itself open to criticism. The Attorney-General says that the result of the elections under the Government of Ireland Act, 1920, afforded no evidence ''of any call by anybody in Southern Ireland to be taken out of the Free State or to have the 1920 Act put into operation.'' But it is obvious that when the elections took place in May, 1921, there was no opportunity for a demand from anyone in Southern Ireland to be taken out of the Free State as the Free State did not then exist. Nor was there any opportunity for voters in Southern Ireland who took part in the elections of May, 1921, to put forward a demand that they should be included in Northern Ireland.

If, however, the Commission is to go into the historical facts with regard to the question of excluding Ulster in whole or in part from a self-governing Ireland, why should the story of events prior to the passing of the Government of Ireland Act, 1920, which first provided for the partition of Ireland, be excluded from consideration? Further, the British delegates, who took part in the negotiations for the Treaty and signed the Treaty, were all members of His Majesty's Government of the United Kingdom, and undertook to submit the Treaty for the approval of the Parliament of the United Kingdom. As a Government they were constitutionally responsible for the government of Ireland, to the extent of the functions reserved to the United Kingdom under the Government of Ireland Act, and the Parliament to which they had to submit the Treaty for ratification was a parliament which under the law included members representing all parts of Ireland, and, though the great majority of the members elected to represent constituencies in Southern Ireland had abstained from taking their seats, there were actually sitting in that Parliament members from Southern Ireland as well as from Northern Ireland. It is clear that the British Government and the British Parliament of 1921 owed a duty to all the inhabitants of Ireland, and that though the Treaty was described as a Treaty between Great Britain and Ireland, the British delegation and the British Parliament were bound, so far as their action with regard to the Treaty was concerned, by constitutional obligations to the inhabitants of Ireland as well as to the inhabitants of Great Britain. Serjeant Hanna in his argument with regard to Article XII said " supposing the British had not put this clause in. It was put in to protect their own supporters ; and it is obvious, without referring to contemporaneous history at all, that it was put in to avoid what would happen in any other country in circumstances which amounted in fact to a rebellion of one section of the community against the established government and desiring to establish their own." If the British delegation were putting this clause in to protect that section of the population of Northern Ireland to which Serjeant Hanna refers as " their own supporters," why should they shut their eyes to the interests of their own supporters on the Southern side of the border? The fact that there was a " mixed population," that is a population divided by political and religious differences, on the Southern side as well as on the Northern side of the border, was a notorious fact established by successive elections and by the census returns.

In this examination of the arguments on behalf of the Irish Free State I have so far concentrated attention on the contention, to which the greater part of that argument was more especially devoted, that Article XII does not empower the Commission to determine the boundary in such a way as to take from the Free State any territory which is on the Free State side of the existing border—in other words, that the existing boundary can only be shifted one way, namely, so as to reduce the existing area of Northern Ireland. The other main question raised as to the scope of the Commission's functions in determining the boundaries is a closely allied question, and much of what has been said has a bearing on this question also.

The Free State Government urge that determination of the boundaries involves a reconsideration of the whole area of Northern Ireland, and that the Commission in such a reconsideration must not be influenced by the existing boundary, except for the purpose of restricting the limits of its enquiry to the northern side of it, but must start *de novo*. If, in accordance with the view above expressed, the Commission's enquiry is not restricted to the existing area of Northern Ireland, and the Commission has authority to make transfers of territory either way, then obviously there can be no difference in the scope of the Commission's enquiry on the two sides of the existing boundary, and whatever it is proper for the Commission to do in Northern Ireland it must also do in the Irish Free State. What has already been said on the question of interpreting the words " determine the boundaries between Northern Ireland and the rest of Ireland " is sufficient to show that the theory, that it is the duty of the Commission to start *de novo* on a reconstruction of the map without any regard to the existing boundary, is in my opinion quite untenable. The Article does not say the Commission is to decide what areas are hereafter to constitute " Northern Ireland " and " the rest of Ireland," but that the Commission is to " determine the boundaries between Northern Ireland and the rest of Ireland." In dealing with " Northern Ireland " and the " rest of Ireland," the Commission is dealing not with vague geographical abstractions but with two ascertained territorial entities consisting, respectively, of " Northern Ireland " and " Southern Ireland " as constituted by Section *one* of the Government of Ireland Act, 1920. The fact that the term " the rest of Ireland " is used instead of " Southern Ireland " does not affect the position; in relation to Northern Ireland " the rest of Ireland " can only mean the area constituted by the Government of Ireland Act as Southern Ireland. No doubt the use of the name " Southern Ireland " was avoided because under the terms of the Treaty that name was to disappear.

The Commission must therefore start its examination of the whole question on the basis of the division as marked by the existing boundary between these two entities, must treat that boundary as holding good where no sufficient reason can be shown for altering it, and must only vary that boundary where the factors which Article XII directs it to take into account justify such variation.

As to the limits of such variation, the Article fails to give any specific direction. This is one of the many points on which the Article may be contrasted with the provisions for settlement of boundaries contained in the Versailles Treaty—Articles 88, 94–97 and 109. Those provisions contain precise directions as to the limits of the areas to be dealt with, as to who are to be regarded as inhabitants, as to the expression of the wishes of the inhabitants by votes taken for the purpose, and as to the units of area in which wishes are to be ascertained by this taking of votes.

On all these points Article XII fails to give any directions. It would seem, therefore, that these points are left to the discretion of the Commission, but it is necessary to consider closely the terms of the Article for the purpose of ascertaining whether it does not lay down, either expressly or by implication, principles which govern the exercise of such discretion.

I have suggested that the words to be supplied in Article XII after " the inhabitants " are some such words as " of the regions or areas concerned," and that the regions or areas concerned are boundary regions or areas, that is regions or areas within range of boundary variations—which may be directly affected by a revision of boundaries.

The fact that the wishes of the inhabitants are to be taken into account in the determination of the Boundary suggests that the areas to be considered are not to be merely areas insignificant in size, such as might be dealt with for the purpose of correcting minor irregularities in the line, and removing what might be called economic or geographic inconveniences. The principle of following the wishes of the inhabitants is a principle capable in itself of very wide application, and, if the inhabitants of one area are entitled to have their wishes considered, the denial of a similar privilege to the inhabitants of an adjoining area would involve an apparent discrimination against the latter which would require justification. If therefore the principle of following the wishes of the inhabitants is to be recognised in the revision of a boundary, what is to prevent us from applying that principle so as to include within the limit of boundary variations all areas in which the "wishes of the inhabitants," however that term may be understood, point in the direction of a change? Economic and geographic conditions are specified as factors which are to limit attempts to make the boundary follow the "wishes of the inhabitants"; that is where the inhabitants of an area wish that area to be placed on one side of the line, but giving effect to such wishes would cause economic or geographic inconvenience, that inconvenience, if sufficiently serious, will prevent effect being given to the wishes of the inhabitants. So much seems clear. Do the terms of the Article point to any considerations other than those arising from economic and geographic conditions which limit the areas within the range of boundary variation? I have already expressed the opinion that it is not the duty of the Commission to start de novo on a reconstruction of the map without any regard to the existing boundary, and that the Commission, having to deal with two ascertained territorial entities, must start on the basis of the division between them as marked by the existing boundary. Article XII also makes it clear, I think, that when the Commission has finished its work, these two territories with which it is dealing must each retain its own identity, that is, Northern Ireland when its boundaries have been determined must still be recognisable as the same provincial entity, and be capable of carrying on as a separate province of the United Kingdom with its own parliament and Government for provincial affairs under the Government of Ireland Act. The same principle applies mutatis mutandis to "the rest of Ireland," which must after a determination of the boundary retain its identity as the Irish Free State as constituted under the terms of the Treaty and be in a position to function accordingly, as a self-governing Dominion "in the Community of Nations known as the British Empire."

It is convenient to refer here to two arguments, which have been advanced from opposite points of view, with reference to this question of the extent of the areas which should be regarded as falling within the range of boundary variation. The first is an argument based on Section one (2) of the Government of Ireland Act, 1920, which is advanced by those who urge that the Commission is not authorised to do more than make minor alterations of the existing boundary. I understand the argument to be that as this section, which provides that Northern Ireland is to consist of the six parliamentary counties and two parliamentary boroughs therein named, stands unrepealed, the Commission has no power to make an alteration of the boundary which would involve the transfer to the Irish Free State either of the whole, or of the greater part, of any one of these eight units. The power to determine the boundaries of Northern Ireland conferred on the Commission by Article XII necessarily involves, however, power to vary the provisions of the section referred to, and I am therefore unable to assent to the argument that, because Section *one* (2) has not been expressly amended or repealed, the Commission must in carrying out its work respect each of the individual units of which Northern Ireland consists.

The question whether or not the Commission has power to make an alteration of the boundary which would involve the transfer to the Irish Free State of the whole, or the greater part, of any of the counties or boroughs mentioned in Section *one* (2) of the Government of Ireland Act, is a question which must in my opinion be considered in relation to the identity of Northern Ireland as a whole; and the question to be asked from this point of view, in regard to any such proposed alteration, is whether or not such alteration would destroy the identity of Northern Ireland as a whole, or so reduce its area and resources as to render it impossible for it to continue as a province of the United Kingdom governed under the provisions of the Government of Ireland Act. The fact that there is a list of units contained in Section *one* (2) of the Act does not appear to me in itself to prove that the maintenance of each of the units so named as a constituent part of Northern Ireland is essential to the maintenance of the identity of Northern Ireland.

The second argument to which I wish to refer is an argument, advanced by Counsel on behalf of the Irish Free State in dealing with the question of the inference to be drawn from the declaration contained in Article XII, that "the provisions of the Government of Ireland Act, 1920, . . shall so far as they relate to Northern Ireland continue to be of full force and effect." Counsel urged that the powers given to the Northern Government and Parliament by that Act were of a restricted and limited character, and were nothing more than "enlarged local government powers." With regard to this description it is clear that, just as the constitution of Northern Ireland under the Government of Ireland Act with its provision for two Houses of Parliament, and for Ministers responsible to Parliament, is not in form the constitution of a mere local government authority, so also the powers and responsibilities of the Government and Parliament of Northern Ireland are considerably in excess of the powers and responsibilities which we are accustomed to regard as attaching to local government authorities; if therefore they can be correctly described as enlarged local government powers, the enlargement is very considerable. But, whether or not this description can be regarded as fitting the powers conferred on the Government and Parliament of Northern Ireland by the Government of Ireland Act, the nature of these powers, and of the constitution under which Northern Ireland exists to-day, must, I think, be borne in mind in considering the extent to which its territory might properly be diminished under the provisions of Article XII.

I think a further conclusion follows from the view that the duty of the Commission is not to reconstitute the areas of Northern Ireland and of the Irish Free State, but to provide a better boundary between them. The Commission, starting its examination of the question on the basis of the existing boundary, must first consider the wishes of the inhabitants adjacent to that boundary, and where it finds an area, of sufficient size and population to merit separate consideration, which is at present on the right side of the border, that is on the side where its inhabitants wish to remain, the existence of that area will in itself be a reason against making an alteration which would involve its transfer to the wrong side, and will thus afford some guidance as to where a line should be drawn, and enable a point to be fixed beyond which alterations intended to give effect to the wishes of the inhabitants should not extend.

Where the area in question deserves to be ranked as "homogeneous" in the sense indicated below, the case against disregarding its wishes will of course be all the stronger. But it is impossible I think to lay down any precise rule as to the requirements which must be fulfilled in the case of individual areas, in order to entitle the wishes of their inhabitants to prevail. The conditions of an individual area cannot be considered alone, but must be examined in relation to conditions in adjacent areas. Overwhelming majorities in surrounding areas which desire a change may, in some cases, be sufficient to justify the disregarding of the wishes of an "island" community which is strongly against a change, though the same island, if situate in a region where parties were more equally divided, would serve to provide a fixed point marking the limit beyond which any change should not extend.

I propose now to deal with two further questions, which are of importance in themselves, and which also have a bearing on this question of the areas on either side of the existing border with which the Commission is authorised to deal:

(1.) In considering the wishes of inhabitants with regard to the determination of boundaries, what is the position with regard to majorities and minorities? Is unanimity to be required, or is a bare majority one way or the other to be sufficient?

(2.) What is the relation between the three different factors mentioned as affecting the determination of boundaries—wishes of inhabitants and economic and geographic conditions?

(1.) *Majorities.*

In considering the wishes of inhabitants with regard to the determination of boundaries, what is the position with regard to majorities and minorities? Is unanimity to be required, or is a bare majority one way or the other to be sufficient?

The Article says that the Commission is to determine the boundaries "in accordance with the wishes of the inhabitants so far as may be compatible with economic and geographic conditions." I have already remarked on the generality of these terms. The reference to "the wishes of the inhabitants" is not followed, as in the case of similar articles of the Versailles Treaty, by any detailed provisions as to the principles or methods to be adopted in the determination of boundaries on this basis: nor is any further guidance given as to the relation between the different factors mentioned— namely, wishes of inhabitants and economic and geographic conditions.

The wishes of the inhabitants which the Commission has to take into account fall, when considered in relation to the existing boundary, into two classes:

(1.) Wishes in favour of maintenance of the existing boundary:

[13849]

(2.) Wishes in favour of a change of the existing bounaary involving transfer of territory to the Irish Free State or to Northern Ireland, as the case may be.

I have already expressed the view that the Commission must treat the existing boundary as holding good where no sufficient reason can be shown for altering it. The onus is therefore on those who desire a change to prove that the facts justify a change.

The case for a change of the existing boundary may rest either (1) on the wishes of the inhabitants, or (2) on economic conditions, or (3) on geographic conditions, or (4) on a combination of considerations arising from these different factors.

Where the case for an alteration is based on the wishes of the inhabitants alone, it is obvious that the case will not be made out unless the evidence shows that a majority of the inhabitants is in favour of the proposed alteration. The Treaty says nothing as to the measure of agreement required among the inhabitants in support of any proposed determination of the boundary in order to entitle the Commission to regard such proposed determination as '' in accordance with the wishes of the inhabitants.'' It does not prescribe any particular majority as the majority required in order to make a verdict of inhabitants one way or the other decisive. It avoids this question just as it avoids defining the inhabitants who are to be entitled to have their wishes considered, the areas within which inhabitants' wishes are to be ascertained, and the unit of area which is to be adopted for the purpose of such ascertainment. It does not, in my opinion, follow from the omission of any reference to this question of a majority either (a) that the Commission can only accept a verdict which is unanimous, or (b) that the Commission is required to accept the verdict of a majority however small. It appears to me that the question of what majority is to be considered sufficient to justify a change of the existing boundary is left to the discretion of the Commission. If the Commission were to make a change in the boundary involving the transfer of an area containing 1,999 inhabitants simply in order to gratify 1,000 of such inhabitants at the cost of offending the other 999, such a proceeding would obviously be unreasonable. It would likewise be unreasonable if the Commission were to decline to make a change involving the transfer of an area containing, say, 1,000 inhabitants, of whom all save two or three desired the change merely because of the opposition of this insignificant minority. But in view of the fundamental character of the change involved in a transfer of territory from one jurisdiction to another, and of the dis-location of established conditions which must inevitably result from any such change, there is, I think, much to be said for adopting a rule that, where the case for a change of the existing boundary rests solely on the wishes of the inhabitants, and is not fortified by any economic or geographic considerations, the Commission would not be justified in making a change unless the majority in favour is substantial—i.e., represents a high proportion of the total number of inhabitants of the area concerned. I doubt if it is possible to lay down a definite rule for general application as to the percentage figure which should be regarded as sufficient to constitute a substantial majority. In considering whether or not the evidence showed the existence of a substantial majority in a particular area it would, I think, be right on the grounds indicated in a later paragraph, for the Commission to bear in mind any distinctions which could be fairly drawn between different classes or sections of the population whose wishes were being taken into account, according to the varying degrees of permanence implied by the nature of the ties attaching them to the area, and to allow extra weight to the wishes of those who represented the most permanent element in the population.

In discussing the effect to be given to Article XII the term " Homogeneous " is sometimes used. It is said, or suggested, that it is the duty of the Commission to respect the wishes of homogeneous areas and only to transfer from one side to the other homogeneous areas, which to-day find themselves on the wrong side of the boundary. " Homogeneous area " in this context means, I take it, if strictly interpreted, an area the population of which is of one mind, and which would, if asked to vote, give a unanimous vote in favour of being either in Northern Ireland or in the Irish Free State. In this sense there is probably no homogeneous area of any considerable size to be found on either side of the existing boundary, except perhaps in South Armagh, but an area in which there is an overwhelming majority in favour of one side or the other may be roughly described as homogeneous, and it is obviously desirable that the Commission should, so far as possible, respect the wishes of an area homogeneous in this sense which is so situated and of such a size as to form a unit fit for separate consideration.

The application of the principles above suggested will, in effect, mean that changes made in the existing boundary by the Commission on the basis of the wishes of the inhabitants should, generally speaking, be limited to cases where there are communities or districts predominantly of one character on the wrong side of the existing line, and that the wishes of the inhabitants taken alone would not be regarded as sufficient to justify a change in mixed communities, or districts where the evidence points to only a small percentage of advantage on one side or the other.

I am inclined to add that the greater the importance of the change demanded, in its effect on territory or population, the higher the percentage of inhabitants who can be regarded as supporters of the change which should be required to justify it. For instance, the transfer of an important town will cause a dislocation and disturbance of existing conditions far more serious than the transfer of a small agricultural district, and this circumstance should be taken into account, whether it is regarded merely as an economic factor affecting the case for transfer, or as a factor lending extra weight and importance to the wishes of those who are against transfer.

With reference to the question of the measure of respect with which the existing boundary should be regarded, it is right to mention the contention, which has been urged upon the Commission, that this particular boundary has none of the sanctity which would ordinarily attach to an existing state boundary. In support of this contention it has been pointed out that this boundary is not an ancient historical boundary, but only dates from the Act of 1920, and that this Act which first established the boundary was lacking in moral authority, because the inhabitants of the country were not directly consulted, the great majority of their representatives were actively opposed to it, and the minority only gave a tardy and reluctant acquiescence.

I think the answer to this contention is that, whatever can be said as to the circumstances in which the Government of Ireland Act, 1920, was passed, the boundary fixed by that Act was a boundary legally fixed, and is therefore entitled to be respected as such, and the establishment of this boundary, which had already come into legal operation when the Articles of Agreement for a Treaty were signed, immediately gave rise to certain vested rights and interests which should not be lightly interfered with. The interests created by the establishment of that boundary have of course developed and extended during the four years which have now elapsed since it first took effect. The point has been made that this period of delay was not contemplated by the Treaty, but was due to a failure to carry out the provisions of the Treaty as to the appointment of the Commission, for which the Government of the Irish Free State was in no way responsible, and that this delay should therefore not be allowed to prejudice the interests of that Government and its supporters in relation to the application of Article XII.

From an examination of dates, and of the terms of the Treaty, it appears, however, that the boundary first became operative on the 19th April, 1921, the appointed day under Section 73 of the Government of Ireland Act; that while the Treaty was dated the 6th December, 1921, the Commission could not in any case have been appointed before December, 1922, when the Act of Parliament ratifying the Treaty was passed, and the Address of both Houses of the Parliament of Northern Ireland provided for in Article XII was presented; and that the date of the despatch announcing the nomination by the Government of the Irish Free State of their member of the Commission was the 19th July, 1923, two years and three months after the date when the boundary established by the Government of Ireland Act first became operative. The Commission was actually constituted fifteen months later on the 29th October, 1924.

It thus appears that of the total period of three years and six months, which intervened between the date when the boundary first became operative and the date of the constitution of the Commission, nearly half had elapsed before it became legally possible to appoint the Commission, and nearly two-thirds had elapsed before the nomination of their member by the Government of the Irish Free State.

In considering the question whether it was the intention of Article XII that the Commission when determining the boundary " in accordance with the wishes of the inhabitants " should accept the wishes of a bare majority as decisive one way or the other, it is necessary to bear in mind the further point that the Commission is given no special powers for the purpose of ascertaining the wishes of inhabitants, and has therefore no means of arriving at precise figures as to such wishes.

This point is dealt with below.

(2.) *Relation between wishes of inhabitants and economic and geographic conditions.*

What is the relation between the three different factors mentioned as affecting the determination of boundaries—wishes of inhabitants and economic and geographic conditions?

The Commission has to start its examination of the question on the basis of the existing boundaries, but it has to re-settle those boundaries in the light of the factors to which the proviso to Article XII refers. What is the comparative importance of these different factors, namely, wishes of the inhabitants, and economic and geographic conditions? Some of the representations received urge that under the terms of the proviso the wishes of the inhabitants are to be regarded as "paramount." But I do not think this view can be accepted as correct. The terms of the proviso show clearly that it may be the duty of the Commission to overrule the wishes of the inhabitants owing to considerations arising from economic and geographic conditions. The Commission is only to give effect to the wishes of the inhabitants "so far as may be compatible" with such conditions. It would perhaps be correct to say that, by the terms of the Article, the wishes of the inhabitants are made not the paramount but the primary consideration: that is, the first point for the Commission to look at in dealing with a particular area is the question of the wishes of the inhabitants of that area. The Commission must first ascertain the wishes of the inhabitants, and must next consider whether economic and geographic conditions are such as to allow of effect being given to those wishes.

I have already dealt with the question of majorities, and the distinction to be drawn between wishes for and against transfer. Where there is a substantial majority in favour of transfer, economic or geographic conditions may be such as to prevent effect being given to the wishes of the majority. Where there is not a substantial majority in favour of transfer, and the position as to the wishes of the inhabitants is therefore such as to point to the conclusion that an area should be left where it is, economic and geographic conditions may nevertheless be such as to require or justify a transfer, in spite of the absence of a demand on the part of the inhabitants for such a transfer. In other cases again where there is a majority in favour of transfer, but where owing to the smallness of the majority the case for transfer would be too weak if considered in relation to the wishes of the inhabitants alone, economic and geographic conditions in favour of transfer may give such additional weight to the wishes of the majority as to justify the Commission in regarding the case as made out when the three factors are taken together. It may therefore be right and necessary either to override the wishes of the inhabitants, whether in favour of transfer or against transfer, by reason of economic or geographic considerations, or to use these considerations for the purpose of adding extra weight to wishes expressed on one side or the other. As the onus is on those who seek to make out a case for transfer, it is obvious that economic and geographic considerations in favour of transfer must be very strong in order to justify the transfer of an area which is contrary to the wishes of the inhabitants of that area. It seems likely that areas, the transfer of which will be justified on economic and geographic considerations, where the wishes of a majority of the inhabitants of the area itself are against transfer, will normally be small areas which affect communications or drainage. It may often be possible even in such cases to justify the transfer on the basis of the wishes of the inhabitants by showing that, geographically or economically, the area to be transferred belongs to a larger unit, of which the inhabitants by a majority wish to be on the other side of the boundary to which the small area is to be transferred, and that, if a reasonable unit consisting of territory on both sides of the existing border were to be constituted for the purpose of self-determination, the necessary majority in favour of transfer would be found to exist.

Economic and Geographic Conditions.

On the question of the effect to be given to the words "so far as may be compatible with economic and geographic conditions" a further point has been raised to which it is necessary to refer.

The contention has been advanced by the Government of the Irish Free State that these words are to be read as referring only to economic and geographic conditions of any particular area whose claim for inclusion in the Irish Free State is being considered, and that economic or geographic conditions of other areas which might be affected by such inclusion are not to be taken into account. This contention is of course to be viewed in relation to their general contention that the Commission has no power to include in Northern Ireland any territory on the Irish Free State side of the present boundary.

This point has been raised more particularly in connection with objections to inclusion in the Irish Free State of certain areas in Northern Ireland from which Northern Ireland towns draw their water supply. The most conspicuous case is the case of the water supply of Belfast. The Belfast City and District Water Commissioners have waterworks in the Mourne Mountains in the southern part of County Down, and have submitted a representation to the Commission objecting to the inclusion in the Irish Free State of the area in which these waterworks are situate, on the ground of the alleged prejudicial effect of such inclusion on the interests which they represent.

The Government of the Irish Free State make the following submission with regard to the general question involved:

"The representation dealing with the waterworks which supply the City of Belfast, submitted to the Boundary Commission by the Belfast City and District Water Commissioners, appears to be based on a misconception of the Boundary Commission's terms of reference as contained in Article 12 of the Treaty.

"That representation suggests that effect should not be given to the wishes of the inhabitants of the area from which the water supply is derived, on the grounds of possible inconvenience to the consumers of the water in Belfast, an area which is not in dispute.

"It is submitted that the reference to economic and geographical conditions in the Treaty is intended as a corrective to the possible absurdities of a line based solely on the distribution of the population, and drawn regardless of the economic hardships which might be inflicted on the people whom it was intended to relieve. It is submitted that the provision regarding economic conditions is confined to economic conditions affecting the particular area in question, and in which it is being applied as a corrective, and that it does not entitle the Commission to consider possible economic inconvenience which may be suffered by persons in another area whose exclusion from the Free State is not in dispute."

The Attorney-General in his argument admitted that the economic conditions of any particular area could not normally be considered except in relation to other areas. The following extract from the proceedings relating to this point indicates the view which he put forward:

The Chairman.—I understand you say with regard both to economic conditions and geographic conditions that the only conditions to be looked at are the conditions of the area the wishes of whose inhabitants are being considered.

Attorney-General.—Yes.

The Chairman.—Of course economic conditions imply a relation between two persons or two areas—a buyer and a seller. Economic conditions suggest a relation of some kind.

Attorney-General.—Undoubtedly they suggest that.

The Chairman.—Therefore the position of two areas, A. and B. where there is only a one-sided economic interest, so to speak, would be an unusual position. I do not know if we could find an example of it. I understand the real gist of your contention about this question of economic conditions, so far as interpretation is concerned, is that we are to restrict our study of economic conditions in relation to any particular area to the area itself.

The Attorney-General.—I do not quite suggest that, because it might be impossible for you to determine what were the economic conditions in a particular area without considering the conditions of surrounding areas to some extent. A consideration of the economic conditions in any particular area might involve, and probably would involve, to some extent at any rate, the examination of the economic conditions of surrounding areas. To that extent, so far as your examination is concerned, it may have to go outside a particular area. What I suggest is this, that when you apply that provision as a corrective, so as to prevent your giving effect to the wishes of the inhabitants considered alone, then you are restricted to the economic conditions affecting that particular area which is the subject of your decision.

The Chairman.—We are to look at economic conditions generally as affecting the relation between the area under consideration and adjoining areas, but where it comes to a question of economic interest, the only interest that is to be protected is that of the area whose inhabitants have expressed a wish that something should be done with them, or not done with them as the case may be?

The Attorney-General.—Yes.

The Chairman.—It becomes almost a question of application rather than of interpretation. Taking the term " economic conditions " generally, you say we could not consider the economic conditions of a particular area in isolation because its economic conditions would inevitably involve its relations with other areas, so that we cannot restrict our examination of conditions to a particular area.

The Attorney-General.—No.

The Chairman.—You urge that when we come perhaps to a further stage and consider economic interests, the only interests to be protected are the interests of the area the wishes of whose inhabitants we are considering?

The Attorney-General.—Yes, that is my suggestion.

This extract indicates that the Free State contention, as explained by the Attorney-General in the course of his argument, becomes a contention as to the principles to be adopted by the Commission in applying the terms of Article XII, rather than a contention as to the interpretation of those terms as they stand. For it is admitted that the Commission cannot examine the economic conditions of any particular area except in relation to other areas.

There appears to me to be nothing in the Article which supports the contention either in its original or in its modified form; and the one-sided limitation, which it is sought to impose on the regard which the Commission should pay to the economic interests of different areas, seems to me to be a limitation which is unreasonable in itself and inconsistent with the intention of the Article.

The reference to economic and geographic conditions is general. The intention of the Article as indicated by this reference appears to me to be that the Commission should not look at particular areas in isolation from one another, but should take into account the economic and geographic relations between them, and should seek to avoid drawing a boundary line which, by its defiance of economic or geographic conditions, would involve, as the result of its adoption, serious economic detriment, or geographic isolation, to communities on either side of it. The Commission should therefore, in my opinion, consider the economic effect of any proposed boundary on areas situate on either side of it, and should not set one area above another so far as the claim for consideration of its economic interests is concerned, but should treat all areas whose interests are affected by the drawing of the boundary on a like footing.

There remain some further questions, already indicated in an earlier paragraph, which necessarily arise in interpreting and applying the provision that the boundary is to be determined " in accordance with the wishes of the inhabitants." I have suggested that the words to be supplied after " the inhabitants " are some such words as " of the regions or areas concerned," and that the regions or areas concerned are boundary regions or areas, that is, regions or areas within range of boundary variations, and I have indicated certain considerations which are of assistance in defining the limits of such areas.

The questions with which I now have to deal are :—

(1.) Who are the persons who are entitled as " inhabitants " to have their wishes considered in respect of boundary regions or areas?

(2.) How are their wishes to be ascertained?

(3.) Are all such persons to have an equal voice?

(4.) What is the unit of area in reference to which the wishes of inhabitants should be ascertained?

I will take these questions in order.

(1.) *Meaning of Term " Inhabitants."*

This question was discussed by Counsel for the Free State in the course of their argument. Serjeant Hanna referred to a judicial decision by which the term " inhabitants " had been interpreted as meaning " a person having a permanent residence." (*R. v. Mitchell* 10 East 511 (1809)). The question in this case was whether certain men who were serving in the Militia and were quartered at Colchester, but whose homes were at Norwich, were " inhabitants " of the City of Norwich, and so entitled to vote for elections to corporate offices there. Lord Ellenborough in giving judgment drew the distinction between temporary and permanent residence in these words:

" Of what other place but Norwich could these men be said to be inhabitants at this time? They had their own dwelling houses or homes there, in which they left their families dwelling, and to which they returned from time to time when they obtained leave of absence from their Regiment. They had no other abiding place than this, for the place where the Regiment happened to be quartered could not be considered as such."

In other cases it has been pointed out that the term " inhabitant " has no fixed meaning, but must be interpreted according to the context and the nature of the subject matter (*A. G. v. Foster* 10 Vesey 339 (1804) *King v. Mashiter* 6A x E 153 (1837)). There can I think be no question that in the context of Article XII the persons, who are entitled as "inhabitants" to have their wishes considered on the question as to whether a particular area should be included in the Irish Free State or in Northern Ireland, are persons having something that can be called a permanent connection with the area concerned, that is a permanent home within the area, though not necessarily a fixed home. It is clear that temporary or casual residence within an area cannot be regarded as qualifying a person to have his wishes considered on the question as to whether the permanent destiny of the area is to be in one country or another. But in making the distinction between temporary and permanent residence it is advisable to avoid the technicalities of the Law of Domicile and to remember that a person may have what may fairly be described as a "permanent" home within an area without being domiciled within the area in the strict legal sense of that term (cf. Dicey Conflict of Laws, p. 92). The term "permanent" is used rather loosely to describe a residence which is something more than temporary or occasional, but there are varying degrees of permanence, and it is not easy to find a satisfactory test, or to say exactly where the line should be drawn between "temporary" and "permanent." Whatever the test, and wherever the line is drawn, among those allowed to rank as permanent residents some will have a stronger claim than others to that description. The ties that bind a person to a particular area, apart from the mere fact of actual residence therein at a particular moment, may be ties of business, property or sentiment: each of these different ties may vary in strength, and they may or may not co-exist: the stronger the ties that bind a person to residence within a particular area, the greater his interest in its future, and the clearer his title to have a say as to that future.

(2.) *Method of Ascertainment of Wishes of Inhabitants.*

The Article says nothing as to this, and confers on the Commission no special power by which such wishes can be ascertained. The only means of arriving at precise figures with regard to the wishes of the inhabitants would be a plebiscite. It is clear that without special powers of a far-reaching character the Commission cannot conduct a plebiscite. Legal provisions of a very stringent and comprehensive nature would be necessary in order to ensure that only persons entitled to vote as inhabitants took part, that all inhabitants were free to vote, and that the secrecy of the vote was maintained, and guarantees as to the proper enforcement of such provisions would be required. The Treaty makes no provision whatever for a plebiscite, and the Commission has therefore no power to carry out a plebiscite. The absence from Article XII of any provision enabling the Commission to conduct a plebiscite affords ground for inferring (1) that it was not the intention of the parties to the Treaty that the Commission should ascertain the wishes of the inhabitants in that manner, and (2) that it was not intended that the Commission should, in seeking to give effect to the wishes of the inhabitants, rely on the verdicts of bare majorities. If the same question is looked at from a practical point of view the Commission in fact finds itself debarred from acting on the verdicts of bare majorities for the sufficient reason that it has no adequate means of verifying the existence of such majorities.

As it is not open to the Commission to ascertain the wishes of the inhabitants by means of a direct vote, the Commission must have recourse to other sources of information, such as election results and census returns, and evidence of persons claiming to speak on behalf of inhabitants or to have knowledge of their views. Where the wishes of the inhabitants have to be ascertained from such data and evidence it is clear that a considerable margin must be allowed for possible error. Parties who have appeared before the Commission to give evidence have laid great stress on the census returns as affording a good indication of the wishes of the inhabitants of the different districts concerned. The latest census returns available are those of 1911. The data contained in these returns to which most importance is attached are the religious statistics. It is claimed by leading representatives of both parties that Roman Catholics can be reckoned as wishing to be under the Government of the Free State, and that all others, who are with insignificant exceptions included in the returns as members of one or other of the Protestant denominations, can be reckoned as wishing to be under the Government of Northern Ireland. Assuming that this claim is well founded, the following points have to be borne in mind :

(1.) The question of the extent to which the numbers or composition of the population of any particular district may have changed since 1911.

(2.) The question of the extent to which the census returns include persons who are temporary residents and are not properly to be reckoned as inhabitants, *e.g.*, migratory labourers of the servant boy type who leave their own districts to hire themselves out for six-monthly periods in other districts, and the effect on the balance of parties in any particular district of the presence of such a temporary element at the date when the census was taken. Members of the Special Police (A Specials) are as a rule quartered outside the districts to which they really belong, and on the principle above stated do not appear to be entitled to be reckoned as inhabitants of the districts in which they are serving. This point does not arise in connection with the census returns as no such force existed in 1911, but it has to be borne in mind in connection with statements furnished as to the number of inhabitants or voters of different parties or denominations now residing in particular districts.

(3.) The extent to which the census returns include persons under age and lunatics, or other persons not qualified to vote as inhabitants, but who are all included in the census returns as members of particular denominations. The presence of a school or a lunatic asylum in a particular district may conceivably have an important effect on the balance of party strength in that district as reflected by the census returns. Further reference will be made to some of these points. I have only referred to them now in this general way for the purpose of making it clear that, in examining census returns for the purpose of ascertaining the wishes of inhabitants, allowances must be made for many factors which cannot be determined with precision.

(3.) *Are all Persons ranking as Inhabitants entitled to an Equal Voice ?*

If the decision were to be by vote every person entitled to vote would, apart from express provision to the contrary, have an equal say—every voter would count for one and no voter for more than one; but if the wishes of the inhabitants are not to be ascertained by means of votes, but in some less direct way, a distinction may, I think, fairly be drawn between different classes of the population, on the principle that the more permanent elements of the population of a particular area have a greater interest in the destiny of that area, and that their wishes are therefore entitled to greater weight. If the Commission has to proceed not on the basis of a vote taken for the purpose, in which persons only with prescribed qualifications participate, but on the basis of census returns which make no distinction between temporary and permanent inhabitants, it becomes more important to examine the position in the light of such a principle. But the principle can of course only be applied where information is available which renders it possible to distinguish between different classes on the ground that one forms a more permanent element in the population than another. There will be room for a good deal of difference of opinion in any attempted classification of inhabitants of an area according to degrees of permanence. It may however be possible to lay down one or two general rules as to the making of such a classification; for instance, it is probably safe to say that owners and lessees of land or house property, including under the term lessees tenants of agricultural property, whether " bought " or " unbought," and tenants of dwellinghouses for periods of, say, a year and upwards, are the most permanent elements in the population of any particular area, and that in considering the wishes of inhabitants more weight may fairly be attached to the wishes of a number of persons having such interests in land than to the wishes of an equivalent number of persons who have no such interests.*

It is obviously difficult to formulate any rule allowing for a definite percentage to be added to the votes of persons thus roughly classed together as owners and lessees of land or house property, but such a difficulty does not, I think, relieve the Commission of the duty of attempting to make some fair assessment of the allowance to be made, in each case where the data available justify the drawing of a definite conclusion as to the views of such persons, as distinguished from other elements in the population.

(4.) *Unit of Area.*

It now remains for me to deal with the question of the unit of area, *i.e.*, the unit of area in relation to which the wishes of inhabitants

---

* *Cf. Dicey, " Conflict of Laws," pp.* **145, 147.**

Page 145, *Rule* **17.**—" Residence in a country is *primâ facie* evidence of the intention to reside there permanently (*animus manendi*) and in so far evidence of domicil " . . .

" *Time.*—Time or length of residence does not of itself constitute domicil." . . .

Page 147.—" *Mode.*—The effect of residence in a country as evidence of a man's intention to continue residing there depends, to a great extent, on the manner of his residence.

If D. not only lives in France but buys land there, and makes that country the home of his wife and family, there is clearly far more reason for inferring a purpose of residence on his part than if he had merely taken lodgings in Paris, and lived there alone."

. . . " *Rule* 18.—Residence in a country is not even *primâ facie* evidence of domicil, when the nature of the residence either is inconsistent with, or rebuts the presumption of an intention to reside there permanently (*animus manendi*)."

The instance is quoted of an Ambassador.

are to be ascertained. The Article gives no direction on this point. It was suggested in argument by Counsel for the Free State that guidance might be obtained from the provisions of the Versailles Treaty. Provisions were quoted from that Treaty providing for the ascertainment of the wishes of inhabitants by communes.*

It was suggested that the area in Northern Ireland which most nearly corresponded to the commune was the Poor Law Union, which was described as " the smallest administrative area." This description of the Poor Law Union as the smallest administrative area is not accurate. Apart from the Cities of Belfast and Londonderry, Northern Ireland is divided for local government purposes into rural districts and urban districts. The Free State has hitherto been similarly divided into rural districts and urban districts. Each rural district and each urban district has a council of its own. Some Poor Law Unions are coterminous with a rural district, but a Poor Law Union in Northern Ireland normally includes one or more urban districts in addition to a rural district: the Newry Union in addition to two urban districts (Newry and Warrenpoint) includes two rural districts, one in Down and one in Armagh, and prior to the taking effect of the Act of 1920 the Londonderry, Strabane, Ballyshannon, Enniskillen, Clones and Castleblayney Unions each included two rural districts, one on either side of the boundary as established by that Act. The Poor Law Union is the smallest administrative area for Poor Law Union purposes, but not for other purposes of local administration. It does not appear that the proposition, that Poor Law Unions in Ireland correspond, as administrative areas, to the communes in territories dealt with under the Versailles Treaty, is one which can be seriously supported. Apart from this suggested analogy, the Commission was asked to adopt the Poor Law Union as the unit of area on (1) administrative and (2) economic grounds. Some witnesses considered that on administrative grounds the County and not the Union should be accepted as the unit. With regard to the arguments in favour of the County or the Union based on administrative grounds, it is sufficient to say that Article XII does not mention administrative convenience as one of the factors to be taken into account, and the Commission is not entitled to take into account considerations of administrative convenience except so far as they coincide with economic and geographic considerations. Economic conditions may afford arguments against the breaking up of a particular administrative area. But if the Commission were to adopt a rule that the County or the Union must, on grounds of administrative convenience, be treated as indivisible, it would find itself compelled, in cases where the wishes of a majority of the inhabitants in one

* It appears on reference to the Versailles Treaty that while in other cases the Treaty provides—Articles 88 and 94–97—for ascertainment of the wishes of the inhabitants by communes, in the case of the boundary between Germany and Denmark provision is made (Article 109) for dividing the whole of the area involved into two sections, and the result in the first section is to be determined by the majority of votes cast in the whole of the section, while in the second section the result is to be determined by communes. In the Treaty of St. Germain-en-Laye (The Austrian Treaty), which deals in Article 49 with the Klagenfurt area, where a boundary had to be drawn between Austria and the Serb-Croat-Slovene State, provision is similarly made for dividing the area into two sections or zones, and the result of the vote is to be determined by the majority of votes in the whole of each zone.

portion of a County or Union were in opposition to the wishes of the majority of the inhabitants of the whole County or Union, to override the wishes of the inhabitants of the particular portion concerned for the sake of administrative considerations; in other words, the Commission would be setting up a new factor, "administrative considerations," as superior to the wishes of the inhabitants.

The claim, that the Poor Law Union was entitled on economic grounds to be treated as a unit, was based on the theory that the division of the County into Poor Law Unions had originally been based on the market areas of the principal towns, and that the limits of the Unions still coincide in the main with the limits of market areas. In particular cases there is no doubt a rough correspondence between the market area of a particular town and the Poor Law Union, which consists of the town itself and the district surrounding it. But the evidence has failed to show any such general correspondence between Poor Law Unions and market areas as would justify the adoption of the Poor Law Union as an indivisible economic unit. Other areas which have been tentatively suggested for the consideration of the Commission as units are the old parliamentary divisions as existing prior to the 1920 Act, and parishes. Separate figures for the old parliamentary divisions are given in the 1911 census returns, but these divisions can now only be regarded as of historical interest. Parishes are no longer recognised for purposes of civil administration, and the 1911 census returns do not contain separate figures for parishes. Each denomination is free to adopt its own system of divisions for ecclesiastical purposes: to some extent the old parochial boundaries still serve for such purposes, but the ecclesiastical parish boundaries are varied from time to time, and there is no uniformity of practice as between the different denominations. The County, the Parliamentary Division, and the Poor Law Union are, as units of area for the purposes of the Commission's work, all open to the objection that they are, from the point of view of population, unduly large. The County in Northern Ireland with the smallest population, Fermanagh, had in 1911 a population of 61,836; and Down, which is, with the exception of the County Borough of Belfast, the county with the largest population, had a population in 1911 of 204,303. The old Parliamentary Divisions had populations varying from about 30,000 to over 50,000. The smallest of the old Poor Law Unions (as existing prior to 1920) (Castlederg) had a population of 11,161, while the largest, excluding Belfast and Londonderry, (Lurgan) had a population of 53,609. Of the twenty-nine Poor Law Unions included in whole or in part in Northern Ireland, twenty-one had populations of more than 20,000, and eight had populations of less than 20,000.

The Commission, being required to determine the boundaries in accordance with the wishes of the inhabitants, should, I think, in selecting its units of area, seek to follow the wishes of the inhabitants as closely as is reasonably possible, and should therefore be prepared to take as a unit the smallest area which can fairly be entitled, having regard to its size and situation, to be considered separately, and with regard to which separate data are available. The smallest areas, in respect of which separate data as to the religion of the inhabitants are available in published returns, are the old District Electoral Divisions as existing in 1911, each of which is separately dealt with in the census returns for that year. These areas are, as their name implies, nothing more than divisions of the country for voting purposes. The Divisions are utilised as voting areas both for parliamentary and local government elections. Each Poor Law Union contains a number of such divisions. Their boundaries do not cross the boundaries of local government areas, but the whole of each division is situate in one local government area. The divisions vary in size, but an examination of the census returns for the Counties of Down, Armagh, Tyrone, Fermanagh, Londonderry, Donegal and Monaghan shows that, of the District Electoral Divisions in those Counties, about one-half have a population of over 1,000, while only a small proportion have a population of less than 500. The divisions with the smaller populations are in the more sparsely inhabited districts. Each District Electoral Division contains as a rule a number of "Townlands," which are the ancient historic land units of the county. The Commission has obtained access to documents in the Census Office which give the particulars, required for the religious census, for the population of each townland, and from those particulars has been able to have prepared a detailed religious map, showing the proportions of Catholics and Protestants in each townland. This enables distinctions to be drawn between different parts of a District Electoral Division which were not discernable so long as the only figures available showing the religious census were for each electoral division as a whole.

The Commission, being now in possession of this detailed information, which throws further light on the wishes of the inhabitants in different areas, is in a position to mark out for itself areas which can conveniently be treated as units in the light,—

(1.) Of the evidence as to numbers and wishes of inhabitants :
(2.) Of economic conditions :
(3.) Of geographic conditions :—

and I think it should therefore hold itself free to mark out convenient units in the light of these considerations as its work proceeds.

The townlands have no uniformity as regards area or population, and many of them are very small, and have very few inhabitants, while some have none at all. Generally speaking, it appears to me that it may be a good working rule to start on the basis of considering separately each District Electoral Division, and only to vary these units by combination or division where sufficient reasons can be advanced for such variation. Such reasons will normally be based either on considerations as to the size of the particular electoral division, i.e., that it is either too big or too small for treatment as a unit, or on data available as to the wishes of inhabitants in particular parts of the division or of adjoining divisions, or on economic or geographic considerations. It may ultimately prove advisable in the light of such considerations to make very wide departures from the original units, and to adopt others which will in some cases be larger and in other cases smaller than the electoral divisions; and, when I speak of starting on the basis of electoral divisions, I do not wish it to be supposed that I regard the boundaries of electoral divisions as being in themselves worthy of any special respect.

DRAFT CONCLUSIONS.*

I.

The intention of Article XII is that, if the Address therein referred to is presented, Northern Ireland shall continue to exist as a province of the United Kingdom in accordance with the provisions of the Government of Ireland Act, 1920, subject to the revision of boundaries, for which machinery is set up under the proviso, and that the several Articles of Agreement for a Treaty shall be modified, so far as necessary, to give effect to the provisions of Article XII.

II.

The Commission is required to determine the boundaries between Northern Ireland and the rest of Ireland. Until the boundaries have been altered by the Commission " Northern Ireland " is the region constituted as such by Section 1 (2) of the Government of Ireland Act, 1920; that is to say the region consisting " of the parliamentary counties of Antrim, Armagh, Down, Fermanagh, Londonderry and Tyrone, and the parliamentary boroughs of Belfast and Londonderry "; and the rest of Ireland is the region constituted as " Southern Ireland " by the same section—that is to say, the region consisting of " so much of Ireland as is not comprised within the said parliamentary counties and boroughs." The Commission having to deal with these two ascertained territorial entities must start from the existing boundaries of those entities; that is, it must start its examination of the whole question on the basis of the division marked by the existing boundary, and must treat that boundary as holding good where no sufficient reason, based on considerations of which the Commission can properly take account, is shown for altering it.

III.

In determining the boundaries between Northern Ireland and the rest of Ireland under the terms of the proviso, the Commission has power to shift the existing boundary line in either direction,—it has no more and no less authority to take land from the Northern side of the existing boundary and give it to the Free State, than it has to take land from the Free State side and give it to Northern Ireland. It has the same authority and duty in each case, namely, to make whatever transfer of territory is involved by a determination of the boundary in accordance with the terms of the Article.

IV.

The Commission is to determine the boundaries " in accordance with the wishes of the inhabitants, so far as may be compatible with economic and geographic conditions." The inhabitants to whose wishes effect is to be given are the inhabitants of boundary regions; that is of regions which may be directly affected by a revision of boundaries. The extent of the boundary regions, and the areas which are to be taken as units for the purpose of deciding as to the wishes of the inhabitants, are matters left to the discretion of the commission in the light of the terms of the clause itself, and of such circumstances as the Commission's examination of the actual position in the territories adjacent to the existing border may reveal.

---

* These " draft conclusions " were appended to the Memorandum as handed by the Chairman to his colleagues on the 11th September, 1925. They are printed here so that the complete Memorandum may be available in its original form, but the greater part of these " draft conclusions " is now included in substance in Chapter II in the form of answers to the questions stated in that Chapter.

.[13849]

V.

The fact that the wishes of the inhabitants are to be a determining factor shows that the scope of the Commission's work is not limited to a mere correction of irregularities in the present boundary; at the same time no wholesale reconstruction of the map is contemplated by the proviso—the Commission is not to reconstitute the two territories, but to settle the boundaries between them. Northern Ireland must, when the boundaries have been determined, still be recognisable as the same provincial entity; the changes made must not be so drastic as to destroy its identity or make it impossible for it to continue as a separate province of the United Kingdom with its own Parliament and Government for provincial affairs under the Government of Ireland Act. The same principle applies *mutatis mutandis* to the "rest of Ireland," which must after the determination of the boundaries retain its identity as the Irish Free State as constituted under the terms of the Treaty, and be in a position to function as a self-governing Dominion " in the community of nations known as the British Empire."

VI.

The Commission starting its examination of the question on the basis of the existing boundary must first consider the wishes of the inhabitants adjacent to that boundary, and where it finds an area of sufficient size and population to merit separate consideration, which is at present on the right side of the boundary, that is on the side where its inhabitants wish to remain, the existence of that area will in itself be a reason against making an alteration which would involve its transfer to the wrong side, and may thus enable a point to be fixed beyond which alterations intended to give effect to the wishes of the inhabitants should not extend.

VII.

It follows from the principle stated above (§ II) (that the existing boundary should be regarded as holding good where no sufficient reason is shown for altering it) that the onus is on those who propose any specific alteration to show that the conditions justify such alteration.

The case for an alteration may rest either (1) on the wishes of the inhabitants, or (2) on economic conditions, or (3) on geographic conditions, or (4) on a combination of considerations arising from these different factors. The question of what majority of inhabitants is sufficient to justify an alteration is left to the discretion of the Commission, and, in view of the fundamental character of the change involved in a transfer of territory from one jurisdiction to another, and of the dislocation of established conditions both in the area directly concerned and in adjoining areas resulting from any such change, it may be advisable for the Commission to take the line that, where the case rests solely on the wishes of the inhabitants, it will not regard the case as made out unless the majority in favour of the change is a substantial majority, *i.e.*, a majority representing a high proportion of the total number of persons entitled to rank as inhabitants of the district.

VIII.

The application of the principles suggested above will mean that changes made in the existing boundary by the Commission on the basis of the wishes of inhabitants should, generally speaking, be limited to cases where there are communities or districts predominantly of one character on the wrong side of the existing line, and that the wishes of the inhabitants taken alone should not be regarded as sufficient to justify a change in mixed communities or districts where the evidence points to only a small percentage of advantage on one side or the other. It is further suggested that the greater the importance of the change demanded in its effect on territory and population, the higher the percentage of inhabitants who support the change which should be required to justify it,

IX.

Under the terms of the Article the wishes of the inhabitants are made the primary but not the paramount consideration. It may be the duty of the Commission in some cases to override the wishes of inhabitants, whether for or against transfer, by reason of economic or geographic considerations. In other cases such considerations may give extra strength to a case for transfer which rests in part on the wishes of the inhabitants, but where the majority in favour of transfer is not sufficient to be regarded as decisive.

IX (A).

The reference to economic and geographic conditions in Article XII is in general terms, and the intention of the Article as indicated by this reference is that the Commission should take into account the economic and geographic relations between different areas, and should seek to avoid drawing a boundary line which, by its defiance of economic or geographic conditions, would involve, as the result of its adoption, serious economic detriment, or geographic isolation, to communities on either side of it.

X.

"Inhabitants" in Article XII means persons having a permanent connection with the area concerned. Temporary or casual residence within an area cannot be regarded as qualifying a person to have his wishes considered on the question whether the permanent destiny of the area is to be in one country or another. Among persons entitled to rank as inhabitants of an area some will be found to be united by stronger ties to the area than others.

XI.

The Commission while directed to determine the boundaries in accordance with the wishes of the inhabitants, so far as may be compatible with economic and geographic conditions, is given no special powers for the purpose of ascertaining the wishes of the inhabitants. The absence from the Article of any provision enabling the Commission to conduct a plebiscite affords ground for inferring (1) that it was not the intention of the parties to the Treaty that the Commission should ascertain the wishes of the inhabitants in that manner, and (2) that it was not intended that the Commission should, in seeking to give effect to the wishes of the inhabitants, rely on the verdicts of bare majorities. (*Cf.* § VII.)

XII.

The Commission has been invited by both parties to the boundary controversy to rely upon the census returns of 1911 showing the religious denominations to which inhabitants belong, as affording an indication of the wishes of the inhabitants, the members of Protestant denominations being reckoned as wishing to be in Northern Ireland and Roman Catholics as wishing to be in the Irish Free State.

In examining these census returns for the purpose of ascertaining the wishes of inhabitants, allowance must be made for many factors which cannot be determined with precision.

XIII.

In considering whether the evidence available shows the existence of a substantial majority in a particular area in favour of transfer, the Commission should bear in mind any distinctions which can fairly be drawn between different classes or sections of the population according to the varying degrees of permanence implied by the nature of the ties attaching them to the area, and allow extra weight to the wishes of those representing the more permanent elements in the population, *e.g.*, owners of land or house property, tenants of agricultural holdings, and tenants of dwelling houses for periods of, say, a year and upwards.

XIV.

The Commission being required to determine the boundaries in accordance with the wishes of the inhabitants should seek to follow the wishes of inhabitants as closely as is reasonably possible, and should therefore be prepared to take as a unit of area in relation to which the wishes of inhabitants are to be ascertained the smallest area which can fairly be entitled, having regard to its size and situation, to be considered separately, and with regard to which separate data are available.

If the Commission were to adopt a rule, as suggested in some quarters, that the County or the Union should on administrative grounds be regarded as an indivisible unit, it would find itself compelled on such grounds to refuse to treat separately particular portions of a County or Union where the inhabitants differed from the majority in the County or Union as a whole, and therefore to override the wishes of the inhabitants of these portions. The Commission would thus in effect be setting up a new factor, administrative considerations, as superior to the wishes of the inhabitants.

The Commission should hold itself free to mark out convenient units in the light of the three factors which it is entitled to take into account—wishes of inhabitants, economic and geographic conditions—as its work proceeds; but it may probably be a good working rule to start on the basis of considering separately each District Electoral Division, and only to vary these units by combination or division where sufficient reasons can be advanced for such variation. Such reasons will usually be based either on considerations as to the size of the particular district electoral division, (*i.e.*, that it is either too big or too small for separate treatment as a unit) or on data available as to the wishes of the inhabitants of particular parts of the division, or of adjoining divisions, or on economic or geographic considerations.

CHAPTER IV.

EVIDENCE RELATING TO GENERAL QUESTIONS.

1. Value of Census Figures and other Statistics.

As already indicated above (Chapter II, section dealing with Question 5) the religious statistics for different areas, included in the published returns of the 1911 census, the latest held in Ireland, were referred to in many of the representations received by the Commission, and in much of the evidence heard, as throwing light on the wishes of the inhabitants of such areas in relation to the boundary.

Such references were freely made by representatives of both sides. The following statements are typical of a large number made by leading members of the two parties who gave evidence before the Commission :—

" Experience at all elections shows that the results conform with mathematical accuracy to the census returns according to religions, viz., that Catholics invariably show themselves desirous of remaining within the Free State, while the others almost invariably desire exclusion therefrom."

" Although there are exceptions, the terms ' Catholic ' and ' Protestant ' are synonymous with the terms ' Nationalist ' and ' Unionist ' in Northern Ireland."

" The term ' Unionist ' is practically synonymous with ' Protestant,' and the terms ' Nationalist,' ' Free State ' and ' Republican ' with ' Roman Catholic.' "

" In this County every man votes as he is born."
" Catholics would be unanimously for the Free State; Protestants would
be unanimously Unionist."
" There is no doubt about it that all Catholics vote Nationalist and
Protestants vote Unionist. I never knew of a Catholic that would vote
Unionist, though there may be a stray Protestant, the old Protestant Home
Rulers, who would vote Nationalist."

Such references have been based on two general assumptions.
(1) That in the areas concerned religious and political divisions
to-day, broadly speaking, correspond; and (2) that in such areas,
subject in each case to comparatively few exceptions, if the question
could be put to the vote, members of Protestant denominations
would vote in favour of being in Northern Ireland, and Roman
Catholics would vote in favour of being in the Irish Free State.
These assumptions appear to be almost universally accepted.

Different views have been urged as to qualifying considerations,
some general in their application, and some limited to particular
localities, subject to which the religious statistics of the 1911 census
should be read as reflecting in the light of such assumptions, " the
wishes of the inhabitants " at the present date.

Among such considerations it was urged :—

(1.) That the results of the most recent elections showed a
certain degree of change in the proportions of Unionist
and Nationalist voters in certain constituencies; though
it was contended, on the Nationalist side, that, in certain
areas account must be taken of difficulties experienced by
Nationalist Agents in the carrying on of registration
work, and of the inconvenience of the positions of the
polling stations assigned to certain Nationalist areas.

(2.) That a comparison of the numbers of Catholic and
Protestant electors on current registers in certain districts
also indicated a certain degree of change, as compared
with the proportions between the denominations based
on census figures. In this connection it was contended
that in certain areas, in weighing the value of the
evidence based on electoral registers, account must be
taken of registration difficulties, and of the fact that
certain classes of temporary residents would be included
in the registers.

(3.) That the census tables include temporary residents, persons
under age, and other persons who would not be entitled
according to electoral laws to express their wishes by a
vote.

(4.) That in certain areas one party or the other had gained by
immigration or lost by emigration during the period
1911–1925.

(5.) That in certain areas the proportion of school children of
one or other party, who were attending elementary
schools, showed an increase since 1911, though in these
cases it was contended that account should be taken of
such possibilities as the better observance of the school

attendance laws, and of the fact that figures available were not always exactly comparable.

(6.) That if a vote could be held on the boundary issue alone economic considerations would influence a considerable proportion of the voters, such as the desire to be in the same jurisdiction as their market town or their market area; the desire to obtain the advantages peculiar to one or other state under its existing laws, relating to land purchase or old age pensions; and the prospect of higher prices or a lower cost of living. It was noticeable however that while witnesses contended that voters holding opposite political views to their own would be influenced by such considerations to depart from their adhesion to their party, they rarely if ever admitted that members of their own party might be so influenced.

Such contentions were advanced as indications of the margin of error which must be allowed for in basing calculations as to "the wishes of the inhabitants" on religious statistics contained in the census returns; but, while allowances have to be made in varying degree for the various factors mentioned, the evidence heard from both sides, taken as a whole, shows a wide measure of agreement that such statistics afford, generally speaking, an approximate indication of the present wishes of the inhabitants of different areas in relation to the boundary.

In view of this general consensus of opinion as to the value of the religious statistics of the census of 1911, the Commission took steps to obtain copies of the detailed figures showing the religious persuasions of the inhabitants of the Townlands in the areas which required close consideration in detail. These figures, which had formed the basis of the published statistics for larger areas, but had not themselves been published, were made available for inspection, at the General Registry in Dublin, by an official of the Commission, who made the necessary extracts from them. Maps were then compiled on the basis of these figures so as to show the religious complexion of each Townland in the districts considered. With the aid of these maps and the figures from which they were constructed, the Commission was enabled to determine with a high degree of accuracy the local limits of the various areas in which Roman Catholics or Protestants predominated.

The degree to which areas with Catholic and Protestant majorities are intermixed is shown in a general way by the Outline Map on the $\frac{1}{4}''$ scale, distinguishing, by colours, between areas which showed Catholic majorities and areas which showed non-Catholic majorities in the religious statistics of the 1911 census. (Appendix VII.) This map has been prepared, as regards certain areas adjacent to the existing border (enclosed within dotted lines on the map), on the basis of the unpublished figures for Townlands. In these areas the degree of intermixture is therefore more accurately shown than in the areas more remote from the border, in which the colouring is based on the published figures for District

Electoral Divisions. The figures for these larger Divisions disguise local variations, which are shown in cases where the colouring is based on Townlands, and therefore suggest a higher degree of uniformity among the population than a more detailed study would show. The colouring of the map takes no account of the size of majorities, either actual or proportionate, any majority however small being sufficient to fix the colour for the unit concerned; except that urban districts are coloured proportionately. The map does not show, except for the hachuring of Urban Districts, the comparative density of population as between towns and villages on the one hand, and sparsely inhabited rural areas on the other. The map is therefore useful rather as an indication of the degree of intermixture, than as affording any accurate measure of the comparative strength of the Catholic and Protestant sections of the population in different areas.

A number of informal enumerations of the inhabitants of certain districts, notably in County Tyrone, the results of which were submitted to the Commission by Committees of members of one or other party, tended on the whole to confirm the validity of the figures of the 1911 census, published and unpublished, as still reflecting the conditions existing in 1925. In these enumerations, which had been recently compiled, the inhabitants were again classified by religious denominations. In cases in which the unofficial enumerations, which were in each case compiled exclusively by members of one party only, diverged to an appreciable extent from the figures of the census of 1911, such tests as the Commission was able to apply showed that reliance could not be placed on the enumerations.

It may be added that a comparison with the records of the five previous censuses shows that the variation in the proportions as between Catholics and Protestants from decade to decade has been generally of such slight magnitude as to show the improbability of any substantial change in the general situation having taken place since the Census of 1911. The following table gives the proportion of Roman Catholics to the total population in the 6 censuses 1861–1911 in each of the counties to which the claims considered by the Commission related :—

	Roman Catholics in proportion to total population.						Change in per cent. in 50 years.
	1861.	1871.	1881.	1891.	1901.	1911.	
Co. Armagh	48·8	47·5	46·4	46·1	45·2	45·3	− 3·5
Co. Donegal	75·1	75·7	76·5	77·0	77·7	78·9	+ 3·8
Co. Down	32·5	31·7	30·9	29·7	31·3	31·6	− 0·9
Co. Fermanagh	56·5	55·9	55·8	55·4	55·3	56·2	− 0·3
Londonderry City ...	57·6	55·0	55·1	55·3	55·2	56·2	− 1·4
Co. Londonderry ...	45·3	44·4	44·4	44·6	41·4	41·5	− 3·8
Co. Monaghan	73·4	73·4	73·7	73·3	73·4	74·7	+ 1·3
Co. Tyrone	56·5	55·6	55·5	54·6	54·7	55·4	− 1·1

2. Nature of Wishes Expressed.

Political Wishes.

In the course of their evidence witnesses gave various reasons for their wishes to be in one or other of the States. In general it appeared that the primary reason for wishing to be on one side or the other of the border lay in the desire which many witnesses expressed to be in "their own country," that is, in the country in which persons of their own religious or political complexion were in a majority, and in the case of Nationalists, where they could satisfy their national aspirations under the most complete form of self-government.

Other less general reasons were also given. Many Nationalist witnesses from districts in Northern Ireland said that they wished to be in a country where there were no "Special Police," and where they would get "fair play" as a political party. In this latter connection frequent reference was made to the disadvantages resulting to the Nationalist Party from the abolition of proportional Representation and the recent redivision of constituencies for the purpose of Local Government elections. Witnesses on both sides maintained that in the Free State or in Northern Ireland as the case might be, economic prospects were brighter, the cost of living was or would be cheaper, and employment better.

In a large number of cases witnesses expressed the opinion that their real desire was for the unity of Ireland, some witnesses saying that the reason for which they wished for large tracts to be transferred to the Free State was that they thought that by that means the unity of Ireland would be soonest attained. Witnesses on both sides freely said that their real wish was that there should be no boundary either political or fiscal.

When the issue of partition was raised, the Commission pointed out that its duty under its terms of reference was to determine a boundary, and not to decide the question whether there should be a boundary or not.

Economic Wishes.

This was however only one side of the evidence, and the subject of national, or religious, or political aspirations, was in most cases only referred to in reply to direct questioning. The majority of witnesses except in answer to questions spoke rather of their economic desires than of their political aspirations, which they seemed to expect the Commission to take for granted. Much of evidence volunteered was directed to emphasising the importance of free access being secured or maintained between market towns and the regions claimed as their respective market areas. Witnesses representing the rural population of the border districts impressed upon the Commission the inconvenience suffered owing to their being separated by a customs barrier from their market towns. Of 61 witnesses from East Donegal 54 laid primary stress on this point.

On the other hand the chief point made in the evidence of many witnesses from the towns of Londonderry, Newry, Keady, Clones, Pettigoe, Aughnacloy, and Strabane was the desire of the townsmen that they should not be separated from their natural market area.

From the mass of evidence accumulated on this point one or two facts emerged with something approaching definiteness—

(a.) That the market area of a market town practically corresponds to its retail trade area; this point is important in the neighbourhood of a customs barrier, as farmers bringing produce to market wish to take home their supplies. When these are subject to customs dues the extra expense and the delay involved in passing them through the barrier seriously increases their cost.

(b.) That the proportion of the inhabitants of market towns who obtain their living directly or indirectly from trade with the surrounding market area varies in inverse proportion to the importance of the industries, if any, situated in the town and its immediate neighbourhood.

(c.) That the size of the market area of a town depends on its distance from the nearest market towns of comparable or greater size. A market area appears normally to extend from about 6 to 10 miles from the town. In the case of larger towns like Londonderry, Enniskillen or Newry, the trading area extends further in some directions owing to the absence of any other centres of importance. In such cases the important town appears practically to control the business of a small number of subordinate centres which for most purposes may be considered to be within its market or trading area.

(d.) That market areas and retail trading areas of particular towns show a considerable measure of adaptability to changes in conditions, such as the advent of a railway; the interposition of a customs border; or the introduction of motor transport.

The question of a choice between transfer to the State in which they wished to live and separation from their market town or market area seemed rarely to have been faced by witnesses and was seldom dealt with spontaneously.

When witnesses said they wished to be on one side or the other of the border it was clear that in almost all cases they were assuming that their homes and market centres would be on the same side. In cases where the point was expressly raised that the satisfaction of a claim made on political grounds might involve separation from a convenient market centre, the witness showed signs of being presented with a dilemma which he had not thought out.

One witness said: "What I should like is that either Derry should be in Donegal, or Donegal should be with the Six Counties. Either would suit me."

It appears that the interposition of a customs barrier between a market town and a portion of its market area results in partial interruption of communication as follows :—

(a.) That the passage of loaded carts through the border posts, even when containing no dutiable goods, entails delay sometimes running into hours.

(b.) That the customs posts are only open between certain definite hours, so that in many cases only one return journey can be performed in a day instead of two.

(c.) That customs posts are only situated on certain main roads designated as "approved" roads. Only very limited categories of traffic can utilise unapproved roads. Such categories do not include any class of motor vehicles, or vehicles conveying goods other than farmers' carts conveying the farmers' own produce. Other traffic which before the institution of the customs border had utilised unapproved roads now has to make a detour of varying length in order to pass a customs post, in some cases an additional distance of 10 or even 20 miles being involved in a single journey.

A large volume of evidence heard on this question tended to indicate that other circumstances being equal a boundary following either a mountain range or a stretch of river crossed by few bridges possessed great advantages from the point of view of economic conveniences over a boundary passing through closely inhabited areas and intersecting a relatively large number of roads.

Interference with wholesale trade areas though entailing additional expense on wholesale houses appeared to have affected the volume of their trade decidedly less than that of retail traders. There was however some evidence of a similar dilemma which presented itself to witnesses who were asked whether they would desire a political change which would involve the interposition of a customs barrier between their trading centre and part of their area of distribution. A wholesale trader, who was asked whether he wished his town to be in the Free State if one half of its market area remained in Northern Ireland said, " as an ex-politician, yes. As a merchant, no. That is a frank answer."

3. GENERAL EVIDENCE AS TO DISTRIBUTION OF POPULATION.

An examination of the areas involved in the claims for wide mixed regions showed that, while these regions, in some cases, included areas of considerable extent which showed uniform majorities, either Catholic or Protestant. these were on the whole the exception ; and, generally speaking, in the areas involved in large claims Catholic and Protestant districts were intermingled.

In particular the claim put forward by a group of Nationalists, including representatives of all but one of the six counties, suggested the transfer of an area which comprised the whole of the counties of Tyrone and Fermanagh, the city and the greater part of the county of Londonderry, rather more than half of the county of Armagh, and portions of the county of Down. This area taken as a whole contained, according to the Census of 1911, a population of 464,145 persons, of whom 258,617 were Catholics and 205,528 members of other denominations.

It is necessary to make some analysis of this claim, as it is the most notable instance of a type which is to a great extent common to the majority of claims for wide areas.

The population figures for the areas claimed are as follows :—

CITY OF LONDONDERRY.

	Total.	Catholics.	Non-Catholics.	Majority. Catholics.	Majority. Non-Catholics.
City of Londonderry	40,780	22,923	17,857	5,066	...

CO. LONDONDERRY.

Groups.	Number of District Electoral Divisions.	Total.	Catholics.	Non-Catholics.	Majorities. Catholics.	Majorities. Non-Catholics.
Northern part of Limavady Union	12 (1 U.D.)	13,345	5,088	8,257	...	3,169
Southern part of Limavady Union	6	5,756	3,835	1,921	1,914	...
Eastern part of Londonderry No. 1 Rural District	4	4,599	2,971	1,628	1,343	...
Western part of Londonderry No. 1 Rural District	8	9,814	3,944	5,870	...	1,926
Western part of Magherafelt Rural District	8	10,041	7,747	2,294	5,453	...
Central part of Magherafelt Rural District	12	16,445	5,643	10,802	...	5,159
Eastern part of Magherafelt Rural District	5	9,621	5,749	3,872	1,877	...
Totals (i.e., exclusive of Coleraine Union and of Londonderry City)	...	69,621	34,977	34,644	333 (net majority)	...

CO. TYRONE.

Groups.	Number of District Electoral Divisions.	Total.	Catholics.	Non-Catholics.	Majorities.	
					Catholics.	Non-Catholics.
South-Western— Castlederg–Newtown Stewart	20	17,380	7,153	10,227	...	3,074
Trillick–Fintona	20	15,780	9,665	6,115	3,550	...
Seskinore Fivemiletown	10	8,615	3,605	5,010	...	1,405
	50	41,775	20,423	21,352	...	929 (net majority)
Eastern— Cookstown ...	10 (1 U.D.)	14,361	4,735	9,626	...	4,891
Munterevlin ...	2	3,764	3,025	739	2,286	...
Dungannon ...	5 (1 U.D.)	13,403	8,693	4,710	3,983	...
South-Eastern ...	15	16,875	6,294	10,581	...	4,287
	31 (3 U.D.'s)	48,403	22,747	25,656	...	2,909 (net majority)
Central	35 (1 U.D.)	35,995	25,682	10,313	15,369	...
Cullamore ...	2	1,508	1,073	435	638	...
Killeter	3	2,915	2,258	657	1,601	...
Strabane	1 (1 U.D.)	6,984	5,030	1,954	3,076	...
Donemana ...	5	5,085	1,802	3,283	...	1,481
Totals for county ...	128 (4 U.D.'s)	142,665	79,015	63,650	15,365 (net majority)	...

CO. FERMANAGH.

Groups.	Number of District Electoral Divisions.	Total.	Catholics.	Non-Catholics.	Majorities.	
					Catholics.	Non-Catholics.
Western	18	9,751	7,550	2,201	5,349	...
South-Eastern ...	28	20,662	14,172	6,490	7,682	...
Northern and Central	40 (1 U.D.)	31,423	13,018	18,405	...	5,387
Totals ...	86 (1 U.D.)	61,836	34,740	27,096	7,644	...

CO. ARMAGH.

Groups.	Number of District Electoral Divisions.	Total.	Catholics.	Non-Catholics.	Majorities.	
					Catholics.	Non-Catholics.
Armagh City ...	1 U.D.	7,356	3,965	3,391	574	...
Keady-Middletown	3 (1 U.D.)	6,631	4,753	1,878	2,875	...
Rest of area claimed in Armagh Rural District	14	18,458	8,137	10,321	...	2,184
Northern part of Newry No. 2 Rural District	4	5,139	1,397	3,742	...	2,345
Rest of Newry No. 2 Rural District	8	15,811	12,746	3,065	9,681	...
Newtown–Hamilton	1	1,369	478	891	,,	413
Rest of Crossmaglen Rural District	8	8,072	7,276	796	6,480	...
Totals ...	38 (2 U.Ds.)	62,836	38,752	24,084	14,668 (net majority)	...

CO. DOWN.

Groupo.	Number of District Electoral Divisions.	Total.	Catholics.	Non-Catholics.	Majorities.	
					Catholics.	Non-Catholics.
Catholic section of Downpatrick Rural District	17	25,826	15,808	10,018	5,790	...
Protestant section of Downpatrick Rural District	8	13,370	3,421	9,949	...	6,528
Northern part of Kilkeel Union	3	2,943	2,079	864	1,215	...
Central and Eastern part of Kilkeel Union	3 (1 U.D.)	9,365	3,953	5,412	...	1,459
Western part of Kilkeel Union	4	5,769	3,969	1,800	2,169	...
Northern part of Newry No. 1 Rural District	3	4,395	1,613	2,782	...	1,169
Remainder of Newry No. 1 Rural District	8	10,148	7,208	2,910	4,268	...
Warrenpoint ...	(1 U.D.)	1,938	1,081	857	224	...
Newry	(1 U.D.)	11 963	8,924	3,039	5,885	...
Totals	46 (3 U.Ds.)	85,717	48,056	37,661	10,395 (net majority)	...

This claim, so far as it is based on indications of the wishes of the inhabitants of the areas concerned, relies on the assumption that the wishes of the inhabitants of large areas, in which the majority of the population are opposed to the suggested transfer of jurisdiction, should be overruled in favour of the wishes of the inhabitants of other areas, on the ground that if the whole group of areas is taken together the wishes of a majority of the inhabitants are shown, on the basis of the religious statistics, to be in favour of such a transfer of jurisdiction.

The question of the respect to be paid to areas situated in the jurisdiction in which the majority of their inhabitants wish to remain has been considered above in Chapter III.

The general method, adopted in this claim, of using majorities in one area, who are in favour of a change, to overrule the wishes of the majority in another who wish to remain where they are is inconsistent with the view stated by the Commission as to the interpretation of Article XII and the principles which should govern its application.

The adoption of the line suggested in the claim under consideration would, on the basis of the census figures, gratify the wishes of 258,617 persons and be contrary to the wishes of 205,528 others, so that on balance the number of persons whose wishes would be gratified would be 53,089. In other words, if the 205,528 persons who would be displeased by transfer are taken as cancelling an equivalent number of persons who would be pleased, in order to achieve the net result of pleasing 53,089 persons, it would be necessary to transfer a total of 464,145 persons, or nearly nine times as many.

If reference is made to the table given below in Part 3 of this report it will be seen that the number of persons transferred by the Award from one jurisdiction to another is 38,913, of whom a net balance of 22,301 persons, on the basis of the census figures, will find their wishes gratified by the changes. Thus the number of persons whose wishes are gratified on balance represents more than half the number of those transferred as against approximately one-ninth in the case of the suggested transfer which is under consideration.

A further point which emerges from the above analysis is the fact that in certain districts there is a great concentration of the Catholic population. Among other areas of which this is true are (1) the southern part of the district of Newry No. 2 in Co. Armagh; (2) an area in and adjacent to the Sperrin Mountains, consisting of parts of the Rural Districts of Strabane, Omagh, Cookstown and Magherafelt; and (3) certain outlying parts of Co. Fermanagh. The large Catholic majorities concentrated in these areas have the effect of disguising the real position as to the distribution of population in the remainder of the counties or other districts concerned. In these remaining areas it is true as a general proposition that the numbers are more evenly balanced, some districts showing Catholic, and some Protestant majorities. This fact that the two parties are so often nearly of even strength explains the intense interest which is taken in many areas in the registration of electors.

PART II.—AREAS CONSIDERED.

CHAPTER I.

LONDONDERRY AND NORTH-EAST TIRCONAILL.

1. INTRODUCTORY.

The City of Londonderry is situated on the river Foyle about 5 miles above the point at which the river enters Lough Foyle, and about 20 miles from the open sea.

According to the Census of 1911 the city had a population at that time of 40,780 inhabitants, of whom 22,923 or 56·2 per cent. were Catholics and 17,857 or 43·8 per cent. were members of other denominations.

Figures were submitted to the Commission which tended to show that the population of the city had increased since the date at which the Census was taken. The assertion was made that the proportion of Catholics in the total population of the city had increased; but while it appeared probable that, owing to the immigration of factory workers from Donegal during the war, there had been some increase in the Catholic proportion, no definite figures on the subject were obtainable.

The city is divided into five wards, of which four are situated on the left bank of the river and include the original walled town, the greater part of the harbour, almost all the shirt and collar factories, the municipal buildings, and the larger working-class districts. The fifth, or Waterside ward, situated on the right bank of the river, includes one or two industrial establishments, but has mainly the character of a suburb. It is connected with the main portion of the city by the Carlisle Bridge, which in addition to the road provides a means of passage for railway goods wagons.

The city is the county town of the county of Londonderry, which, exclusive of the city itself, contained in 1911, 99,845 inhabitants, of whom 58,367 or 58·5 per cent. were non-Catholic and 41,478 or 41·5 per cent. were Catholics.

The city lies at the western end of the county being only separated from Tirconaill by a strip of territory, averaging about 3 miles in width, which is known as the "Liberties."

The port of Londonderry is the principal port for the North-West of Ireland. The goods handled at the port in the year 1924 amounted to 414,991 tons, 336,311 tons being imports and 48,680 tons exports; in addition 90,988 head of cattle, 25,744 sheep, and a quantity of other live-stock were exported.

The city has four railway termini. On the city side of the river are the stations of the Great Northern main line from Omagh, Enniskillen, and Dublin, and of the light railway which runs to Inishowen and to Letterkenny and Burtonport. On the right bank are the termini of the railway from Belfast viâ Coleraine, and of the light railway which runs to Strabane and from thence to Glenties, Killybegs, and Ballyshannon.

The city and the "Liberties", together occupy approximately half the width of the isthmus between the river Foyle and Lough Swilly, which connects the peninsula of Inishowen with the rest of Tirconaill. The communications which utilise this isthmus are on the east the main road through Londonderry; on the west the main road and light railway through Burt and Tooban Junction respectively. The centre of the isthmus is occupied by a group of hills rising to between 800 and 900 feet above sea level. The population of Inishowen, according to the Census of 1911, was 27,576, of whom 23,875 were Catholics, and 3,701 non-Catholics.

Tirconaill, or Co. Donegal, is itself almost isolated by the border from the rest of the Irish Free State, with which its only existing point of contact is an isthmus from 4 to 6 miles broad at the southern end of the county. No railway traverses this isthmus, and the only road connection is that which crosses the bridge over the River Erne at Ballyshannon.

The total population of Tirconaill in 1911 was 168,537, of which 133,021 or 78·9 per cent. were Catholics and 35,516 or 21 per cent. non-Catholics.

The portion of Tirconaill, which adjoins the River Foyle, and formed the former rural districts of Londonderry No. 2 and Strabane No. 2, has a mixed population and contained a number of District Electoral Divisions which had Protestant majorities in 1911. This area, which includes the district known as "the Laggan," lay, before the establishment of the border, in the market areas of Londonderry and Strabane. The population of the remainder of the District Electoral Divisions of the county showed almost uniformly Catholic majorities.

2. CLAIMS AND CONTENTIONS.

The chief representations received in respect of the city and its neighbourhood were submitted by—

(a.) A Committee of Nationalist inhabitants of the City of Londonderry;

(b.) A Committee of Nationalist inhabitants of the Londonderry Poor Law Union;

(c.) The City Corporation of Londonderry;

(d.) The Honourable the Irish Society;

(e.) The Londonderry Port and Harbour Commissioners;

(f.) The Londonderry Members of the Shirt and Collar Manufacturers' Federation;

(g.) The County Donegal Protestant Registration Association;

(h.) A Group of County Donegal business men.

The Committee of Nationalist inhabitants of the city claimed, firstly, that the desire of the majority of the inhabitants was the unity of all Ireland; secondly, that failing the unity of Ireland the majority of the inhabitants wished that the city should be included in the Irish Free State. The Committee based its claim on the fact that the majority of the inhabitants as Catholics had always desired to be associated with an autonomous Government in Dublin, and on the contention that the economic life of the city was largely dependent on its connection with Tirconaill. In the course of the hearing of evidence certain witnesses put forward by the Committee substituted for this claim an alternative scheme in favour of a boundary following the line of the Foyle, and dividing the city so as to include the Waterside Ward in Northern Ireland and the remainder in the Irish Free State.

The Committee of Nationalist inhabitants of the Union of Londonderry claimed that the Union, consisting of the city and of Londonderry No. 1 Rural District, should be included in the Free State on the ground that taken as a whole a majority of the inhabitants of the Union were Catholics and consequently desired to be in the Free State.

The claims put forward for the transfer of the city were opposed—

    (*a*) on legal grounds—

        (1) that the city is mentioned in the Government of Ireland Act 1920 as a constituent part of Northern Ireland;

        (2) that no part of the city actually touches the present boundary;

    (*b*) on economic grounds—

        (1) that the transfer would endanger the prospects of the city's industries;

        (2) that the greater part of the trade of the city and its port is with Northern Ireland;

        (3) that the city is closely linked economically with the Protestant districts to the East.

The City Corporation claimed that certain small readjustments should be made in the boundary in favour of Northern Ireland. The Port and Harbour Commissioners also claimed certain minor adjustments of the boundary. The statement submitted by the Irish Society outlined the historical position in regard to Lough Foyle, which it contended was wholly included in the County of Londonderry.

The Londonderry members of the Shirt and Collar Manufacturers' Federation contended that this industry imported its material from and exported the bulk of its products to Great Britain, that many of its factories were allied with British undertakings, and that its continued prosperity depended on costs being kept at a level which would enable the Derry factories to hold their own against English factories.

It was urged that if Londonderry were included in the Irish Free State there was a serious risk that the costs of the industry might be adversely affected, and that British undertakings which at present manufacture partly in Great Britain and partly in Londonderry might prefer to concentrate their operations at British centres.

[13849]

The Donegal Protestant Registration Association claimed that the Unionist inhabitants of Tirconaill desired that it should be included in Northern Ireland, and that the economic difficulties occasioned by the boundary would thereby be removed.

The Association further claimed that in certain areas adjoining the boundary the majority of the inhabitants, including almost all the farmers and landowners, were Unionists, and that in other neighbouring areas the majority of the landowners and farmers were Unionists. The areas specially claimed in the neighbourhood of Londonderry, were the former Rural Districts of Londonderry No. 2 and Strabane No. 2, with small additional areas adjoining them.

The Committee of Donegal Business Men supported the claims made for the inclusion of Londonderry, or of that part of the city situated on the west bank of the Foyle, in the Free State on the ground of economic connection between the city and Tirconaill. The Committee opposed the claims for the inclusion of any portion of Tirconaill in Northern Ireland.

Lough Foyle.

In three representations received by the Commission the contention is put forward that the whole of Lough Foyle, inside a line drawn between Magilligan Point and Greencastle, is included within the present limits of Northern Ireland, and that the existing boundary between Northern Ireland and the Irish Free State therefore runs along the high-water mark on the Donegal shore of the Lough. (Representations of (1) the Hon. the Irish Society; (2) the Corporation of the City and County Borough of Londonderry; (3) the Londonderry Port and Harbour Commissioners.)

As appears from the representation of the Irish Society, this contention is based on the view that under the provisions of the Charter of Charles II granted to the Society in 1662, as interpreted by a decision affecting the fishery rights of the Society given in a case heard in the Irish Courts in 1856 (*Allen* v. *Donnelly*, 5 Irish Ch. Reports, p. 229 and p. 452), the whole of Lough Foyle inside a line so drawn is included in the County of Londonderry.

Extracts from these three representations were forwarded to the British Government and to the Government of the Irish Free State, with a request for any information which these Governments might be in a position to give as to the existing boundaries of the Irish Free State and Northern Ireland in relation to the waters of Lough Foyle.

The British Government stated in its reply that it was not in a position to express a view as to where the present boundary does in fact run, but forwarded a letter, dated the 20th March, 1923, from the Secretary to the Cabinet of Northern Ireland in which the question was dealt with. The following is an extract from that letter :—

" The Government of Northern Ireland wish to put forward the view that the question of Lough Foyle is not governed by any rule of international law, but that the Lough has always formed part of Northern Ireland as delimited in the opening section to the Government of Ireland Act."

In addition to relying on the terms of the Charter already referred to, the Government of Northern Ireland quote an Act of the Parliament of the United Kingdom of the year 1838 (1 & 2 Vic. Ch. 87) entitled "An Act for Draining and Embanking certain Lands in Lough Swilly and Lough Foyle in the Counties of Donegal and Londonderry." The Preamble to this Act contains a recital to the effect that Lough Foyle is situated in Co. Londonderry : this recital begins as follows :—

" Whereas there are in the Lakes or Loughs called respectively Lough Swilly and Lough Foyle situate respectively in the counties of Donegal and Londonderry . . ."

The Government of Northern Ireland further contend that Lough Foyle if included in the " County " of Londonderry is also included within the " Parliamentary County " of Londonderry, which is the unit named in Section 1 (2) of the Government of Ireland Act, 1920.

The Government of the Irish Free State in their reply state that Lough Foyle is not included either in Co. Londonderry or in Co. Donegal. With regard to the Charter of 1662 they say :—

" So far as the Charter of 1662 is concerned, they desire to point out that it was no part of the real object of that Charter to alter the then existing Boundaries of counties nor do they admit that it could have the legal effect contended."

They further refer to an Act of the Parliament of the United Kingdom of 1825 (6 George IV. Ch. 99) entitled " An Act to repeal an Act of the last Session of Parliament relative to the forming Tables of Manors, Parishes and Townlands in Ireland, and to make provision for ascertaining the Boundaries of the same," and state that a general survey of Ireland was carried out under that Act whereby the boundaries of Counties, Baronies and other divisions of land in Ireland were fixed and determined. They refer to the maps prepared as a result of this survey, and state that such maps show that no part of Lough Foyle is included in the County of Londonderry. The Government of the Irish Free State also lay stress on the use of the term " parliamentary county " and not " county " in Section 1 (2) of the Government of Ireland Act, 1920.

3. Distribution of Population.

An examination of the Census figures of 1911 in detail reveals the following particulars :—

(a.) The five wards into which the city is divided showed the following distribution :—

	Total.	Catholic.	Non-Catholic.
North	10,788	4,729	6,059
South	7,683	4,935	2,748
East	4,409	1,603	2,806
West	8,730	8,038	692
Waterside ...	9,170	3,618	5,552

(*b*.) The population of the Liberties was as follows :—

Total.	Catholic.	Non-Catholic.
3,147	1,216	1,931

(*c*.) The population of the remainder of the rural district of Londonderry No. 1 was as follows :—

Total.	Catholic.	Non-Catholic.
11,266	5,699	5,567

(*d*.) The population of the area within 5 miles of the centre of the city was as follows :—

	Total.	Catholic.	Non-Catholic.
1. In Northern Ireland	7,742	3,101	4,641
2. In Tirconaill ...	1,914	754	1,160
3. Total	9,656	3,855	5,801
4. Total including city	50,436	26,778	23,658

(*e*.) The population of the area within 10 miles from the centre of the city was as follows :—

	Total.	Catholic.	Non-Catholic.
1. In Northern Ireland	17,533	7,301	10,232
2. In Tirconaill ...	10,607	5,427	5,180
3. Total	28,140	12,728	15,412
4. Total including city	68,920	35,651	33,269

In the eastern part of Tirconaill the following District Electoral Divisions, which together form a group adjacent to the existing border, contained, according to the census of 1911, non-Catholic majorities : in the north the divisions of Birdstown and Kilderry; in the south-west the divisions of Killea, Castleforward, Newtown-cunningham, Treantagh Mucklagh, St. Johnstown, Feddyglass, Raphoe, Figgart and Kincraigy. The total figures for these divisions taken together were in 1911 4,441 Catholics and 5,841 non-Catholics.

An inspection of the figures showing the religious denominations of the populations of townlands in this area provided the Commission with the means of determining more accurately the boundary between areas with Catholic and non-Catholic majorities. A non-Catholic majority was found, for instance, in the eastern part of the division of Burt. On the other hand it was found that the southern part of the area with Protestant majorities was separated from the town of Strabane by a considerable district containing Catholic majorities.

The Committee of Nationalist inhabitants of the city submitted figures giving the numbers of Catholic and non-Catholic electors on the latest Parliamentary and Local Government registers for the city alone. These were :—

	Catholic.	Non-Catholic.
Parliamentary	9,745	7,976
Local Government	7,578	6,485

Thus there was a Catholic majority of 1,769 on the Parliamentary Register, and a Catholic majority of 1,093 on the Local Government Register, the proportions being :—

			Catholic. Per cent.	Non-Catholic. Per cent.
Parliamentary	...	...	55	44
Local Government	...	...	54	45

The Commission was informed that the voting in the Parliamentary elections for the city as a separate constituency had been as follows in recent elections :—

1900	Conservative	...	2,361	Nationalist		...	2,294
1910	,,		... 2,435	,,		...	2,378
1910	,,		.. 2,415	,,		...	2,310
1913	Liberal ...	...	2,699	Unionist	...	...	2,647
1918 {	Sinn Fein ...	...	7,335	,,		...	7,020
	Nationalist	...	120				

The Commission was further informed that in elections for the City Council, except under Proportional Representation, three wards had always returned Unionist members, while two wards had always returned Nationalist members. Under Proportional Representation a different ward system had been used under which the Nationalist party obtained 21 members and the Unionist party 19.

4. ECONOMIC AND GEOGRAPHIC CONDITIONS.

A large quantity of material was furnished to the Commission on the subject of the economic alliance of the city both with the surrounding districts and with more distant areas.

Much evidence was heard as to the dependence of the surrounding rural districts both in Northern Ireland and in Tirconaill on their connection with the city as their only possible market town and source of supplies.

A large number of witnesses from districts in Tirconaill in the neighbourhood of Londonderry, most of whom were farming on their own account as owners or tenants, laid great stress on the hardships caused to them by the existence of a customs barrier between them and the city. Out of 61 witnesses from East Donegal 54 laid primary emphasis on this point. Of this number 46 stated that their desire was to be on the same side of the border as the city of Londonderry, the remaining 8 witnesses stated that they desired to be on the same side of the border as the town of Strabane.

It was noticeable that the long delays and the additional expenditure caused by the necessity for passing the customs barrier were especially felt by persons who lived in the districts nearest to the border, who had been accustomed in many cases to send produce to and from the city twice or even three times in the day.

It is clear that economic considerations in respect of this area and its relations with its market centre give extra strength to the case for transfer based on the wishes of the inhabitants.

Evidence was given by many witnesses on the subject of the area served by the Port and by the wholesale traders of the city.

From this evidence it appeared that the area served by the Port was fairly well defined, it being limited in the East by the range of mountains extending southwards from a point between Limavady and Coleraine to Pomeroy, and from thence south-west so as to include Clogher and the bulk of Fermanagh. Beyond this area, particularly in the south, further areas appeared to use the Port for some purposes, more especially for traffic to Scotland.

The chief imports are grain from America, coal from Great Britain, and manufactured articles mainly from Great Britain; the chief exports are cattle, sheep, and other live stock sent to Great Britain. As mentioned above, the imports in the year 1924 amounted to 366,311 tons, and the exports to 48,680 tons exclusive of live stock; live stock included 90,988 head of cattle and 25,744 sheep.

The wholesale trade of the city appeared not to extend quite so far as the traffic of the Port; Limavady, Omagh, Enniskillen and the town of Donegal being approximately the limits of its normal sphere.

The principal industry of the city is the shirt and collar manufacturing industry, which was originally founded there at a time when skilled labour in the neighbourhood was abundant, and was set free by the decay of the home industry. It was stated that the industry now has no special advantages in maintaining its connection with Londonderry, except the skill of the workers and the reputation which the Londonderry manufacturers have made for themselves. It was stated to the Commission that the proportion of the inhabitants of the city who depended on the shirt and collar making industry might be estimated at about 50 per cent.

Some attempt was made to define the comparative proportions of the trade of Londonderry with Northern Ireland and its trade with parts of the Irish Free State. Trade with the Irish Free State was estimated by certain witnesses at as high a figure as 75 per cent. of the total. This figure appeared to be a conjecture. Such figures as were submitted to the Commission tended to show that the larger part of the trade of the Port of Londonderry in the goods to which the figures related was trade with areas situated in Northern Ireland.

The dependence of Tirconaill on the city's market area, and the economic connection of the Peninsula of Inishowen with Londonderry were emphasised by many witnesses. Other witnesses emphasised the dependence of the city upon the trade of Tirconaill. On the whole the evidence tended to show that retail trade was most severely hit by the institution of the Customs barrier. Wholesale trade appeared to have suffered to an appreciable but relatively small extent. It did not appear that the trade of the Port itself had hitherto diminished in consequence of the boundary.

5. GENERAL POSITION AND CONCLUSIONS.

The Commission has not found it necessary to decide the legal question which was raised in the representation submitted by the

Corporation of the City of Londonderry as to whether the powers of the Commission to "determine the boundaries between Northern Ireland and the rest of Ireland" are sufficient to cover such an alteration of the existing boundary as the inclusion in the Irish Free State of the City of Londonderry would involve.

It is clear that the City of Londonderry cannot be considered apart from the portion of the county known as the "Liberties" on the west bank of the Foyle; and further that, if the City and Liberties were to be included in the Irish Free State, a portion of the county adjoining the City on the east bank of the Foyle, which could not reasonably be separated from the City, would also have to be included.

The Census figures for the City itself, and the Liberties taken together, show a Catholic majority of 4,351 corresponding to a Catholic proportion of 54·9 per cent. The Protestant majorities in the districts surrounding the City go some way towards counter-balancing this majority, as is shown by the Census figures for the areas included in a 5-mile or 10-mile radius. It is clear that the figures quoted and referred to do not, even when allowance is made for any probable increase in the proportion of Catholics in the City since 1911, afford evidence of the existence of such a majority as would be sufficient to justify the Commission in holding that the case for so great a change had been made out on the basis of the wishes of the inhabitants.

The argument in favour of a change based on economic and geographic conditions is the argument as to the mutual dependence of the City of Londonderry and Tirconaill. If a case had been made out for the inclusion in the Irish Free State of the counties of Fermanagh and Tyrone or the greater part of those counties, this argument would have been strongly reinforced. But as the Commission has decided for reasons stated below that those counties, with the exception of certain limited areas, should continue to be included in Northern Ireland, the case of the connection between Londonderry and Tirconaill has to be considered alone. Though owing to the closeness of the economic relations between the two resulting from natural geographic conditions, long-continued commercial intercourse, and the construction of railway systems which make Londonderry the chief railway terminus for Tirconaill, their separation by a customs barrier is an economic misfortune for both, the separation of the City of Londonderry from Northern Ireland would obviously involve a fresh defiance of geographic conditions, and a new series of economic misfortunes both to the City itself, and to the counties of Tyrone and Fermanagh and to a portion of the county of Londonderry, and the attempt to remedy existing difficulties by such an operation would make economic conditions worse instead of better.

In view of the position as thus broadly stated it is unnecessary to enter in detail into questions which have been raised as to how the inclusion of the city in the Irish Free State would affect the shirt and collar making industry on which a large portion of the population of the city depends for its livelihood. But the evidence given as to the circumstances of the industry indicated that such a change would involve grave risk to the continued prosperity of the industry which relies almost entirely on its export trade, and is closely associated with English factories.

The Commission examined the alternative proposal, put forward and supported by some Nationalist witnesses during the hearing of evidence, that instead of the city of Londonderry as a whole being included in the Irish Free State, the city should be divided and the boundary drawn down the River Foyle so as to leave the Waterside Ward on the east bank of the river in Northern Ireland, but was satisfied that apart from the fact that a line so drawn would distinguish between the part of the city which had a Catholic majority, and the part which had a Protestant majority, this suggestion had nothing to commend it, and that such a division of the city and port was from the economic and geographic point of view wholly impracticable.

The Commission considered that a case had been made out, on behalf of the adjacent Protestant areas in Tirconaill, for an alteration of the boundary on the west side of the city which would include in Northern Ireland a portion of East Donegal, such an alteration enables the customs frontier, now within 3 miles of the city, which interrupts the regular flow of traffic to and from farms in the immediate neighbourhood, to be shifted to a greater distance, so as to reduce the area suffering the inconvenience and expense of such interruption. The line adopted by the Commission includes in Northern Ireland such portion of the area of East Donegal adjoining the city as shows uniform Protestant majorities, and as can be detached from Tirconaill without cutting the railway and main road connecting the Peninsula of Inishowen with the rest of the County.

Lough Foyle.

With reference to the question raised, as to whether Lough Foyle is or is not included in the County of Londonderry, the Commission has carefully considered the various contentions put forward, and the Commission's Chief Technical Assistant has inspected the maps, referred to by the Government of the Irish Free State as maps prepared as a result of the survey made under authority of the Act of 1825, together with other maps and documents available in the Ordnance Survey offices of Dublin and Belfast.

The interpretation given to an admittedly obscure passage in the Charter of 1662 by the decision in *Allen v. Donnelly* (*Allen v. Donnelly* 5 Irish Ch. Reports, p. 229 and p. 452, 1856) lends some support to the view that the whole Lough up to a line drawn from Greencastle to Magilligan Point forms part of the County of Londonderry; but the question of the boundaries of the County and the effect of the Charter in determining such boundaries did not arise directly in that case. The Act of 1838 for the reclamation of Slob-lands in Lough Swilly and Lough Foyle, besides containing in its preamble the recital already quoted, also contains other provisions which are consistent with this recital. It does not appear, however, that either the recital itself or any other provision of the Act can be regarded as conclusive on the point raised.

The maps prepared in accordance with the survey conducted under the Act of 1825 do not appear to settle the question of the county boundaries. The terms of the Act itself do not clearly show that the Act was intended to have the effect of fixing the boundaries of counties.

The report received by the Commission from its representative as to the maps prepared under the Act is as follows—

" The maps relied on, for the purpose of proving that Lough Foyle is not included in the County of Londonderry, are five Parish maps dated 1830 to 1832 showing the Townlands bordering Lough Foyle on the East in the Parishes of Faughan Vale (2 maps), Tamlaght-Finlagan and Magilligan (2 maps). These maps show that no portion of Lough Foyle was included in the said Parishes, but do not give any information as to the position of the County Boundary in that neighbourhood except on the assumption, which has not been proved, that the County Boundary and the Parish Boundaries along Lough Foyle are coincident."

Other maps and documents inspected in the Ordnance Survey offices of Dublin and Belfast appear, however, to show that in the opinion of the Ordnance Survey authorities of the time when the relevant maps were prepared Lough Foyle was not included either in Co. Donegal or Co. Londonderry. The following are extracts from the report of the Commission's representative upon the material available in these offices—

" The presumption from the study of the documents at Dublin is that Lough Foyle is excluded from the Counties of Donegal and Londonderry (evidence—revised Area Book) and still more definitely that it is excluded from the County of Donegal (evidence—Boundary Sheet), with the exception of the Islands . . ."

" There is nothing to show in any of the Ordnance Survey documents at Belfast that Lough Foyle is either wholly or in part in either County Londonderry or Donegal. The presumption from the examination of these documents would be that Lough Foyle was excluded from the two counties . . ."

Enquiries have been made by the Commission as to whether any rates have been levied on the Fisheries or other property of the Irish Society in the Lough by the rating authorities of Co. Londonderry or Co. Donegal. It appears that no such rates have been levied, and that such property is not mentioned in the valuation books.

As the case stands on the information before the Commission, the question whether the whole of Lough Foyle should be regarded as having been included in the County of Londonderry is left in doubt.

The question which has been raised as to the use of the term " parliamentary county " in Section 1 (2) of the Government of Ireland Act, 1920, as distinguished from the term " county," is also a question of some difficulty, but, after an examination of the various statutes bearing on the question of the meaning to be given to the term " parliamentary county," the Commission is disposed to take the view that whatever portion of the Lough is to be regarded as having been included in the "County" should also be regarded as included in the "Parliamentary County."

The entrance to Lough Foyle between Greencastle and Magilligan Point is about one mile wide : the Lough extends south-westward for a distance of 15 miles to Culmore Point. It appears that, whatever the position as to the boundaries of the Counties on either side of the Lough, the internal waters of the Lough should be regarded as having, until 1920, formed part of the national territory of Ireland, and that the territorial waters, strictly so called, that is, the waters of the marginal belt along the coast, only begin at the point where the Lough meets the open sea.

Whether the waters of the Lough are to be regarded as "national" or "territorial" waters, the Commission considers that, if the whole of the waters of the Lough are not included in the County of Londonderry, the existing line dividing Northern Ireland from the Irish Free State must be regarded as passing through the Lough, either through the middle of the waters of the Lough, or along the median line of the principal navigation channel.

Whatever may be the correct view of the position as it has hitherto existed, the Commission considers that a line should now be drawn which recognises the practical requirements of the geographical situation as affected by the Articles of Agreement for a Treaty. A line drawn along the high-water-mark on either shore of the Lough would obviously be an inconvenient line to adopt from the point of view of administration and criminal jurisdiction.

The navigation channel in the territorial waters outside the Lough by which ships approach the Lough, and the navigation channel in the northern portion of the Lough itself afford means of access to the port of Moville and Carrickarory Pier, both situated in the Irish Free State. Beyond Carrickarory Pier the navigation channel is the means of access to the Port of Londonderry, and a considerable part of it consists of the dredged channel in which dredging work is constantly carried out by the Port Authorities of Londonderry. The line drawn by the Commission runs down the middle of the navigation channel so far as Carrickarory Pier head, and from that point the line is drawn so as to include in Northern Ireland the whole of the navigation channel, while including a strip of the foreshore and waters of the Lough in the Irish Free State. By this arrangement the navigation channel so far as it is required for affording means of access to ports in both territories is divided between Northern Ireland and the Irish Free State, while that portion which only affords access to the Port of Londonderry and includes the whole of the dredged channel is included in Northern Ireland.

SECTION A.

Particulars by District Electoral Divisions and portions of District Electoral Divisions, according to the Census of 1911, of the area in Eastern Tirconaill adjacent to the Liberties of Londonderry.

(Transferred to Northern Ireland.)

County.	District Electoral Division.	Catholics.	Non-Catholics.	Area.
TIRCONAILL ...	Kilderry (portion) ...	179	369	3,422
	Birdstown (portion) ...	149	270	2,632
	Burt (portion)... ...	153	270	3,199
	Castleforward (portion)	163	335	3,388
	Killea (whole)	555	853	7,569
	Treantagh Mucklagh (portion)	176	402	4,409
	St. Johnstown (portion)	509	641	4,434
	Feddyglass (portion)...	35	90	1,242
		1,919	3,230	30,295

CHAPTER II.

CO. TYRONE.

1. INTRODUCTORY.

Tyrone, the largest county in Northern Ireland, occupies a a central position, in which it is contiguous to six of the eight remaining counties of the Province of Ulster, among these being four of the five remaining counties of Northern Ireland. It stretches from Lough Neagh to the Foyle, and from the Sperrin Mountains to within a few miles of Lough Erne. It is interposed between Co. Fermanagh and the rest of Northern Ireland.

Geographically the county has no very prominent natural divisions. It is a country of hills and valleys. The northern and north central districts are mountainous. The county contains little level ground, apart from a strip of land bordering on Lough Neagh. Considerable areas, principally in the southern and central parts of the county, are covered with peat-bogs.

2. CLAIMS AND CONTENTIONS.

The chief representations received in respect of the county were submitted by :—

(*a*.) A committee of Nationalist inhabitants of the county. Separate representations were submitted for the eastern and western halves of the county.

(*b*.) The Tyrone Boundary Defence Association.

The Committee of Nationalist inhabitants claimed that the county as a whole should be included in the Irish Free State, on the following grounds :—

(1) that according to the Census of 1911 the Roman Catholics then had a majority of 15,365 over other denominations in a total population of 142,655 corresponding to a Catholic proportion of 55·4 per cent. :

(2) that in the elections of November 15, 1922, for the combined constituency of Tyrone and Fermanagh, the Nationalist candidate who secured most votes gained a majority of 6,596 over the leading Unionist candidate :

(3) that in each of the 6 rural districts, into which the county is divided and in 3 out of its 4 urban districts, the Census shows a majority of Catholics :

(4) that economically and geographically the county is intimately connected with Londonderry, in which it was claimed a majority of the population desired to be included in the Irish Free State; and with the county of Fermanagh, which also had a Catholic majority.

The Committee's claims were supported by representations submitted on behalf of the Omagh Urban District Council, by Committees of Nationalist inhabitants of the Clogher Rural District, of Aughnacloy, and of the Union of Magherafelt (Co. Londonderry).

The Tyrone Boundary Defence Association contended in opposition to the claim put forward by the Nationalist Committee—

(1) that the Unionist population predominated in the borders of the county and surrounded the chief Nationalist areas which lay at a distance from the border; the Nationalist areas could not, it was contended, be transferred to the Irish Free State without involving both the Unionist districts and the county of Fermanagh :

(2) that in the election of October 29th, 1924, in which no Nationalist candidate stood for election, and the contest lay between Unionist and Republican candidates, the leading Unionist candidate for the combined constituency of Tyrone and Fermanagh had polled more votes than the leading Nationalist candidate had polled at the previous election :

(3) that the severance of Tyrone from Northern Ireland would leave the county without a natural port or trade centre :

(4) that although the Unions of Clogher, Castlederg and Dungannon, and the rural district of Strabane, contained Catholic majorities according to the Census, there are actually Unionist majorities in the current Parliamentary register in these areas;

and that in the Cookstown Union, and in the Omagh Union with the exception of the mountainous area, the parties are nearly balanced in the register.

The Association's contentions were supported in further representations submitted by the—

> Unionist inhabitants of the Union of Cookstown;
> The Clogher Rural District Council;
> The Dungannon Urban District Council;
> The Dungannon Board of Guardians;
> The North-west Tyrone Boundary Defence Committee;
> The Town Commissioners of Aughnacloy;
> and others.

Representations were further received by the Committee in respect of—

(a) the Union of Magherafelt (Co. Londonderry), claiming inclusion of that area in the Irish Free State; and

(b) the former Rural District of Strabane No. 2 (Tirconaill) claiming that the district should be included in Northern Ireland.

Finally evidence was submitted on behalf of the Urban District Council of Strabane by delegates representing both parties, who agreed in claiming that the former Rural District of Strabane No. 2, in Tirconaill, lay in the market area of the town.

3. Distribution of Population.

The county as a whole had a population in 1911 of 142,655, of which 79,015, or 55·4 per cent., were Catholics and 63,650, or 44·6 per cent., non-Catholics. Catholic and Protestant districts are mingled in a definite but complicated pattern. The town of Strabane and the north-central area, including the Sperrin Mountains, are strongly Catholic; the remainder of the county is more evenly divided, but shows Protestant areas for the most part on the outer parts of the county surrounding Catholic areas in the interior. If the District Electoral Divisions existing at the time of the census be taken, the county falls into seven main sections :—

(a) a Protestant area in the North-west, bordering on Co. Londonderry;

(b) a Protestant area in the West centre, touching Tirconaill at its north-west corner, and touching both Tirconaill and Co. Fermanagh at its south-west corner;

(c) a Protestant area in the south, bordering on Co. Fermanagh and touching Co. Monaghan;

(d) a Protestant area in the south-east, bordering on Co. Monaghan and on Co. Armagh;

(e) a Catholic area south-west of Omagh;

(f) a large Catholic area north and east of Omagh;

(g) a Protestant area to the north-east with its centre at Cookstown;

The town of Omagh itself forms a Catholic link between (e) and (f).

Besides these areas three smaller Catholic areas exist on the edges of the county (1) at Strabane; (2) westwards from Killeter in the Castlederg Rural District; and (3) on the shore of Lough Neagh.

With the exception of Killeter area and the town of Strabane, the District Electoral Divisions adjoining the county boundary, where it coincides with the boundary of Northern Ireland, are, in almost every case, Divisions with Protestant majorities.

The town of Strabane had a population in 1911 of 5,107, of whom 3,750 (or 73·4 per cent.) were Catholics and 1,357 (or 26·6 per cent.) were non-Catholics. Protestant areas lie north and south of the town; Catholic areas (in Tirconaill) on the west; while immediately to the east lies a mixed area, intervening between Strabane and the extensive Catholic area of north-east Tyrone. Beyond the Catholic area in Tirconaill centering at Lifford, a small town immediately facing Strabane on the west bank of the River Foyle, lies a Protestant area including Raphoe and the northern part of the Rural District of Strabane No. 2.

Taking the region surrounding Strabane on either side of the existing border, the area within a radius of five miles from the town shows a Catholic majority; but if the whole area within a 10-mile radius of the town be considered, apart from the town itself, it shows a Protestant majority.

4. Economic and Geographic Conditions.

Economically the county has no single leading commercial centre. The old border divides the market areas of the towns of Strabane and Aughnacloy. The south-west of the county deals to some extent with Irvinestown and Enniskillen. The rest of the county's retail trade centres in the towns of Omagh, Dungannon, Cookstown, Fintona, Ballygawley, Newtown Stewart and Castlederg and other towns.

As regards wholesale trade and oversea traffic, the trade of the western part of the county, including Omagh, and amounting to roughly two-thirds of the whole county, tends to be centred in Londonderry, while that of the remaining eastern part of the county appears to be divided between Belfast and Newry. The line of division roughly follows the watershed between the Foyle basin and that of the rivers flowing into Lough Neagh.

The county is mainly agricultural, but there are linen and flax mills at Sion Mills, Cookstown and Dungannon, and smaller industries at Strabane, Coalisland and Donaghmore.

The town of Strabane, which had a slightly larger population in 1911 than the county town, Omagh, and was thus the largest town in Tyrone, is an important market centre for the adjoining districts on both sides of the border. Its natural market area includes practically all the two rural districts of Strabane No. 1 (Co. Tyrone) and Strabane No. 2 (Tirconaill), with additional areas on both sides of the border. It is an important railway centre for Tirconaill as traffic from Dublin or Belfast is transferred at

Strabane from the Great Northern Railway's main line to the narrow-gauge railways running to Donegal, Glenties, Killybegs and Letterkenny. The village of Lifford situated on the opposite bank of the Foyle, and connected with Strabane by road and railway bridges, is closely associated economically with Strabane. It has served as the administrative centre of Tirconaill. Since the setting up of the Customs border, Strabane traders have tended to establish depots in Lifford, from which they conduct their trade in Tirconaill, and additional shops have been opened there. It is noteworthy that more than one Strabane merchant, in giving evidence before the Commission, stated that he considered the boundary between Lifford and Strabane to be better from his point of view than one moved a few miles to the west, as he could conduct a depot at Lifford by means of his existing staff, whereas a depot five miles further from Strabane would require additions to his staff and to the cost of his business. A short canal unites Strabane with the Foyle at a point lower down the river. By means of this canal, and the railways and roads which connect the town with Londonderry on both banks of the river, a close economic connection is maintained between the two towns, Londonderry serving both as port for Strabane and to a great extent as a wholesale centre for Strabane and its market area.

5. GENERAL POSITION AND CONCLUSIONS.

As appears from what has been said above, the general position in Co. Tyrone itself is that there are blocks of Catholic districts and blocks of Protestant districts. The Catholic blocks are on the whole larger than the Protestant blocks, but the Catholic blocks are in the interior of the county, while the Protestant blocks are mostly near the borders of the county. In the southern portion of Co. Tyrone there is one Catholic region in the neighbourhood of Trillick bordering on Co. Fermanagh, but to the east and west lie Protestant regions. On the western side of Co. Tyrone along the Donegal border, districts containing Protestant majorities are continuous except for (1) the projecting western portion of the Castlederg Rural District, and (2) the Urban District of Strabane and the District Electoral Division of East Urney immediately to the south of it. The Catholic area at the western end of the Castlederg Division is the only area which is conveniently placed from the point of view of making it possible to meet the wishes of the inhabitants by transferring them to the Irish Free State without at the same time transferring Protestant districts. The Protestant region round Castlederg almost meets the Protestant region to the north of Strabane, one district electoral division with a small Catholic majority intervening. The region immediately to the east of Strabane is a mixed region showing both Catholic and Protestant electoral divisions; but further east lies a large Catholic area which occupies the centre of the northern portion of the county. No serious concrete suggestion has been made to the Commission as to how this large Catholic area could be included in the Irish Free State by carving out a section of Co. Tyrone from the west with a division line starting somewhere in the neighbourhood of Strabane. A study of the map shows clearly that this Catholic region in the northern centre of Co. Tyrone and the adjoining Catholic region in the south of Co. Londonderry cannot be separated from the southern part of Co. Tyrone and Co. Fermanagh.

The case of the town of Strabane is also necessarily involved with that of the rest of Co. Tyrone. While the town itself has a Catholic majority, it lies, as already pointed out, between Protestant areas to the north and to the south with a mixed area immediately to the east. Any attempt to include the town in the Irish Free State with a reasonable portion of its market area in Co. Tyrone would involve taking considerable sections of these areas, and would involve the drawing of a line which could only be described as geographically impossible. The small town of Lifford which owing to its situation near Strabane where the railways of Tirconaill meet, has been used as the administrative centre of the County for County purposes, faces Strabane on the Irish Free State side of the border, on the western bank of the River Foyle : it seems probable that, if the border remains as at present in the Foyle between Strabane and Lifford, Lifford may develop as a commercial and industrial centre for East Donegal. Some Strabane merchants have already opened depots at Lifford for the purpose of carrying on their trade with Tirconaill. The proximity of Lifford to Strabane, which facilitates the supervision of such depots, makes it possible for the Strabane merchants to retain their trade of Tirconaill by adopting this plan. The Commission was informed that the opening of a clothing factory in Lifford was also contemplated by a Strabane manufacturer. It is clear that both Strabane itself and the region in Co. Tyrone which it serves as a market and retail centre would suffer severely if the frontier line were brought across the river so as to include in the Irish Free State the town of Strabane without the area surrounding it. As already pointed out Strabane's trade connections for the purpose of obtaining wholesale supplies are largely with Londonderry.

We have thought it right to discuss the position in Co. Tyrone itself, for the purpose of examining the possibility of dealing with sections of the County by alterations in the existing boundary of Northern Ireland, where it coincides with the western boundary of Co. Tyrone, but, as the foregoing summary indicates, the claim put forward by the Nationalist inhabitants of Co. Tyrone was for the inclusion of the County as a whole in the Irish Free State. Those who put forward this claim recognised that the claim for Co. Tyrone could not stand alone. Co. Tyrone lies between Co. Fermanagh and the rest of Northern Ireland; the inclusion either of the whole of Co. Tyrone, or of western and central Tyrone, in the Irish Free State would necessarily involve also the inclusion in the Irish Free State of the whole of Co. Fermanagh. Those who claimed the inclusion of Co. Tyrone in the Irish Free State were compelled therefore to claim the inclusion of the whole of Co. Fermanagh as well. Further, the economic connection between Londonderry and

Co. Tyrone and Co. Fermanagh was urged in Co. Tyrone as showing that economic considerations added weight to the wishes of the inhabitants of Londonderry in favour of the City's inclusion in the Irish Free State. It was generally recognised that the transfer of the City would also involve the transfer of a considerable undefined portion of the western part of Co. Londonderry, apart from the Union of Magherafelt, a Catholic region bordering on Co. Tyrone on the north-east, for which a separate claim was made.

The claim for the inclusion of Co. Tyrone in the Irish Free State therefore involved large areas and populations in addition to those of Co. Tyrone itself. As the claims for the City of Londonderry and the adjoining portion of Co. Londonderry, and for Co. Fermanagh, are separately dealt with, it is unnecessary to go over the same ground in dealing with the claim for Co. Tyrone; but it is necessary to say something here, by way of anticipation, as to the dominating feature of the position as regards distribution of population in Co. Fermanagh, in order that the relation between the two counties may be appreciated.

The northern portion of Co. Fermanagh which borders on Co. Tyrone is predominantly Protestant. This northern region of Co. Fermanagh forms part of a Protestant block in the northern and central portions of the county consisting of forty district electoral divisions and one urban district (Enniskillen). Each of these forty Divisions showed a Protestant majority in 1911 with the exception of four isolated Divisions with Catholic majorities and one in which the population was evenly divided. Enniskillen itself has a small Catholic majority but is surrounded by district electoral divisions showing Protestant majorities, and the area immediately between Enniskillen and the south-western border of the county is mainly Protestant. According to the census figures this Protestant block in the northern and central parts of Co. Fermanagh numbered in 1911 31,423, rather more than half of the total population of the county, and consisted of 13,018 Catholics and 18,405 Protestants. The Catholic majority in Co. Fermanagh taken as a whole may be said to depend for its strength on the border districts in the west, south-west and east of the county. The contention that the large block of country showing Protestant majorities in the north and centre of Co. Fermanagh should be included in the Irish Free State is based primarily on the ground that Co. Fermanagh must be dealt with as a whole in accordance with the wishes of the Catholic majority, which according to the census figures represents 56.2 per cent. of the population. An alternative ground on which the contention is based, particularly by representatives of Co. Tyrone, is that the two counties of Fermanagh and Tyrone should be considered together and effect be given to the wishes of the Catholic majority representing 55·6 per cent. of the entire population of the two counties considered as a unit. As a further alternative, if it had been conceded that the Protestant regions in the eastern part of Co. Tyrone should be distinguished from the Catholic regions in the centre and north of the county, it might have been urged that the Catholic majorities in the latter region should be taken with the Catholic majorities shown

[13849]

for Co. Fermanagh as a whole for the purpose of supporting the case in favour of the inclusion in the Irish Free State of this Protestant region in Co. Fermanagh.

The case of Co. Tyrone raises therefore, in concrete form, the general questions discussed in Chapter III as to the scope of the Commission's powers and duties, and as to the principles on which units of area should be chosen or defined for the purpose of ascertaining the wishes of the inhabitants (See Question 2 (C) and Question 6).

It may be asked, is a change on so large a scale in the existing area of Northern Ireland as that which is involved in the claim for inclusion in the Irish Free State of Co. Tyrone, that is, a change involving the removal from Northern Ireland of the two entire Counties of Tyrone and Fermanagh with the possible addition of the City and a portion of the County of Londonderry, or, at the lowest estimate, involving the whole of Co. Fermanagh and the whole of Co. Tyrone with the exception of the Cookstown and Dungannon areas to the east bordering on Lough Neagh, a change which falls within the scope of the Commission's powers, or is it outside the scope of those powers as interpreted by the answer given to Question 2 (C)? In that answer we laid down the principle that "no wholesale reconstruction of the map is contemplated by the proviso—the Commission is not to reconstitute the two territories, but to settle the boundaries between them." We do not think it necessary to give a definite answer to the question thus raised, because it appears to us that the question of the claim for the inclusion in the Irish Free State of Co. Fermanagh and the western and central parts of Co. Tyrone is a claim which must be rejected on the basis of the actual distribution of population within the area claimed, in accordance with the further principle laid down in Chapter III, that where the Commission "finds an area of sufficient size and population to merit separate consideration which is at present on the right side of the boundary, that is on the side where its inhabitants wish to remain, the existence of that area will in itself be a reason against making an alteration which would involve its transfer to the wrong side, and help to indicate the point beyond which alterations intended to give effect to the wishes of the inhabitants should not extend."

It is clear that the northern and central parts of Co. Fermanagh, in which Protestants have the majority, form an area of sufficient size and population to merit separate consideration, which is at present on the right side of the border, that is, on the side where its inhabitants wish to remain. In the opinion of the Commission it would clearly be unjustifiable to use Catholic majorities in adjoining areas for the purpose of overwhelming the Protestant majority in this area, and to override, on the basis of the total Catholic majority so obtained, the wishes of the majority of the inhabitants of this area in favour of remaining on their present side of the border. The existence of this Fermanagh area adjoining the southern border of Co. Tyrone affords, in the opinion of the Commission, a conclusive reason against making the suggested alteration of the existing boundary which would involve the inclusion in the Irish Free State of the whole of Co. Fermanagh and at least the western and central parts of Co. Tyrone. The Protestant district in the north and centre of Co. Fermanagh must by virtue of its geographical position be recognised as a governing factor not only in respect of Co. Fermanagh itself but also in respect of Co. Tyrone.

In view of the considerations above stated the alterations made by the Commission in the existing boundary of Northern Ireland, where it coincides with the western boundary of Co. Tyrone, are limited to—

(1) the Killeter region in the western portion of the Castlederg Rural District, which is transferred to the Irish Free State;

(2) the townland of Fearn, which is transferred to Northern Ireland.

Particulars of the areas transferred are appended.

Particulars, according to the Census of 1911, by District Electoral Divisions and portions of District Electoral Divisions, of the Areas which, in consequence of the adoption of the Boundary Line as determined by the Commission, are transferred from one jurisdiction to the other jurisdiction.

SECTION B (i).

Area in Tirconaill forming part of the District Electoral Division of West Urney.

(Transferred to Northern Ireland.)

County.	District Electoral Division.	Catholics.	Non-Catholics.	Area (acres).
TIRCONAILL ...	West Urney (portion)	...	60	819

SECTION B (ii).

Area in County Tyrone forming part of the Rural District of Castlederg.

(Transferred to Irish Free State.)

County.	District Electoral Division.	Catholics.	Non-Catholics.	Area (acres).
TYRONE	Corgary (whole) ...	728	166	17,758
	Magheranageeragh (portion)	644	154	4.904
	Killeter (whole) ...	688	205	11,030
	Killen (portion) ...	5	...	43
	Lisnacloon (portion) ...	98	28	493
		2,163	553	34,228

[13849]

CHAPTER III.

COUNTY FERMANAGH AND PORTIONS OF SOUTHERN TIRCONAILL AND SOUTH-WEST MONAGHAN.

1. Introductory.

County Fermanagh forms a projection so placed that it is flanked on three sides by portions of the Irish Free State. In the West its extreme point reaches to within 6 miles of the Atlantic Ocean, at Donegal Bay, thus nearly separating Tirconaill from the rest of the Free State.

The population of the County in 1911 was 61,836, of which 34,740 or 56·2 per cent. were shown as Roman Catholics, the remainder, namely, 27,096 or 43·8 per cent. belonging to all other denominations.

The County has more geographic individuality than most counties. The Upper and Lower Lough Erne occupy a depression running from end to end of the County, and the land both North and South for the most part slopes downwards to the lough from ridges or plateaux which roughly follow the limits of the County, except in the south-west and south-east, where the border lies beyond them.

The county town of Enniskillen is situated at the principal bridge across the Erne at a point where a section of river connects the upper and lower lakes. It is the market and trading centre for the whole of the central part of the County, whose trade is concentrated in an unusually high degree at a single centre.

2. Claims and Contentions.

The chief representations received in respect of the County were submitted by (a) a Committee of the Nationalist inhabitants, and (b) the County Council which owing to the abstention of the Nationalist party from the last elections was virtually a Unionist body.

Both these groups put forward a large number of witnesses from all parts of the County.

Besides these bodies a certain number of individuals made representations and were heard as witnesses.

The Nationalist Committee claimed that in view of the fact that the Census showed a Catholic majority of 7,644 in the County in 1911 the County should be transferred as a whole to the Free State. The Committee supported this claim by reference to the parliamentary election of 1918 in which 13,041 votes were given for Nationalist candidates as against 11,292 given for Unionist candidates; and by reference to the Local Government elections of 1920 when 52 Nationalist members were elected on the three District Councils and one Urban Council as against 48 Unionist members.

The inclusion of the County in the Free State would, the Committee claimed, remove the numerous economic and geographic inconveniences occasioned by the existing border. Among these were—

(1.) The fact that the present border separated parts of the market areas of Clones, Belturbet, Ballyconnell, Pettigoe, Swanlinbar and Ballyshannon from their natural market towns ;

(2.) The fact that the existing border cut the Sligo, Leitrim and Northern Counties Railway into two sections ;

(3.) The fact that the existing border had interrupted the connection of Enniskillen as a distributing centre with adjoining parts of neighbouring Free State counties.

The Committee urged that the County being economically and geographically a natural unit should not be divided by the new boundary. In particular, the Committee urged, there were strong reasons why Lough Erne and its drainage system should be preserved under one jurisdiction.

The Fermanagh County Council contended that the County should be wholly retained in Northern Ireland, and that in order to remedy the economic and geographic inconveniences caused by the existing border certain portions of the adjoining Free State counties should be placed in Northern Ireland, notably the town and neighbourhood of Pettigoe, the bridge and sluice gates at Belleek, and the district electoral division of Drummully (Co. Monaghan), which was practically enclosed by portions of the county of Fermanagh.

The Council claimed that the Census returns of 1911 did not accurately represent the present proportion, as between Catholics and non-Catholics, of the population of the county. There had been a considerable Protestant immigration, and recent elections had shown that the electors of the county were approximately equally divided as between Unionists and Nationalists, the Nationalist majority having been very much reduced since the time at which the Census was taken. It was claimed that over 1,400 votes had been gained on the Local Government Register by the Unionist side since 1920.

The Council further urged that the strength of the Nationalist party in the County was largely concentrated in certain frontier tracts, namely, in the western section of the County adjoining Tirconaill and Leitrim, and in the south-eastern section of the County adjoining Monaghan and Cavan. Enniskillen, the Council maintained, was the centre of a Protestant area comprising twelve out of a total of twenty County Electoral Divisions. The chief Nationalist strength, it contended, lay in the four new county divisions of Inishmacsaint, Holywell, Rosslea and Doon. The Council also urged that a division of the County would not be in accordance with its economic and geographic conditions. The Council pointed out that practically every road in the County led to Enniskillen in which town practically the whole business of the

County was done. The Council also urged that it would be a serious mistake in any way to split up Lough Erne, or to separate the lake, whose borders were, it was claimed, inhabited by Unionists on both sides for practically its entire length, from the sluice gates at Belleek by which the level of the lake was controlled.

3. Distribution of the Population.

Both the Nationalist Committee and the County Council submitted figures giving the total numbers of Catholic and non-Catholic electors on the latest Parliamentary and Local Government registers for each of the newly formed District Electoral Divisions and County Electoral Divisions.

These tables placed the Commission in a position to check the figures contained in the Census showing the religious distribution of the population according to the former District Electoral Divisions.

Maps were also prepared showing the distribution of the population according to the particulars obtained concerning the religious denominations of the inhabitants of townlands, the effect of which was to show a marked distinction between different sections of the County. The sections, into which the County and the adjoining regions of Tirconaill and Co. Monaghan, which it is necessary to consider, are thus divided, are :—

(i.) A northern section, consisting of the District Electoral Divisions of Tirconaill which adjoin the border of Co. Fermanagh. In the eastern part of this area (Pettigo and Grousehall) the census figures show Protestant majorities; the western part shows Catholic majorities.

(ii.) A western section, comprising nearly all the former Rural District of Belleek and a small portion of that of Enniskillen was found to be a predominantly Catholic region extending eastwards from the existing border as far as Derrygonnelly, but not including the western shore of Lower Lough Erne, which is bordered by a belt of Protestant communities.

(iii.) A southern section south-west of Upper Lough Erne was found to constitute a second Catholic region rather smaller in area. This region extends from a point south-east of Florence Court to a point some distance short of Crum.

(iv.) A south-eastern section, comprising the former Rural District of Clones No. 2 and a portion of the Rural District of Lisnaskea. In this section the Catholic and Protestant sections of the population are intermingled in varying proportions; and the section may be divided into four sub-sections.

(a.) The District Electoral Divisions of Clonkeelan and Derrysteaton, which show a marked Catholic predominance. These divisions isolate the District Electoral Division of Drummully (Co. Monaghan) from contact with the rest of the Irish Free State. This division contained in 1911 a population of 449 of whom 264 were Catholics and 185 non-Catholics, 9 out of the townlands of which it is composed showing Catholic majorities, and 7 Protestant majorities. Communication between Drummully and the rest of Co. Monaghan is only possible through Northern Irish territory. The main road and railway from Clones to Belturbet and Cavan both pass through Drummully, but both before and after doing so they pass through portions of Co. Fermanagh lying in the Divisions of Clonkeelan and Derrysteaton respectively;

(b.) The present District Electoral Divisions of Rosslea and Eshnadarragh at the eastern extremity of Co. Fermanagh which show an overwhelming Catholic majority;

(c.) A belt of territory with smaller but appreciable Protestant majorities stretches from Crum on the south of Upper Lough Erne in a north-easterly direction to Dresternan, and runs south of Rosslea into Co. Monaghan.

(d.) Between this belt of Protestant majorities and the Lisnaskea –Fivemiletown area lies a belt of districts with Catholic majorities containing a smaller population but a larger majority.

(v.) The remainder of the County embraces all the Northern and Central districts extending to the edge of the County south-west of Enniskillen. This area forms a Protestant region. The census figures show Protestant majorities in 35 District Electoral Divisions while in one other division the population was evenly divided The town of Enniskillen, which in a population of 4,847, shows a Catholic majority of 529 corresponding to a Catholic proportion of 55·5 per cent., is enclosed by this region; and there are Catholic districts on its outer edges.

This Protestant region adjoins the border of Co. Tyrone, and extends on the north-west up to the Tirconaill border in the neighbourhood of Pettigoe. The adjoining section of Co. Tyrone mainly consists of areas with Protestant majorities, particularly in the west where these extend northwards to Castlederg and Newtown Stewart, and in the east where they extend practically without interruption across the southern part of Co. Tyrone to the borders of Co. Armagh.

Evidence was given in support of the statement that there had been a considerable immigration into the county since the taking of the Census in 1911. The names and addresses of several hundred Protestant families were submitted to the Commission containing a total of 2,117 persons who had settled in the county since 1920. It was not in most cases possible to determine how far this immigration constituted a net increase of the Protestant population. The number given did not include a considerable number of Protestant members of the Special Constabulary, who had been transferred to Co. Fermanagh from other districts. As regards these members of the Special Constabulary it was contended that allowance should be made, in examining the voters' rolls, for the fact that their names were included in the registers.

4 (a). Economic and Geographic Conditions.

A considerable amount of evidence was heard by the Commission on the subject of the market areas of the market towns both in Fermanagh and in the adjoining districts of the Free State. From this evidence it became clear that the towns of Clones and Pettigoe had been hard hit by the existing border, while Ballyshannon, Ballyconnell and Belturbet had been hit to a less extent.

It appeared that in certain cases the course of trade had in some degree adapted itself to the conditions imposed by the new border, but there remained considerable districts in which under any circumstances it appeared that very considerable hardship would be caused unless a substantial restoration of the natural market areas could be effected.

The economic difficulties of the town and neighbourhood of Pettigoe are peculiar inasmuch as the town itself was divided by the border and the greater part of the town is cut off by the border from the more important part of its market area. A further part of this market area lies in the valley of the Termon river in which the existing border follows the course of the stream. The road, however, continually crosses and re-crosses the river and so passes from one territory into another. The inhabitants of the upper part of the valley thus have to cross the frontier several times in order to reach Pettigoe.

The main road round the northern shore of Lower Lough Erne and the Bundoran branch of the Great Northern Railway both pass through Pettigoe where they run for a stretch of about 2 miles through Free State territory; thus in order to pass from Kesh to Letter along either road or railway the border has to be crossed twice.

It has been an additional, though no doubt a removable, hardship to the inhabitants of Pettigoe that this main road has not been classed as an "approved" road for traffic between Pettigoe and Kesh. In order to travel with a motor-car from the portion of Pettigoe situated in Tirconaill, or from the Termon Valley, to the neighbouring market town of Kesh, some six or seven miles distant, it is necessary to travel round viâ Belleek and Enniskillen, a distance of some forty or fifty miles for the single journey.

The situation caused by the existing border at Belleek is also peculiar. At the town of Belleek both the north and south banks of the river are in Northern Ireland except for a small wedge of Free State territory which included the bridge over the river and some three hundred yards of road leading from that bridge to the Fermanagh border on the south bank.

Of the sluice gates by which the level of Lough Erne is controlled two are situated in Co. Fermanagh and the remaining two in Tirconaill. The house of the gatekeeper is situated on an island which forms part of Tirconaill.

The position at Belleek further affects communication between Tirconaill and the rest of the Irish Free State, inasmuch as the only point of contact by road under existing conditions is the bridge over the river Erne at Ballyshannon. Some eight hundred yards of Northern Irish territory divides the bridge at Belleek from the point at which a road again enters Free State territory north of the town.

Many witnesses, both among those put forward by the Nationalist Committee and among those brought forward by the County Council, laid emphasis on the importance to County Fermanagh of the control of the level of Lough Erne and the drainage of the areas which border on the two lakes and the stretch of river connecting them. It appeared that unity of control was rendered more important by the existence of a certain conflict of interests between the owners of land bordering on the Lower Lake, who with the urban authorities of Enniskillen were interested in the maintenance of the statutory level, and the owners of land bordering on the Upper Lake, who would prefer to see a reduction of the level.

In this connection it may be noted that the Upper Lough Erne extends for a short distance south-eastwards beyond the border of Co. Fermanagh into Co. Cavan and Co. Monaghan. The following table showing the number of riparian landowners in the three counties at the date of the drainage operations, and the value of the improvements, effected by the drainage scheme of 1880–91 in each county, serves to indicate the relative importance of the sections of the lake concerned.

	Riparian Landowners.	Value of Improvements.
		£ s.
Co. Fermanagh	230	4,133 0
Co. Cavan	60	579 0
Co. Monaghan	5	3 10
	295	4,715 10

It may be added that among the riparian owners in 1891, taking both lakes together, 217 owned land bordering on the Upper Lake as against 87 who owned land bordering on the Lower Lake.

4 (b). GEOGRAPHIC CONDITIONS.

The enquiry brought out the existence of certain well defined geographic barriers at various points in the County :—

(1.) In the neighbourhood of Pettigoe the geographic barrier lies rather on the heights north-west of the town than in the comparatively well populated valley in which the existing border runs;

(2.) South of Lough Erne the mountain ridge of Cuilcagh forms a natural line of division. Between Lower Lough Macnean and the western extremity of Lower Lough Erne a range of rather lower heights and plateaux separates the Erne basin from that of Lough Melvin and Lough Macnean;

(3.) At the northern end of the eastern border of the County a well defined ridge runs more or less south-west from Slieve Beagh which for a few miles is sufficiently well marked to form a recognisable barrier.

5. Conclusions.

The above description of the position as existing in Co. Fermanagh and its adjacent areas is sufficient to make clear, in the light of the general principles already stated, the grounds of the Commission's decisions with regard to this region, as set out in the different sections of Part III. The line has been drawn on the basis of the distribution of the population as above described, with due regard to the economic and geographic conditions as set out, and as further explained in Part III under the heading " Economic and Geographic Results."

The outline given of the situation of Pettigoe and its neighbourhood, as affected by the existing boundary, shows the serious disadvantages suffered by the inhabitants owing to the existence of the barrier which at present separates their area from the adjacent areas of Fermanagh on the east, as well as the general geographical inconvenience of this section of the boundary ; economic and geographic considerations thus support the case made on the basis of the wishes of the inhabitants for the inclusion of this area in Northern Ireland. Belleek, where the present geographical frontier also involves grave inconvenience, shows a strong Catholic majority, and the wishes of this majority in favour of inclusion in the Irish Free State are in accord with geographic considerations. These two changes, the inclusion of Pettigoe in Northern Ireland and of Belleek in the Irish Free State, involve on the whole a substantial improvement in the position as to communications on both sides of the border.

In dealing with the south-eastern region where a difficult problem was presented by the intermingling of the Catholic and Protestant sections of the population, the Commission has drawn the line so as to retain in Northern Ireland all but a small part of the Fermanagh portion of the belt of Protestant territory stretching northwards from Crum into Co. Monaghan beyond Dresternan ; and the greater part of what may be described as the mixed area in south-eastern Fermanagh with its centre at Newtown Butler is thus also retained in Northern Ireland.

In this region the line includes in the Irish Free State—

(1) all but the north-western corner of the pocket of Monaghan territory consisting of the District Electoral Division of Drummully ;

(2) adjacent areas of Fermanagh on the east, south and west of Drummully ;

(3) the small remaining Fermanagh portion of the Protestant belt intervening between the village of Rosslea and Co. Monaghan, together with an area further south and

south-east where the Protestant belt extends into Co.
Monaghan; and
(4) the village of Rosslea and the Catholic area lying
immediately to the north of it.

Particulars of the areas transferred are appended.

Particulars, according to Census of 1911, *by District Electoral
Divisions and portions of District Electoral Divisions, of the
Areas which, in consequence of the adoption of the Boundary
Line as determined by the Commission, are transferred from
one jurisdiction to the other jurisdiction. The figures given
under the heading " area " refer in each case to acres.*

Section C (i).

*Area in Tirconaill including the town of Pettigoe and District
Electoral Division of Grousehall.*

(Transferred to Northern Ireland.)

County.	District Electoral Division.	Catholics.	Non-Catholics.	Area.
TIRCONAILL ...	Grousehall (whole) ...	225	256	6,300
	Pettigoe (portion) ...	241	543	4,788
	Templecarn (portion)...	31	43	422
		497	842	11,510

108

Section C (ii).

Areas in Western portion of County Fermanagh including Belleek, Garrison and Belcoo.

(Transferred to Irish Free State.)

County.	District Electoral Division.	Catholics.	Non-Catholics.	Area.	Catholics.	Non-Catholics.	Area.
Two areas to the North-East of and around Belleek.							
FERMANAGH	Mallybreen (portion)	48	...	1,024			
	Castlecaldwell (portion)	230	7	2,330			
	Belleek (portion)	504	53	3,032	782	60	6,386
Area East of Lough Melvin and Lough MacNean.							
FERMANAGH	Inishmacsaint (portion)	1,780	224	15,667			
	Church Hill (portion)	50	9	2,002			
	Roogagh (portion)	283	42	4,948			
	Garrison (whole)...	377	326	4,968			
	Lattone (whole) ...	524	16	5,159			
	Doagh (portion) ...	24	7	674			
	Old Barr (portion)	50	3	992			
	Glenkeel (portion)	13	...	1,668			
	Holywell (whole)	585	38	5,062			
	Gardenhill (whole)	203	15	4,030			
	Gortahurk (portion)	17	...	94	3,906	680	45,264
					4,688	740	51,650

SECTION C (iii).

Area in Tirconaill comprising Belleek Island.

(Transferred to Northern Ireland.)

County.	District Electoral Division.	Catholics.	Non-Catholics.	Area.
TIRCONAILL ...	Carrickboy (Belleek Island) (portion)	...	...	3

SECTION C (iv).

Two areas in Southern part of County Fermanagh lying East and North of Swanlinbar and Ballyconnell.

(Transferred to Irish Free State.)

County.	District Electoral Division.	Catholics.	Non-Catholics.	Area.
FERMANAGH ...	Cuilcagh (portion) ...	40	15	1,619
	Derrylester (portion)...	186	28	1,562
	Kinawley (portion) ...	568	112	2,775
	Springtown (portion)...	276	18	1,852
	Doon (portion)... ...	249	8	1,779
	Aghyoule (portion) ...	707	145	4,994
	Crum (portion) ...	196	43	1,586
		2,222	369	16,167

SECTION C (v).

Five areas in Eastern part of County Fermanagh mainly in the District Electoral Divisions of Clonkeelan, Magheraveely and Rosslea.

(Transferred to Irish Free State.)

County.	District Electoral Division.	Catholics.	Non-Catholics.	Area.	Catholics.	Non-Catholics.	Area.
Area South of Newtown Butler.							
FERMANAGH	Crum (portion) ...	14	3	237			
	Derrysteaton (portion)	608	161	4,651			
	Newtown Butler (portion)	9	2	71			
					631	166	4,959
Area South-West of Clones.							
FERMANAGH	Clonkeelan (portion)	392	226	2,986			
	Magheraveely (portion)	71	9	268			
					463	235	3,254
Area North-West of Clones.							
FERMANAGH	Magheraveely (portion)	...	...	...	21	7	151
Area North of Clones.							
FERMANAGH	Magheraveely (portion)	...	...	...	8	8	37
Rosslea and Eshnadarragh.							
FERMANAGH	Dresternan (portion)	243	8	1,041			
	Rosslea (portion)	1,781	237	9,181			
					2,024	245	10,222
					3,147	661	18,623

SECTION C (vi).

Area in County Monaghan forming part of District Electoral Division of Drummully.

(Transferred to Northern Ireland.)

County.	District Electoral Division.	Catholics.	Non-Catholics.	Area.
MONAGHAN ...	Drummully (portion)...	13	38	336

CHAPTER IV.

SOUTH TYRONE AND NORTH MONAGHAN.

1. Introductory.

In the section of the existing boundary between the point where it leaves the border of County Fermanagh and the point where it reaches the border of County Armagh, the boundary follows the county border between County Tyrone and County Monaghan. At a point about halfway between these two points the course of the border forms approximately a right angle, the northern end of County Monaghan forming a salient, which is enclosed on both sides by parts of County Tyrone.

On the western side of the salient the border follows the high ground sloping north-eastward from the top of Slieve Beagh until it sinks into the valley of the Blackwater at the apex of the salient. On the eastern side of the salient the border follows the river Blackwater which here flows in a south-easterly direction as far as Caledon, where the border of County Armagh is reached.

The Clogher Valley runs parallel to the border a few miles within County Tyrone on the western side of the salient. The Clogher Valley Light Railway, which runs through the valley, is continued on the eastern side of the salient from Ballygawley to Tynan.

2. Claims and Contentions.

Claims and contentions received in respect of Co. Tyrone as a whole have already been summarised above in Chapter 2.

Claims received in respect of the territory situated in Co. Monaghan in this section were :—

(1.) A proposal submitted on behalf of the Clogher Rural District Council, that a strip of territory bordering on the river Blackwater opposite the town of Aughnacloy, should be included in Northern Ireland on account of the economic connection between this district and Aughnacloy;

(2.) A proposal submitted by a group of Protestant inhabitants of Glasslough and district, who pointed to the geographical difficulties of the present position and urged that for the purpose of removing these difficulties changes should be made with due regard to the wishes of the Protestant inhabitants.

It was contended in a representation submitted on behalf of Nationalist inhabitants of Glasslough and district that a majority of the inhabitants of Glasslough and its neighbourhood were Catholics, and that the district was economically connected with the town of Monaghan. It was contended on this ground that no part of the district should be removed from the jurisdiction of the Irish Free State.

Particular claims in respect of territory situated on the Tyrone side of this section of the border were :—

(1.) A claim, submitted by Nationalist inhabitants of the Clogher Rural District, that the Rural District should be included as a whole in the Irish Free State on the grounds that a majority of the inhabitants were Catholics, corresponding to a Catholic proportion of 50·8 per cent.

(2.) A claim, submitted by Catholic inhabitants of Aughnacloy, that the town should be included in the Free State on the grounds that the trade of the town was largely with adjoining districts in Co. Monaghan and that the Town Council had recently shown a majority of Nationalist Councillors.

It was contended in a representation submitted by the Clogher Rural District Council that no part of the area controlled by the Council should be transferred to the Irish Free State, on the grounds that a majority of the electors on the register of voters in that area were Protestants and that economically the interests of the area were bound up with Northern Ireland.

It was contended in a representation submitted by the Aughnacloy Town Commissioners that the town should not be included in the Free State on the grounds that a majority of the inhabitants were Protestants; that a majority of the voters on the current register were Protestants; and that economically the more important portion of the town's market area consisted of the surrounding Protestant districts in Co. Tyrone.

3. POPULATION.

The general distribution of the population in Co. Tyrone has already been discussed above in Chapter 2 (County Tyrone). The District Electoral Divisions adjacent to this section of the border on the Tyrone side show Protestant majorities with the exception of that of Cullamore, which shows a large Catholic majority. This division, though it adjoins the border, stretches back from it across the Clogher valley. In the town of Aughnacloy the population was almost evenly divided, the Census showing 510 non-Catholic inhabitants as against 500 Catholic.

On the southern, or Co. Monaghan side, of the border in this section the population is predominantly Catholic in each District Electoral Division, except in the District Electoral Division of Glasslough which is situated on the Co. Monaghan side of the border at a point at which the counties of Tyrone and Armagh meet. This division has a small Protestant majority, according to the Census of 1911. An examination of religious figures for townlands shows that in the Glasslough Division townlands with Catholic and Protestant majorities are intermixed in such a way that the majority of the Protestant townlands are not adjacent to the existing border. Generally speaking, the portions of Co. Monaghan in which there are Protestant majorities lie further to the south and west, and are separated from the existing border by districts containing Catholic majorities.

4. Economic Conditions.

The areas situated on the Tyrone side of the existing border in this section are served by a number of minor economic centres which are linked together by the Clogher Valley Railway. These are from west to east, Fivemiletown, Clogher, Augher, Ballygawley, Aughnacloy and Caledon.

The town of Aughnacloy (population 1,010 in 1911) is situated about half a mile from the border. It has a market which served the adjacent area in County Monaghan. With this exception 'the country on the Monaghan side of the border in this section has its economic centre in the town of Monaghan.

5. General Position and Conclusion.

In the region where Co. Tyrone meets Co. Monaghan to the north of the Monaghan salient, the existing frontier divides Protestant districts of south-east Tyrone from Catholic districts of Northern Monaghan, except where the District Electoral Division of Cullamore makes a break in the line of Protestant districts. Any alteration of the frontier so as to include this division, or the greater part of it, in the Irish Free State would involve interference with means of communication in the Clogher Valley, and smaller changes would also be open to economic and geographic objections. There is no practicable method by which the wishes of the Catholic inhabitants of this division can be gratified without including considerable areas from neighbouring divisions which show Protestant majorities. The position of the frontier town of Aughnacloy is an unfortunate one from the point of view of its prosperity as a market centre, but the distribution of population in the neighbourhood as well as geographical conditions render it impossible for the Commission to make any change for the purpose of relieving its difficulties.

CHAPTER V.

COUNTY ARMAGH, EASTERN COUNTY MONAGHAN AND COUNTY DOWN.

1. Introductory.

County Armagh.

The County of Armagh, which lies between Co. Down on the East and Co. Tyrone on the West, had, according to the Census of 1911, a population of 120,291 of whom 54,526 were Catholics and 65,765 non-Catholics.

The north-eastern side of the County forms an outlying part of the Belfast industrial area.

[13849]

The County contains five Urban Districts, namely, those of Portadown, Armagh, Lurgan, Keady and Tanderagee. Further, the Urban District of Newry (Co. Down) includes an area which formerly formed part of Co. Armagh.

The County is divided into four Rural Districts, namely, those of Armagh, Lurgan, Tanderagee and Newry No. 2. The area included in the last-named district previously formed two rural districts, namely, Newry No. 2 and Crossmaglen.

Of the Urban Districts in the County, Armagh (population 7,356) and Keady (population 1,434) contain Catholic majorities. Of the Rural Districts those of Newry No. 2 and Crossmaglen contain Catholic majorities. The remainder of the Urban and Rural Districts contain Protestant majorities.

The chief economic centres for the County are Armagh, Portadown, Lurgan and Newry; among the subordinate centres are Keady, Newtownhamilton, Bessbrook and Tanderagee.

The section of the existing border which divides the counties of Armagh and Monaghan roughly follow in its northern portion the division between the market areas of Monaghan and Armagh. Further south the region of Mullyash forms a minor salient of Co. Monaghan lying between the towns of Keady, Newtownhamilton and Castleblayney. Again further south the existing border separates Castleblayney and Dundalk from portions of their market areas.

County Down.

The County of Down roughly comprises the portion of Northern Ireland lying between the Great Northern Main Line from Belfast to Newry and the sea.

The County as a whole contained in 1911 a population of 204,303 of whom 64,485 were Catholics and 139,818 non-Catholics. The County contained nine Urban and eight Rural Districts, of which seven Urban and six Rural districts showed Protestant majorities. The remaining Urban districts, namely, Newry and Warrenpoint, and the remaining Rural districts, namely, those of Kilkeel and Newry No. 1 showed Catholic majorities.

The chief industrial areas of the County are in the north-western region and in the neighbourhood of Newry. At the southern extremity of the county the Mourne Mountains form a tract of high open country between Newcastle and Carlingford Lough, which is mainly uninhabited. To the south of the mountains lies a well-populated area between the mountains and the sea.

2. CLAIMS AND CONTENTIONS.

The following are the principal claims of a positive character included in representations submitted to the Commission :—

(1.) The claim for inclusion of Middletown and neighbourhood (Co. Armagh) in the Irish Free State, submitted by Nationalist inhabitants of the district.

(2.) The claim for inclusion of Keady and neighbourhood (Co. Armagh) in the Irish Free State, submitted by Nationalist inhabitants of the district, supported by the Keady Urban District Council.

3.) The claim for inclusion of Mullyash (Co. Monaghan) in Northern Ireland made by inhabitants of the district.

(4.) The claim for the inclusion of the Urban District of Armagh in the Irish Free State, submitted by the Armagh Urban District Council, and by Nationalist inhabitants of the city.

(5.) The claim for inclusion in the Irish Free State of Newry Union and Kilkeel Union consisting of—

(a.) Rural District of Newry No. 2 (including Cross-maglen), i.e., the southern portion of Co. Armagh.

(b.) Urban District of Newry.

(c.) Rural District of Newry No. 1, Urban District of Warrenpoint and Kilkeel Union, i.e., the southern portion of Co. Down.

The claim for these areas was submitted by the Newry Urban District Council and by a Committee of the Nationalist inhabitants of the Unions of Newry and Kilkeel.

(6.) The claim for inclusion in the Irish Free State of an area based on the former Parliamentary Division of East Down, submitted by a committee of inhabitants of East Down.

Representations were submitted by the Armagh County Council, the Rural Disrict Councils of Armagh, Newry No. 1, Newry No. 2 and Kilkeel, and the Kilkeel Board of Guardians, in opposition to the claims for the transfer of any part of their areas. A representation was submitted by the Newry Chamber of Commerce, in opposition to the claims made for the transfer of Newry and any part of the adjoining districts. Representations were further received from the Bessbrook Spinning Company, the Belfast City and District Water Commissioners, the Portadown and Banbridge Water Works Board, and the Camlough Water Works Trustees, in opposition to the claims for the transfer of the areas in which their works were situated.

Further, the Urban District Council of Warrenpoint submitted a claim for the inclusion of that town in the Irish Free State. This claim was opposed in a representation submitted by a group of property owners, traders and inhabitants of the town.

Armagh Urban District.

The representation of the Armagh Urban District Council claimed that the city should be included in the Irish Free State on the ground that, in the city's total population of 7,356, 3,965 representing a proportion of 53·9 per cent. were Catholics, and that two out of the three wards into which the city was divided returned

[13849]

Nationalist councillors. The City is surrounded by Protestant districts, and it was suggested that it should be connected by a narrow corridor, about two miles long, consisting of three townlands, with the old constituency of South Armagh, the whole of which they urged, should be treated as a Catholic area.

Keady–Middletown Area.

In the representation claiming the transfer to the Irish Free State of Keady, Middletown and neighbourhood, it was suggested that an area should be transferred including the District Electoral Divisions of Middletown, Derrynoose and Keady Urban and Rural, with portions of those of Tynan, Brootally, Crossmore and Armaghbrague, on the ground that in the total area so claimed the population showed a Catholic majority.

It was further contended that the area claimed had little, if any, economic connection with Armagh or other places in Northern Ireland.

In support of the claim respecting the town of Keady it was contended that merchants of Keady had suffered appreciable losses by the interposition of the Customs barrier between the town and an area in Co. Monaghan with which trade had been carried on. It was further urged in support of the claim that the Keady Urban Council, which was an exclusively Nationalist body, had been elected on the understanding that it would demand from the Commission the right to be included in the Irish Free State, or, alternatively, that the boundary be eliminated.

Mullyash Area.

The group of inhabitants of Mullyash claimed that this District Electoral Division of Mullyash and some neighbouring townlands should be transferred to Northern Ireland on the ground that the census figures of 1911 showed a Protestant majority for such areas.

Unions of Newry and Kilkeel.

The representations in which it was claimed that the Unions of Newry and Kilkeel should be transferred to the Irish Free State based this claim on the following grounds :—

(1.) That in the towns of Newry and Warrenpoint, and the Rural Districts of Newry No. 1, Newry No. 2, Crossmaglen and Kilkeel, the majority of the population in each case was Catholic ;

(2.) That the following elected local authorities had, since their creation in 1898, contained Nationalist majorities :—

1. Newry Board of Guardians.
2. Newry Urban District Council.
3. Warrenpoint Urban District Council.
4. Newry No. 1 Rural District Council.
5. Newry No. 2 Rural District Council.
6. Crossmaglen Rural District Council.

7. Kilkeel Board of Guardians.
8. Kilkeel Rural District Council.

> It was stated that the above authorities all passed resolutions repudiating the authority of the Belfast Parliament to govern them, and were consequently suppressed. At subsequent elections for these bodies with the exception of the Urban Councils of Newry and Warrenpoint no representatives of the Nationalist party were put forward as candidates. It must be understood therefore that the Representations submitted on behalf of the various local bodies mentioned, other than the two Urban District Councils, expressed the views of Unionist members only.

(3.) That the constituencies of South Armagh and South Down for many years always returned Nationalist members. The same had been true of Nowry Town until it ceased in 1918 to be an independent constituency;

(4.) That the unions of Newry and Kilkeel were economically to a large extent interdependent and self-contained, the town of Newry being their principal source of supply; and that it would be "highly injurious, in fact almost disastrous . . . . if any portion of that area were cut off from contact with Newry, or if Newry was cut off from it."

It was contended by representatives of the Newry Chamber of Commerce that neither the town of Newry, nor any portion of South Down or South Armagh should be transferred to the Irish Free State, on the ground that the economic interests of those areas were "irrevocably united" to the Northern Government and that any transfer would be highly detrimental to the best interests, financial and otherwise, of the inhabitants, and cause loss of trade, increased taxation and unemployment.

In the representation of the Kilkeel Rural District Council it was contended that the area controlled by the Council should not be transferred to the Irish Free State on the following grounds :—

(a.) That the trade connections of the area were mainly with Belfast, and that only a very trifling percentage of its trade was with the Irish Free State;

(b.) That Carlingford Lough formed a natural boundary;

(c.) That the rural district contained the principal reservoirs which supplied water to Belfast, Portadown, Banbridge, and other centres in Northern Ireland.

The Rural District Councils of Newry No. 1 and Newry No. 2 represented that the trade and business of the areas controlled by them lay with Northern Ireland, and that the agricultural, business, and financial interests of the district were bound up with the Northern area.

In the representations submitted by the Belfast City and District Water Commissioners, it was contended that no part of County Down should be transferred to the Irish Free State on the following grounds :—

(1.) That Carlingford Lough formed a natural boundary.

(2.) That any land boundary drawn on the northern side of the Lough would expose the Commissioners' Works to the risk of attack.

(3.) That a transfer of the area containing the Commissioners' Works in the Mourne mountains would involve risk of interference with the undertaking, and of restrictions in the use of water and increased taxation; and would make it difficult for the Commissioners to finance their undertaking.

The Portadown and Banbridge Joint Water Works Board opposed the transfer of the district in which their works were situated on the ground that their undertaking would be prejudiced if placed under a jurisdiction different from the jurisdiction of those for whose benefit the Water Works were provided.

In the representations submitted by the Bessbrook Spinning Company it was contended that it would be incompatible with economic conditions to put any portion of the undertaking of the Company into the Irish Free State on the ground that the industry carried on by the Company was essentially a Northern Irish industry, having practically no connection with the Irish Free State. Nearly all the goods produced by the Company were sent to Belfast and other Northern centres, through which the Company received its raw material and machinery. A customs barrier between Bessbrook and Northern Ireland would expose the undertaking to additional taxation and additional expense and delay, and would separate the industry from its natural base at Belfast and the associated undertakings of which in reality the Bessbrook Company formed a part.

In the Representation submitted on behalf of a committee of inhabitants of East Down, it was claimed that the area comprised in the Parliamentary constituency of East Down should be included in the Irish Free State on the ground that a majority of the inhabitants of the area were Nationalists.

3. Distribution of the Population.

Middletown–Keady–Newtown Hamilton Area.

The area claimed in the west of Co. Armagh, including Middletown, Keady and Derrynoose District Electoral Divisions, and portions of the neighbouring divisions, appears to have had in 1911 a total population of 8,916, of which 5,751 or 64 per cent. were Catholics, and 3,165 or 36 per cent., non-Catholics. In the area claimed in this section of the county the town of Keady had a population of 1,438, of which 1,082 or 75 per cent., were Catholics. The town is exactly on the dividing line between a predominantly

Catholic area in the west and south-west, and a predominantly Protestant area in the north-west, north, east and south-east; so that the trading area of the town lies divided between Catholic and Protestant regions. The area claimed is made up, in addition to the town of Keady, of the three District Electoral Divisions of Middletown, Derrynoose and Keady Rural, each of which showed Catholic majorities, and of some 24 additional townlands, of which 14 showed Protestant majorities, nine Catholic majorities, while in one the Protestants and Catholics were equal in number.

The area to the south-east of Keady forms a group of Protestant districts and townlands, including the District Electoral Divisions of Armaghbrague and Newtown Hamilton. These two divisions together had in 1911 a population of 2,775, of which 1,088 were Catholics and 1,687 non-Catholics. If in addition to these two divisions part of the division of Mullyash (Co. Monaghan) and neighbouring Protestant townlands in Co. Armagh and Co. Monaghan be included, the total population of this group of Protestant districts was 4,606, of which 1,695 were Catholics and 2,911 non-Catholics.

Newry No. 2 Rural District, including Crossmaglen.

The total population of Newry No. 2 Rural District, including Crossmaglen was in 1911 30,391, of which 21,897 were Catholics and 8,494 non-Catholics. The northernmost District Electoral Divisions in the Rural District showed Protestant majorities, viz., those of Newtown Hamilton, which has been referred to, Mount Norris, Poyntzpass, Tullyhappy and Mullaghglass. Certain of the northern townlands in the adjoining District Electoral Divisions to the South also showed Protestant majorities. With the exception of a few townlands in the neighbourhood of Bessbrook and Newry, and one or two other isolated townlands, the remainder of the Rural District of Newry No. 2, including Crossmaglen, showed uniformly Catholic majorities. Thus, the line of division between Catholic and Protestant areas runs from a point South of Newtown Hamilton to a point on the border of the Urban District of Newry. Between Newtown Hamilton and Bessbrook the Catholic area extends somewhat further to the north than elsewhere. Bessbrook itself, with its population, according to the Census, of 2,888, of which 1,467 or 50·8 per cent. were Catholics, is exactly on the line of division.

Newry Urban District.

The town of Newry was in 1911, with 11,963 inhabitants, the fifth largest town in the Six Counties which now constitute Northern Ireland. Its population was divided as between religions into 8,924 Catholics (74.6 per cent.) and 3,039 non-Catholics (25.4 per cent.).

Newry No. 1 Rural District.

In the Rural District of Newry No. 1 figures for the old District Electoral Divisions show Protestant majorities in Donaghmore

(64.8 per cent.), Ouley (57.2 per cent.) and Rathfryland (65.1 per cent.).

The remainder of the divisions have Catholic majorities, those in Crobane and Newry Rural being slight while those in the remainder are substantial.

Protestant majorities are shown in all but one of the townlands in the northern part of Newry Rural, and in all but two townlands in the northern part of Crobane.

Thus, in Newry No. 1 Rural District the line of division between Catholic and Protestant regions starts from a point on the border of the Urban District of Newry. The townland figures show that it then runs slightly north of east and continues to the east between Rathfryland and Hilltown. Isolated Catholic townlands are found north of this line and isolated Protestant townlands are found to the south of it.

Kilkeel Union.

In the Kilkeel Union the total population in 1911 was 18,077, of which 10,001 were Catholics and 8,076 Protestants. The figures for the old District Electoral Divisions show a division of the Rural Districts into three sections. The actual population was as follows :—

Western Section—	Total.	Catholics.	Non-Catholics.
Rosstrevor	2,050	1,457	593
Killowen	509	445	64
Greencastle	1,644	1,143	501
Mourne Park ...	1,566	924	642
Southern and Eastern Section—			
Kilkeel	3,208	1,311	1,897
Ballykeel	1,764	724	1,040
Mullartown	2,628	1,198	1,430
Newcastle U.D. ...	1,765	720	1,045
Northern Section—			
Fofanny	1,218	981	237
Bryansford	1,063	735	328
Maghera	662	363	299

Downpatrick Union.

In the Union of Downpatrick the population was almost equally divided between Catholics and non-Catholics. Total figures for the Union were : Catholics 19,229, non-Catholics 19,967.

In the former parliamentary constituency of East Down which excludes certain District Electoral Divisions of Downpatrick Union and includes certain divisions of the Banbridge and Kilkeel Rural Districts, the total population according to the census of 1911 consisted of 21,901 Catholics, as against 18,043 non-Catholics.

General Résumé.

Thus if we regard the southern portions of the counties of Armagh and Down as a whole, it is found that there is a small

Catholic district on the western border stretching from Middletown to Keady, and that there are large Catholic districts (i) in South Armagh in the Rural District of Newry No. 2 and (ii) in South Down in the Rural District of Newry No. 1 and the western part of the Rural District of Kilkeel.

In the eastern and northern parts of the Rural District of Kilkeel and in the Union of Downpatrick the population is mixed; some District Electoral Divisions show a Catholic majority and others a Protestant majority. In the whole group taken together the population is almost equally divided. On the whole, in this group the District Electoral Divisions in the eastern part tend to have a larger Catholic proportion, while those in the west tend to show a larger Protestant proportion.

4. Economic and Geographic Conditions.

(A.) *Middletown–Keady–Newtown Hamilton Area.*

Evidence was given to the effect that the market area of Keady included the District Electoral Divisions of Middletown, Keady Rural, and Crossmore; part of that of Armaghbrague and a strip of Co. Monaghan from two to five miles in width.

There was some conflict of evidence as to the market area in which Middletown was included. It appears that the District Electoral Division of Middletown being nearly equidistant from the market towns of Monaghan, Keady and Armagh, can use any of these markets more or less indifferently, except in as far as one or two of them specialise in certain commodities, such, for instance, as flax and pig markets in Armagh.

On the whole it would appear that before the establishment of the boundary the dividing line between the market area of Keady on the one hand and the market area of Castleblayney and Monaghan on the other, had been situated about midway between the two towns in each case, and that thus a small strip of Co. Monaghan had tended to trade rather with Keady than with Castleblayney, and perhaps a smaller strip further north tended to trade with Keady as much as with Monaghan; but it appears that in a fairly wide marginal area farmers went to one or other of these market towns according as prices were more attractive or as they obtained credit more easily.

As regards Keady market and its trade as a whole, it was stated on the other hand that Keady had no proper market place or proper market facilities. The representation submitted by the Armagh Urban District Council spoke of Keady as being within the Armagh market area, and it was maintained that the market area of Armagh for pork, flax, grain and grass seed, extended as far as Castleblayney and Monaghan. The present importance of Keady market was stated to be a matter of recent development since the advent of the railway to Keady. Formerly, it was said, Keady and Newtown Hamilton markets had been of equal importance; now Keady market was much better than that of Newtown Hamilton.

The Linen Industry was stated by witnesses on both sides to be the only industry in the Keady district that was of present day importance. Of four factories in the area, one in Keady had been closed for four or five years, a second in Dundrum had been closed for apparently a long period. It was stated that at the most important mill in the area which was now working, namely, Darkley, the spinning of yarn and the manufacturing of linen was carried out, but the finishing and marketing was done in other parts of Northern Ireland to which the half finished products were sent.

Newtown Hamilton is a small town of 612 inhabitants with a monthly fair and a weekly market. The area served by the Newtown Hamilton market was stated to include parts of the District Electoral Divisions of Armaghbrague, Ballymyre, Dorsy and Lisleitrim, as well as part of that of Mullyash (Co. Monaghan). Evidence tended to show however that for some purposes residents in these areas used the more distant markets of Keady, Armagh, Castleblayney or Newry.

The most important towns in the neighbourhood of Newtown Hamilton and their distances from it are as follows :—

						Miles.
Armagh ...	...	...	...	...	...	12
Newry ...	...	...	...	...	...	12
Dundalk	...	...	...	...	...	16
Markethill	...	...	...	...	...	8
Castleblayney	...	...	...	...	...	10
Keady ...	...	...	...	...	...	8

For communications by rail recourse must be had to the stations at one or other of these towns.

It may be noted that the main roads from Keady to Newry, and from Armagh to Dundalk intersect one another at Newtown Hamilton.

(B.) *Newry and District.*

As regards economic conditions Newry has to be considered under three aspects :—

(1) as a market town and distributive centre;
(2) as a centre of industry;
(3) as a port.

It was stated to the Commission that as far as the numbers of persons employed in various industries were concerned the order of importance in Newry was :—

(1) the textile trade;
(2) shipping and coal business:
(3) timber, iron, slates, granite, &c.;
(4) flour, meal, &c.

This classification is generally confirmed by the occupation figures of the census of 1911, which show the persons employed in the four chief groups of occupations as :—

(1) flax-spinning, weaving, &c.—1,035 persons;
(2) retail trade—1,016 persons;
(3) port, railway and cartage (exclusive of general labourers) —407 persons;
(4) building, stone quarrying, and timber—354 persons.

(i.) (a.) *Newry as a wholesale centre.*

The wholesale trade of Newry, apart from the marketing of the produce of its industries and the coal trade originating from its port, is of limited importance. No wholesale distributing houses appear to exist in the town for branches of retail trade other than the grocery trade.

The area within which the wholesale distribution is carried on from Newry appears to be practically restricted to the present Union of Newry, the western half of the Union of Kilkeel, and a small portion of the north of Co. Louth.

(b.) *Newry as a market town and retail centre.*

Evidence given to the Commission seems to bear out the contention advanced that the extent of a market area roughly corresponds to half the distance between the market town and the nearest important centre in each direction. The evidence showed that Newry's market area extends six or seven miles towards Dundalk (13 miles distant); slightly further in the direction of Banbridge (13 miles distant); about 10 miles towards Portadown (19 miles distant); and eight to nine miles towards Armagh (18 miles distant). In the latter two cases the delimitation is not so well defined owing to the existence of small markets in Markethill and Tanderagee, which to some extent draw custom from the northern part of Newry No. 2 Rural District.

In the west Newry market area appears to extend for some purposes to a distance of about eight miles; but this is subject to qualification as Dundalk, Castleblayney, and Newtown Hamilton, also attract trade from parts of this area. It appears that, although there is no market in Bessbrook, the farmers of Camlough sell some of their produce to dealers and purchasers in Bessbrook, while the inhabitants of Bessbrook itself divide their custom between local shopkeepers and those of Newry.

In the south the market area appears to include Killevy (Co. Armagh) and Omeath (Co. Louth). In the east the Newry market area appears to extend in some sense as far as Hilltown but stops short of Rathfryland.

In the south-east Newry appears to be the market town either directly or indirectly for an area including Warrenpoint, Rosstrevor and Killowen, though here the qualification must be made that the retail shopping of Warrenpoint, Rosstrevor and Killowen is to a great extent done in Warrenpoint and Rosstrevor. East of Killowen, though Newry's wholesale area appears to extend as far as the town of Kilkeel, its market area does not appear to reach beyond the Causeway Water.

On the basis of the detailed evidence received it is possible to estimate the population of the Newry market area, exclusive of the town itself, at approximately 34,500. Of this population some 1,300 are separated from Newry by the existing border. Of the 33,200 persons, who are resident in districts on the Northern Ireland side of the existing border, about 12,900 would be cut off from Newry by a line following as far as possible the exact division between Catholic areas and Protestant areas. Such a line would leave Newry with a market area containing 20,300 + 1,300 or altogether 21,600 inhabitants. The line considered by the Commission to contain the minimum area which would have to be transferred with Newry, if Newry were to be included in the Irish Free State, would have left Newry with a market area containing altogether about 27,700 persons. The line adopted by the Commission leaves a market area containing about 28,300 inhabitants.

The northern portion of Newry's market area, estimated on the lines above indicated, has a proportionately higher valuation for rating purposes than the southern portion. The area north of the line dividing the Catholic regions to the south from the mixed and Protestant regions to the north, while it only includes one-third of the population of the Newry market area, contains districts which together are rated at only a fraction under a half the rateable value of the whole market area.

The area which the Commission, as appears below, regards as the area which must share the fate of the town, has a valuation for rating purposes equivalent to 57 per cent. of the rateable value of the whole market area. The line adopted by the Commission leaves Newry with a market area rated at about 89 per cent. of the total market area. In each case the figures given relate to the market area of Newry considered apart from the town itself.

(ii.) *The port of Newry, its Traffic, and the Area served by it.*

The port of Newry is controlled by the Newry Port and Harbour Board, which consists of 15 members, of whom nine are elected by the Newry Urban District Council and the remaining six by traders.

The Port and Harbour Board controls—

(a) the Port itself;

(b) the Newry Canal, which extends from Newry to Portadown and Lough Neagh;

(c) the Ship Canal from Newry extending down at the side of the Newry River as far as the Victoria Lock three miles below Newry;

(d) the Newry River from the Victoria Lock to a point in Carlingford Lough midway between Warrenpoint and Omeath.

From this point to the sea the channel through Carlingford Lough is under the control of the Carlingford Lough Commissioners.

Railway Facilities.

Both the Great Northern and the London Midland and Scottish railways have railway lines leading on to the quays at the harbour. The London Midland and Scottish Railway runs only to Greenore and thence to Dundalk. The Great Northern Railway serves Dublin, Belfast and most of the former province of Ulster, but has the disadvantage that all trains have first to run four miles north from Newry Port to Goraghwood before reaching the main line.

The area for which the Port of Newry is in the most favourable position as regards railway rates includes Portadown, Dungannon, Cookstown, Armagh, Keady, Monaghan, Banbridge, and all stations on the railways between these places and Newry. Lurgan is nearer Belfast; Omagh and Enniskillen are nearer Londonderry; Clones and Enniskillen are nearer Dundalk.

A distinction must be drawn between Portadown, Dungannon, Cookstown and Banbridge on the one hand, and the rest of the area described on the other hand; since although these places, and especially their industrial establishments, are valuable customers for Newry coal, Newry has not a secure hold on their custom as they are only six miles nearer to Newry than they are to Belfast, and slight advantages in port charges or sea freights enable Belfast to compete with Newry on equal terms for their trade. The area in which Newry is by distance easily the most favourable port is confined to the towns of Monaghan, Armagh and Tanderagee, and the places situated along the railways between Newry and these towns. In a southerly direction Dundalk, Greenore and Warrenpoint have the advantage over Newry.

Goods Carried.

The traffic at Newry Port is confined to goods. The returns for the past four years show that the relation of imports to exports in weight is approximately as 12 to 1. Among imports coal represents about 80 per cent. of the traffic, maize represents about 12 per cent., flour about 4 per cent., and general cargo the rest (4 per cent.). These figures are exclusive of goods carried by the Dundalk and Newry Steamship Co., which does not carry coal. This Company carries general cargo consisting mainly of all kinds of goods from Great Britain for the supply of retail shops, including food, hardware, clothing, &c.

Exports.

The chief items are potatoes, which form about 50 per cent., in some years 70 per cent., of the total exports. The bulk of the remainder of the exports consists of granite in various forms and a certain amount of timber.

Disposal of Imports : (a.) *Coal.*

Figures submitted to the Commission indicate that in 1924 62 per cent. of the coal imported at Newry Harbour was sent to stations or wharves in Northern Ireland, 22 per cent. used locally and 15 per cent. sent to stations in the Irish Free State. Of the quantities sent to stations in Northern Ireland approximately 95 per cent. was sent to stations lying outside the adjacent area claimed for inclusion in the Irish Free State, *i.e.,* the area comprised in the Unions of Newry and Kilkeel. The total quantity of coal imported during the year ended March 31, 1924, was given as 177,272 tons, the total imports of all kinds during the same period, exclusive of goods carried by the Dundalk and Newry Steam Packet Company, being 223,653 tons.

(b.) *Grain and Flour.*

Estimates as to the proportion of Newry's distributive trade in grain and flour, which is sent to places in the Irish Free State, varied from 45 per cent. to 60 per cent. An analysis of detailed figures submitted for the year ending the 30th November, 1922, showed that of the quantity of grain and flour despatched from Newry by rail in that year 4,491 tons were sent to stations in Northern Ireland and 18,868 to stations in the Irish Free State, chiefly in the counties of Monaghan and Cavan. The great majority of the stations in the Irish Free State to which these quantities of flour and grain were sent are so situated that the nearest route from Newry lies viâ Dundalk; Newry firms appear to possess some advantage in regard to the handling of grain which enables them to compete with Dundalk firms in areas so situated that the nearest route by rail lies viâ Dundalk so that they are some 20 miles nearer to Dundalk than Newry.

Prospects of Newry Port.

(a.) It was contended by persons with long experience of the shipping business at Newry that the interests of the Port were irrevocably bound up with Northern Ireland :—

(i.) Owing to the character of the Newry coal trade, and the position of the region supplied by it;

(ii.) Owing to the fact that Newry only had a slight advantage in railway rates over Belfast, in respect of the industrial areas which were its important customers:

(iii.) Because Newry's hold on this trade was in any case precarious since freights to Newry from some important ports were higher, access to the port was difficult, and the cost of unloading the coal was higher than in Belfast;

(iv.) Because the trade of Newry was bound to be with the parts of Northern Ireland north of the town of Newry, including Armagh, Banbridge and Portadown. It was stated that if the town were placed in the Free State it would lose most of its coal trade, and would find no fresh economic " hinterland " in the Free State to compensate for its losses.

(*b*.) It was contended that the trade in grain, foodstuffs, &c., which was the only trade of importance between Newry and areas at present in the Free State, was extremely precarious, as the areas served were for the most part readily accessible from Dundalk.

Much evidence was heard by the Commission in respect of the need for an improvement of the approaches to Newry Port; the Ship Canal from Newry to the Victoria Lock being so shallow that it could not be used by ships of modern dimensions when fully loaded.

It was expected that the trade of the Port would inevitably decline in the near future unless some large scheme of improvement could be carried out. The necessary work would be so costly that it could only be undertaken with the assistance of a Government subsidy. It was contended by Nationalist witnesses that the Government of the Irish Free State would be more likely to provide such a subsidy, as Newry to some extent competed with Belfast, and a Government whose headquarters were in Belfast would, it was suggested, hesitate to provide the money for equipping a rival port.

On the other hand, it was contended by other witnesses that the Government of Northern Ireland would be far more likely to supply the funds necessary for equipping a port which, by its natural position, was the nearest port for a large portion of Northern Ireland than the Government of the Irish Free State, in whose territory lay two adjacent and rival ports and whose territory, even with the addition of the Union of Newry, would include only a very small proportion of the railway stations to which the goods imported at Newry were sent.

Textile Trade.

Three spinning or weaving mills are situated in or adjacent to the town of Newry. The total number of persons employed in the three mills at the time of the enquiry was stated to be 700. Besides these three mills it was stated that 300 persons living in Newry worked regularly at Bessbrook. It was stated that two of the three Newry mills were managed and financed from Belfast, while all purchases were made and produce marketed there; in the third case it was stated that all but a very small quantity of the purchases were made through Belfast, London or Dundee, and that practically all the products were sold in Northern Ireland and Scotland.

In addition to these three mills there are large mills at a distance of about three miles from Newry, belonging to the Bessbrook Spinning Co. In these mills altogether some 2,500 persons are employed, so that the total number of persons employed in the industry in Newry and its neighbourhood is about 3,200. The village of Bessbrook, in which the Bessbrook Co.'s mills are mainly situated, is connected with Newry by an electric tramway. The tramway is used by the Company for the conveyance both of its raw material and its products to and from the Great Northern line and of coal from the Port. It is also largely used by the factory workers and residents in Bessbrook for travelling to and from Newry, where most of their purchases are made.

Representations were made on behalf both of the Bessbrook Spinning Co. and of the three mills in and near Newry contending that any transfer of the mills to the Irish Free State would be attended with grave risk to the industry.

It was urged that the industry was essentially a Northern Ireland industry, having practically no connection with the Irish Free State. Almost all goods produced were sent to Belfast and other Northern centres, while machinery and requisites were obtained from Northern Ireland or Great Britain. The interposition of a customs barrier would inevitably entail expense and delay, and possibly customs duties on raw materials, machinery and other necessary supplies; and new difficulties might be caused with regard to the transport of raw materials, half-finished products, finished products and machinery between the mills and Belfast or Great Britain.

It was further stated that it would be in itself a serious handicap to the industry that it should be carried on under a separate jurisdiction, with possibilities of different legislation both financial and industrial, from the main body of the industry. Moreover, if the area were placed in the Free State, it would be placed at a disadvantage in the Belfast market, as if two manufacturers quoted the same price the one whose works were situated in Northern Ireland would receive the order rather than the one whose works were under another jurisdiction.

On these economic grounds representations were made to the Commission on behalf of the bodies controlling all the mills in Newry and its neighbourhood, urging that their works should not be transferred from the jurisdiction of Northern Ireland. The Bessbrook Company stated that the Company would prefer to see the erection of a customs barrier between their works and Newry, with all the additional expense and delays that would be entailed thereby, rather than face the risks which they felt would be involved in a separation of their works from Northern Ireland.

(C.) *Kilkeel.*

The Union of Kilkeel consists of the greater part of the Mourne Mountains, and the area between the mountains and the sea.

The town of Kilkeel (population 1,620) is a market town and shopping centre for this area. It has a small harbour through which coal supplies are obtained for the district, and certain other supplies including flour.

The town is a centre for the herring fishing industry, and the herrings are partly distributed by road in Northern Ireland and partly cured locally and sent to Great Britain. There is a large

number of granite quarries in the Mourne Mountains. The granite
is mostly sent by sea from the nearest harbour to Great Britain.

No railway runs through the district, the nearest stations being
Newcastle in the east and Warrenpoint in the west. The eastern
part of the area comes to some extent within the region for which
Belfast serves as economic centre. The western end of the district
comes within the region for which Newry serves as economic centre.
The areas of economic influence of Belfast and Newry appear to meet
at the town of Kilkeel. Reference has already been made to the
fact that the Mourne Mountains contain reservoirs from which the
water is supplied to Belfast, Portadown, Banbridge, and other
towns.

The whole region from Newcastle to Warrenpoint is a favourite
holiday resort for the population of Belfast and other northern
centres.

(D.) *East Down.*

The parliamentary constituency of East Down, which includes
the north-eastern part of Kilkeel Rural District and reaches to the
town of Newcastle, is served by the Belfast and County Down
Railway which connects directly wih Belfast, and by the Great
Northern Railway Company's branch rom Banbridge to Castlewellan
and Newcastle which connects it with Banbridge, Portadown and
Belfast. The district has no direct railway communication with
Newry. At its eastern end the district includes the southern part of
the Ards Peninsula on the further side of Strangford Lough.
Communication with this Peninsula is obtained by ferry between
Strangford and Portaferry.

The market centres for the district are Downpatrick, Castlewellan,
and Ballynahinch.

5. General Position and Conclusions.

The chief problem as to the future of this region centres in the
town and port of Newry. Before entering into considerations
affecting the basis of Newry's economic life, which, in the opinion of
the Commission, preclude the transfer of Newry to the Irish Free
State, it is necessary to state the position with regard to the various
other areas involved in the Counties of Armagh and Down in order
that the true character and limits of the Newry problem may be
clearly appreciated.

Any decision as to Newry must necessarily have an important
effect one way or the other on the fate of large areas both in County
Armagh and County Down; but a distinction has to be drawn
between the two counties. If Newry is not included in the Irish
Free State it necessarily follows that no portion of County Down*
can be so included; on the other hand there are important areas in

* That is no portion of the mainland: three islands in Carlingford Lough
form part of County Down.

[13849]

the west and south of County Armagh which have been claimed for inclusion in the Irish Free State, and which can be so included independently of Newry, though the transfer of Newry to the Irish Free State would necessarily also involve the transfer of some or all of such areas.

The areas to be considered in addition to Newry itself may therefore be regarded as divided into three classes :—

(1.) Armagh areas which can be included in the Irish Free State independently of Newry;

(2.) Armagh areas which are so closely and directly dependent on Newry that Newry could not be included in the Free State without them nor they without Newry;

(3.) Areas in County Down.

(1.) *Areas in Armagh not directly dependent on Newry.*

The Commission has come to the conclusion that, whatever the decision with regard to Newry, the following areas in western and southern Armagh should be included in the Irish Free State :—

(i.) Western area consisting of parts of District Electoral Divisions of Tynan, Middletown and Derrynoose;

(ii.) Southern area consisting (*a*) of the former Rural District of Crossmaglen with the exception of Newtownhamilton and certain areas east and west of it, and (*b*) of the adjoining southern portion of Newry No. 2 Rural District between Crossmaglen and the Newry River.

Particulars of these areas are contained in the statistical statement appended.

A line drawn so as to include these areas in the Irish Free State will retain in Northern Ireland the towns of Keady and Newtownhamilton and their surroundings. These two centres, one Catholic and the other Protestant, cannot conveniently be separated. No line can be drawn between them which will not adversely affect the market areas of one or both, and the interests of the population in the intervening area, which is mainly Protestant. The position of Keady on the dividing line between the Catholic areas to the west and south of the town and the Protestant areas to the north-west, north, east and south-east of the town has already been referred to. The inclusion of Keady in the Irish Free State would in any case involve a considerable part of these Protestant areas. If Keady remains in Northern Ireland the line can be drawn so as to include in Northern Ireland the Protestant area in Co. Monaghan lying to the south of Keady Rural District Electoral Division consisting of the greater part of Mullyash District Electoral Division and certain adjoining townlands. The Commission considers that if the Protestant areas lying to the north-east and east in the District Electoral Divisions of Armaghbrague, Lisleitrim and Newtownhamilton (Co. Armagh) remain in Northern Ireland, this adjacent area in Co. Monaghan should then be united with them and also be included in Northern Ireland. The triangular block of country having its southern apex at Oram in the Mullyash District Electoral Division including the two centres of Keady and Newtown Hamilton and their surroundings exclusive of the Armagh areas which are to be transferred to the Irish Free State as already mentioned, but including the portion of the Mullyash district which should be transferred to Northern Ireland if Keady remains in Northern Ireland, shows a census population which has been calculated at about 10,000 in which the numbers of Catholics and Protestants appear to be almost exactly equal. If the portion of the Mullyash district referred to were not reckoned as part of this block the total population would be reduced by just under 1,000, and there would be a Catholic majority of about 400 corresponding to a Catholic proportion of 52 per cent. for the remaining portion of the block. Whichever way the figures are taken, it is clear they are not such as to justify any change so far as Keady and Newtown Hamilton are concerned. This block, which in view of the circumstances above stated has been considered as a whole, should therefore form part of Northern Ireland.

For the greater part of the southern area in Armagh to be transferred Dundalk is the most convenient market centre, while a smaller portion on the west falls within the market area of Castleblayney. This southern area also includes, however, a portion of the Newry market area lying in the hilly district to the south-west of the town in the direction of Dundalk. The limits of this southern area, which is intended to include as much of the Catholic district south and west of Newry as can be transferred to the Free State without Newry, have been fixed so as to avoid interference with the Catchment area of the Camlough lake on which Newry town and Bessbrook and other mills depend for their water supply, and so as to place the frontier, where it comes nearest to Newry, on the Fathom Mountain, an outlying spur of the hilly region which shuts in Newry on the south. It is clear that this area cannot be extended further in the direction of Newry.

(2.) *Areas in Armagh directly Dependent on Newry.*

As already pointed out Newry is situated on the northern edge of the Catholic districts of South Armagh and South Down. An examination of the townland figures, which form the basis of the religious statistics of the 1911 census, shows that in both counties there are strong Catholic majorities to the south of Newry and Protestant majorities immediately to the north; there is a Catholic area in Co. Armagh to the west and north-west of Bessbrook; there are also one or two small Catholic areas further north on the eastern side in Co. Down; but with these exceptions areas which have Protestant majorities are continuous to the north right up to Portadown and Belfast. A population line therefore drawn so as to divide the areas in the south-east of Co. Armagh and the south-west of Co. Down in which the Roman Catholics have majorities from the areas in which the numbers of Catholics and Protestants are equally balanced or in which the Protestants have

[13849]

majorities would come immediately to the north of Newry, would pass between Newry and the important factory centre of Bessbrook, and would separate Newry from the richest portion of its market area lying to the north, leaving it with less than two-thirds of its market area as considered on the basis of numbers of population and about half its market area as considered on the basis of rateable value. Such a line would seriously prejudice Newry's position as a market town and centre of retail trade, and would cause great inconvenience to the inhabitants of the areas in the immediate neighbourhood of Newry which would thus be cut off from it. The custom of 2,300 Bessbrook employees, most of whom live in Bessbrook while only about three hundred live in Newry, is alone estimated to be worth approximately £75,000 a year to the retail trade of Newry. The owners of the Bessbrook factory have stated emphatically through the witness who represented them that if they have to choose between inclusion in the Irish Free State and severance from Newry, they prefer the latter, looking at the question solely from the point of view of their business interests and the prosperity of their industry. The evidence given on behalf of the Protestant inhabitants who form the majority in the rural districts immediately to the north of Newry, was to the effect that they would prefer separation from Newry to inclusion in the Irish Free State, but it is clear from the point of view of business convenience they would much prefer to be in the same jurisdiction as Newry, and that their opposition to the adoption of a boundary which would include their districts in the Irish Free State is based on political views which are so strongly held as to lead them to disregard such business considerations. On economic grounds we have therefore come to the conclusion that a line following the population line to the north of Newry has to be dismissed as impossible. If Newry were included in the Irish Free State it would be necessary to take a line further north. A line taken immediately to the north of Goragh Wood station, which is the railway junction for Newry, would greatly improve the position so far as Newry's market area is concerned, but would still separate Newry from a considerable portion of the richest part of its market area to the north, this line would involve the inclusion with Newry of an area in Co. Armagh to the north of the population line above indicated with a population of about 4,700 in which the numbers of Catholics and Protestants are almost evenly balanced though there appears to be a slight Protestant majority.

If the whole of Newry's market area were to be included in the Irish Free State the boundary would have to run some miles further north in the neighbourhood of Poyntzpass, and would involve areas having substantial Protestant majorities which may be regarded as within reach of Northern market towns such as Banbridge and Tanderagee. It is clear that the overriding of the wishes of Protestant majorities in such additional areas for the purpose of protecting the economic interests of Newry as a market centre would not be justified.

(3.) *Areas in Co. Down.*

In discussing areas in Co. Armagh falling under the head last mentioned some reference to the position in Co. Down has been unavoidable. It is now necessary to examine more closely the position in that County. A limit on the eastern side of the area in Co. Down which could be regarded as open to consideration by the Commission with a view to inclusion in the Irish Free State is imposed—

(i) by the existence of a Protestant majority in the eastern portion of Kilkeel Union consisting of the District Electoral Divisions of Kilkeel, Ballykeel and Mullartown and of the Urban District of Newcastle;

(ii) by the situation in the Mourne Mountains of the waterworks which supply the Northern industrial centres of Belfast, Portadown and Banbridge.

Separation of the centres named, and particularly of Belfast, from the sources of their water supply by a boundary drawn so as to include in the Irish Free State that portion of the Mourne Mountains in which their waterworks are situate is open to grave objection; the mere fact that such works were situate in another jurisdiction beyond the control of their own government would inevitably tend to produce among the inhabitants of these centres a sense of anxiety and insecurity as to this vital necessity of their economic and industrial life, and would also give rise to difficulties, with regard to any future legislation required for the development of their undertakings, owing to the fact that the corporations concerned, though themselves subject to the jurisdiction of Northern Ireland, would necessarily have to approach the Oireachtas for the purpose of obtaining authority to carry out new works in the Irish Free State. These circumstances have led the Commission to adopt the view that such a separation must be avoided. The eastern limit to the area in Co. Down fixed in accordance with the conditions above stated would pass from a point about two miles east of Hilltown over the Mourne Mountains descending to the sea in the District Electoral Division of Greencastle about $1\frac{3}{4}$ miles west of Kilkeel. The northern line in Co. Down fixed to coincide with the line already referred to in Co. Armagh passing immediately north of Goragh Wood would run to the north of Damolly, and in a general south-easterly direction about half way between the two small towns of Rathfriland and Hilltown. The area in Co. Down defined by the lines indicated includes a total census (1911) population without Newry of 14,426, of which 9,831 are Roman Catholics and 4,595 are Non-Catholics. This area includes Warrenpoint and its immediate neighbourhood in which the numbers of Catholics and Protestants are almost equally balanced, though the Catholics have a slight majority, and also a northern belt containing a total population of 2,464 of which 1,252 are Non-Catholics and 1,212 Roman Catholics, but with these exceptions large Catholic majorities prevail throughout the area.

Newry with dependent areas (Cos. Armagh and Down).

The position as to the total additional areas in County Armagh and County Down, which, if Newry were included in the Free State, should in accordance with the scheme above outlined be included with it, can now be stated as follows :—

	Total Population.	Roman Catholics.	Non-Catholics.
Area in Co. Armagh ...	9,288	5,888	3,400
Area in Co. Down ...	14,426	9,831	4,595
Newry itself	11,963	8,924	3,039
Total ...	35,677	24,643	11,034

It appears therefore that the transfer of Newry to the Irish Free State would involve a total population with Newry which may be stated in round figures at 35,600, of whom 24,600 are Catholics and 11,000 Protestants. By reason of the economic necessities already stated the unit so arrived at includes an area to the north of Newry lying partly in Co. Armagh and partly in Co. Down above the line referred to as " the population line " containing a total population of about 7,100 in which the wishes of the inhabitants are not shown to be in favour of inclusion in the Irish Free State.

We have assumed for the purpose of our consideration of the question as to whether or not Newry and its surrounding area should be included in the Irish Free State that such a change is within the powers of the Commission notwithstanding the large area and the considerable population involved. The majority shown on the basis of the census figures for the area as a whole in favour of inclusion in the Free State is a substantial majority, but the Commission has had to consider whether a decision giving effect to a change of jurisdiction in accordance with the wishes of the inhabitants as indicated by these figures would be compatible with economic and geographic conditions of a more general character than those hitherto referred to.

So far as geographic considerations are concerned the Commission has been strongly urged to maintain the present position by recognising the natural boundary in Carlingford Lough as a far more suitable boundary than any artificial land boundary which could be found in Co. Down. There is some force in this contention, but, in view of the character of the land boundary in other portions of the country, the mere fact that the inclusion of a portion of Co. Down in the Irish Free State would involve the substitution of a certain length of land boundary not marked by natural features for the existing boundary in Carlingford Lough cannot in itself be regarded as conclusive. It has been urged that on economic grounds there would be some advantage in adopting a boundary which would have the effect of including all the waters of Carlingford Lough within the same jurisdiction, as vessels would thereby be enabled to call in succession at the small ports in the Lough and at Newry without undergoing Customs formalities. Other geographical considerations enter so closely into the economic question that they can best be dealt with in conjunction with that question.

The economic position of Newry as a market town has already been referred to at some length and it has been noted that the line to the north of Goragh Wood which has been indicated as the line which would have to be taken for the purpose of securing to Newry a reasonable share of its natural market area to the north would still cut off an important part of the region, between Goragh Wood and Poyntzpass, for which Newry at present serves as a market centre. The separation from Newry of some portion of its market area, either north or south, is however involved in each of the alternative proposals under consideration.

The larger economic considerations on which the Commission has based its decision have now to be stated.

The deciding consideration with respect to Newry and the area involved with it as above described has been the economic position of Newry—

(1) as a port, and
(2) as forming, together with the industrial villages of Bessbrook and Damolly, an industrial centre for the flax-spinning and linen-weaving industry.

The Commission has come to the conclusion that the economic interests of Newry are bound up with the industrial life of Northern Ireland, and that to sever Newry from Northern Ireland would be to separate it from the country to which in an economic sense it belongs, and to expose it to economic disaster. The evidence of the map itself shows clearly that the future of Newry as a port is bound up with Northern Ireland. It is only necessary to refer to its situation on the Newry River 8 miles beyond the head of Carlingford Lough, to its position in relation to the railway system which necessitates goods despatched by rail from Newry to destinations in the Irish Free State being sent north as far as Goragh Wood before starting in a southerly direction; to the existence of the Newry Canal which links Newry to the northern industrial centres of Portadown and Banbridge; and to the position in relation to Newry of the competing ports of Dundalk and Greenore in the Irish Free State, which have the advantage over Newry in respect of access by sea, and are far better placed than Newry for serving County Louth and the area to the south of it, as well as a considerable part of Southern Armagh.

The situation of Newry is therefore such that, except in the northern part of Monaghan, it can hardly be said to have any hinterland in the Irish Free State which it can effectively serve as a port, and that its prosperity as a port depends on its trade with Northern Ireland.

The conclusion derived from a study of Newry's situation as shown on the map is supported by the evidence available as to the actual trade of the port, to which reference has been made in the earlier part of this chapter.

The governing features of Newry's geographical situation in relation to its means of communication with the surrounding country must be borne in mind. The town lies on the Newry River in a valley easily approachable from the neighbouring valley of the Bann and the valleys of the Blackwater and the Lagan further to the north : these river valleys provide practicable gradients from Newry to Armagh, Auchnacloy, Portadown, Dungannon, Lurgan, Belfast, Banbridge and the district round Rathfryland, and hence have resulted railway, rcad and canal facilities which draw Newry's trade in these directions. The hill barriers to the west, south-west and south have obstructed the provision of railway connections leading directly from the town to places situate beyond these barriers and have restricted the road connections. The character and limitations of the present system of communications, which facilitate Newry's transport by road, rail and canal north-westward, northward and north-eastward, but impose on Newry's transport by rail to the Irish Free State, westward and southward, a detour to the north, are therefore not accidental, temporary and easily remediable, but the direct result of natural geographic features.

The question naturally arises as to whether Newry is in a sufficiently strong position as a port, in relation to Northern Ireland, to retain and expand its existing trade even if it finds itself in another jurisdiction. The information available points to the conclusion that this question must be answered in the negative. The coal import trade is the mainstay of the port of Newry, from which more than half of the revenue of the port is derived : it is clear that Belfast is a formidable competitor for this trade ; that, while Newry has an advantage as regards railway rates in respect of certain areas, this is largely counter-balanced by its higher freight and port charges ; that in a considerable part of the area in which Newry competes with Belfast as a centre for the supply of coal the difference between the prices that can be quoted is very small ; and that the maintenance of Newry's existing share in the coal trade depends not only on keeping its port and landing charges down to the present figure, but also on the retention of the commercial goodwill of the customers who draw their coal supplies from Newry. The severance of Newry from Northern Ireland is likely to involve both the raising of charges owing to the effect on wages rates of the differences in the system of taxation, and the loss of such custom as is in some degree the result of the existing political connection.

The position of Newry as a Free State port in relation to the area in Northern Ireland which it serves to-day would therefore be very different to the existing position of the port of Londonderry in relation to the greater part of Donegal. To-day Londonderry retains its trade with Donegal because there is no other available port which can effectively compete with it for that trade, but Newry would be faced with the competition of Belfast, which is already effective in respect of a considerable part of its area of supply. and which in the circumstances supposed might prove fatal to the bulk of its shipping trade.

Considerations which apply to the trade of the port of Newry also apply in some measure to the town and port of Warrenpoint which competes with Newry in the supply of coal to some of the inland centres. Newry's decline as a port would also affect detrimentally its position as a market centre for certain agricultural products, such as grass seed and potatoes, which are shipped from Newry to Great Britain.

With regard to Newry's position as a centre of the flax-spinning and linen-weaving industry, the factors which have to be taken into account are those which arise not from the necessities of a particular geographic situation but from the conditions of a highly organised industry concentrated in Northern Ireland. It is necessary to consider what results would follow from the separation of the Newry group of mills and factories from the jurisdiction in which the rest of the industry is carried on, and from Belfast which is the centre for its organisation and control, and for the sale and export of its products. It is impossible in such a case to predict results with certainty, but it is necessary to take account of probabilities. The evidence shows that this industry relies entirely on its export trade, that competition is very keen, and that the industry is subject to recurring periods of depression. The Newry group of mills and factories is already handicapped by distance from Belfast, which involves extra freight charges, but this handicap is counteracted, in part at least, by the lower standard rate of wages recognised in the district. There is, nevertheless, evidence of a tendency towards increased concentration of the spinning and weaving industry in the immediate neighbourhood of Belfast. To subject the Newry group of mills and factories to the handicaps involved in separation by a customs barrier from their centre for organisation, and for distribution of their products, and to place them in a different customs area to their competitors, in which the system of taxation has a distinctly protective character, exposes them to special risks. A small increase in their costs of production as compared with those of their competitors, or even the fear of such an increase, may lead to the partial or complete closing down of the local undertakings. Such risks, which affect the employment and livelihood of large numbers of the population and the prosperity of the town as a trading centre, cannot in the opinion of the Commission be disregarded. Any serious curtailment of the operations of the flax-spinning and linen-weaving industry in Bessbrook, Newry, and the neighbourhood would inevitably damage Newry's present position as a centre of retail trade, and as a market centre for the agricultural produce of the adjoining districts.

In view of the above considerations the Commission has come to the conclusion that the change which would be involved in the separation of Newry and its surrounding area from the rest of Northern Ireland cannot be regarded as a change which is "compatible with economic and geographic conditions." The two different sets of factors which the Commission is directed to take into account—the wishes of inhabitants, and economic and geographic considerations—are thus found to be definitely in conflict with respect to this area, and under the terms of Article XII economic and geographic considerations must prevail.

The Commission has therefore adopted the line which transfers to the Irish Free State the western and southern areas in Co. Armagh already specified and to Northern Ireland the above-described Monaghan area in the neighbourhood of Mullyash, and which does not involve the transfer of any part of Co. Down to the Free State with the exception of a small island in Carlingford Lough. Particulars of the areas transferred are appended.

Particulars, according to the Census of 1911, by District Electoral Divisions and portions of District Electoral Divisions. of the Areas which, in consequence of the adoption of the Boundary Line as determined by the Commission, are transferred from one jurisdiction to the other jurisdiction.

Section E (i).

Area in County Armagh comprising parts of District Electoral Divisions of Tynan, Middletown and Derrynoose.

(Transferred to Irish Free State.)

County.	District Electoral Division.	Catholics.	Non-Catholics.	Area.
ARMAGH... ...	Tynan (portion) ...	23	10	205
	Middletown (portion)...	896	247	4,215
	Derrynoose (portion)...	845	79	4,508
		1,764	336	8,928

Section E (ii).

Area in County Monaghan comprising parts of District Electoral Divisions of Mullyash, Church Hill and Carrickaslane.

(Transferred to Northern Ireland.)

County.	District Electoral Division.	Catholics.	Non-Catholics.	Area.
MONAGHAN ...	Mullyash (portion) ...	262	552	5,336
	Church Hill (portion)...	58	102	814
	Carrickaslane (portion)	15	6	129
		335	660	6,279

SECTION E (iii).

Area in Southern part of County Armagh including greater part of former Rural District of Crossmaglen and adjoining portion of that of Newry No. 2.

(Transferred to Irish Free State.)

County.	District Electoral Division.	Catholics.	Non-Catholics.	Area.
ARMAGH ...	Lower Greggan (whole)	1,245	29	5,238
	Moybane (whole) ...	854	10	3,027
	Crossmaglen (whole) ...	1,931	113	4,769
	Cloghoge (whole) ...	530	155	2,961
	Cullyhanna (whole) ...	630	26	3,008
	Lisleitrim (portion) ...	456	93	2,481
	Dorsy (portion) ...	1,192	53	5,039
	Newtown Hamilton (portion)	2	6	40
	Camly (portion) ...	206	31	1,447
	Ballybot (portion) ...	312	3	1,007
	Killevy (portion) ...	1,547	14	4,973
	Jonesborough (whole)	1,741	101	6,018
	Latbirget (whole) ...	1,344	6	5,764
	Forkhill (whole) ...	1,507	114	5,737
	Camlough (portion) ...	339	55	2,021
	Belleek (portion) ...	23	8	161
		13,859	817	53,694
DOWN	Island in Carlingford Lough	—	—	—

PART III.—SKETCH OF PROPOSED NEW BOUNDARY AND ITS EFFECTS.

I.

Sketch of the General Character of the Boundary Line as about to be determined by the Commission.

This Sketch is to be read as in all respects subject to the terms of the Commission's formal award.

(In this Sketch the references to District Electoral Divisions relate to such Divisions as existing in 1911.)

A.

LONDONDERRY AND NORTHERN TIRCONAILL (COUNTY DONEGAL).

THE Boundary Line begins at the limit of territorial waters off Inishowen Head whence it runs in a south-westerly direction following the middle line of the navigation channel past Magilligan Point to Moville and the Pier about three-quarters of a mile south of Moville known as Carrickarory Pier. From this point as far as a point between Ture and Muff it takes the form of a chain of straight lines, based on posts used to mark the navigation channel, but so arranged as to include in Northern Ireland the whole of the dredged channel leading to the Port of Londonderry, while including a strip of the foreshore and water of Lough Foyle in the Irish Free State.

The land boundary begins at a point south of Ture. From Lough Foyle to Burnfoot it runs in a general westerly direction, including the Ture House–Church Town–Burnfoot road in the Irish Free State, and including Muff and Birdstown in Northern Ireland.

From Burnfoot the line runs south-west to Speenoge, including the Burnfoot–Speenoge road in the Free State, and including Bridge End in Northern Ireland.

From Burt the Line runs southward over Greenan Hill, in such a way as to include the Grianan of Aileach in the Free State. It then turns southwestward, including Castleforward and Newtown Cunningham in the Free State. Continuing southwestward it includes the crest of Dooish mountain in Northern Ireland, but includes the Letterkenny–Tooban Junction railway wholly in the Free State.

At a point west of Dooish mountain the Line turns southward. It then runs south until it approaches the road leading from Raphoe to the ferry on the river Foyle 2½ miles south of St. Johnstown.

From this point the Line runs eastward to the river Foyle, crossing the Great Northern Railway at a point about midway between St. Johnstown station, which is included in Northern Ireland, and Porthall station, which is included in the Free State. From the point where it reaches the river Foyle the Line follows the existing boundary which passes up the median line of the river.

B.

COUNTY TYRONE.

From the point at which the Boundary reaches the river Foyle, it follows the existing border between the counties of Tyrone and Tirconaill, along the median channel of the river, passing between Strabane and Lifford as far as Clady. South of Clady the Line continues to follow the existing boundary as far as the northern slope of Fearn Hill. It there diverges from the existing border over a short distance so as to include in Northern Ireland the greater part of the townland of Fearn, which forms a salient projecting into County Tyrone. The Line then follows the existing boundary westward along the high ground north of the town of Castlederg until it approaches the Killygordon–Killeter road. From this point the Line runs south through County Tyrone to the North-eastern angle of the salient of Tirconaill formed by the District Electoral Division of Grousehall. It here rejoins the existing border. The Line thus includes in the Free State the District Electoral Divisions of Corgary and Killeter, the greater part of Magheranageeragh, and one townland of Lisnacloon.

From the point where it regains the existing border the Line follows the old border westward along the mountain ridge as far as a point north-west of Grousehall Hill.

C.

COUNTY FERMANAGH AND SOUTHERN TIRCONAILL.

The general course of the Boundary Line in County Fermanagh and the adjoining region is as follows :—

The Line leaves the border of County Tyrone at a point north-west of Grousehall Hill, whence it runs southward between the high ridges which divide the Termon valley from the Derg basin, including the town of Pettigoe and its immediate neighbourhood, together with the District Electoral Division of Grousehall, in Northern Ireland. The Line then re-enters County Fermanagh, divides the District Electoral Division of Mallybreen, and runs south and west, at a short distance from Lough Erne, including in the Irish Free State the greater part of the District Electoral Divisions of Castlecaldwell and Belleek.

The Line includes in Northern Ireland the shore of Lough Erne, and the river Erne as far as, and including, the sluice gates at

Belleek. The town of Belleek and the south bank of the river Erne between Belleek and Rosscor are included in the Free State. From Rosscor to Lower Lough Macnean the Line traverses the range of hills and high plateaux which run north-west and south-east in this section of the county : the villages of Garrison and Belcoo being thus included in the Free State.

From Lower Lough Macnean to Cuilcagh mountain the Line follows the existing border. It then re-enters County Fermanagh and runs in such a way as to include in the Free State areas adjacent to Swanlinbar and Ballyconnell, while including in Northern Ireland the Kinawley–Derrylin–Teemore–Crum road.

In the south-east of the county the Line includes in the Free State practically the whole of the District Electoral Divisions of Derrysteaton, Drummully (County Monaghan), and Clonkeelan, with three townlands of the Division of Magheraveely.

Further north the Line includes in the Free State the village and neighbourhood of Rosslea and the region of Eshnadarragh : it rejoins the existing border three miles south of Slieve Beagh.

D.

NORTHERN COUNTY MONAGHAN.

From Slieve Beagh to Tynan the Boundary follows the existing border between the counties of Monaghan and Tyrone.

E.

COUNTY ARMAGH.

From the point at which the boundaries of Counties Tyrone, Monaghan and Armagh meet, the Line follows the existing boundary as far as a point about $\frac{3}{4}$ mile north of Middletown where it turns eastward, including the village and its immediate neighbourhood in the Free State. The Line then turns south-eastward and runs approximately parallel to the Tynan–Kiltubbrid–Sheetrim–Carnagh road, which is included in Northern Ireland, while portions cf the District Electoral Divisions of Middletown and Derrynoose situated to the west of that road are included in the Irish Free State. The Line crosses the existing border in the neighbourhood of the point at which it cuts the Keady–Castleblayney railway. It then traverses the salient of County Monaghan formed by the District Electoral Division of Mullyash, the greater part of that Division and a few adjoining townlands being included in Northern Ireland. The Line then re-enters County Armagh so as to include in Northern Ireland the townlands of Cortamlat and Altnamackan (District Electoral Division of Lisleitrim), and all but a small south-eastern section of the District Electoral Division of Newtown Hamilton.

The Line then runs roughly eastward, at a short distance to the south of the Newtown Hamilton–Belleek–Camlough road, as far east as Sugarloaf Hill. It then turns south-east and runs over high ground to Hill 1155, which is an outlying spur on the north-east flank of Slieve Gullion. From the crest of Hill 1155 the Line runs eastward over Carn Hill and the northern slope of Fathom mountain to a point on the slope of the escarpment immediately west of the Newry canal. From this point as far as a point south of the Victoria Lock the Line runs between the mountain road and the valley road so as to include the former in the Free State and the latter in Northern Ireland.

At a point south of the Victoria Lock the Line cuts the Newry–Greenore railway and the road which runs parallel with it, and follows the bank of the river until it reaches the existing border between the counties of Armagh and Louth. From the point where it reaches the existing border the Line follows the median line of the navigation channel down the Newry river through Carlingford Lough, and through the channel connecting the Lough with the open sea as far as the limit of territorial waters.

The Line thus includes in the Irish Free State the District Electoral Divisions of Cloghoge, Lower Creggan, Crossmaglen, Cullyhanna, Moybane, Forkill, Jonesborough and Latbirget, the larger part of those of Lisleitrim, Dorsy and Killevy, and portions of those of Camly, Belleek and Camlough. It includes the town of Newry in Northern Ireland.

The total length of the new Boundary Line, exclusive of Lough Foyle and Carlingford Lough, is shorter by 51 miles than that of the old line, the respective lengths, as taken from the 1-inch map, being approximately 229 and 280 miles.

II.

Statistical Statement.

Acreage and Population, according to the Census Returns of 1911, of the areas which, as the result of the substitution of the Boundary Line about to be determined by the Commission for the boundary as existing prior to such determination, will be transferred from one jurisdiction to another.

This statement includes particulars obtained from published returns of the 1911 census, supplemented by further detailed information derived from the original returns made separately for each townland existing in the archives of the Census Office in Dublin (which have been rendered available for examination by the Commission), showing the numbers of Roman Catholics and the numbers of members of Protestant denominations in the areas above referred to.

The religious statistics for different areas, included in the published census returns, have been referred to in many of the representations received by the Commission, and in much of the evidence heard, as throwing light on the wishes of the inhabitants of such areas in relation to the boundary. Such references have been freely made by representatives of both sides, and the general assumptions on which such references have been based, that in the areas concerned religious and political divisions do to-day, broadly speaking, correspond, and that in such areas, subject in each case to comparatively few exceptions, if the question could be put to the vote, members of Protestant denominations would vote in favour of being in Northern Ireland, and Roman Catholics would vote in favour of being in the Irish Free State, appear to be almost universally accepted as established propositions. Different views have been urged as to qualifying considerations, some general in their application, and some limited to particular localities, subject to which the religious statistics of the 1911 census should be read as reflecting, in the light of such assumptions, "the wishes of the inhabitants" at the present date, but the evidence heard from both sides, taken as a whole, shows a wide measure of agreement that such statistics afford, generally speaking, an approximate indication of the present wishes of the inhabitants of different areas in relation to the boundary.

Section A.

Area in Eastern Tirconaill adjacent to the Liberties of Londonderry. (Transferred to Northern Ireland.)

Acreage	...	30,295	Roman Catholics	...	1,919
Population	...	5,149	Other Denominations	...	3,230

Section B (i).

Area in Tirconaill forming part of the District Electoral Division of West Urney. (Transferred to Northern Ireland.)

Acreage	...	819	Other Denominations	...	60
Population	...	60			

(ii.)

Area in County Tyrone forming part of the Rural District of Castlederg. (Transferred to Irish Free State.)

Acreage	...	34,228	Roman Catholics	...	2,163
Population	...	2,716	Other Denominations	...	553

Section C (i).

Area in Tirconaill including town of Pettigoe and District Electoral Division of Grousehall. (Transferred to Northern Ireland.)

Acreage	...	11,510	Roman Catholics	...	497
Population	...	1,339	Other Denominations	...	842

(ii.)

*Area in Western portion of County Fermanagh including Belleek,
Garrison, and Belcoo. (Transferred to Irish Free State.)*

Acreage	...	51,650	Roman Catholics	...	4,688
Population	...	5,428	Other Denominations	...	740

(iii.)

*Area in Tirconaill comprising Belleek Island. (Transferred
to Northern Ireland.)*

Acreage ... 3 (Sluice-gates and gatekeeper's lodge)

(iv.)

*Area in Southern part of County Fermanagh. (Transferred to
Irish Free State.)*

Acreage	...	16,167	Roman Catholics	...	2,222
Population	...	2,591	Other Denominations	...	369

(v.)

*Areas in Eastern part of County Fermanagh. (Transferred to
Irish Free State.)*

Acreage	...	18,623	Roman Catholics	...	3,147
Population	...	3,808	Other Denominations	...	661

SECTION C (vi.)

*Area in County Monaghan forming part of District Electoral Division
of Drumnully. (Transferred to Northern Ireland.)*

Acreage	...	336	Roman Catholics	...	13
Population	...	51	Other Denominations	...	38

SECTION D.—*Nil.*

SECTION E (i.)

*Area in County Armagh comprising parts of District Electoral
Divisions of Tynan, Middletown, and Derrynoose. (Transferred
to Irish Free State.)*

Acreage	...	8,928	Roman Catholics	...	1,764
Population	...	2,100	Other Denominations	...	336

[13849]

(ii.)

Area in County Monaghan comprising parts of District Electoral Divisions of Mullyash, Church Hill, and Carrickaslane. (Transferred to Northern Ireland.)

Acreage	...	6,279	Roman Catholics	...	335
Population	...	995	Other Denominations	...	660

(iii.)

Area in Southern part of County Armagh including greater part of former Rural District of Crossmaglen and adjoining portion of that of Newry No. 2. (Transferred to Irish Free State.)

Acreage	...	53,694	Roman Catholics	...	13,859
Population	...	14,676	Other Denominations	...	817

Note.—In certain cases, where townlands are divided, and in the case of two District Electoral Divisions (Camlough and Belleek in Co. Armagh), in which no particulars concerning the religious denominations of the inhabitants of the townlands were available, the figures shown in the columns headed " Roman Catholics " and " Other Denominations " are, in default of detailed information, based on figures which have been calculated on a proportional basis for the townlands, or parts of townlands concerned.

Summary of Transfers to the Irish Free State.

Number in above Schedule.	Acreage.	Population.	Roman Catholics.	Other Denominations.
B (ii)	34,228	2,716	2,163	553
C (ii)	51,650	5,428	4,688	740
C (iv)	16,167	2,591	2,222	369
C (v)	18,623	3,808	3,147	661
E (i)	8,928	2,100	1,764	336
E (iii)	53,694	14,676	13,859	817
Total	183,290	31,319	27,843	3,476

Summary of Transfers to Northern Ireland.

Number in Schedule.	Acreage.	Population.	Roman Catholics.	Other Denominations.
A	30,295	5,149	1,919	3,230
B (i)	819	60	...	60
C (i)	11,510	1,339	497	842
C (iii)	3	...	...	...
C (vi)	336	51	13	38
E (ii)	6,279	995	335	660
Total	49,242	7,594	2,764	4,830

III.

Local Economic and Geographic Results.

The Boundary Line above described will involve the following local economic and geographic results :—

A.

LONDONDERRY AND NORTHERN TIRCONAILL (CO. DONEGAL).

The area west of the Foyle, which by its situation necessarily depends on Londonderry as its market town and source of retail supplies, is mainly included under the same jurisdiction as the city itself.

The rail conections, viâ Tooban Junction, between the peninsula of Inishowen and the rest of Tirconaill, and the road connection between the same regions viâ Burnfoot, Speenoge, and Newtown Cunningham, are included wholly in the Free State. Communication by road between the Letterkenny–Burnfoot–Buncrana road and the localities situated along Lough Foyle from Ture to Moville is secured by the inclusion in the Free State of the road north of Birdstown.

The area to which the city of Londonderry furnishes wholesale supplies, and which it serves as a port, remains divided by the boundary, and the position of semi-isolation, from the economic point of view, of Tirconaill in general and of the Inishowen peninsula in particular, remains unaltered in its main features. On the other hand, the city remains under the same jurisdiction as the areas in the counties of Londonderry, Tyrone and Fermanagh, which it serves as a wholesale centre and port.

The shirt and collar industry, in which the industrial workers of the city are mainly engaged, is included in the same customs jurisdiction as the immediate sources of its raw material and the chief market for its finished products.

The areas from which the city draws its water supply are now wholly included in Northern Ireland.

By the division of the navigation channel from Carrickarory Pier to the sea free access is secured to the Pier and to the harbour of Moville. On the other hand, by the inclusion in Northern Ireland of the whole of the channel from Carrickarory to the mouth of the river Foyle, the portions of the channel which are maintained by dredging are included in the same jurisdiction as the port of Londonderry which the channel exists to serve.

B.

COUNTY TYRONE.

The Line, continuing to run along the river Foyle, and passing between the towns of Lifford and Strabane, leaves the economic position of these two towns essentially unaltered. The position, in relation to the boundary, of the railways which meet at Strabane station, and of the town's connections by road and canal, remains in general unchanged. The inclusion in Northern Ireland, however, of the direct road to Castlederg, through Fearn, affords an improvement of the communication between Strabane and the area to the south-west. The main road from Londonderry through Strabane to the south remains in Northern Ireland. By the inclusion of the Great Northern Railway Company's station at Porthall in the Free State, the traders of Tirconaill retain the possibility of sending and receiving goods direct to and from Dundalk or Clones and beyond, without the necessity for customs formalities or for a change of gauge at Strabane.

From the point where it leaves the river Finn the Line runs through high and for the most part sparsely inhabited country, except where it crosses the Derg valley below Killeter. The inclusion in the Irish Free State of the area west of Killeter, restores the former connections of part of this area with the centres of Ballybofey and Stranorlar; while the inclusion of Killeter in the Free State leaves to this area its own local centre with its creamery. The Killeter–Killygordon road, which is included wholly in the Free State, affords connection with the Donegal railway system.

C.

COUNTY FERMANAGH AND SOUTHERN TIRCONAILL.

The inclusion in Northern Ireland of the market town of Pettigo and its immediate neighbourhood removes anomalies of the existing border in the Termon valley, restores the town to its principal market area, and re-establishes connection by road and rail between the two sections of County Fermanagh which are situated on the northern bank of the lake.

The town and bridge of Belleek are included in the Free State, which by this means obtains a second line of communication between County Tirconaill and the rest of its territory.

The river Erne from Rosscor to Belleek is included under the control of Northern Ireland. The Line also includes in Northern Ireland the two sluice gates at Belleek situated in County Fermanagh, the two sluice gates previously situated in the Irish Free State, and a strip of territory on the north bank of the river between Lough Erne and Belleek providing connection with the sluice gates. Full power to deal with questions affecting the control of the level of the lake is thus vested in the Government in whose jurisdiction the whole of Lower Lough Erne and the greater part of Upper Lough Erne are situated. By leaving in Northern Ireland the north and south banks of Lower Lough Erne at Rosscor, where a bridge is in course of construction, the Line allows of the establishment of road communication across the two sides of the lake.

South of the western extremity of Lower Lough Erne the Line runs along the mountainous plateau stretching from Rosscor to

Lower Lough Macnean. The Line leaves in Northern Ireland the eastern slope of the range and the low-lying area between it and Lower Lough Erne, maintaining the connection of this area, including the village of Derrygonnelly, with the remainder of the region bordering on the lake and with its principal market centre, Enniskillen. The villages of Garrison and Blacklion are thus included in the Free State, as is the whole of Lough Melvin and the line of communication Ballyshannon–Belleek–Garrison–Belcoo–Blacklion.

In the southern part of the County the Line includes in the Irish Free State a portion of the area lying between the present boundary and the shores of Upper Lough Erne. The Line traverses the northern foothills of Slieve Rushen. A portion of the market area of Ballyconnell, which was severed from its market town by the existing border, is thus restored. The Line includes in Northern Ireland the Enniskillen–Derrylin–Teemore–Crum road, and the area to the east of that road, with its ferry connections with Lisnaskea, thus preserving the economic connections of the division of Crum and the southern bank of Upper Lough Erne with Lisnaskea and Enniskillen.

The Line restores to the town of Clones a section of that part of its market area which had been cut off by the existing border. It also leaves free to the inhabitants of Derrysteaton their connection with Belturbet, and restores to those of Rosslea and its neighbourhood free communication with Clones, Smithborough and Monaghan.

The Line removes the anomalies connected with the Drummully enclave, which, though part of County Monaghan, was deprived by the existing border of any direct communication with the Free State. Road and rail connection between Clones and Belturbet are placed entirely in Free State territory.

D.

COUNTY MONAGHAN AND SOUTH TYRONE.

The maintenance of the old border in this area involves the continuance of the existing economic and geographic conditions.

The market areas of the towns of Monaghan, Dungannon, Ballygawley, and Fivemiletown remain undisturbed. The market area of the town of Aughnacloy remains divided by the boundary.

The Clogher Valley Railway, which runs from Tynan via Caledon and Aughnacloy to Ballygawley, and thence via Augher, Colgher, Fivemiletown and Brookeborough to Maguire's Bridge, is included wholly in Northern Ireland.

The boundary in this section is well marked geographically. For some miles north-west from the summit of Slieve Beagh it follows the crest of the hills. Over the greater part of the rest of its course in this section its follows the river Blackwater.

[13849]

E.

COUNTY ARMAGH.

The section of the Line affecting County Armagh and eastern County Monaghan has the following economic and geographic results :—

The market areas of Monaghan and Armagh are included within the same jurisdiction respectively as the towns themselves, subject to the qualification that the region, in which the two market areas overlap, is necessarily divided.

Portions of the market areas of Keady and Castleblayney are cut off from these towns by the boundary. On the other hand, certain areas previously separated from these towns by the boundary are brought within their range. The area served by the smaller market of Newtown Hamilton is mainly included on the same side of the border as the town.

The barrier interposed by the existing boundary between the town of Dundalk and the area in the south of County Armagh, which it served as market town and source of supplies, is removed.

The Line severs from the town of Newry a portion of its market area in the southwest in the direction of Dundalk, most of which lies beyond the watershed over which the Great Northern Railway passes between these two towns. The distance from Dundalk to the most northerly part of this area is approximately 11 miles.

On both sides of the Newry–Dundalk road and of the Great Northern Railway the boundary runs in mountainous country at a considerable height above the sea level.

The inclusion in Northern Ireland of Newry, together with its immediate surroundings, leaves the town in the same jurisdiction as both the area north of the town which it serves as principal market centre and source of retail supplies, and the area, limited in the south-east by the Mourne mountains, in which Newry shares these functions with Warrenpoint, Rostrevor and Hilltown.

The local flax and linen mills which are the principal industrial enterprises situated in the town and its immediate neighbourhood are included under the same jurisdiction as the business centre of the linen industry, the immediate source of its supplies, and the market and export centre for its products.

The port of Newry is included within the same jurisdiction as the principal area which, by its geographical situation and its railway and canal communication, it is fitted to serve. Out of 37 railway stations, exclusive of those at Newry and Bessbrook, and those on the Clogher Valley Light Railway, for which Newry is the nearest port, the Line includes all except three (situated in Co. Monaghan) within the same jurisdiction. The areas north of Newry, on whose support as customers for coal supplied through Newry Harbour the port is dependent for the chief part of its principal import trade and thus indirectly for a large proportion of its annual revenue, are included on the same side of the border as Newry.

The Newry river, above the point at which the old boundary reaches it, remains wholly included in Northern Ireland, as also the entire course of the Newry Canal and the Victoria Lock.

The navigable channel through Carlingford Lough and as far as the open sea, which provides access both to Newry and to the several lesser ports on each side of Carlingford Lough, is divided between Northern Ireland and the Irish Free State.

The Line includes the water supplies of the towns of Newry, Portadown, Banbridge, Hilltown, Rathfryland, and Belfast, and the Bann Reservoir, under the same jurisdiction as the districts dependent on these supplies.

Of the group of ports comprising the three harbours of Newry, Greenore, and Dundalk, which are all situated within an area measuring 13 miles by 9, the Line thus includes one port as at present in Northern Ireland, and two as at present in the Irish Free State.

PART IV.—CONCLUSION.

The narrative contained in Chapter I of Part I brings the account of the Commission's proceedings up to its meeting on the 5th November, 1925. The original date suggested for the conference with representatives of the Government of the United Kingdom and the Government of the Irish Free State, for which at that meeting it was decided to make proposals, was Thursday, the 19th November. Owing to the engagements of Dr. MacNeill in Dublin in connection with debates in the Dail affecting his Department, it became necessary, in order to meet his convenience, to postpone the conference for a few days, and Tuesday, the 24th November was suggested to the two Governments as the date to be substituted for that originally proposed. It was necessary for the Commission to meet again before the conference with the Governments, and such a meeting was fixed to take place on Friday, 20th November. At the commencement of this meeting, after the confirmation of Minutes, but before any other business had been transacted or discussed, Dr. MacNeill informed his colleagues that he had decided to withdraw from the Commission, and to tender his resignation of his position as a member of the Commission to the Executive Council of the Irish Free State. Discussion ensued, but it appeared that his decision was unalterable, and he withdrew. Since then Dr. MacNeill has taken no further part in the proceedings of the Commission. From the time when the decisions of the Commission, as recorded without dissent in the Minutes of the Meeting of the 17th October, were reached, up to the 20th November, the date of Dr. MacNeill's withdrawal, it had been definitely understood between the three members of the Commission that the Award was to be a unanimous Award; and during the intervening period the whole work of the Commission had proceeded on that basis. Our Award has now to appear without a third signature. We regret that Ireland has been deprived of the benefits of a unanimous Award after such a result of our long enquiry had apparently become assured.

It was contemplated that a statement should be issued at the same time as the Award indicating that the members of the Commission had agreed to sink individual differences of opinion for the purpose of arriving at a unanimous Award, but not specifying any point on which such differences had arisen. The draft of such a statement had been prepared by the Chairman prior to the meeting of the 20th November for submission to his colleagues, and was at that meeting read to the Commission by the Chairman, after Dr. MacNeill had announced his decision to withdraw, as showing the stage which had been reached by the Commission, and the completeness of the understanding existing with regard to unanimity. This draft statement was in the following terms :—

DRAFT SUGGESTED STATEMENT.

In spite of the difficulties of our task and the different views held with regard to it we have been able finally to record a unanimous decision.

It is our earnest hope that the issue of this Award, at the end of a long and full enquiry, bearing the signatures of all three Commissioners, may be accepted by Irishmen as definitely marking the close of the Boundary controversy, and as helping to open the way to improved relations between the Irish Free State and Northern Ireland, whatever form those relations may ultimately take, and to a better understanding between all sections of the people on both sides of the border. The publication of detailed evidence and arguments would inevitably tend to keep old controversies alive. We have therefore ventured to advise the Governments concerned that, apart from the Memorandum which is being issued for publication simultaneously with the Award, the Proceedings of the Commission should not be published either now or for a long time to come, but should be deposited under seal for a fixed term of years.

As appears from the terms of this statement the Commission had contemplated the issue of a memorandum for publication simultaneously with the Award, but had not contemplated the presentation of a detailed report. The memorandum, which was already in draft on the 20th November and included in the Agenda for that date, was to contain a chronological summary of the Commission's proceedings on the lines of the narrative now contained in Chapter I, but less complete, and such information as to the line adopted by the Commission and its effects as is contained in Part III of this Report.

The Award of the Commission embodies the line agreed upon at the meetings at which Dr. MacNeill was present : this Report, however, has been prepared subsequent to Dr. MacNeill's withdrawal. The Commission had taken the view that a unanimous Award would render unnecessary and undesirable the publication of a formal report entering into the pros and cons of the various questions raised before it and into local detail; but in the opinion of the two Commissioners who since the 20th November have continued the Commission's work and intend to attach their signatures to the Award, the withdrawal of Dr. MacNeill has rendered it necessary that such a report should be presented and published.

Owing to the sudden change of plans necessitated by circumstances this Report has been compiled under pressure as to time ; the chief object we have had in view has been to make clear the principles on which we have proceeded, the manner in which those principles have been applied, and the considerations which have governed their application, and we have felt that it was more important to achieve this object within a reasonable time than to delay for the purpose of elaborating local detail.

While any settlement of a boundary line such as we have been called upon to make must inevitably be open to numberless criticisms on points of detail, we put forward the decisions which we have adopted in the confident and sincere belief that they are in accordance with the provisions of Article XII of the Articles of Agreement for a Treaty, which contains our terms of reference, and have been arrived at on a fair estimate, based on the information available and the evidence received, of the various factors which we are required by that Article to take into account.

The documents accumulated by the Commission are necessarily voluminous. They include 130 Representations received; written Observations by many of the different parties concerned on opposing Representations; Witnesses' Statements, and the Verbatim Reports of the proceedings during the sittings held for the hearing of evidence. We have directed the excision from the proceedings of certain small portions of evidence which were given under pledge of secrecy and the destruction of anonymous documents, and other documents which were sent in with a request for secrecy. Apart from these the Secretary has copies of all the Commission's documents, and we have directed him to complete the task of putting these documents in order, and to hold copies at the disposal of the three Governments concerned.

From our personal point of view as members of the Commission we should welcome the giving of the fullest publicity to our proceedings, but it is necessary to say that in the privacy of the Commission's sittings witnesses were encouraged to speak frankly to us, and that many spoke freely and apparently without reserve. In view of the present state of feeling in the districts concerned, we do not recommend publication of the evidence in detail.

STAFF.

We cannot speak too highly of the services rendered to the Commission by Mr. F. B. Bourdillon, C.B.E., who has been responsible as Secretary for the general conduct of the Commission's work, including the organisation of the enquiry in Ireland, and by Major R. A. Boger, R.E., who, as Chief Technical Assistant, has been in charge of all the work connected with maps, which has involved the most careful preliminary study of the situation in the different districts, as well as the preparation of the detailed description and complete sets of maps showing the line adopted.

Both these Officers have brought special skill and experience to bear on the peculiar difficulties of our work, and have been of the greatest assistance to us in collecting and tabulating information and providing the material necessary to enable us to reach our decisions, and finally to prepare the draft Award and this Report.

CONCLUDING STATEMENT.

The main part of the above Report was already in print, and the preparation of the remainder was almost complete, on December 3rd, when the further Agreement supplementing the Articles of Agreement for a Treaty between Great Britain and Ireland of 1921 was entered into. In view of this new Agreement we are withholding our signatures to the draft Award, which had been prepared, and a copy of which is annexed (Appendix V). We assume that the new Agreement will be confirmed by the British Parliament and by the Oireachtas of the Irish Free State. We have stated to the Governments concerned that we consider that, notwithstanding this Agreement, our complete Report should still be presented, and it has been agreed that it should be presented to the British Government.

The Report has now to be read as referring to the Award which, prior to the signature of the new Agreement of December 3rd, 1925, we had intended to make, but which, if that Agreement is duly confirmed, will not now be made. Though we regret that all idea of making any of the changes in the existing boundary which are dealt with in the Report, even those which while involving the transfer of comparatively small areas with few inhabitants would remove serious economic and geographic inconveniences affecting a considerable number of inhabitants on both sides of the border, is for the present abandoned, we recognise that the purpose of the new Agreement is to secure a general settlement, and to establish peace in Ireland on a secure foundation, and we earnestly hope that this larger settlement for which the Agreement provides may bring to the people of Ireland benefits far greater than any which could have resulted from a new determination of boundaries.

It is therefore to be understood that, in signing this Report, we are not making an Award determining the boundaries between Northern Ireland and the rest of Ireland, nor are we now contemplating making such an Award. The Report now is presented only for the purpose of showing how the boundaries would have been determined, had we been called upon to make an Award, and for the purpose of explaining and justifying such proposed determination.

(Signed)   RICHARD FEETHAM,
Chairman.

JOSEPH R. FISHER,
Commissioner.

(Signed)   F. B. BOURDILLON,
Secretary.

6, *Clement's Inn, London,*
December 9, 1925.

APPENDICES.

55328

APPENDIX I.

HEARING OF COUNSEL
Representing the Government of the Irish Free State*

December 4th and 5th, 1924

At 6, Clement's Inn, London, W.C.2

FIRST DAY.

The SITTING opened at 11.20 a.m.

PRESENT:

MR. JUSTICE FEETHAM (*in the Chair*),
MR. J. R. FISHER,
DR. E. MacNEILL, Litt.D., T.D.,
MR. F. B. BOURDILLON (*Secretary*),
MR. C. BEERSTECHER, (*Private Secretary to Mr. Justice Feetham*),
MR. ALFRED MARSHALL, (*Shorthand Writer*).

The following were present representing the Government of the Irish Free State:—

MR. JOHN O'BYRNE (*Attorney-General of the Irish Free State*),
SERJEANT HANNA, K.C.,
MR. PATRICK LYNCH, K.C.,
MR. CECIL LAVERY, B.L.,
MR. MURNAGHAN (*Instructing Solicitor*),
MR. STEPHENS (*Secretary of the North-Eastern Boundary Bureau*).

The CHAIRMAN, in welcoming Counsel, said the Commission had decided, for the present at any rate, to hold its meetings in private. Statements as to its proceedings were issued to the Press from time to time.

The COMMISSION thought that it could best do its work under these conditions of comparative privacy, and that the questions with which it had to deal could be discussed with greater freedom if the discussion were not reported in detail. He therefore invited the co-operation of Counsel in the Commission's efforts to maintain the privacy of the proceedings. He added that a full record of the proceedings would be kept, and that if desired a copy would be sent to Counsel, through the medium of the Government of the Irish Free State, for confidential use.

Mr. JOHN O'BYRNE, Attorney-General, stated that he and his colleagues would on their part maintain the privacy of the proceedings.

(The hearing of Counsel then commenced.)

---

* A copy of the verbatim Report of the Proceedings at the hearing of Counsel on December 4th and 5th, 1924, was sent to the Government of the Irish Free State on January 3rd, 1925, with a request that it should be placed in the hands of Mr. Attorney-General O'Byrne in order that he might make any necessary corrections. A copy was returned with his corrections, and two copies of the verbatim Report embodying these corrections were forwarded to the Government of the Irish Free State on the 2nd February, 1925. The Report as printed below embodies the corrections made.

The ATTORNEY-GENERAL: A statement has been submitted on behalf of the Irish Free State, which no doubt each of the Commissioners has read, and my colleagues and myself do not desire to take up unduly the time of the Commission; consequently we do not propose to go into the various matters dealt with in that statement in detail, but if there is any portion of it which the Commission would like us to elaborate or to deal with particularly, we shall be prepared to do so. Is there any matter the Commission would like us to go into?

The CHAIRMAN: The best course would be for us to hear what you have to say to us and to ask you to supplement it by any points you have not dealt with.

The ATTORNEY-GENERAL: The statement deals shortly with the historical aspect of this question, and it shows that for upwards of 100 years, from the time of the Act of Union, there has been a continued controversy going on in Ireland, having for its object the setting up of a Parliament in Ireland and a Government responsible to that Parliament. That controversy has been carried on in many ways. It was carried on in the British Parliament; it was carried on throughout the country, and on a few occasions it led to armed outbreaks. I would just allude in passing to the events of 1848 and 1867. Then we come down to the more recent controversy, which ultimately resulted in the passing of the Government of Ireland Act, 1914. Now, as set out in the Statement, that Act was passed into law on the 18th day of September, 1914, but on the very same day was passed the Suspensory Act, 1914, which provided that " the Government of Ireland should not be put into operation until the expiration of 12 months from the passing of the Act or such later date, not being later than the end of the European War, as might be fixed by Order in Council."

The controversy which led to the passing of the Government of Ireland Act of 1914 had been a long and bitter one. Hopes had been raised, and, when it seemed as though these hopes were about to be realised, they were dashed to the ground by this Suspensory Act, and very great discontent and dissatisfaction was aroused throughout Ireland. That will largely explain the events of the immediately succeeding years. Two years subsequently (in 1916) there was an armed outbreak in Ireland, very severe fighting took place in Dublin for about a week and a certain amount in other parts of the country. The outbreak was suppressed and a great many executions followed. A great number of prisoners were taken and removed. Subsequently—about Christmas of that year, I think —most of these prisoners were released, but the feeling which had been growing very tense in Ireland prior to 1916—prior to the outbreak at Easter, 1916—was accentuated by the events connected with the suppression of that revolt and by the executions which followed. The movement which had been on foot in Ireland, having for its object the effectuation of Self-Government for Ireland, became more and more pronounced, and got a very decided impetus from the events of 1916. In December, 1918, an election was proclaimed for the British House of Commons. At that time the Act of 1914 was still on the Statute Book, but still suspended by the Suspensory Act. The matters to which I have alluded will probably explain the result of the election of December, 1918. Altogether 105 members were elected to represent Irish constituencies; but of these 105 members only 32 ever attended the British House of Commons. The remainder met in Dublin, some time in January—I think 19th January—1919, and they set up the First Dail. That assembly acted as a Parliament for the whole of Ireland. It set up certain departments of State, which functioned with reasonable success, and it proceeded to act as a properly-constituted Parliament of the country. The assembly known as the First Dail included certain members representing constituencies in the six counties which now constitute Northern Ireland. In the following year a Bill was introduced into the British House of

Commons for the government of Ireland, and it was passed into law by the Government of Ireland Act, 1920, on the 23rd December of that year. It is a singular thing that not a single Irish member voted in favour of it; even of the 32 members from Ireland who attended the British House of Commons not a single one voted in favour of that Bill. That Act provided for the setting up in Ireland of two Parliaments: one a Parliament for Northern Ireland (which, under the Act, consisted of the Parliamentary Counties of Antrim, Armagh, Down, Fermanagh, Londonderry, and Tyrone, and the Parliamentary boroughs of Belfast and Londonderry), and another Parliament for the rest of Ireland (called " Southern Ireland " in that Act). Under that Act elections were proclaimed in May and held in Ireland on 24th May, 1921. When these elections were proclaimed the First Dail passed a resolution dissolving itself and accepted the elections held under this Act of 1920 as and for elections to a Second Dail. The Parliament of Southern Ireland was summoned for the 17th June, and of the members elected to sit in the House of Commons for Southern Ireland not a single member attended except the representatives of Dublin University. The Parliament, of course, never functioned in Southern Ireland—it never could function. The Act was repudiated *in toto* by Southern Ireland. The Parliament of Northern Ireland was called on the 22nd June. Of the 52 members elected to sit in the House of Commons in Northern Ireland, 40 altogether, I believe, attended. Twelve members did not attend then or at any times. These 12 members, like their fellow members in the rest of the country, refused to recognise the Act of 1920. It is interesting to note the constituencies which these 12 members represented: four of them were for the counties of Fermanagh and Tyrone, two for County Armagh, one for County Antrim, one for West Belfast, two for County Down, and two for Londonderry (including the Borough).

The First Dail, by resolution, had dissolved and had agreed to accept these elections as elections for a Second Dail. That Second Dail met on the 16th August, 1921, and comprised the members elected to represent constituencies in Southern Ireland (except Dublin University members) and certain members elected to represent constituencies in Northern Ireland. That Second Dail, like the First Dail, proceeded to act as a Parliament for the whole of Ireland.

I might allude in passing to certain other events which had taken place in Ireland for the two or three years previous to this. There had been a very considerable amount of fighting between British troops and armed forces raised in Ireland, which were generally known as the Irish Republican Army. A truce was arranged in July of 1921 between the General Officer Commanding the British Forces in Ireland and the Officers Commanding the Irish Republican Army. On 14th September (two months afterwards) the Second Dail appointed five plenipotentiaries to negotiate a Treaty of Accommodation and Peace with representatives of the British Government. From July to September there had been a lengthy correspondence between Mr. Lloyd George and Mr. de Valera. Subsequently plenipotentiaries were appointed in September, and they came to London to negotiate this Peace. The plenipotentiaries were Mr. Arthur Griffiths (Chairman), Mr. Michael Collins, Mr. R. Barton, Mr. Duggan and Mr. G. Gavan Duffy. The Chairman represented the Counties of Tyrone and Fermanagh in Northern Ireland, and Mr. Collins represented the County of Armagh; so that of the five plenipotentiaries two represented seats in Northern Ireland. The result of their negotiations is embodied in the Treaty, with Article 12. of which we are dealing. It was signed in London on 6th December, 1921, and was duly ratified later on.

The Second Dail claimed to represent all Ireland; the plenipotentiaries appointed by it claimed to represent all Ireland, and were undoubtedly accepted on that basis by the representatives of the British Government. The Treaty which they arranged and signed was undoubtedly a Treaty for the whole of Ireland and not for any part of Ireland. It is only necessary to look at the first Article of the Treaty in order to see this. The document itself is called " Articles of Agreement for a Treaty Between Great Britain and Ireland ", and it provides in the first Article that " Ireland shall have the same constitutional status in the Community of Nations known as the British Empire as the Dominion of Canada, the Commonwealth of Australia, the Dominion of New Zealand, and the Union of South Africa, with a Parliament having powers to make laws for the peace, order and good government of Ireland and an Executive responsible to that Parliament, and shall be styled and known as the Irish Free State." But though the Irish plenipotentiaries claimed to act for Ireland, and were accepted here as acting for Ireland, it was present to their minds—as it was present to the minds of the representatives of the British Government—that a problem existed in the north-eastern corner of Ireland which would have to be faced.

The Parliament of Northern Ireland set up by the Act of 1920 had met and functioned—not completely, because 12 of its members had refused to recognise it—but it had nevertheless met and had proceeded to act as a Parliament and had set up a Government, and that constituted a difficulty which the persons who signed the Treaty on both sides had to face. If the six counties constituting Northern Ireland had contained a homogeneous population unanimously in favour of maintaining the status acquired by them under the Government of Ireland Act, the problem would not have been nearly so difficult as it was. It did not contain such a population; it contained a mixed population, some of whom were in favour of maintaining the position set up by the Government of Ireland Act, 1920, and some of whom had repudiated that Act and were in favour of accepting the Treaty and working it. That was the difficulty—a mixed population; some in favour of the Treaty and some against it. The Treaty dealt with that problem in this way : it gave the people of this area the option of accepting the Treaty or rejecting it, It gave the period of one month for the exercise of that option. Article 11 of the Treaty makes provision for this. (*Article* 11 *was here quoted.*) Article 12 provides for the manner in which the option is to be exercised. (*Article* 12 *was here quoted.*) The other alternative is provided for in Article 14, which is based on Northern Ireland wishing to remain under the jurisdiction of the Parliament and Government of the Irish Free State. (*Article* 14 *was here quoted.*) That would have been the result if Northern Ireland had elected to remain under the jurisdiction and control of the Parliament and Government of the Irish Free State; in other words, if they had not presented such an address as is contemplated in Article 12. In that event, the Parliament and Government of Northern Ireland would have continued with the same powers and jurisdiction as in the Act of 1920, but as regards all matters outside their jurisdiction they would have come under the control of the Parliament and Government of the Irish Free State. In that event, they would have maintained the entire of the six counties mentioned in the Government of Ireland Act as constituting Northern Ireland. On the very day on which the Constitution of the Irish Free State was formally promulgated both Houses of the Parliament of Northern Ireland presented the address contemplated by Article 12 : in other words, they elected to go out of the jurisdiction of the Parliament and Government of the Irish Free State. Their going out was subject to an important qualification, which is provided for in Article 12. They were entitled to go out, but they were not to take out all the territory which constituted Northern Ireland under the Government of Ireland Act. They elected to exercise the powers conferred on them by the earlier part of Article 12, but the exercise of those powers was qualified by the Proviso to Article 12, which is as follows : (*The Proviso to Article* 12 *was here quoted*).

There you have the genesis of the Commission. The necessity for that Commission I have tried to explain. They had to deal with an area comprising a population some of whom were in favour of being under the jurisdiction and control of the Parliament and Government of the Irish Free State and some of whom were anxious to remain under the restricted powers of Parliament and Government of Northern Ireland and the superior powers of the British Parliament and Government. It is, as I would submit, for this Commission to determine what portions of that population are anxious to be under the jurisdiction of the Irish Free State and what portions are anxious to be under the jurisdiction of the British Parliament.

Under the Treaty *the entire of the area* was part of the Irish Free State—it still is—but there were those provisions to which I have alluded restricting the exercise of the powers of the Parliament and Government of the Irish Free State in that area. In the first place, there was the restriction for the first month to give the Houses of Parliament of Northern Ireland an opportunity of exercising this option, of making up their minds whether they would go out or remain in. There was the further restriction that if they presented the Address mentioned in Article 12 then the powers of the Parliament and Government of the Irish Free State should no longer extend to Northern Ireland and that the provisions of the Government of Ireland Act 1920 should continue to exist within that area subject to the setting up of the Commission. I suggest that, pending the operations of the Commission, the presenting of the Address was sufficient for the moment to prevent the exercise of the powers of the Parliament and Government of the Irish Free State— *pending the operation of the Commission.*

It is now for the Commission to determine, in accordance with the wishes of the inhabitants, subject to the qualification as to economic and geographic conditions, what portions of that area (of the six counties) are now entitled to go out permanently from the jurisdiction of the Parliament and Government of the Irish Free State. These six counties form part of the Irish Free State just as much as the County of Cork and County of Kerry; they contain a very large population who are as strongly in favour of being under the jurisdiction of the Parliament and Government of the Irish Free State as are any other portion of the population of Ireland. The wishes of the inhabitants have been recognised by this Treaty just as the wishes of the inhabitants of portions of the Continent of Europe were recognised by the Versailles Treaty. It is the wishes of the inhabitants that constitute the dominant factor in determining this whole question; and the primary and principal work of this Commission is to ascertain the wishes of the inhabitants. This is their primary and very important work. They have first to ascertain the wishes of the inhabitants and, having done that, to ascertain in accordance with those wishes what portions of Northern Ireland are entitled to go out of the jurisdiction of the Irish Free State.

The CHAIRMAN : Will you deal more fully with the interpretation to be put on the Proviso to Article 12? I would like you to develop your argument that the " wishes of the inhabitants " referred to in that Proviso are the " wishes of the inhabitants of Northern Ireland ".

The ATTORNEY-GENERAL : The Article deals with Northern Ireland.

Before I come to the actual words, may I say that every document must be construed by reference to the circumstances in which it was entered into and by reference to the matter with which it was intended to deal. This is particularly so in the case of a Treaty, which is always construed in a much more liberal manner than an ordinary contract between two individuals and is construed chiefly with a view to giving effect to the objects of the persons entering into that agreement and so as to meet and deal with the problem which it is intended to solve.

What was the problem intended to be solved by these Articles? It was this: that you had an area of six counties with a mixed population: a Parliament and Government had been set up for these six counties which had acted to a certain extent, but in a halting and maimed manner, because of the 52 elected representatives only 40 had ever attended the

Parliament. You had portions of that area in which the inhabitants were almost unanimously in favour of being under the jurisdiction and control of the Irish Free State: you had portions which were opposed to that. I start off with this proposition: That the problem which was intended to be solved by Article 12 and Article 14 of the Treaty was the problem of a mixed population in these six counties.

The CHAIRMAN: So far as the question of mixed population is concerned, may there not be evidence that there is a mixed population on the other side of the border as well?

The ATTORNEY-GENERAL (continuing): Immediately after the Act of 1920 had been put into operation, or after an attempt had been made to put it into operation, of the persons elected to represent constituencies in Southern Ireland no one attended except the representatives for Dublin University. You cannot very well take Dublin University by itself. Not a single representative of the 26 counties attended. That was in June of 1921. The Parliament was summoned for June of 1921 (the 17th, I think). Where is there any evidence there of any call by anybody in Southern Ireland to be taken out of the Free State or to have the 1920 Act put into operation? Please mark the sequence of events: 17th June —abortive meeting of the House of Commons of Southern Ireland; early in July—negotiations for a truce which was arranged, and came into operation on 11th July; correspondence between Mr. Lloyd George and Mr. de Valera up to September; plenipotentiaries appointed in September, who come immediately to London; and the Treaty signed in December. I say—and I do not think I can be contradicted in this—that the sequence of events from June to December shows that the Treaty, or some arrangement of that kind, was necessitated by the event arising out of the Government of Ireland Act. The manner in which the Government of Ireland Act was accepted and treated in Ireland showed the absolute necessity for a new method of dealing with Ireland.

Now coming to the actual words of Article 12 (Article 12 was here quoted). What " inhabitants " are referred to? You have a position brought about by the action of the people of Northern Ireland through their representatives. You have an Article put in there expressly for the purpose of providing for the difficulty created in Northern Ireland. You have an Article dealing, on the face of it, with Northern Ireland. Then you have a Commission set up to ascertain the wishes of the inhabitants. What inhabitants? Surely the inhabitants of Northern Ireland —the place that is being dealt with by this Article; the place which has created the difficulty and which made it necessary for the Treaty to deal specially with. Right through the beginning of that Article you have the words " Northern Ireland " repeated. Even if you leave out all the circumstances—all contemporaneous circumstances, all the circumstances leading up to it; if it were merely a question of grammatical construction —may I suggest that the construction to be put on " inhabitants " there is " the inhabitants of Northern Ireland "? But when you are dealing with an instrument of this kind—a Treaty, which according to every canon of construction is to be construed in a liberal manner and so as to give effect to the intentions of the High Contracting Parties to it—when taking the Treaty in that way, considering the problem which it was intended to solve, how can it possibly be suggested that this Commission was intended to deal with any other area than the six counties of Northern Ireland? I have shown my reference to the circumstances leading up to it that it must be recognised that at the date of the passing of the Treaty there was a large portion of the population of Northern Ireland that had never accepted the Government of Ireland Act, and they were anxious to be under the same jurisdiction and control as the population of the remaining part of the country. This is further recognised— and recognised in the most express manner—upon the face of the Treaty itself. I have already alluded to the two different positions contemplated by the Treaty; the position that the North would remain under the jurisdiction and control of the Parliament and Government of the Irish Free State, or that it would elect to go out. I have pointed out that in the event of their electing to remain under the jurisdiction of the Parliament and Government of the Irish Free State that the entire of the six counties would have continued to constitute Northern Ireland. But, see what follows. If that had been the position, if the Houses of the Parliament of Northern Ireland had elected to remain under the jurisdiction of the Irish Free State, what would have happened? One of the things contemplated was that a Convention would have been entered into for safeguarding the rights of minorities in Northern Ireland.

I will deal now with Article 15. Article 14 contemplated Northern Ireland remaining within the jurisdiction of the Irish Free State. It is immediately followed by Article 15. (*Article 15 was here quoted*). Subsection (*d*) of that Article deals with "Safeguards for minorities in Northern Ireland". There is no question of minorities in the rest of Ireland. There were minorities in Northern Ireland recognised —as they were bound to be recognised—having regard to the course of events leading up to this Treaty. It was recognised that the existence of these extensive minorities in Northern Ireland was a difficulty, a serious problem. It was recognised that these minorities would have to be dealt with and protected. How are they protected? If Northern Ireland had remained under the jurisdiction of the Irish Free State, and consequently kept the entire of her territory, they would have been protected by this Convention contemplated by Article 15.

The CHAIRMAN: That was to be a Convention between the Governments of Northern and Southern Ireland?

The ATTORNEY-GENERAL: Yes.

It was recognised that once the territory of the six counties was left intact, as set up by the Government of Ireland Act, that some provision would have to be made with reference to these large minorities in Northern Ireland. It was done by Article 15, which contemplates safeguards in this way. The other alternative is Article 12, which contemplates the North going out. In that event there is no suggestion for any Convention of this kind, because, may I suggest, it was contemplated that in that event the work of this Commission would be to bring these minorities— these large minorities—within the jurisdiction of the Parliament and Government of the Irish Free State.

The CHAIRMAN: Do I understand that the position you take up is that the Proviso requires the Commission to exclude from Northern Ireland, as hitherto defined, such portions as may be selected for exclusion after ascertaining the wishes of the inhabitants?

The ATTORNEY-GENERAL: Yes.

The CHAIRMAN: The difficulty which suggests itself is that the terms of the Article do not say "exclude" from Northern Ireland. It says "determine the boundaries,"—which might mean either exclusion or inclusion.

The ATTORNEY-GENERAL: Your work consists in ascertaining, in accordance with the wishes of the inhabitants, what portions of the six counties are entitled to go permanently out of the jurisdiction of the Irish Free State. When once the work of the Commission is finished and that has been determined, the portions so determined shall constitute Northern Ireland for the purpose of the Government of Ireland Act 1920 and of the Treaty.

The CHAIRMAN: You say it should be "what portions of Northern Ireland are to be permanently included in Northern Ireland." Or you would say "what territory included in the present limits of Northern Ireland is to constitute the permanent territory of Northern Ireland?"

The ATTORNEY-GENERAL : That is just it; the present arrangement is a purely temporary one. First, a month to give them an opportunity for exercising the option; secondly, the arrangement now existing, which is purely temporary and pending the operations of this Commission.

The CHAIRMAN : The new territory is to be " Northern Ireland " for the purpose of the Government of Ireland Act, 1920, and should be capable of maintaining a Parliament and Government.

The ATTORNEY-GENERAL : It is to be such as can show within it a homogeneous population in favour of the position set up by the Government of Ireland Act. It is, may I suggest, for the Commission to determine what areas in Ireland have a population in favour of the continuance of the position set up by the Government of Ireland Act, 1920. It is only that area which will constitute Northern Ireland for the purpose of the Act of 1920 and of this Treaty. I do not know that the consideration which you suggested a moment ago is a proper suggestion for this Commission.

The CHAIRMAN : Which—the consideration that it is to be an area capable of maintaining a Parliament and a Government?

The ATTORNEY-GENERAL : I think the work of the Commission consists in ascertaining the wishes. I suggest that it is not a proper consideration in this Article which, I think, defines within pretty clear limits that the Commission is to consider the boundary in accordance with the wishes subject to possible rectification by economic and geographic considerations. If the Commission does consider the other question to which you have alluded it must be remembered that it is a Parliament and Government with very restricted powers, a local Parliament and Government with certain delegated powers under the immediate control of another Parliament and Government from whom these powers are derived. You must not consider it from the point of view of a more or less independent State; that would be an absolutely false analogy. Northern Ireland, under the Government of Ireland Act, elects representatives to the Parliament of Northern Ireland with certain limited delegated powers; it also elects representatives to the British Parliament. At the present time Northern Ireland, or such portion as the Commission may subsequently determine to be Northern Ireland, takes up the position of desiring to be joined on to Great Britain as a part of the system of Great Britain, and accordingly I say that if you consider at all the consideration to which you, Mr. Chairman, have referred, you must take it in that very restricted way : that it is only a local Parliament and Government with very restricted delegated powers. You must remember that that area, whatever it may be, will continue to have representatives in the British Parliament. May I summarise the reasons why I suggest that this Article must be considered solely with reference to the area included in Northern Ireland? First, the circumstances leading up to this Treaty and the unquestioned and unquestionable fact that the problem which Article 12 was designed to solve was the problem existing in the six counties of North Eastern Ireland. You have next the Proviso to Article 12, which sets up this Commission, which was a qualification upon the right of the six counties to go out of the jurisdiction of the Irish Free State. This Commission is not set up by an independent Article : it is set up by a condition put in the nature of a qualification upon the right of Northern Ireland to go out, and it is contained in an Article dealing with Northern Ireland.

You will, of course, remember this : The Irish Free State is a self-governing power within the British Commonwealth of Nations, with full and absolute powers of legislation.

Dr. MacNEILL : Are there not some limitations mentioned with regard to religion and some other things?

The ATTORNEY-GENERAL : There are some express limitations to which the Free State has agreed. Subject to these, of course, it is a State with full powers; and may I suggest that I do not think this

Commission or any other body will have power to come in or to interfere in any way with its territory.

The CHAIRMAN: Surely that is begging the question. Whatever we do must, of course, be done under that Article (12); our jurisdiction to do that will be the same as our jurisdiction to do anything else.

The ATTORNEY-GENERAL: You cannot forget that consideration; especially you cannot forget the consideration that you are dealing here on the one side with the Irish Free State and on the other side with Great Britain—Ireland and Great Britain. Then as a part of the Parliamentary system of Great Britain you have this area—whatever it may be determined to be—in Northern Ireland. At the present time there are six counties under that jurisdiction—the jurisdiction of the Parliament of Great Britain. I would suggest that it is for this Commission to ascertain of these six counties how much is really entitled to remain under that jurisdiction.

Mr. FISHER: Has your attention be directed to the arguments of the Judicial Committee of the Privy Council?

The ATTORNEY-GENERAL: I have not considered that.

Mr. FISHER: The point was argued with regard to the powers of the British Government to appoint a Commissioner over the heads of the Northern Irish Government.

The ATTORNEY-GENERAL: The Irish Free State were not concerned in that, and have not considered it. I may refer to a section of the Government of Ireland Act. According to Section 75 of the 1920 Act, the position in Northern Ireland is that "the supreme authority of the Parliament of the United Kingdom shall remain unaffected and undiminished over all persons, matters, and things in Ireland and every part thereof". (*Section 4 of the Government of Ireland Act, 1920, dealing with legislative powers of Irish Parliaments, was here also quoted by the Attorney-General.*)

(*The hearing was adjourned at 1 p.m.*)

————————

(*The hearing was resumed at 3 p.m.*)

Mr. FISHER: The Attorney-General spoke repeatedly of areas which may be entitled to withdraw from the Irish Free State. Has he considered: —

(1) That in the Treaty there is no mention of such areas to be created within Northern Ireland, but solely of existing areas: — Northern Ireland and the " Rest of Ireland ", whose boundaries are to be defined?

(2) That Northern Ireland is spoken of as an autonomous State already in existence with legislative and executive powers which have never been suspended for a moment—a territory defined county by county in the Act of 1920, which by the Treaty continues of full force and effect?

The ATTORNEY-GENERAL: It is true that the Treaty does not refer to areas entitled to withdraw; but may I submit that the proper and reasonable construction of the Treaty amounts to that, and for this reason: —You start with the entire of Ireland as the Irish Free State under the Treaty. That is a simple matter beyond all question. You have only to read the first Article. (*This Article was here quoted.*) Therefore, when you come to consider " What is the Irish Free State as a geographical entity?" It is the entire of Ireland.

We come now to Article II :—

> " Until the expiration of one month from the passing of the Act of Parliament for the ratification of this instrument, the powers of the Parliament and the Government of the Irish Free State shall not be exerciseable as regards Northern Ireland——"

" The powers shall not be exerciseable "—not that they do not exist, but that for this period of one month, to enable this area to make up its mind, " the powers shall not be exerciseable ". I suggest that the logical method of dealing with it would be to go on to Article 14. (*Article 14 was here quoted.*)

Coming to Article 12 :—

> " If before the expiration of the said month, an address is presented to His Majesty by both Houses of Parliament of Northern Ireland to that effect, the powers of the Parliament and Government of the Irish Free State shall no longer extend to Northern Ireland——"

Even then this portion of the country does not cease to be part of the Irish Free State nor, as a matter of fact, are the powers of the Parliament and Government of the Irish Free State completely withdrawn, because you will find that the provisions of the Government of Ireland Act with reference to the Council of Ireland continue in Northern Ireland—not in the rest of the country, but in Northern Ireland.

Mr. FISHER : Is the Council of Ireland elected by the two Provinces—the North and the South—so that the powers of the Council of Ireland are the powers belonging to the North and South?

The ATTORNEY-GENERAL : The Act of 1920 contemplated the Council of Ireland as a body set up to deal with certain services throughout Ireland; this Council to be constituted by, I think, 40 members—20 to be elected by the two Houses of Parliament of Southern Ireland and 20 by the two Houses of Parliament of Northern Ireland. Now under the Treaty there cannot be any such body within the territory under the jurisdiction of the Irish Free State, because within that territory the Parliament of the Irish Free State has complete power as regards these matters. But it still continues in Northern Ireland, and it is constituted in this way : that the Parliament of the Irish Free State steps into the shoes of the Parliament of Southern Ireland and appoints its 20 members on the Council of Ireland; so that in Northern Ireland the Parliament of the Irish Free State, through its representatives, exercises powers in these counties.

Mr. FISHER : Under the Act of 1920.

The ATTORNEY-GENERAL : Under the Treaty.

Mr. FISHER : It embodies the Act of 1920.

The ATTORNEY-GENERAL : Not by force of the Act of 1920 which has been repudiated, and the repudiation of which had led to the Treaty and caused the necessity for it, but it exists by virtue of the Treaty.

Mr. FISHER : Which revives it for that particular purpose.

The ATTORNEY-GENERAL : Which revives it. Even within these counties constituting Northern Ireland the powers of the Free State are not completely withdrawn.

Then you come to consider what is to be the work of this Commission.

The CHAIRMAN : It is worth while to note this in relation to the emphasis you laid on " the powers shall no longer extend to Northern Ireland ". I think you said just now that " Even then Northern Ireland does not cease to be part of the Free State ". I do not know if we shall get very far on that. The first part of Article 12 ends with the words :— (*The portion of Article 12 referred to was here quoted.*) Note, " subject to the necessary modifications "—to the modifications rendered necessary by the powers of the Parliament and Government of the Irish Free State ceasing to extend to Northern Ireland and by the maintenance of the provisions of the Government of Ireland Act 1920, in so far as they relate to Northern Ireland.

The ATTORNEY-GENERAL: As modified by the Treaty.

The CHAIRMAN: All the modifications necessary have to be read into this instrument, in the event of the Address referred to in Article 12 being presented.

The ATTORNEY-GENERAL: Of course.

One of these modifications is the one to which I alluded. Within Northern Ireland this Council of Ireland continues to exist, but as regards the 20 members which were to have been appointed by the Houses of Parliament under the Act of 1920, these are now elected by the Parliament of the Irish Free State.

The CHAIRMAN: That is expressly mentioned in Article 13.

Mr. FISHER: Does it not come to this:—The two, as we know, are required to elect members to this Council of Ireland? The Act of 1920 having ceased to apply to Southern Ireland, this clause expressly indicates that although its other powers are gone the duty of electing 20 members on the Council of Ireland still continue?

The ATTORNEY-GENERAL: No; the power of the Parliament of Southern Ireland has gone completely.

The CHAIRMAN: This is entirely a new body on which these powers are conferred. The powers of the Parliament of Southern Ireland are now conferred on the Parliament of the Irish Free State.

The ATTORNEY-GENERAL: Please remember this modification:—— that as originally contemplated the Council of Ireland was a body having jurisdiction over the entire of the 32 counties of Ireland. It is kept alive for Northern Ireland only; and in Northern Ireland the Parliament of the Irish Free State has exactly the same powers as the Parliament of Northern Ireland as regards electing representatives on this Council of Ireland. It can elect 20 representatives, just as the Houses of Parliament of Northern Ireland can elect their 20, for the purpose of dealing with these matters within the jurisdiction of the Council of Ireland in the counties constituting Northern Ireland.

The CHAIRMAN: Yes; I wanted those words not to be overlooked in the interpretation of Article 12.

The ATTORNEY-GENERAL: We come to the Proviso to Article 12, which gives Northern Ireland the power to withdraw, and that power is given subject to the qualification contained in this proviso. The qualification is that if they go out they go out not with the entire territory, as would have been the case under Article 14—the area subject to the jurisdiction of the Parliament of Northern Ireland will not be the entire of the six counties, as it would have been under Article 14, but such portion of it as the Commission may determine:—

" . . . a Commission consisting of three persons, one to be appointed by the Government of the Irish Free State, one to be appointed by the Government of Northern Ireland, and one who shall be the Chairman to be appointed by the British Government shall determine in accordance with the wishes of the inhabitants, so far as may be compatible with economic and geographic conditions, the boundaries between Northern Ireland and the rest of Ireland . . . "

What is the meaning of that, unless it be that the Commission is to determine what *areas* within these six counties are entitled to withdraw? There is a clear reference—a clear reference by implication—to " areas " of some kind, because the matter is to be determined by the wishes of the inhabitants. The question as to whether an area is to be under the jurisdiction of the Parliament of the Irish Free State or under the jurisdiction of the Parliament of Northern Ireland is to be determined by the wishes of the inhabitants of that area, subject in case of necessity to the qualification in connection with economic and geographic conditions. For that reason I suggest that though the word " areas " is not expressly referred to Article 12, it is referred to by implication when you are directed to ascertain the wishes of the inhabitants; because that is clearly indicated in Article 12 as being the dominant factor in determining this boundary.

(This concluded the Attorney-General's address.)

Serjeant HANNA then addressed the Commissioners.

He said—I shall supplement very briefly, and I hope concisely, the arguments put forward by the learned Attorney-General, approaching it perhaps in some respects from a different point of view. I would ask the Commission to regard this from the standpoint of international law as a *secession* of a section of the inhabitants of the Irish Free State from the Free State, and that you should regard yourselves—as I submit you are— as a tribunal established to determine the extent and method of that secession. For the purpose of establishing that main issue it is necessary in the first place that you should be satisfied that the unit—the fundamental governing unit; the geographic unit—with which you are concerned is *Ireland,* with its existing territorial and geographical boundaries. That I think, and venture to submit, is almost demonstrated by the clauses of the Treaty. The more important clauses were referred to by the learned Attorney-General, more especially Clause 1.

In almost every one of these sections of the Treaty the territory that was being dealt with from a geographical point of view was Ireland; and it is referred to sometimes as " Ireland " and sometimes as " the Irish Free State," the two terms being for the purpose of the Treaty geographically coterminous. Section 1 refers to " Ireland " and says that it shall have a certain status " with a Parliament having power to make laws for the good government of Ireland "—that is the geographical Ireland; the island,—and " it (*i.e.,* Ireland) shall be known as the Irish Free State ". Subject to the point as to what the position of Northern Ireland may be when you have issued your Award, it is clear that until then the whole of Ireland will continue to be the Irish Free State, though a portion of it has a limited Government which may be described quite respectfully as " an exaggerated local Government of its own," the greater and paramount powers being still retained within the grasp of the Imperial Parliament.

Passing from Article 1 to Article 3, we see the method of appointment of the representative of the Crown " in Ireland ".

The CHAIRMAN : You said: " Until the Commission's award the whole of Ireland must be regarded as the Irish Free State ". We will examine that contention later on.

Serjeant HANNA : The whole of Ireland is the Irish Free State with a portion having a limited description to earmark it as " Northern Ireland ". There is nothing until your award is made which will take Northern Ireland out of the Free State. The learned Attorney-General referred to political history. I submit that Ireland is the unit in this Treaty. It is impossible for representatives of Northern Ireland to say that they or that portion of Ireland stood outside this Treaty. They never had any power with reference to Treaties. By Section 4 of the Act of 1920, which gave them the limited powers they have, treaties were excepted from their jurisdiction. Their interests in respect of the Treaty were controlled by the British Parliament and its representatives who dealt with the Irish people in a bargain which took the whole of Ireland as the basis and fundament of these Articles of Agreement. This is a very important point we have in the building up of our argument.

Passing to Article 3 :—

" The representative of the Crown ' in Ireland ' shall be appointed in like manner as the Governor-General of Canada, &c."

Article 4 refers to the " common citizenship of Ireland "—again the geographical entity.

Take Article 5 :—

" The Irish Free State shall assume liability for the service of the Public Debt of the United Kingdom . . . . having regard to any just claims on the part of " Ireland . . . ."

It does not distinguish between the claim of Northern Ireland or the claim of the Free State. The war pensions were to be dealt with on the basis of any equitable set off " on the part of Ireland ". (*The latter part of Article 5 was here quoted.*) That is the whole geographical Ireland, and when we turn to Article 6 and the schedule which was prepared referring to those coastal defences that the British Government is to take over as being subject to the Treaty, we find those in Northern Ireland included. (*The part of the para. in question was here quoted.*) That is the whole of Ireland. I am putting what seem to be small points to satisfy you that the accumulation of these points when we come to Article 12 can, I submit, lead the Commission to no other conclusion than that the bedrock of the Treaty is that the whole of Ireland is the possession of the Free State. Parliament has said that those who desire to secede shall do so through the Boundary Commission.

Let us take the provision as to army; Article 8. (*Article 8 was here quoted.*) They do not say " the population of the Irish Free State ". Why? Because they were dealing with the Irish Free State as being the whole of Ireland, and the proportion of the army which the Irish Free State are entitled to maintain is not the proportion of the Irish Free State or that of the 26 counties; it is the proportion of the population of *Ireland*. This all shows, in the interpretation of this Treaty, the basic idea that the Tribunal will seek for, what is the common thought that runs through the minds of the two parties who are making the Treaty? No interpretation that may be sought to be put on it several years after the contract has been entered into can affect what was the common thought of the two parties when they entered into this Agreement. I respectfully submit that it becomes clearer and clearer that the British Government were dealing with the whole, and that the common thought in their mind was to make provision for the whole of Ireland and for the people who wish to secede from the Irish Free State.

Let us come to a closer interpretation. In the standard English Book, *Westlake*, on " The Interpretation of Treaties " the principle is laid down in Vol. I, p. 283.

" The interpretation of treaties has been considered at much length by many writers on international law, and rules on it have been suggested which in our opinion are not likely to be of much practical use.

" The most important point is to get at the real intention of the parties, and that enquiry is not to be shackled by any rule of interpretation which may exist in a particular national jurisprudence but is not generally accepted in the civilised world."

That is the principle which the Attorney-General indicated was to be given. Westlake says :—" less literally " and " not shackled by any rule of interpretation which may exist in a particular national jurisprudence but is not generally accepted in the civilised world."

Counsel continued to read the extract from Westlake, as follows :—

" On the whole we incline to think that the interpretation of international contracts is and ought to be less literal than that usually given in English courts of law to private contracts and Acts of Parliament. In the first place, English drafting is more minutely careful, and correspondingly English interpretation is more literal, than is common in those countries to which most of the Ministers and Diplomats who are responsible for the wording of international contracts belong. And, secondly, the nature of the matters dealt with by these eminent functionaries and the peculiar conditions under which they work must be considered. A style of drafting accommodated to the expectation of a very literal interpretation would necessitate the suggestion and discussion of so many possible contingencies as would be likely to cause needless friction between the representatives of countries not always very amicable. It seems best in the interest of peace that, when an agreement on broad lines has been reached, it should be expressed in language not striving to hide a felt doubt, but, on the other hand, not meticulously seeking occasions for doubt, and to such a style of drafting, which we believe to be that most common in treaties, a large and liberal spirit of interpretation will reasonably correspond."

The meaning of that is that you seek out the intention of the parties, not binding either of them to a too literal interpretation of the text. It is not merely a question of grammar or logic; it is a question of reading into the Treaty, for the purpose of interpreting it rather than construing it, the entire circumstances which led up to it, so that your minds may be seized of the real problem with which the parties to the Agreement or the Treaty were dealing.

(Counsel here made quotations from Grotius, Vol. II, 16-18 sub-note 1 (b) LXX.)

Counsel also quoted Taylor's " International Law " (1902), p. 305, section 378, as follows:—

" As the primary object of all construction is to discover the common thought in which the minds of the contracting parties met, the entire instrument containing the agreement, no matter whether a contract between individuals or a treaty between nations, must be taken as a whole, and construed according to the natural, fair and received acceptation of the terms in which it is expressed. Despite Cicero's suggestion, quoted by Grotius, that ' when you promise we must consider rather what you mean, than what you say,' it is only from the words actually used that such meaning can be drawn. And yet, in the effort to discover the common intention the spirit rather than the letter should govern, . . ."

You should seek the intention of the parties: you should read into the Treaty the entire circumstances that led up to it, and give due consideration to the language of the whole instrument. The two main principles that we ask you to apply to this document are:—

(1) In considering Article 12 to have regard to all the provisions of the Treaty;

(2) To have regard to what was the subject in dispute between the parties which the Treaty proposed to settle.

Turning now to Article II. Before I read, I venture to make the remark that the Treaty seems to contemplate the Government having powers, and a distinction is drawn between *having powers* and *exercising them*. Bearing that in mind we read:—*(Article 11 was here quoted)*.

What were the powers of the Irish Free State? They had powers to make laws for the good government of the whole of Ireland, including Northern Ireland. That is the extent of their powers. There is a limit put on the " *exercise* " of them:—they " shall not be exercisable as respects Northern Ireland . . ." The Free State had the power in Northern Ireland by virtue of Section 1 of the Treaty. Article 11 only suspends the exercise of them. The word " exercise " is used again in one of the subsequent Articles—I think in No. 14. We have here in Article 11 a word used which supports my argument that the whole of Ireland is the basis of this Treaty, because it says impliedly that although the Free State has these powers it is not to use them in the delimited area of Northern Ireland, "and the provisions of the Government of Ireland Act, 1920, shall, so far as they relate to Northern Ireland, remain in full force and effect . . ." There again we cannot read without having driven home the fact that what we are dealing with is the whole of Ireland and making temporary provisions, as we see from the subsequent sections, for the inhabitants of Northern Ireland who desire to secede from the Free State. Going on we read:—

"If before the expiration of the said month an address is presented to His Majesty by both Houses of the Parliament of Northern Ireland to that effect . . ."

We will see what effect that has:—

". . . the powers of the Parliament and Government of the Irish Free State shall no longer extend to Northern Ireland."

Not that the exercise of the powers is to be taken away, but that the powers themselves are to be deleted as to Northern Ireland.

What I submit to your judgment is this:—That if the Northern Parliament present a petition that the Irish Free State powers should no longer extend to them, the position would then be that the Northern Parliament shall continue their powers under the Act of 1920, but they shall not necessarily have the territory of 1920. And why should they not have that territory? Because of the Treaty, and because, on the Treaty basis of Ireland being the unit, there is a portion of that population who desire to secede from the Free State. The wishes of these "inhabitants" are to be ascertained. The word "inhabitant" implies *territory;* it connotes a geographical habitation. Therefore you cannot deal with inhabitants in this connection save by dealing with an area of territory. When the word "inhabitant" is used it clearly shows that it is a question of the territory which those inhabitants inhabit. The Northern Government, if they put in the petition, were to continue to have the powers under the Act of 1920, but they were not to have the territory, unless it is determined under the Treaty that they are entitled to it. The only territory they are to have will be the territory determined by the Boundary Commission under the Treaty.

(Counsel here quoted the Proviso to Article 12.)

That is a judicial act; that means a judicial determination. ". . . in accordance with the wishes of the inhabitants." There is a definition of the word "inhabitant" in the case of *Rex* v. *Mitchell,* 10 East Reports, as being "a person having a permanent residence."

(Counsel here quoted the Proviso to Article 12 *from the words* "so far as may be compatible . . ." *to the end.)*

Another question that arises is the question as to whether there is any mandate to entitle you to go into the Irish Free State. If anyone were to appear before you and claim that you could go into the Irish Free State and take territory you would ask them: "Where is your authority for that?" It might be on the strictly literal, verbal or grammatical interpretation of the Treaty (we think by straining it it would be) that you might say that altering the boundary means altering it one way or the other.

The CHAIRMAN: I would like you to develop that point. You say that it is straining it. Seeing that the Commission is appointed to determine the boundary of some existing geographical unit, is it straining it to say that means authority to the Commission, or whoever it may be, to determine in either direction; that is, to determine to extend or to diminish?

Serjeant HANNA: Taking in a narrow sense the words which have just been used—"determine the boundaries"—I think in the ordinary case as applied to two civil properties he could go where he liked; but here the interpretation must be in relation to the subject matter. The history that has been put forward by the learned Attorney-General indicates, and the Treaty itself proclaims, that the dispute is a dispute as to delimiting Northern Ireland. Great Britain made no claim in connection with the Treaty or on the face of the Treaty for any of the 26 counties, and as to those in geographical Ulster prior to 1920, Great Britain had placed them outside the pale of the Northern Government in that year.

The CHAIRMAN: We have been asked to take into account historical circumstances. If we take those into account, this point should be considered by you and perhaps dealt with. The Attorney-General referred, and you refer, to certain historical circumstances bearing upon your argument. The Commission, I take it, is expected to keep its eyes open for any historical circumstances which could legitimately be taken into consideration. Can we therefore disregard the fact that there is a mixed population—to use the Attorney-General's phrase—on both sides of the existing border of Northern Ireland, and that the question as to the limit to be assigned to the jurisdiction of the Government and Parliament of Northern Ireland was a question which was a live one at the time that the Act of 1920 was dealt with and had been a matter of very keen controversy before? If there was to be a division, the great point was as to where the dividing line should fall, and there were various claims. I want you to tell me what your contention is as to what the attitude of the Commission should be to that part of history.

Serjeant HANNA: There is no mandate in the Treaty or in Article 12 entitling you to take into consideration the wishes of the population anywhere in the Irish Free State, and I give you my reasons . . .

The CHAIRMAN: Are you basing this on the language of the Article or general circumstances?

Serjeant HANNA: As regards general circumstances, we have confined ourselves to what is contained in Acts of Parliament and international documents.

The CHAIRMAN: The Statement covers other matters than Acts of Parliament; it indicates general history.

Serjeant HANNA: Our contention is that your minds should not be shut to our argument that the subject matter of the Treaty could not be to take territory from the Free State as well as from Northern Ireland, inasmuch as that would be going against the situation as depicted by the Treaty itself. Then again, the question, that the Treaty was to settle by Article 12, was to get rid of the trouble created by the 1920 Act. The Act of 1920 created an impossible situation: Article 12 was to get rid of that. I will tell you why it was impossible using the word in the sense of *unreasonable*. It fixed an arbitrary and artificial area of territory which, regardless of the wishes of the inhabitants, it placed under the government of Northern Ireland. Article 12, we submit, was an admission that the question had to be rectified, as regards those put under the Northern Government. It fell to be rectified; and the occasion came to right it when giving the Irish Free State complete government over Ireland, save such portion as would demonstrate to the Boundary Commission a wish to remain under it; to enable those who claimed that they should not be put into the Irish Free State to secede. The Treaty, as it were, for that purpose wiped out the boundaries of Northern Ireland as if they had never been, and it was as though that map (of Northern Ireland) was put before you and you were to find out in the area that was Northern Ireland the wishes of the inhabitants—those who are willing to stay or who are unwilling to go under the government of the Irish Free State.

The CHAIRMAN: You say the Treaty wiped out the boundary; but you immediately go back to it and say that it is sacrosanct as regards the limits of what is to be excluded?

Serjeant HANNA: The Treaty did not wipe out the Northern Government, and therefore the area still remained temporarily for the purpose of government for the past three years, still when it comes to you to determine whether it is to be a mere alteration of a line or a transfer of a territory, for that purpose that boundary is to be deemed to be obliterated. I am arguing against a mere alteration of a line within narrow limits. Wishes of inhabitants would be almost irrelevant on such a view. It must mean " inhabitants " of an area. " Inhabitants " of a boundary line would be unmeaning.

The learned Attorney-General read and indicated that under Article 15, if Northern Ireland elected to come in, provisions were to be made at a Convention for protecting the people of Northern Ireland—the minorities. Is not that and the absence of a correlative protection to Free Staters a further indication that so far as the secession or non-secession of any area was concerned, it is only the area of Northern Ireland that is to be dealt with?

Article 12 and any clauses that are consequential upon it only deal, and expressly only deal, with Northern Ireland, and there are what seem to be insuperable obstacles to them dealing with anything else because, by the Treaty, Great Britain was giving the Free State plenary powers. Under the Act of 1920, both as regards Northern Ireland and Southern Ireland, the Parliament of Great Britain reserved the paramount powers to themselves in London. That still continues with regard to Northern Ireland. Once the Treaty was passed those paramount powers were transferred to the Irish Free State and were applicable by them to any portion of the Free State and cannot be taken out of them.

The CHAIRMAN: Not unless it is so provided by the Treaty.

Serjeant HANNA: You are to fix the boundary, but I do not think it can be suggested for a moment that in fixing a boundary you are to take out of the Free State a portion of territory over which they have reserved powers, and transfer those powers not to the Government of Northern Ireland but back to the Government of the British Parliament.

The CHAIRMAN: Whatever you do, if that followed, there is nothing in the Treaty to prevent that effect following upon our Award.

Serjeant HANNA: Our construction prevents it, because we have the full plenary powers of government, and the transfer of Northern territory to the Free State does not raise this difficulty.

The CHAIRMAN: If your contention is correct that Article 12 only enables us to make an alteration by way of excluding from what is to be called Northern Ireland portions of what at present, under the Act of 1920, constitutes Northern Ireland, then we have no power to take away from the Irish Free State any territory which is at present under its jurisdiction or to confer any power over such territory on anybody else; it all depends on the interpretation of Article 12. If it means that the Commission has power to determine the boundary in the general sense of the term in either direction, then supposing we exercise that power in such a way as to include in Northern Ireland a portion of what at present is on the Irish Free State side of the existing boundary the result would follow that the territory which went out of the Irish Free State would, under the terms of Article 12, become part of Northern Ireland for all purposes.

Serjeant HANNA: I quite follow. My answer is this: I was using that remark as an argument to convince you that the parties who entered into the Treaty could not have had such a thing in their minds. It cannot be fairly implied from the language. If they had contemplated that you were to restrict—to take away from the Irish Free State—a portion of territory over which they have certain powers, it would not have been expressed as it was expressed in Article 12. *Per contra*, if the only idea was that a portion of territory in Northern Ireland which was within the control and sole jurisdiction for the purpose of transfer of the British

Parliament is to be transferred by the British Parliament, through your Commission, to the Irish Free State, they are transferring something which is governed particularly by Northern Ireland, paramountly by the British Parliament, to a State that has plenary powers, and the plain meaning of Article 12 covers that. I think that the transfer of territory from the Irish Free State to Northern Ireland is in quite a different category from the transfer of territory from Northern Ireland to the Free State, because this fact would come into consideration: If you are to take the wishes of the inhabitants, that is the inhabitants of the Irish Free State, you would have to take the opinion of the people in Cork or Kerry.

The CHAIRMAN: And you say we are to take the opinion of the people of Antrim?

Serjeant HANNA: We might say we did not want you to take the views of the people of Belfast; but if you like to take them it is a matter for the Tribunal.

The CHAIRMAN: Then we need not go to Cork or Kerry?

Serjeant HANNA: The area in which the view is to be taken is the one in which there is a mixed population, but it must be an area.

The CHAIRMAN: You said if the intention of Article 12 was to enable the Commission to transfer territory which at present is in the Irish Free State to the other side of the boundary the language used would have been different. The question of the interpretation of Article 12—allowing for all argument as to the intention and so on—is obviously a very important one for the Commission to consider. Why would not the terms of Article 12 as they stand cover such a transfer; and if the only thing that Article 12 was intended to cover was the transfer of territory to the Irish Free State or the settlement of the question—within the limits of Northern Ireland as defined by the Act of 1920 how much was to remain in Northern Ireland—why was such an expression as " determine the boundaries " used?

Serjeant HANNA: Because it is the boundary of the country that is to be under Northern Ireland. If it had been intended that Free State territory should be transferred to Northern Ireland—or in other words, to Great Britain—if it had been the intention that territory should be transferred from this new State, (the 26 counties), to Great Britain, the people who provided that must be presumed to have understood that the Free State had plenary powers and that the reserved powers would have been introduced on the transfer of any portion of the Free State 26 counties; so that the plenary powers which had been transferred should be re-transferred.

The CHAIRMAN: Is not the reference to the Government of Ireland Act quite sufficient?

Serjeant HANNA: That would be a very inapt and inartistic and unprofessional way of re-transferring powers which were in the Irish Free State.

The CHAIRMAN: You say " re-transferring."

Serjeant HANNA: If they had contemplated taking Free State territory into Great Britain, they would have had supplemental words to indicate that whatever was necessary to make it a legal adjustment would follow.

The CHAIRMAN: Would it be more difficult supposing such a change was made? The boundary fixed by the Government of Ireland Act is maintained until the Commission has decided it for the purpose of government and legislation for the time being. If the result of the Commission's award was to diminish the territory of Northern Ireland, that would mean that various laws which now apply to a portion of

Northern Ireland would cease to apply and the Free State laws would apply instead. If the words of the Article are sufficient for that, are they not also sufficient for a transfer of the other kind?

Serjeant HANNA: I contend they are not; I think it is because there is a difference between the two. This topic arose by my submitting to you that this Commission had no power to transfer to Great Britain the plenary powers over any portion of the Free State which they might determine to transfer back to Great Britain. This Commission has no power to transfer Free State powers back to the British Parliament. I draw a distinction between *having powers* and *exercising them*. We have powers over the whole of Northern Ireland; they are not to be exerciseable unless and until Northern territory comes to us. If it was intended that the reserve powers that we have as regards Northern Ireland, *i.e.*, which Great Britain gave to the Free State, should be re-transferred from the Free State, with any portion of territory you transferred from the Free State, I submit Article 12 would have been differently worded. I base my argument on the Treaty itself to show that the whole issue was:—How much of Northern Ireland wants to secede from the Free State?

The CHAIRMAN: You said it was a question of secession. Then, to take Articles 11 and 12, is the word " secession " quite applicable? You pointed out that in the first 10 articles of the Treaty unity is assumed; there is nothing said about a division. Then take Articles 11 to 15. Article 11 is in the nature of a suspensory Article: the powers are not to be exerciseable over a certain area for a certain time. Article 12 goes further and says that under certain conditions the powers shall no longer extend. You pointed out that that was a stronger expression. This procedure having been, in fact, followed Article 11 only came into operation for a very short time. First of all the powers were not exerciseable, and then they did not extend: the powers therefore have never been exercised. They ceased to exist in respect of this territory. Can you say in respect of the territory where they have never existed as powers which could be exercised that that territory is in a position of seceding?

Serjeant HANNA: I think so, Sir.

The CHAIRMAN: The argument that might be used against you is that they had refused to secede and to separate themselves from Great Britain.

Serjeant HANNA: That would be a repudiation by them of the Treaty. They have no authority to repudiate.

The CHAIRMAN: They have this right under Article 12. I am asking how you would meet the fact that under the Treaty the first 10 Articles never became operative. Can you say there was secession?

Serjeant HANNA: The issue of secession has always depended on the wishes of the inhabitants. You will find in Bouverie's Law Dictionary, under " Secession," a complete compendium dealing with the secession of the 11 States in America which led to the War of Secession. The main point in the first part of the Article is that the bedrock of secession is the wishes of the inhabitants. I would ask the Commission to consider what would have been the position of Northern Ireland if those five Articles had not been put in. The Irish Free State would have been over the whole of the country, and a portion of it refusing to recognise and desiring to repudiate the Government—which is another way of seceding. This is a machinery to avoid a war of secession. Supposing the British had not put this clause in. It was put in to protect their own supporters; and it is obvious, without referring to contemporaneous history at all, that it was put in to avoid what would happen in any other country in circumstances which amounted, in fact, to a rebellion of one section of the community against the established government and desiring to establish their own.

I have referred to three reasons why you have no mandate to go into the Free State. The Attorney-General spoke of the safeguarding of minorities. The dispute between the parties—the "list" that has been settled by this Agreement—was, Northern Ireland—that is what they were dealing with, interpreted with reference to the subject matter. That point, we think, is quite clear.

There is only one other matter. You suggested, Sir, in the course of the address of the Attorney-General, the importance to be attached to the fact that there was an existing autonomy—an existing Government—in Northern Ireland, and that there was a possible construction of Article 12 that sufficient might be left in Northern Ireland for the Government to operate upon. I venture to submit that there are certain considerations which you might have been entitled to take into consideration. You might have been entitled to take into consideration political matters. We submit that this is a political consideration, and as it is a topic on which you invited us to address you I would like to say this:—The powers given to the Northern Parliament were of a restricted and limited character; they were, as I ventured to say, enlarged local government powers. Having regard to the population of any portion of the entire of the six counties, it would be possible to have the same powers in one county or two counties or even just in Belfast itself. Northern Ireland is not a Crown Colony. I think it is fairly described as " a portion of Great Britain that has representation in the Imperial Parliament, but has been given very large powers of local government." So far as I am aware, they can do nothing that can affect anybody except themselves.

Mr. FISHER here quoted the legislative powers of Irish Parliaments conferred by Section 4 (1) of the Government of Ireland Act, 1920 (q.v.).

Serjeant HANNA: They give them that power and then proceed to take it away from them. Section 4 says they shall not have power to make laws except on matters within their jurisdiction. If you limit them to two counties and the City of Belfast, they can still continue to make laws as regards workmen's compensation, local government, factories, and those matters that are domestic matters; but they cannot make any laws with reference to any of these topics that are mentioned in Article 4. I think it is no an unfair description of the Northern Parliament to say that, while it has been designated a Parliament, it has only got substantial enlarged powers of local government.

Coming back to the beginning of the last proposition: the only matters you are entitled to consider are matters when, having found the wishes of the inhabitants (however that may be determined) you come to take account of economic and geographic conditions. It would have been open for the parties to have agreed that you should take " *political* " matters into consideration. That has not been done. The phrase " political expediency or convenience " might have been used. The keynote of the position is that the Treaty decreed that the area of Northern Ireland should be governed by the self-determination of the people in favour of it.

The CHAIRMAN: You say this is a political consideration.

Serjeant HANNA: Of course, I use the word "political" in the higher sense.

The CHAIRMAN: It might be said that this point required to be taken into account in considering the intention of the clause.

Serjeant HANNA: I thought you might have thought it came under the head of " economic conditions." It is after determining the wishes of the inhabitants that economic and geographic conditions may be brought in to adjust a boundary fundamentally determined by the wishes of the inhabitants.

The CHAIRMAN : You mean that it might be said that the question of the possibility of the Province of Northern Ireland being able to continue its existence with greatly reduced territory is an economic consideration? I was not putting it myself from that point of view, but rather from that of this question having to be considered in deciding the general intention of the clause.

Serjeant HANNA : Our answer is that it is not an economic matter. No one would ever say that the continuance of a Parliament is an economic matter. It can always be adjusted to the size of the area. If you are to assume they are to have a huge Parliament for an area that is very much contracted, that would be very uneconomic. We submit that the words " economic and geographic " qualify the findings of the wishes of the inhabitants. When you have the wishes of the inhabitants in certain districts or counties, then you proceed to adjust them on what may be truly called economic and geographic considerations. The continuance of the Parliament of the present extent in Northern Ireland is not a matter that can affect any particular area and is not an economic matter in the truest sense. Lines of railway, etc., may be matters to be considered by the Commission.

The CHAIRMAN : Those other questions you say are not economic questions.

Serjeant HANNA : It will be a case of cutting the coat according to the cloth. If they get a larger area they can run a larger establishment; and if they get a smaller one they must run a smaller establishment. There is no reason why a Government should be limited—as the present Government of Northern Ireland is—to an arbitrary and artificial area. When I say " arbitrary and artificial " I mean an area which apparently nobody approved of.

(This concluded Serjeant Hanna's address.)

The ATTORNEY-GENERAL then proceeded to deal with the question raised in the letter of the Commission of 28th November, 1924.

HE said : There is only one satisfactory manner in which the wishes of the inhabitants may be ascertained on any subject—that is by asking them.

The results of the elections and other things merely furnish certain indications as to what people desire; they are only very vague indications and consequently I submit, on behalf of the Government of the Irish Free State, that it would be necessary for this Commission to take a plebiscite so as to ascertain directly from the people concerned under which jurisdiction they are anxious to be. The proposition seems elementary.

The CHAIRMAN : You will say something as to the method of taking the plebiscite? The Articles of Agreement do not refer to a plebiscite, and do not provide for conferring on the Commission, or on anyone, powers to take a plebiscite.

The ATTORNEY-GENERAL : So far as powers are concerned, might I suggest that that would probably be incidental? The Treaty, which has been ratified by the British Parliament and the Irish Free State Parliament, provides for the setting up of this Commission, one of whose duties it is to ascertain the wishes of the inhabitants; and I would suggest that that in itself confers upon the Commission all powers necessary and incidental for the purpose.

The CHAIRMAN : Do you mean to say that we could go to any part of the country where we thought a plebiscite was desirable for the purpose of this Article and conduct a plebiscite?

The ATTORNEY-GENERAL : Certainly.

The CHAIRMAN : How could we do that? Take an ordinary election. Many provisions are necessary for the conduct of any ordinary election. If we want to take a plebiscite in any portion of the country which might be affected, how could we, without any legal provision existing to that effect, secure that the vote was properly recorded and that the whole thing was properly conducted?

The ATTORNEY-GENERAL: I do not suggest that you would have power to award penalties for persons who personate.

The CHAIRMAN: A plebiscite would be useless unless conducted in a manner calculated to yield a proper result. Great care would have to be taken as to the persons entitled to vote and as to their freedom and right to vote without their vote being public. Secrecy would be desirable.

The ATTORNEY-GENERAL: The Commission, of course, will have to make arrangements, probably fairly elaborate, in connection with the ascertainment of the wishes of the inhabitants. Of course they will be responsible for the preparation of the registers which will have to be compiled, and which will be the foundation of the vote.

The CHAIRMAN: Do you suggest that we could do that without any legal provision conferring on us express powers to do it?

The ATTORNEY-GENERAL: I suggest so.

The Commission, I suggest, are in a position to start the work of the preparation of the necessary registers. They can appoint persons—local persons or committees—for this purpose with rights of appeal to the Commission and with such other provisions as the Commission consider necessary for securing that the register is a true and proper one. It can do all that.

The CHAIRMAN: Can we do any more? You say we have incidentally the power. Can we do more than any private individual?

The ATTORNEY-GENERAL: Surely.

The CHAIRMAN: What can we do?

The ATTORNEY-GENERAL: A private individual will only have his private rights, but this Commission is a Commission set up under the authority of the Parliament of Great Britain and under the authority of the Parliament of the Irish Free State for the purpose of doing a certain thing. Surely the statutes, or the Treaty with statutes, which set up the Commission, contemplated that the Commission in carrying out that work would have all powers which were necessary for the purpose. That seems to be necessarily implied in setting up the Commission.

The CHAIRMAN: What powers have we that ordinary persons have not, resulting from the terms of our appointment?

The ATTORNEY-GENERAL: You are a statutory body having more than statutory powers, because you are set up by this Treaty. Every Court in Great Britain and Ireland would have to recognise you as being set up for this purpose, and so long as you confined yourself to the work which the Article implies and did not interfere with the private rights of individuals it seems to me that the Courts would be bound to recognise you.

The CHAIRMAN: We could ask people to do things by issuing notices and saying: "We would like you to express your wishes on certain days and at certain hours." Any private individual could do that, and may or may not get a satisfactory response. Is it not the case that if we attempted to get a vote it would depend entirely on voluntary compliance by the inhabitants of the district concerned with our requests? Should we be able to order anybody?

The ATTORNEY-GENERAL: Is there anything to prevent the Commission employing people to prepare lists?

The CHAIRMAN: Apart from arrangements by request, and compliance with requests, have we any power to order anything to be done; to say to a man: "You shall or shall not do this; you shall or shall not interfere with a voter coming to vote"?

The ATTORNEY-GENERAL: There are two stages in the ascertainment of wishes; (1) preparation of registers; (2) taking of the vote.

With regard to (1), I do not quite see that there is any power lacking to this Commission which would be necessary for the preparation of a register.

The CHAIRMAN: What power have we got?

The ATTORNEY-GENERAL: You have power to prepare a register of such people as you may find to be inhabitants. You may not have power to order people to do things. I do not see that at that stage it would be necessary to order people to do anything.

The CHAIRMAN: If you take parliamentary or local government registers, there is a law penalising people who give incorrect information; sometimes also requiring them to give information, etc.; a law which confers powers on the registration authority and imposes penalties on those who do not comply with them. We should depend not on powers, but should appoint A. B. C. or D. to get information if they could. If anybody gave them wrong information and stuffed the registers with bogus names they would have no remedy; they would be able to do no more than any private individual who wanted to compile a list of people. If anyone gave them wrong information they would have no remedy.

The ATTORNEY-GENERAL: I can only make the submission that so far at any rate as the compiling of the register is concerned the Commission could proceed to employ local people providing for the issue of notices and advertisements, and for rights of appeal by people left-off, people could be put on, and all that kind of thing. I have no doubt that the Commission will make up their own mind and probably take advice as to their legal powers in connection with that matter.

The CHAIRMAN: I am seeking advice now. I do not gather that you say we have any real power, but that you say we might do these things without power.

The ATTORNEY-GENERAL: There might be some difficulty in connection with the taking of the vote.

The CHAIRMAN: As regards the compilation of the registers, we should not have the usual powers of putting people on their oath, and there would be embarrassment at that stage. Now as to the actual taking of the vote?

The ATTORNEY-GENERAL: That is a somewhat more difficult matter, but this is a Commission set up to perform very onerous and important duties—set up under the authority of two Parliaments—and if the Commission in the course of its work finds that it needs certain further powers necessary for the effective discharge of the duties imposed on it I suggest what will suggest itself to the Commission:— that they should ask for the powers necessary for the purpose.

Mr. FISHER: That is a long job.

The CHAIRMAN: You are inclined to think that the Commission would need some powers conferred on it by law to take a vote? If you refer to the Versailles and Austrian Treaties, the provisions under those Treaties as to plebiscites were most elaborate. But this Treaty says nothing whatever, and makes no provision at all, of the character which is to found in those Treaties. The Commission is simply told to ascertain the boundary in accordance with the wishes of the inhabitants; no direction is given that it is to take plebiscites, and no powers to do so are given. I think that point requires consideration in connection with your contention that the right way of the Commission doing its work, as contemplated by Article 12, is to take plebiscites. If the Article did intend that it stopped very far short of what was really necessary. It contained no clear indication; you have to read it in.

The ATTORNEY-GENERAL: You must consider the difference between the document in question and the Treaty of Versailles. This is a very short document, prepared in a certain amount of hurry, headed " Articles of Agreement for a Treaty."

The CHAIRMAN: Indicating that it was something preparatory?

The ATTORNEY-GENERAL: To a certain extent it indicates that; and it is a very short document. So far as the ascertainment of the wishes of the inhabitants is concerned, it merely sets up this Commission. It is the duty of the Commission to ascertain the wishes of the inhabitants, and the Commission must ascertain the wishes of the inhabitants in a satisfactory manner. How can the wishes of the inhabitants be ascertained in any other manner save by asking each person, each inhabitant, how he wishes to vote on this question? No other satisfactory method certainly suggests itself to me.

The CHAIRMAN: You referred to the question of results of elections and the census records as possible sources of information. I should like to know what you say with regard to both those possible sources of information. Another possible source is to make enquiries and find out what the representative people of districts say.

The ATTORNEY-GENERAL: With regard to making enquiries from representative people, surely the persons you are to consult are inhabitants. Local representative people may give you a pretty fair indication or an indication which is far from accurate, according to the extent of their knowledge; but, however satisfactory it may be, it must necessarily be guesswork to a large extent. Only the man himself can tell you whether he wishes to be put under the jurisdiction of the Irish Free State or under that of the Parliament of Northern Ireland.

As to elections. I take it that this is to be ascertained as the Treaty (of 6th December, 1921) directs, and presumably as at that date. What elections are you to have regard to? You had elections in 1918 to the British House of Commons. A great number of people undoubtedly voted in favour of persons who abstained from that Parliament; certain other persons voted in favour of members who went to that Parliament; but it is quite possible that a person who voted in favour of a member who intended going to the British Parliament at that time would now prefer to be in the Irish Free State—and would in 1921 have preferred to be in the Irish Free State or *vice versa*. Take the elections of 1921. When these elections were held there was serious strife going on in Ireland. That strife has come to an end now, and persons who voted at that time in favour of members who were prepared to sit in the Parliament set up by the Government of Ireland Act may have done so by reason of that strife, and if possible to try to avoid it; whereas now, or in December, 1921, when strife came to an end and the Treaty was entered into, they might vote the other way.

Take the census. I do not know what it would give. It would give religious beliefs according to district electoral divisions.

Mr. FISHER: The census is old; 1911.

The ATTORNEY-GENERAL: Yes; and it only gives you religions.

The CHAIRMAN: To what extent do you regard that as an indication?

The ATTORNEY-GENERAL: It gives a rough indication and no more.

The CHAIRMAN: Apart from the antiquity of the census, supposing you had a recent one? I do not know what the extent of the change is likely to have been since 1911. Can you infer from the existence of a majority, if it was a substantial majority in a particular electoral division of Catholics or Protestants as the case might be, but the votes of the inhabitants (if they voted) would be to go in to the Free State or to remain in Northern Ireland?

The ATTORNEY-GENERAL: I think it would give you a certain loose indication and no more; because there are plenty of Catholics in Northern Ireland who, I think, would vote in favour of being in Northern Ireland, and there are plenty of other religions who would be in favour of being in the Free State. It is an indication and no more.

Mr. FISHER: We come back to a plebiscite for which, I am afraid, we should want an Act of Parliament. I do not see anyone in a disturbed district opening a polling post; the police might simply move them on.

The ATTORNEY-GENERAL: I take it that in taking a vote in the six counties of Northern Ireland the Commission would apply to the British Government for such facilities within the six counties as it may require. Great Britain is a party to this Treaty. This Commission is acting under the Treaty. It is certainly entitled to call upon Great Britain, as one of the parties, for all such facilities within the jurisdiction of the Parliament of Great Britain as it may require for the purpose of carrying out its work. I think it would be the duty of the Commission to call for all such facilities. It may possibly happen that the Commission will require greater powers than the mere granting of facilities of that kind; and if the Commission should find itself in that position, then it should certainly ask for these extra powers, which may possibly necessitate the passing of an Act of Parliament.

The CHAIRMAN: Would you proceed with the suggestions that I understand you were proposing to make with regard to the way in which the plebiscite should be carried out?

The ATTORNEY-GENERAL: The Commission must first ascertain who is entitled to vote. It must make up a register for that purpose of the inhabitants entitled to vote under Article 12. That would necessitate some definition of "inhabitants." Mr. Serjeant Hanna referred in the course of his argument to a case in which an inhabitant was defined as "a person having a permanent residence." I will accept that and put it forward to the Commission.

The CHAIRMAN: What is the test of permanency?

The ATTORNEY-GENERAL: Six months' residence. It would be open to the Commission either to prescribe beforehand what the test was to be or else to leave it to the local body, with the right of appeal to the Commission, to ascertain in each particular case whether or not a person claiming to be put on this register had a permanent residence on the material date. A parliamentary register came into force on 15th December, 1921; that would be a basis to work upon. It has been brought up to date; but I am dealing with this date of 6th December, 1921, as being the material one.

The CHAIRMAN: Do you suggest if we were to compile a register of such persons we should only enter on the register those who had a permanent residence on the 6th December, 1921?

The ATTORNEY-GENERAL: That is my suggestion; that this Treaty must be taken on the date it was entered into. It was ratified by the Dail shortly afterwards and by the British Parliament by Act of Parliament on 31st March, 1922, but had previously been ratified by both Houses by resolution in, I think, December, 1921.

The CHAIRMAN: The Treaty says the Commission is to determine the boundary in accordance with the wishes of the inhabitants, but does not mention a date. If you take that Article as it stands, is it not an instruction to the Commission when it gets to work to consult the wishes of the people who are then inhabitants?

The ATTORNEY-GENERAL: No, no, no; with all respect, it is contemplated that the Commission will operate at once.

The CHAIRMAN: It is a point which requires to be gone into. An authority has said that an Act of Parliament is always speaking; you do not go back. There is nothing in this clause, apart from some general rule, that you suggest that we might perhaps be required to apply. There is no reference to the date; it simply says that if an address is presented the Commission *shall* be appointed and this Commission *shall* determine the boundary in accordance with the wishes of the inhabitants.

The ATTORNEY-GENERAL: Supposing that for certain purposes an Act of Parliament may speak from a certain date. That will depend on the special purpose for which it is made. Here you are dealing with a Treaty providing that a certain thing is to be done: it does not specify any time for doing it. The ordinary presumption is that it is to be done within a reasonable time. Supposing instead of taking the date of the Treaty as the material date you allow several years to elapse and then, when finally ascertaining the wishes of the inhabitants, you ascertain them as at a later date. See the abuses that might give rise to. It may enable one party or another to flood into areas for instance where the balance one way or another was very small.

The CHAIRMAN: Is there any reason to suppose that has been done?

The ATTORNEY-GENERAL: There are, I am told, a great many people who have left Northern Ireland in consequence of various things that have happened there. I would rather base my contention on the broad ground that when a Treaty provides a thing is to be done it should be done promptly, and when it provides for the ascertainment of wishes of people without specifying a date, presumably it must intend as at the date the Treaty was entered into.

The CHAIRMAN: We cannot ascertain the wishes of inhabitants who have died, or as at the date in 1921. The best we could hope is that we could get the wishes of the inhabitants to-day, and those wishes would not be those of 1921. What you are asking us to do is to interpret this so as to put a new difficulty in the way of our work. We are to ask a man " What would you have liked in December, 1921? "

The ATTORNEY-GENERAL: I have no objection to your putting the question in that form.

The CHAIRMAN: You said the thing should be done at once. On the pure questions of interpretation, I would ask you to consider further if the question of the wishes of the inhabitants is not to be taken as meaning the wishes at the time the Commission comes to deal with the matter. You may have some authority we may consider as bearing on that particular question. I foresee extra difficulty in going back.

The ATTORNEY-GENERAL: So far as the practical difficulty of the register is concerned, I do not think there would be any difficulty by taking the 1921 register instead of the 1924 one, because you have a certain basis to work upon, viz., the register of December, 1921. Of course that is very incomplete, but any register you get will be incomplete.

The CHAIRMAN: Do you regard the qualifications which enabled a man or woman to be registered as a voter on the 1921 register as appropriate for the purpose of any vote that may be taken on this question as to boundary?

The ATTORNEY-GENERAL: I think it is very strong *primâ facie* evidence, but I do not think it is complete. One qualification would be business premises as distinct from residence, and I can foresee the possibility of a man living on one side of the border and having business premises on the other and being registered as a Parliamentary voter in respect of the business premises. He could not be held to be an inhabitant on the other side. These cases would not be very numerous.

The CHAIRMAN: It would be an advantage if you could let us know to-morrow any proposal as to who should vote if a vote is taken; as to what modifications (if any) should be made in the qualification for a Parliamentary vote for the purpose of arriving at a suitable qualification for such a vote as you suggest under Article 12.

The ATTORNEY-GENERAL: The question of women would arise. Women are inhabitants just as much as men, and are entitled to vote for the purpose of Article 12 of the Treaty.

The CHAIRMAN: Some women are qualified under Parliamentary qualifications.

The ATTORNEY-GENERAL: Very few; in the first place they have to be over 30.

The CHAIRMAN: We might deal with that in detail if you have a suggestion to make as to what would be a qualification.

The ATTORNEY-GENERAL: What I suggest is: " persons having a permanent residence in the area on the 6th December, 1921." That must be taken subject to some qualifications as to age.

The CHAIRMAN: The qualification in the case of a man is 21, and for a woman 30.

The ATTORNEY-GENERAL: Yes; the important thing is to secure that the persons voting are in a position to make up their own minds. Consequently, when you come to deal with people who in December 1921 were under the age at which the Commission considers a person would be entitled to express preference, and who have since attained that age, my suggestion would be that they should be put on the register; and that you should put on the register people who in 1921 had attained, say, the age of 18 years.

The CHAIRMAN: That is taking advantage of the passage of time.

The ATTORNEY-GENERAL: Not for the benefit of either party.

The CHAIRMAN: I only mean so far as those people are concerned who you treat not as they were in 1921 but as they are now.

The ATTORNEY-GENERAL: The only object in keeping them off in 1921 was that they had not reached the age at which they were entitled to express a preference: now they have reached that age.

Mr. FISHER: It comes to this: we make a register from this date.

The ATTORNEY-GENERAL: Oh, no; instead of putting the age of 21 you put an age of 18. That is my suggestion as to qualification.

The CHAIRMAN: You do not give us any special definition of " permanent residence."

The ATTORNEY-GENERAL: I suggest " residence on the 6th January, 1921." I do not use the term " permanent residence."

The CHAIRMAN: Does it mean that you would fetch people back if we adopted this date? You would say to everybody who had been in the country on 6th December, 1921, and was duly qualified on that date that, though they were no longer inhabitants, they were to come back and exercise the rights of voting?

The ATTORNEY-GENERAL: They would be entitled to do so.

Dr. MacNEILL: Would you do that with an ordinary Parliamentary vote?

The ATTORNEY-GENERAL: Yes. The military and police forces who were there on active service at that time would not, I think, come under the definition of " inhabitants," and they should not be put on the register.

The CHAIRMAN: You say you would take a permanent residence; the men who were at the beginning of 1921 in the country?

The ATTORNEY-GENERAL: Yes; residence from that date up to 6th December, 1921: he must have had some residence there; for instance, a man having his home there who happened on 6th December to be away on business.

Mr. FISHER: If a man is a householder that makes it easy of course.

The ATTORNEY-GENERAL: The cases in which it is difficult are very few as compared to the ordinary cases.

The CHAIRMAN: Is there not a migratory labour population in some parts of the country?

The ATTORNEY-GENERAL: Not to any great extent.

(*The hearing was adjourned at 5.30 p.m.*)

SECOND DAY.

The HEARING was resumed at 11 a.m. on 5th December, 1924, the same persons being present as at the previous day's sitting.

The ATTORNEY-GENERAL: I was dealing yesterday with the question of registers and the ascertaining of persons entitled to vote. I submitted that the material date to be taken into account in compiling that register was the 6th December, 1921. You asked me whether I could refer you to any authority upon that. I have not been able to get any reading in the interval with the exception of a reference in Hall's International Law, paragraph 116, dealing with Treaties, which says:—" Neither party " (to the Treaty) " can make its binding effect dependent on its will upon conditions other than those contemplated at the moment when the contract was entered into." I rely upon that paragraph as showing that it is the conditions applicable when the Treaty was entered into that must be taken into account, and that delay should not be allowed to prejudice the position.

The CHAIRMAN: You see the provisions of Articles 11 and 12 themselves involve the elapse of some time before the Commission can get to work—" Until the expiration of one month from the passing of the Act of Parliament for the ratification of this instrument. . ." The Act of Parliament for the ratification was considered for formal purposes to be the Act approving the Constitution, was it not?

The ATTORNEY-GENERAL: Yes.

The CHAIRMAN: In fact, this Act of Parliament to which reference is made in Article 11 was not passed until December, 1922. Is that correct?

The ATTORNEY-GENERAL: That is correct.

The CHAIRMAN: After that, I am taking the programme of the Treaty which says that the Address is to be presented within one month after the ratification. Ratification took place at the end of 12 months or thereabouts. Then there was the one month. I understand the Address was presented at the beginning of the month. It could only be after that that the Commission could come into existence.

The ATTORNEY-GENERAL: That is what actually happened. There was an interval of one year; but that was not necessarily contemplated by the Treaty.

The CHAIRMAN: It did not fix any time limit.

The ATTORNEY-GENERAL: It did not fix any time limit certainly. By implication I suggest it did fix the period of one year as the ultimate limit, because in Article 17, dealing with the Provisional Government, you will find that: (*Article 17 was here quoted*). That was the ultimate limit of delay.

The CHAIRMAN: You mean the ratification could not be later than 12 months?

The ATTORNEY-GENERAL: Within 12 months it was contemplated that a Parliament and Government of the Irish Free State should be fully constituted and set up; that is, that a Constitution should be enacted in the meantime.

The CHAIRMAN: Was it, as a matter of fact?

The ATTORNEY-GENERAL: Yes.

The CHAIRMAN: The date of the Constitution Act of the Parliament of the United Kingdom was the 5th December, 1922.

Mr. FISHER: One day ahead. It was previously enacted by the Constituent Assembly.

The ATTORNEY-GENERAL: That is the Act we have to look to at the moment.

Mr. FISHER: That meets my point.

The ATTORNEY-GENERAL: It was of course contemplated that there should be some little delay. The most delay that could take place, as contemplated by the Teaty, was one year.

The CHAIRMAN: The most delay that could take place before ratification—sometime after which this had to be done. I am only just trying to see how near you can get to suggesting any fixed date.

The ATTORNEY-GENERAL: Once ratification had taken place, and the Parliament and Government of the Irish Free State had been set up, there was no need for any further delay.

The CHAIRMAN: As soon as the Address had been presented.

The ATTORNEY-GENERAL: There was only a month allowed.

Dr. MacNEILL: Suppose that for some reason that need not be specified, there had been a much longer delay—five, six, or seven years—suppose that some kind of upheaval took place to prevent it. How would you argue in that case?

The ATTORNEY-GENERAL: My argument would be that the lapse of a period of that kind might very seriously prejudice one party or another; and that was not contemplated by the Treaty.

The CHAIRMAN: You say that, apart from any express provision of the Treaty, it might be unfair after delay such as has occurred to take the inhabitants as they are to-day. Do you say that the conditions are such that actually it would be unfair? Have you evidence that the changes which have taken place since the end of 1922—if we take that date—are such that it would be unfair to take the wishes of the inhabitants now?

The ATTORNEY-GENERAL: I think it would be, because certain things have taken place within the six counties of Northern Ireland which have resulted in a great many people going away. I will not go further than that.

The CHAIRMAN: That is a matter that could be dealt with in the definition of the inhabitants who are to be entitled to vote.

The ATTORNEY-GENERAL: It could. Matters like that were dealt with in the Treaty of Versailles in various places.

The CHAIRMAN: Your proposal yesterday was that we should exclude people who are now inhabitants on the ground that they were not inhabitants at this earlier date. I think really you would have to put some evidence before us on this point. It seems rather a question of the working of the Treaty than of its interpretation. You cannot say any date is fixed by the Article as it stands. The Article might have suggested "the inhabitants at a particular date"; it did not.

The ATTORNEY-GENERAL: Possibly evidence with reference to that matter will be put before the Commission at some of its local sittings It is necessary for the Commission to fix some date as the test—whether a date in the past or in the future—they must fix some date.

The CHAIRMAN: It would seem that the natural course for the Commission to take, apart from special representations and in view of the absence of any provision fixing a date, would be to take the position as at the date when it gets to work. You suggest that our considerations should lead us either to take another date or to adopt a special definition of "inhabitant" which would meet the position you outline.

The ATTORNEY-GENERAL: My submission is that the natural date would be the date of the Treaty.

If the persons who entered into the Treaty could at that moment have ascertained all the necessary facts they themselves would have fixed the boundary. They were unable to do it at the moment; they had not the necessary information before them, and they set up this Commission for the purpose of doing that specific thing. My submission is that the Commission should put itself in the position of those who negotiated and signed this Treaty. The Commission has really to fill in gaps which were left in the Treaty by those who signed it.

The CHAIRMAN: You argue that the Treaty was dealing with conditions existing at the time?

The ATTORNEY-GENERAL: Existing at December, 1921.

Dr. MacNEILL: If they had anticipated altered conditions, which are not in evidence at present, they would have made express provision.

The ATTORNEY-GENERAL: Yes, they would have made express provision. If they wanted this boundary to be ascertained at a date some years ahead they would have specified it. The natural date, in my submission, is the date of the Treaty.

The CHAIRMAN: Your submission is that that is the meaning of the Treaty? Supposing the Commission did not put that interpretation which you contended for yesterday on the terms of Article 12, I want to know if you have an alternative submission that under the circumstances actually existing steps must be taken by the Commission to prevent prejudice by the delay?

The ATTORNEY-GENERAL: Certainly.

The CHAIRMAN: That is a point on which you will no doubt consider whether you desire at some later stage to give evidence to the Commission.

The ATTORNEY-GENERAL: Certainly. Generally, in connection with the work of the Commission, may I say that I and the other Counsel who appear here on behalf of the Irish Free State have been to some extent at a disadvantage in this way:—We did not quite understand the matters to which we were to address ourselves. We knew of course in a very general way, but we did not know specifically the points which we were required to discuss here before the Commission, and consequently we submit it would be right to allow us to supplement any written statement that has been put in and any oral statement which we make here by subsequent written or oral statements, should the necessity arise.

The CHAIRMAN: I think the Commission quite understood that from the terms of the letter sent with the formal statement.

The ATTORNEY-GENERAL: On the specific point you put, evidence with reference to this matter could be put before the Commission at some suitable time. I think that is all I have to say with reference to persons entitled to vote.

The next question which would arise in the natural course would be that of local area or, if I may so put it, the local unit within which the wishes of the inhabitants are to be ascertained. In this connection I think it might be useful if I refer shortly to a few of the Articles of the Treaty of Versailles dealing with similar matters. (*Counsel here quoted from Article 88 which defines the area within which the vote is to be taken, and deals with the question of who is to vote.*)

The ATTORNEY-GENERAL (continuing): In the Article dealing with Upper Silesia and other Articles dealing with other areas you will find similar provisions with slight variations. The provisions are identical: that the result of the vote is to be determined by communes according to the vote in each commune. It will be necessary for the Commission to fix some local area, some unit, which will correspond to the Commune. Various areas have been from time to time suggested:—counties, parliamentary constituencies, poor law unions, etc.

Dr. MacNEILL: What are the civil authorities that actually operate within the administrative areas?

The ATTORNEY-GENERAL: The administrative authorities you have are:—The County Council administering a county; the Poor Law Union administering a Poor Law area. The Poor Law Union is the smallest administrative area. I would suggest that that would probably be the area which would most closely resemble the Commune.

The CHAIRMAN: What size is the Poor Law Union area?

The ATTORNEY-GENERAL: They vary in different places.

The CHAIRMAN: How many are there to a county?

The ATTORNEY-GENERAL: Two, three or even more, up to six. In each Poor Law Union area there is a town in which the Union is situated, and the area generally speaking is all round that town; the town is somewhere near the centre.

The CHAIRMAN: May not the Poor Law Union area include several towns?

The ATTORNEY-GENERAL: Sometimes; the principal town is somewhere near the centre of the Union area generally.

Mr. FISHER: The town is the administrative seat.

The ATTORNEY-GENERAL: And is usually the market town as well: the Unions were placed there for convenience. "Union" in Ireland is the name for "workhouse," and you have in them a great number of people from the Union area.

The CHAIRMAN: What relation does the Union area bear to the Rural District?

The ATTORNEY-GENERAL: The Union and the Rural District are identical, subject to this: where you have a Rural District corresponding with the Union and in the centre of that a town of considerable size, the town may constitute an urban area and there is an Urban District Council for the town; but it is surrounded by the Rural District which is administered by the Rural District Council.

Dr. MacNEILL: In that case the Poor Law Union would comprise both.

The ATTORNEY-GENERAL: Yes.

Dr. MacNEILL: I think it means a group of parishes originally.

The CHAIRMAN: Do you say the Communes in Upper Silesia correspond to Poor Law Unions?

The ATTORNEY-GENERAL: They are the smallest administrative area, like the Poor Law Union. So far as size is concerned they vary; some Communes would be smaller and some larger.

The CHAIRMAN: The Rural District is an administrative area for certain purposes—roads and so on, is it not?

The ATTORNEY-GENERAL: Yes, they deal with that.

The CHAIRMAN: The Urban District would also be in a sense an administrative area?

The ATTORNEY-GENERAL: The difficulty in taking an urban district is that it is completely surrounded by the rural district.

The CHAIRMAN: Your submission is that these Poor Law Unions correspond to the Communes? Supposing they do?

The ATTORNEY-GENERAL: The membership of the Poor Law Union is the same as the Rural District Council; the same persons are elected; they sit in a double capacity.

The CHAIRMAN: Assuming that the rural districts correspond with the Communes, does that take us very far? In the Treaty of Versailles the Commune was fixed, and whatever Commission was appointed to deal with the question of plebiscite and so on was bound to that. So far as we are concerned it was not fixed, and we have to consider when we come to deal with areas what is the best unit. The fact that some particular unit was adopted in another Treaty does not in itself take us very far along our path.

The ATTORNEY-GENERAL: It is very strong evidence that this is a convenient unit to take. Consider it from this point of view:—in the first place, it is an area of convenient size and, secondly, it has the great advantage that it is an administrative unit; and if a question of transfer arose it is the unit which could be transferred with the least possible trouble. The unit could be transferred with all its machinery. Though the fact that the Commune was set out in the Treaty of Versailles as the local unit does not bind the Commission in any way, I suggest it is very strong evidence that this is a convenient unit.

The CHAIRMAN: I take it that we have to be guided by the conditions of the country with which we have to deal.

The ATTORNEY-GENERAL: Certainly.

Mr. FISHER: In arranging these units was it not kept in mind as much as possible to keep a balance of religions and parties? They were not intended to be a pocket of any party or creed?

The ATTORNEY-GENERAL: I think not. 1838 was the foundation of them. I think they were formed entirely from the point of view of the convenience of local administration.

In another Article of the Treaty of Versailles (Article 48) dealing with the Saar Basin, where the frontier was merely delimited on the spot without ascertaining the wishes of the inhabitants, it is nevertheless provided in the second and last paragraph of the Article:

"In those parts of the preceding line which do not coincide with administrative boundaries the Commission will endeavour to keep to the line indicated, while taking into consideration, so far as is possible, local economic interests and existing communal boundaries."

In every way the Treaty tried to avoid interfering with these local administrative units, because in the case in which the wishes of the inhabitants were ascertained, they were ascertained by reference to the local administrative units, and in cases where the wishes of the inhabitants were not ascertained, the Commissioners were directed to take into consideration the existing communal boundaries.

It stands to reason that when a question of transfer arises, if local administrative areas are split up there will be considerable dislocation: statutory provisions will have to be made for linking up these dismembered portions with some other units; whereas if the administrative unit is dealt with as a whole it can be transferred without the slightest difficulty, taking all its machinery with it.

The CHAIRMAN : The administrative conditions are one of the things we should take into account in defining our areas, you say? Do you include them under economic or geographic conditions?

The ATTORNEY-GENERAL : No; the way I would use them is that the Commission must fix some unit, and I suggest that this is the most convenient one, for the reasons I have stated. The unit has not been prescribed by the Treaty itself; therefore the Commission must fix it.

The CHAIRMAN : The Commission, under the terms of the Treaty, must use its discretion in the matter. I want to see where we are with regard to the terms of the Treaty. The terms actually refer to the wishes of the inhabitants and to the economic and geographic conditions : they do not mention administrative conditions. The question will arise if you can take a smaller unit; whether that does not enable you to follow more closely the wishes of the inhabitants than when you take a larger unit.

The ATTORNEY-GENERAL : In considering this question of unit, economic and geographic conditions will not come in at all at this stage.

The CHAIRMAN : But surely they do. Supposing we take a most unreasonable unit which defied geography and economics? That would be a serious thing.

The ATTORNEY-GENERAL : The Commission must act with reason.

The CHAIRMAN : If we treat each unit we take as a suitable subject for transfer or for placing wholly on one side or another, in selecting the unit you cannot blind yourself to the economic or geographic conditions.

The ATTORNEY-GENERAL : I was dealing with the provision under Article 12 regarding economic and geographic conditions and was merely suggesting that that provision did not operate at this particular moment, for the reason that consideration is to be given to these conditions in Article 12 only after the wishes of the inhabitants have been ascertained.

The CHAIRMAN : I do not see why we are to wait until that stage. Why are we to blind ourselves?

The ATTORNEY-GENERAL (*quoting from Article* 12) : The Commission " shall determine in accordance with the wishes of the inhabitants, so far as may be compatible with economic and geographic conditions . . ." You first ascertain the wishes of the inhabitants, according to my submission, and where you find that a boundary fixed solely with regard to the wishes of the inhabitants would have grave consequences from an economic or geographic point of view, then you alter the boundary so as to fit in with the economic and geographic conditions. It is only in this case that the provision in Article 12 operates.

The CHAIRMAN : If you take the wishes of the inhabitants with reference to a unit which is bad economically and geographically, you have not advanced your purpose much, have you?

The ATTORNEY-GENERAL : Of course not; and the Commission must fix their unit in accordance with reason and good sense; they must take a convenient unit. In fixing your unit, geographic and economic conditions would come in as aiding good sense. My only submission was that this provision here does not apply at that stage. The Poor Law Union area suggests itself to me as a reasonable and suitable unit for this purpose.

In the Treaty of Versailles you find the vote is to be taken by Communes, subject to the economic and geographic conditions. You will find it in several places.

(*Counsel here referred to Article* 97 *of such Treaty, dealing with East Prussia; and to Article* 88, *dealing with the boundary between Germany and Poland; also to Clause* 5 *of the annex to the latter Article.*)

There will be various other questions as to the manner in which the votes will be taken which will arise subsequently.

The CHAIRMAN: Before you leave the question of the unit of area, I think you ought to deal perhaps with possible alternatives. You have mentioned one area as the one you suggest: there are other possible units of area. We should like to hear what you have to say about those other units. There are smaller and also larger units.

The ATTORNEY-GENERAL: There is no smaller administrative unit.

Mr. FISHER: The polling district? That is only a section of the Poor Law area, is it not?

The ATTORNEY-GENERAL: It is not a unit for any purpose save for that of convenience of recording votes.

The CHAIRMAN: The rural district electoral division returns members to rural district authorities. Inside the rural district electoral division there are polling districts.

The ATTORNEY-GENERAL: There is only one polling booth for each area. Each electoral division returns one member, and there is only one polling booth within that area. He is returned as a member of the Rural District Council and also as a member of the Board of Poor Law Guardians which control the Poor Law Union.

The CHAIRMAN: I thought these rural districts varied in size. One Poor Law Union would include a considerable number of District Electoral Divisions?

The ATTORNEY-GENERAL: Yes.

The CHAIRMAN: It is therefore a much smaller unit than your Poor Law Union?

The ATTORNEY-GENERAL: Very much smaller; but it is not a unit in any sense. It is not put together from any geographic or economic point of view.

The CHAIRMAN: You have to consider geography in polling, do you not?

The ATTORNEY-GENERAL: It is so small.

The CHAIRMAN: Your strong point for the Poor Law unit is that it is an administrative unit, and you are contending that the best course to take is to deal with administrative units. I quite understand that. The Poor Law Union appears to be a large unit. If we are to follow the wishes of the inhabitants, there is something to be said for a smaller unit —for Rural District Electoral Divisions. In the figures this unit bulks largely, and if you say it is not a suitable unit to take I want to know why it is not suitable. One is that it is not an administrative unit.

The ATTORNEY-GENERAL: Taking a vote in that way would lead to endless confusion. You have a vote taken in each District Electoral Division of a Poor Law Union; there are, say, 40 District Electoral Divisions in the Union. You have, say, 22 voting one way and 18 the other way, and they are mixed up amongst one another. It would be, I suggest, impossible to take such a small unit as that.

The CHAIRMAN: Where elections are held for Poor Law Unions, they are held at polling stations in each of these District Electoral Divisions?

The ATTORNEY-GENERAL: Yes.

The CHAIRMAN: Supposing the voting is organised for our purpose and we followed the usual custom; then again they would be voting in District Electoral Divisions at the polling place to which the voter belonged. In getting the vote we should get the particulars of the voting in the District Electoral Divisions if we chose to have the results counted separately. That is so, is it not?

The ATTORNEY-GENERAL: Yes.

The CHAIRMAN: That would be, in fact, our voting unit, whatever effect we gave to the information derived from it. Unless we took pains to have the voting papers mixed up, we should be in possession of information as to how each District Electoral Division had voted.

The ATTORNEY-GENERAL: If you take the vote at each place which is a voting place for a Poor Law Union, and if the votes are counted separately, you will have the votes for the divisions and also for the Union. It would have certain conveniences.

The CHAIRMAN: We should be getting this information unless we took pains not to get it. It would be more detailed information as to the distribution in reference to this question.

The ATTORNEY-GENERAL: I think it would be too detailed if taken separately.

The CHAIRMAN: That would mean an examination of these boundaries and so on. I want to be quite clear whether we should say to ourselves beforehand: "We are not to look at anything but information as to totals for Poor Law Unions? Would you say that?

The ATTORNEY-GENERAL: If you consider it a proper unit for transfer, then my submission is that no advantage is gained by having separate returns for District Electoral Divisions.

The CHAIRMAN: Do you think that we could come to that general conclusion beforehand that we would tie ourselves to these units which are shown on this map (*produced*) as sacrosanct units and must deal with each one completely?

The ATTORNEY-GENERAL: I suggest you must fix some unit. The result of the voting in any of these areas can always be rectified by geographic and economic conditions.

The CHAIRMAN: Surely then we want the most detailed information as to the wishes of the inhabitants.

The ATTORNEY-GENERAL: The other two units that have been suggested are Parliamentary constituencies, and counties. I fancy these units are too large.

Mr. FISHER: How do the Parliamentary constituencies stand now; are all the counties lumped together?

The ATTORNEY-GENERAL: Yes.

Dr. MacNEILL:: Have you any information with regard to "Communes" which you quoted as supplying precedent; as to the population and extent of these Communes as compared with areas in Ireland?

The ATTORNEY-GENERAL: Compared with Poor Law Unions some are smaller and some larger: they vary a great deal more than the Poor Law Unions.

Dr. MacNEILL: Roughly speaking, do you think they would correspond?

The CHAIRMAN: I suppose there is some official record of the voting which would show what the Commune was as regards numbers?

The ATTORNEY-GENERAL here produced a document, prepared by an official of the Northern Boundary Bureau, dealing with Communes in different countries on the Continent.

The ATTORNEY-GENERAL: On the subject of District Electoral Divisions, may I say that since 1921 very considerable changes have been made; they have been re-arranged—and re-arranged, as we suggest, for political purposes.

The CHAIRMAN: That is in Northern Ireland?

The ATTORNEY-GENERAL: Yes; in the six counties.

The CHAIRMAN: The census figures relate to the old ones.

The ATTORNEY-GENERAL: Yes. If you take a District Electoral Division I suggest it should be that of 1921.

The CHAIRMAN: I take it these Divisions exist on both sides of the Border; that there is no difference in the system?

The ATTORNEY-GENERAL: Oh no.

Mr. FISHER: The Poor Law system is more or less under transformation in the South.

The ATTORNEY-GENERAL: Completely transformed.

Mr. FISHER: Do they vote by Counties, or by proportional representation?

The ATTORNEY-GENERAL: There is an Act going through at the present time. At the present time the Rural District Council has not been abolished in the Free State, but the Act will have that effect.

In a great many cases the District Electoral Division is merely a congregation of a few town-lands—5, 6 or 8 town-lands.

The CHAIRMAN: Town-lands is a smaller unit?

Dr. MacNEILL: That is the old unit; more or less arbitrary. They originated in a variety of ways and they change. The owner, the landlord, had the power to change town-lands. They do not correspond to anything.

Serjeant HANNA: The D. E. D. register is made up by town-lands, and though its results might be open to criticism, under the present system you can still eliminate from them the voting of the town-lands in respect of the boundaries of the D. E. D.'s.

Dr. NacNEILL: Census statistics are collected by town-lands, are they not?

The ATTORNEY-GENERAL. Yes.

Mr. FISHER: Are the voters described by town-lands?

The ATTORNEY-GENERAL: Yes. Referring to the written statement submitted to the Commission, page 3. You will find as a result of the Parliamentary elections of 1921 in Northern Ireland, 12 members refused to take any part in the proceedings of that Parliament, as follows:—4 for the counties of Fermanagh and Tyrone, 2 for Co. Armagh, 1 for Co. Antrim, 1 for West Belfast, 2 for Co. Down, and 2 for Londonderry.

Taking that as an index, I suggest that a vote must be taken in the Counties of Fermanagh, Tyrone, Armagh, Down, and Londonderry.

The CHAIRMAN: You omit two places. One was returned for the County of Antrim and one for West Belfast.

The ATTORNEY-GENERAL: It is well known that in a portion of the County of Antrim there is a very considerable community who would be strongly in favour of being under the jurisdiction of the Irish Free State; but I am afraid that they are so much cut off by a population whose views are the other way that for geographical reasons it would be impossible for them to come in.

Prima facie, I would suggest that the vote should be taken over the entire of Northern Ireland; but at the moment I do not ask you to take a vote over any portion of the County of Antrim or in the City of Belfast. That is of course without prejudice to any claims which may be made by local persons or local bodies.

The CHAIRMAN: Without prejudice to the Commission considering any claims that they may receive from other parties; but so far as the Government of the Irish Free State is concerned you do not ask us to take a vote in those areas?

The ATTORNEY-GENERAL: That is so.

Dr. MacNEILL: Following your argument of yesterday, what it would point to was that the voting should be over the entire area of the six counties. Do you think there are practical reasons which would enable the Commission to come to a conclusion that would not be likely to be disputed? You are suggesting that the evidence of these Parliamentary elections would be suitable evidence to enable the Commission to restrict the area of voting?

The ATTORNEY-GENERAL: Yes.

The CHAIRMAN: In that case then you indicate the view that it would be undesirable to ask people to vote if, as a matter of fact, the vote could not affect their destiny.

The ATTORNEY-GENERAL: In that case it would be useless.

The CHAIRMAN: I want you to consider this position: the fate of one district of course may depend (whatever unit you take) on what is done with another. There is the possibility of a change which may be desired in one region being barred by the fact that another region is against it. In considering the question of a vote, should not that consideration be taken into account? Might it not be advisable to proceed by steps in respect of any particular area and not to start by taking votes everywhere, many of which might be quite ineffective owing to the fact that certain decisions which might be taken with regard to other areas would bar anything being done with respect to some of the areas?

The ATTORNEY-GENERAL: I suggest that on this evidence alone there is an unanswerable case for taking the vote in the five counties I have mentioned simultaneously.

The CHAIRMAN: Is the voter in the best possible position for coming to a decision on the question asked him? He has no idea what is going to happen to the other counties and towns. Ought we not to try to put him in a position to judge in a more practical way?

The ATTORNEY-GENERAL: That is not contemplated by the Treaty.

The CHAIRMAN: From the practical point of view, is there not something to be said for giving the voter a chance to make up his mind on the facts of the situation?
In the Austrian Treaty there are two zones in which votes are to be taken. The vote was to be taken successively, first in one and then in another; but if the vote in the first zone went in a particular direction no vote was to be taken in the second zone.

The ATTORNEY-GENERAL: There may have been very strong local reasons for that. I am aware of the provision but not aware of the local conditions that suggested the course.

The CHAIRMAN: Was it not that it was impossible to transfer the second zone if the first one was not transferred?

The ATTORNEY-GENERAL: I mean I have no knowledge of the local conditions so far as the voting and the likelihood of the result of the voting was concerned.

The CHAIRMAN: There were two strips of territory which were dealt with as two separate units. The fate of one unit was inevitably decided by the decision of the other, if that decision was of a particular character.

The ATTORNEY-GENERAL: That is so, of course.

The CHAIRMAN: I only wanted you to consider whether similar circumstances might not render advisable a similar procedure.

Mr. FISHER: We might go back to the practical point we were discussing yesterday about our powers.

The CHAIRMAN: As to existing evidence of the wishes of the inhabitants. I understand the Government of the Irish Free State was concerned in the publication of the " Handbook of the Ulster Question."

I notice on p. 46 the following statement with regard to the wishes of the inhabitants:—

"The wishes of the inhabitants of Ulster by population as regards inclusion in the Free State, or within the territory subject to the Belfast Parliament, are here shown in accordance with the census of their religious opinions, 'Catholics' being regarded as on the side of the Free State, and 'All Others' as on the side of the Belfast Parliament."

You said yesterday the figures of religious censuses could be taken only as a rough indication.

The ATTORNEY-GENERAL: Yes.

The CHAIRMAN: That statement says that the classification based on these figures is only approximate. It suggests that the figures on the census would be favourable to Northern Ireland; they would put the case at the worst against yourselves?

The ATTORNEY-GENERAL: That is so, assuming the statement to be accurate.

The CHAIRMAN: Will you consider whether if we want evidence as to the weight to be attached to census figures you will be able to give us any such evidence?

The ATTORNEY-GENERAL: I shall certainly consider that. It is not a matter on which I can even offer any views.

The CHAIRMAN: It is rather a matter for evidence; we might, I think, want particular information which should be given in the form of evidence?

The ATTORNEY-GENERAL: No matter what evidence you may produce on a question of that kind the result will necessarily be very vague, and possibly very inaccurate. Evidence of that kind might be sufficient to enable the Commission to make up its mind as to whether there was a prima facie case for a vote in certain areas. It is not sufficient for carrying out the express directions of the Treaty that the boundary is to be fixed according to the wishes of the inhabitants.

The CHAIRMAN: If the position is that it might be sufficient to make out a prima facie case, then I think it might be an advantage to the Commission to have evidence on the point, and you may be in a position at some stage to offer evidence on the question.

The CHAIRMAN (referring to the Handbook): These figures date back to 1911. This map is attached. (The Chairman here referred to the map of Northern Ireland, which accompanies the Handbook.)

The ATTORNEY-GENERAL: It is based on the Census figures of 1911 regarding religion; the green squares representing Catholics and the yellow squares representing the other religions.

The CHAIRMAN: The heading assumes that the religious and political division is the same.

Mr. FISHER: It is an attempt to produce the census in a graphic form.

Dr. MacNEILL (to the Attorney-General): Whilst having that prima facie value you say?

The ATTORNEY-GENERAL: Yes.

The CHAIRMAN: There was a question affecting the future procedure of the Commission, and we said we were quite prepared to discuss the question of procedure with you. Is there any matter you wish to discuss or any suggestion you wish to make?

The ATTORNEY-GENERAL: I had intended before the sitting concluded to ask the Commission for some information as to what their procedure would be.

The CHAIRMAN : I can only go thus far at present : We have, as you may have seen, issued advertisements in the Irish newspapers inviting written representations from public bodies, associations, or individuals with reference to the work with which the Commission is charged, and we have indicated a date by which those representations should be received (31st December, 1924). We have asked those who send in such representations to intimate whether they wish to appear before the Commission, and we have said that we contemplate holding sittings in Ireland after we have these replies for the purpose of receiving evidence. Our actual plans for a visit to Ireland for that purpose will have to await, I think, the receipt of these communications. The idea of the Commission was that it will probably be most convenient to sit in Ireland for the purpose of receiving evidence. If we pay such a visit—as we hope to do—possibly you might desire to offer evidence during that visit, you might have evidence to offer affecting the work of the Commission. You have not, of course, said very much as to wishing to offer evidence. You have asked the Commission to go and gets its own. No doubt you will consider that question further, and we might arrange for a further appearance by you before we went to Ireland for the purpose of receiving evidence, at some date after these replies have been received and when our plans have taken rather more definite shape. There are various matters with which you dealt during these last two days with regard to which you might perhaps furnish us with official records; for instance, the results of the elections of 1918 and 1921.

The ATTORNEY-GENERAL : So far as the actual returns are concerned there will be no difficulty.

The CHAIRMAN : Generally speaking, where you wish us to take into account happenings of which we cannot be expected to have knowledge you could supply us with that in some official record, and we should be much obliged.

The ATTORNEY-GENERAL : I alluded yesterday to some of the proceedings of Dail Eireann. Most of these proceedings were in private.

Mr. FISHER : Before the Treaty; now I presume there is an official record?

The ATTORNEY-GENERAL : Yes.

The CHAIRMAN : You referred to the fact that delegates were appointed and so on.

With regard to the oral evidence you might offer, are you waiting for the Commission to tell you what they would like you to offer, or have you any evidence you would like to offer spontaneously?

The ATTORNEY-GENERAL : I have not. The Government for which we appear contemplated that the Commission would proceed to take a vote. After that vote has been taken there may be necessity for evidence regarding, say, economic or geographic conditions in different localities. For the moment the Government has not seen the necessity of putting in evidence before the Commission. If, however, there is any matter on which the Commission desire them to offer evidence we shall certainly consider it.

The CHAIRMAN : We have not at the present moment the powers necessary to enable us to take a vote. The Commission contemplates paying a visit to Ireland, and one object of that visit would be to ascertain what can or cannot be done with the information that is available without a vote, and evidence bearing on this question might then be tendered. Will you consider that? You will consider what evidence you would like to offer and would be prepared to let us know? We will consider what evidence we should like from you, and at some later date we may be able to give you some indication as to that in time to enable you, if you are willing, to get or prepare such evidence, so that we may receive it when we take evidence in Ireland.

The ATTORNEY-GENERAL: You suggested that a further meeting of the Commission would probably take place here at which the Government of the Irish Free State would be invited to be present before you proceed to Ireland to take evidence. Do you contemplate that evidence should be submitted here at that sitting?

The CHAIRMAN: I was not contemplating that, but it might be, if there was any that it was more convenient for us to take here. If you like to suggest that, we will be prepared to consider it. The idea is to take the bulk of the evidence in Ireland, but we do not preclude the possibility of taking evidence here.

Serjeant HANNA: Could facts be verified by a Statutory Declaration?

The CHAIRMAN: That would be quite sufficient.

Serjeant HANNA: Some witnesses might not like to give evidence *viva voce*, but to make a Statutory Declaration.

The CHAIRMAN: No power has been expressly given to the Commission to take evidence on oath, and I do not think we can assume we have such powers. The taking of evidence will not be the taking of sworn evidence so far as we know at present.

The ATTORNEY-GENERAL. I take it that at the proposed meetings at which evidence is being produced by one side or the other there will be a possibility of cross-examining witnesses?

The CHAIRMAN: That is another question—a point we shall no doubt consider before we take the evidence. It may be that the Commission will rely on its own powers of cross-examination.

Serjeant HANNA: You might not have all the necessary information for that purpose.

The CHAIRMAN: I did not mean we shall be necessarily well qualified, or as well qualified as others, but it may be the best course in the interests of the Inquiry. We have to consider that. If we do give opportunities for cross-examination, your Government might wish to be present, but that is a point we shall have to decide.

With regard to the record of proceedings, a copy will be sent to the Government of the Irish Free State for confidential use; and the Commission would be glad if any corrections you may wish to make could be suggested within a reasonable time after the transcript reaches the Government. The Commission may at some stage wish to publish a report of these proceedings, and it is therefore important that they should have your suggested corrections.

The ATTORNEY-GENERAL: The fact that the proceedings are private does not prevent any Counsel appearing here communicating to their Government what has taken place?

The CHAIRMAN: Oh no.

The HEARING was concluded at 1 p.m.

APPENDIX II.

The Government of the Irish Free State, believing that a just appreciation of the events leading up to and the circumstances surrounding the conclusion of the Treaty between Great Britain and Ireland entered into at London on the 6th December, 1921, will be of assistance to the Boundary Commission, places the following statement before them. In doing so, it has endeavoured to avoid all controversial matters and to confine the statement to facts which are either matters of history or else are evidenced by public statutes and Parliamentary records.

The Act of Union between Great Britain and Ireland was never approved of or accepted by the people of Ireland. It gave rise to great and continuous discontent, resulting from time to time in armed revolt against the Government established under that Act. There was at the same time a continued constitutional agitation carried on in the Parliament of the United Kingdom and throughout the country generally, having for its object the setting up in Ireland of a Parliament for Ireland and a Government responsible thereto. This agitation resulted, on the 18th day of September, 1914, in the passing of the Government of Ireland Act, 1914 (4 & 5 Geo. V. c. 90), but on the same day was passed the Suspensory Act, 1914 (4 & 5 Geo. V. c. 88) providing that the Government of Ireland Act should not be put into operation until the expiration of 12 months from the passing of the Act, or such later date (not being later than the end of the War) as might be fixed by Order in Council. The suspension of the Government of Ireland Act, 1914, accentuated the pre-existing discontent, and created the belief in Ireland that the British Government were not observing good faith with Ireland.

In these circumstances an election was proclaimed in December, 1918, for the election of members to the British House of Commons. The Act of 1914 was still on the Statute Book, but, owing to the Suspensory Act, had not been put into operation.

The election was held in December, 1918, and the new House of Commons met in January, 1919. Of 105 members elected to represent Irish constituencies only 32 attended that Parliament. The remaining Irish members met in Dublin and established the First Dail Eireann, which claimed to act for the whole of Ireland. This assembly included three members who had been elected to represent constituencies in the six North-Eastern Counties, which now comprise " Northern Ireland," namely, Mr. Arthur Griffith, who represented North-East Tyrone, Mr. Eoin MacNeill, who represented Derry City, and Mr. Sean O'Mahony, who represented South Fermanagh.

On the 25th day of February, 1920, a Bill was introduced into the British House of Commons for the Government of Ireland. It became law as the Government of Ireland Act, 1920 (10 & 11 Geo. V. c. 67) on the 23rd day of December, 1920. No Irish member voted in favour of that Bill. The Government of Ireland Act, 1920, provided for the setting up of a Parliament for " Northern Ireland," consisting of the Parliamentary Counties of Antrim, Armagh, Down, Fermanagh, Londonderry and Tyrone, and the Parliamentary boroughs of Belfast and Londonderry, and another Parliament for " Southern Ireland," consisting of so much of Ireland as was not comprised in " Northern Ireland."

Early in May, 1921, elections were proclaimed by the Lord Lieutenant for the House of Commons for " Southern Ireland " and for the House of Commons of " Northern Ireland." The First Dail Eireann, by resolution, agreed to dissolve and to accept the foregoing elections as elections for a new Dail Eireann. The elections were held on the 24th day of May, 1921.

The Parliament of " Southern Ireland " was summoned for the 17th day of June, 1921. Of the persons elected to represent constituencies in " Southern Ireland " none attended save the members elected to represent Dublin University, and accordingly that Parliament was unable to function and never, in fact, did function.

The Parliament of " Northern Ireland " was opened on the 22nd day of June, 1921, but 12 members elected for constituencies in " Northern Ireland " refused to recognise the jurisdiction of that Parliament, and never participated in any of its functions. The said 12 members were distributed as follows, namely, four were elected for the Counties of Fermanagh and Tyrone, two for the County of Armagh, one for the County of Antrim, one for West Belfast, two for the County of Down, and two for the County of Londonderry (including the Borough of Londonderry).

The new Dail Eireann, known as the Second Dail Eireann, met in Dublin on the 16th day of August, 1921. It comprised all the members elected to represent constituencies in " Southern Ireland " (except the members for Dublin University), and certain members elected to represent constituencies in " Northern Ireland." The Second Dail Eireann, like the First Dail Eireann, claimed to represent and to act for the whole of Ireland.

On the 14th day of September, 1921, the Second Dail Eireann appointed five plenipotentiaries to negotiate and conclude a Treaty of accommodation and peace with representatives of the British Government. The plenipotentiaries were Mr. Arthur Griffith, Mr. Michael Collins, Mr. Robert Barton, Mr. Eamon Duggan and Mr. George Gavan Duffy. Of these plenipotentiaries Mr. Arthur Griffith and Mr. Michael Collins had both been elected in May, 1921, to represent constituencies in " Northern Ireland " Mr. Griffith represented the Counties of Fermanagh and Tyrone and Mr. Collins the County of Armagh.

The Treaty was concluded and signed on the 6th day of December, 1921, and was subsequently duly ratified.

The Irish plenipotentiaries claimed to speak and act on behalf of Ireland, and were dealt with on that basis by the British representatives. The Treaty is a Treaty with the whole of Ireland and not with any part of it. Its first Article is :—

" 1. Ireland shall have the same constitutional status in the Community of Nations known as the British Empire as the Dominion of Canada, the Commonwealth of Australia, the Dominion of New Zealand, and the Union of South Africa, with a Parliament having powers to make laws for peace and order and good government of Ireland and an executive responsible to that Parliament, and shall be styled and know as the Irish Free State."

Though the Irish Free State, as set up by the Treaty, thus comprises the whole of Ireland, it was nevertheless recognised that a real problem existed in the North-Eastern corner of Ireland, and that special provisions were required to deal with that problem. The real difficulty of the problem arose from the fact that, whilst some of the inhabitants of that area were anxious to avail themselves of the advantages secured for them by the Treaty, others preferred to stand by the Act of 1920, and to maintain the position created by that Act. The wishes of the inhabitants of the area were recognised to be the dominant factor, and accordingly it was provided that the powers of the Parliament and Government of the Irish Free State should not be exercisable in " Northern Ireland " for the period of one month, so as to give the people in that area, through their Houses of Parliament, the right of choosing between the alternatives comprised in Articles 12 and 14 respectively of the Treaty.

Article 14 was based upon the Houses of the Parliament of " Northern Ireland " electing to remain under the jurisdiction of the Irish Free State. In such event, it was provided that the Parliament and Government of " Northern Ireland " should continue to exercise, as regards the whole of " Northern Ireland," the powers conferred on them by the Government of Ireland Act, 1920, but that the Parliament and the Government of the Irish Free State should, in " Northern Ireland," have the same powers as in the rest of Ireland, in relation to matters in respect of which the Parliament of " Northern Ireland " had not the power to make laws under the said Act of 1920. In the foregoing event, the boundaries of " Northern Ireland " would have remained intact, but provision was made by Article 15 for safeguarding the rights of the minorities in " Northern Ireland."

Article 12 of the Treaty provided for the possibility of the Houses of Parliament of " Northern Ireland " electing not to remain under the jurisdiction of the Parliament and Government of the Irish Free State. It provided that in such event the powers of the Parliament and Government of the Irish Free State should no longer extend to " Northern Ireland," but that thereupon a Commission (being the Commission to whom this statement is addressed) should be set up to determine, in accordance with the wishes of the inhabitants, so far as might be compatible with economic and geographic conditions, the boundaries between " Northern Ireland " and the rest of Ireland; and it was declared that, for the purposes of the Government of Ireland Act and of the Treaty, the boundary of " Northern Ireland " should be such as might be determined by that Commission.

It is provided by the concluding words of Article 12 that " for the purposes of the Government of Ireland Act, 1920, and of this instrument, the boundary of Northern Ireland shall be such as may be determined by such Commission." That boundary has not yet been determined. The presentation of the address mentioned in Article 12 of the Treaty had the effect of staying for the moment, and pending the operations of the Boundary Commission, the powers of the Parliament and Government of the Irish Free State in " Northern Ireland "; but it was not contemplated by the Treaty that any area within " Northern Ireland " should have the right to withdraw permanently from the jurisdiction of the Irish Free State, unless the majority of the inhabitants of such area were in favour of this course.

This Government considers that it is in the position of a trustee for such of the inhabitants of " Northern Ireland " as wish to remain within the jurisdiction of the Irish Free State. It submits that the work of the Commission consists in ascertaining the wishes of the inhabitants of " Northern Ireland," with a view to determining, in accordance with such wishes, so far as may be compatible with economic and geographic conditions, what portions of that area are entitled to withdraw permanently from the jurisdiction of the Irish Free State.

APPENDIX III.

Irish Boundary Commission,
5-6, Clement's Inn, W.C. 2.
2nd February, 1925.

SIR,

I AM directed to refer to the proceedings before the Commission on the occasion of the hearing of Counsel on behalf of your Government as recorded on pages 64 and 80-85 of the official transcript, and especially to the remarks made by the Chairman as appearing on page 64 and pages 82, 84, and 85.

The Commission has now received a large number of representations, in response to the invitation issued in the Press, with reference to the work with which the Commission is charged.

*   *   *   *   *   *

The representations received include many expressions of opinion as to the conclusions which should be drawn from existing data, such as are available in Census figures and election returns, as to " the wishes of the inhabitants " referred to in Article XII. of the Articles of Agreement for a Treaty, and some of the evidence offered will no doubt be directed to this question. The Commission will be glad to know whether your Government wishes to offer any evidence on this subject during the course of the Commission's sitting in Ireland.

It does not appear to the Commission, as at present advised, to be necessary that Counsel on behalf of your Government should appear before the Commission again before the proposed sittings are held in Ireland. If, however, your Government desires to submit any further statement to the Commission, the Commission will, of course, be glad to receive such statement. If your Government desires at any time further opportunity of being heard by Counsel, the Commission will be glad to consider the question of arranging a further hearing.

*   *   *   *   *   *

I have the honour to be, Sir,
Your obedient Servant,
(Signed)   F. B. BOURDILLON,
Secretary to the Commission.

D. O'Hegarty, Esq.,
Secretary to the Executive Council,
President's Office,
Upper Merrion Street, Dublin.

---

* In the case of the first five letters the relative portions only are printed.

Roinn an Uactarain,
Sraid Muirbtean Uac,
Baile Ata Cliat (Dublin).
19th February, 1925.

S. 4150.
The Secretary,
Irish Boundary Commission,
6, Clement's Inn,
London, W.C. 2.

SIR,

REFERRING to your letter of the 2nd instant, I am to state that my Government note that the representations received by the Irish Boundary Commission include many expressions of opinion as to the conclusions which should be drawn from data, such as are available in Census figures and election returns, as to the " wishes of the inhabitants " referred to in Article 12 of the Treaty.

My Government desire to offer evidence on this subject during the course of the Commission's sittings in Ireland, and they will be glad to receive information as to when and where it will be convenient for the Commission to hear such evidence.

It is suggested that inasmuch as this evidence will be of a general character and not referring particularly to any local area, it might be conveniently given in some such place as Dublin rather than at a local centre. In order that such evidence may deal with all the points covered by the representations received by the Commission, my Government desire that copies of all such representations should be forwarded to them.

They assume that, in accordance with the terms of the paragraph of the Circular quoted in your letter, there will be no objection to Counsel on behalf of the Irish Free State being present while such evidence is being given; they feel that this course will facilitate the Commission in the taking of evidence.

* * * * * *

I have the honour to be, Sir,
Your obedient Servant,
(Signed)   DIARMUID O'HEIGCEARTUIGH,
Secretary to the Executive Council.

6, Clement's Inn,
London, W.C.2.
24th March, 1925.

The Secretary to the Executive Council
of the Irish Free State,
President's Office,
Upper Merrion Street,
Dublin.

SIR,

I AM directed by the Irish Boundary Commission to refer to your letter of the 19th February (S.4150.) and to say that the Commission would be glad to hear the evidence which the Government of the Irish Free State desire to offer on the subject of the conclusion which should be drawn from data such as are available in Census figures and Election returns as to the wishes of the inhabitants referred to in Article 12 of the Articles of Agreement for a Treaty between Great Britain and Ireland.

With regard to the third paragraph of your letter, I am directed to state for the information of your Government that the main points relating to this subject dealt with in representations received by the Commission are :—

(1) The extent to which the figures of the Census of 1911 can be relied upon as showing the position to-day.

(2) The extent to which such figures can be checked by comparison with the numbers of voters included in current voters' lists, and what modifications, if any, should be made in such figures in the light of such comparison in order to arrive at the present position.

(3) The question whether in considering the Census figures for the purpose of arriving at the number of inhabitants, there are any classes of temporary residents who should be excluded.

(4) The question of the correspondence between political and re ligious divisions.

(5) The extent to which the division of opinion on the question of inclusion in the Irish Free State or in Northern Ireland follows the lines of existing religious or party divisions.

(6) The light which is thrown on questions (4) and (5) by the results of Parliamentary and Local elections.

The Commission trust that this information will be sufficient for the purpose of assisting your Government to prepare the evidence which it proposes to give.

It has not hitherto been the practice of the Commission to supply copies of representations received, except in the case of representations bearing upon particular localities, which the Commission forwards for the information of other parties making representations in an opposing sense in respect of the same localities, where it appears that the adoption of such a course will facilitate the progress of the enquiry.

*   *   *   *   *   *

With regard to the fourth paragraph of your letter, I am directed to state that though the Commission is quite prepared to hear Counsel on behalf of your Government again, if your Government so desire, it is thought that in the case of the evidence put forward by your Government, the procedure should be the same as that adopted in the case of public bodies, associations and groups which submit evidence to the Commission.

*   *   *   *   *   *

I am, Sir,

Your obedient Servant,

(Signed)   F. B. BOURDILLON,

Secretary to the Commission.

Roinn an Uactarain,
Sraid Muirbtean Uac,
Baile Ata Cliat (Dublin).
6th April, 1925.

The Secretary,
Irish Boundary Commission,
6, Clements Inn, London, W.O.2.

SIR,

WITH reference to your letter of the 24th ultimo.

*   *   *   *   *   *

My Government note that it has not been the practice of the Commission to supply copies of representations received, except in the case of representations bearing upon particular localities, which are forwarded for the information of other parties making representations in an opposing sense in respect of the same localities. It would appear, however, from the communiques issued by the Commission that representations have been received and witnesses heard in support thereof which raise considerations other than such as could be adequately dealt with by local groups and associations. For instance, it is understood that the site of the reservoir for the Belfast Water supply has been advanced as an argument against the fulfilment of the desire of the inhabitants of part of the County of Down to be included in the Irish Free State.

My Government consider that they should be afforded an opportunity of examining the representations made in this and similar cases so that they may be in a position to make submissions to the Commission on matters arising out of the considerations thus put forward. It also appears probable that in the representations received by the Commission from persons and associations within the present jurisdiction of the Irish Free State who make claim to exclusion from that jurisdiction statements or arguments have been made which my Government might desire to controvert, and they feel that copies of the representations in these cases also should be made available to them so that they may be enabled to place before the Commission such evidence or argument as may be appropriate.

*　　*　　*　　*　　*　　*

I have the honour to be, Sir,
Your obedient servant,
(Signed)　　DIARMUID O'HEIGCEARTUIGH,
Secretary to the Executive Council.

6, Clement's Inn,
London, W.C. 2.
7th May, 1925.

The Secretary to the Executive Council,
　　President's Office,
　　　　Upper Merrion Street, Dublin.

SIR,

　　I AM directed by the Irish Boundary Commission to refer to your letter of the 6th April.

*　　*　　*　　*　　*　　*

With reference to the third paragraph of your letter, in which you inform the Commission that your Government desire an opportunity of examining certain representations made to the Commission in respect of the Belfast Water Supply and similar cases, and also representations made in respect to claims for inclusion in Northern Ireland by persons and associations at present within the jurisdiction of the Irish Free State, I am directed to forward for your Government's information copies of the following:—

(a) Representation in respect of Belfast Waterworks.

(b) Representation in respect of Portadown and Banbridge Waterworks.

(c) Portion of representation in respect of the Union of Kilkeel relating to the Bann Reservoir.

(d) Portion of representation in respect of the County of Fermanagh relating to the sluice gates at Belleek.

(e) Representation relating to the district of Glasslough.

(f) Representation relating to the district of Mullyash.

(g) Representation relating to the district of Drummully (Co. Monaghan).

(h) Representation relating to the portion of the Parish of Clogh situated in County Monaghan.

(i) Representation relating to the district of Pettigo.

(7) Representation relating to the County of Tirconaill, and in particular to certain portions of that County adjacent to the borders of the Counties of Londonderry, Tyrone and Fermanagh.

The Commission will be glad to receive any submissions which the Government of the Irish Free State may desire to make on the points raised in these representations.

It is understood that the representations are forwarded only for the information of your Government, and I am to ask that they should not be published unless and until their publication should be authorised by the Commission.

      *   *   *   *   *   *

I am, Sir,
Your obedient Servant,
(Signed)   F. B. BOURDILLON,
Secretary to the Commission.

Department of the President,
Dublin.
11th July, 1925.

The Secretary,
   Boundary Commission,
     6, Clement's Inn,
       London, W.C. 2.

SIR,

WITH reference to your letter of the 7th May last, and 24th ultimo, enclosing copies of representations made to the Boundary Commission in regard to the Belfast Water Works and other similar matters as well as of certain representations made by persons and associations at present within the jurisdiction of the Irish Free State for the transfer of areas to Northern Ireland, I have to transmit herewith copies of a memorandum containing the submissions which my Government desire to make to the Commission on the points raised in the representations in question, and to state that Counsel, on behalf of the Irish Free State, will be prepared to appear before the Commission to supplement by oral exposition the submissions contained in the memorandum.

I am, Sir,
Your obedient Servant,
DIARMUID O'hEIGCEARTUIGH,
Secretary to the Executive Council.

MEMORANDUM CONTAINING SUBMISSIONS WHICH THE GOVERNMENT OF THE IRISH FREE STATE DESIRE TO MAKE TO THE IRISH BOUNDARY COMMISSION ON POINTS RAISED IN VARIOUS REPRESENTATIONS SUBMITTED TO THE COMMISSION.

In this Memorandum representations, copies of which were forwarded by the Commission for the examination of the Government, are taken in the order in which they are set out in the letter of the 7th May, 1925, from the Secretary of the Commission, save that the representation from the Clogher Rural District Council, which was forwarded on the 24th June, is dealt with after other representations which deal with County Monaghan.

(a) *Representation in respect of the Belfast Waterworks.*

The representation dealing with the waterworks which supply the City of Belfast, submitted to the Boundary Commission by the Belfast City and District Water Commissioners, appears to be based on a misconception of the Boundary Commission's terms of reference as contained in Article 12 of the Treaty.

That representation suggests that effect should not be given to the wishes of the inhabitants of the area from which the water supply is derived, on the grounds of possible inconvenience to the consumers of the water in Belfast, an area which is not in dispute. It is submitted that the reference to economic and geographical conditions in the Treaty is intended as a corrective to the possible absurdities of a line based solely on the distribution of the population and drawn regardless of the economic hardships which might be inflicted upon the people whom it was intended to relieve. It is submitted that the provision regarding economic conditions is confined to economic conditions affecting the particular area in question and in which it is being applied as a corrective, and that it does not entitle the Commission to consider possible economic inconveniences which may be suffered by persons in another area whose exclusion from the Free State is not in dispute.

It is further submitted that since the principle of partition was reluctantly accepted by the Irish people as a whole, in order to provide for the wishes of a minority, it follows, as a matter of equity, that any inconvenience arising from the arrangement should fall, as far as possible, on those to meet whose wishes the arrangement was made.

In their summary, at the end of their representation, the Water Commissioners set out the arguments on which their contention is based. They suggest that Carlingford Lough is a natural boundary, and better than any artificial boundary which could be drawn. Far from being a natural boundary, Carlingford Lough is a natural highway of intercourse between the people of South Down and the people of Louth, who are a politically homogeneous community fortuitously divided by the existing boundary.

The Water Commissioners suggest that " any boundary drawn further north, but still south of the Commissioners' Mourne area, would expose the Commissioners' work to easier attack, and necessitate continuous protection." This article depends on the wholly untenable suggestion that the wishes of the inhabitants of the area near the water works are to be overridden by the fact that they live in proximity to this undertaking, and also on the assumption that a state of war exists and is likely to continue in the country.

The Water Commissioners further argue that in the event of the water works area being included in the Free State there will be a risk of interference with the undertaking, of restrictions in the use of water, and of increased taxation. Without admitting that the inclusion of this area in the Free State would involve any such risks, it is submitted that these are not matters which fall within the terms of reference of the Boundary Commission, but are matters for negotiation and arrangement between the Governments concerned.

The Water Commissioners say that the inclusion of the works in the Free State would create difficulties for them in the financing of their undertaking. This view must be regarded merely as a matter of opinion, and, it is submitted, is quite irrelevant to the matters in question.

It is also submitted that the existence of a right in the Belfast Water Commissioners to take water is no argument against a change in governmental jurisdiction.

(b) *Representation in respect of Portadown and Banbridge Water Works.*

The general arguments outlined above, in relation to the representation of the Belfast City and District Water Commissioners, apply with equal force to the representation of the Portadown and Banbridge Joint Water Works Board.

(c) *Portion of the representation in respect of the Union of Kilkeel in relation to the Bann Reservoir.*

The water supplies referred to in this representation are:

    (1) Belfast.
    (2) Portadown and Banbridge.
    (3) Warrenpoint.
    (4) Rathfryland.
    (5) Kilkeel, and
    (6) Newcastle.

The supplies for Belfast, Portadown and Banbridge have been dealt with above; the other places mentioned as being supplied with water from the Mourne areas are all places in which the majority of the inhabitants desire to be included in the Free State, and have submitted claims to this effect to the Commission.

(d) *Portion of representation in respect of the County of Fermanagh relating to the sluice gates at Belleek.*

Clearly inconvenience arises from the fact that the present boundary divides the sluice gates at Belleek. A claim has, however, been submitted to the Commission on behalf of the majority of the inhabitants of County Fermanagh, seeking inclusion in the Free State. The recognition of the right of the people of Fermanagh to be so included would automatically place the Lough Erne system under one jurisdiction, an arrangement which is further desirable on account of the fact that the waters of Lough Erne are available for power purposes after they pass into existing Free State territory. It is understood that proof has been given to the Commission of the Constitution of the Lough Erne Drainage Board and it has been shown that areas in County Cavan are interested in the control of the level of the lough, and that if Fermanagh is not excluded from the Free State the whole matter will be under one jurisdiction.

The further representations deal with claims for inclusion in Northern Ireland by persons and associations within the jurisdiction of the Irish Free State. It is submitted that, for the reasons already put before the Commission, the Commission has no jurisdiction to draw a boundary in such a way as to include in Northern Ireland territory which is within the existing Free State jurisdiction.

It is further submitted that, even if the jurisdiction of the Commission did extend to the inclusion of existing Free State territory in Northern Ireland, there are no districts in the Free State which would, under the Commission's terms of reference, be entitled to be so included.

The following representations deal with areas in County Monaghan, adjacent to the existing boundary:—

(e) *Representation relating to the District of Glasslough;*
(f) *Representation relating to the District of Mullyash;*
(g) *Representation relating to the District of Drummully;*
(h) *Representation relating to the portion of the Parish of Clough.*

These are all small districts which, with the exception of Drummully, have Unionist majorities, but are so surrounded by areas containing Nationalist majorities that, even were they within the Commission's jurisdiction they could not be excluded from the Free State. It must also be pointed out that all these areas in County Monaghan lie south of large areas of Northern Ireland inhabited by Nationalist majorities, on behalf of whom claims for inclusion in the Free State have been submitted to the Commission.

Statement prepared for the Boundary Commission by the Clogher Rural District Council regarding the Western portion of the Tyrone-Monaghan border.

This representation deals with an area in the Free State the majority of the inhabitants of which would be strongly opposed to any such transfer as is suggested. The area dealt with forms part of the market area of Aughnacloy. The cutting off of this area from its market centre has caused, as pointed out in the representation, great inconvenience to the people of Aughnacloy, and of the area in question. The majority of the inhabitants in the Aughnacloy market area are in favour of being, with their market town, included in the Free State. Aughnacloy, moreover, lies to the south of large areas on behalf of the majority of the inhabitants of which claims for inclusion in the Free State are before the Commission. It is submitted that a line drawn in accordance with the wishes of the inhabitants will solve the economic difficulties of the area referred to in the representation, by including its market centre in the Irish Free State.

(i) *Representation relating to the District of Pettigo.*

The Pettigo and Grousehall district, which, according to the last census, had a small Unionist majority, is in a position similar to the above-mentioned districts in County Monaghan. There is no doubt that the people of Pettigo have suffered very great inconvenience from the existing Boundary, from which, it is submitted, they will be relieved by the drawing of the boundary in accordance with the wishes of the inhabitants of adjacent areas at present under the jurisdiction of Northern Ireland.

(j) *Representation relating to the County of Tirconnaill and in particular to certain portions of that county adjacent to the borders of the Counties of Londonderry, Tyrone and Fermanagh.*

This representation begins by drawing attention to the anomalous position of the county, which only adjoins other territory at present under the jurisdiction of the Free State along the Leitrim County boundary, south of Ballyshannon, and seeks to establish a claim for the inclusion of the county in Northern Ireland, based on the allegation that the votes of the more wealthy inhabitants of the county would be in favour of this arrangement.

At the time when the area to be included under the jurisdiction of the Northern Government was being selected, this county was expressly omitted, together with the counties of Cavan and Monaghan, from the claim for separate treatment made by the Northern minority, through their organisation, the Ulster Unionist Council. The Council met on the 10th March, 1920, for the purpose of considering the area for which separate treatment could be claimed. It decided on the six counties, and this area was adopted by the then British Government, without ascertaining the wishes of any other party. In other words the maximum claim of the party for whose accommodation partition was introduced did not extend to the inclusion of this county, or any part of the counties of Cavan and Monaghan, in Northern Ireland. The present anomalous geographical position of County Donegal is due to the fact that the adjoining counties of Tyrone and Fermanagh, and the City of Derry, which is the economic capital of County Donegal, were cut off, contrary to the wishes of their inhabitants, from the county with which they should naturally have been associated. It is submitted that the setting up of the Boundary Commission by the Treaty was agreed to in order to set right this injustice, which had been done contrary to the well-known and often-expressed wishes of the Irish people.

The claim for the inclusion of Donegal in Northern Ireland is not based on the wishes of the inhabitants, but on the contention that the wishes of a very small but more wealthy minority should override the wishes of the majority of the people, who would be violently opposed to the transfer suggested in this representation.

The representation contains a complaint against the extension of the franchise in the Free State, which, coupled with the system of proportional representation secures for all parties a fair share of legislative control.

The agricultural labourer is contemptuously referred to as of the migratory servant boy class. He is not migratory, save in the sense that he, like other workers, is not bound to remain in the service of any one employer.

It is suggested that emigration has affected to a very large extent the Unionist strength throughout the county. If this be a fact, it further diminishes the Unionist minority, which could not, at any time, claim to speak for the county as a whole.

The representation deals with certain areas which it refers to as Unionist strongholds in East Donegal, but it shows, where census figures are given, that the Unionists are in a minority, even in these areas which they themselves selected for consideration.

This representation also deals with the Pettigo district, and the neighbourhood of Belleek, referring to the sluice gates, both of which areas have been referred to above.

The Unionists' claim is (1) that the whole county should be transferred to Northern Ireland, and failing that (2) that the former constituency of East Donegal, and a small portion of North and South Donegal, should be transferred, and failing that (3) that the areas referred to as the Rural Districts of Londonderry No. 2 and Strabane No. 2 and Manorcunningham, Convoy, Cliff and Pettigo, with small adjacent areas, be transferred as a minimum.

None of these claims, even if the jurisdiction of the Commission extended to the inclusion of a portion of Donegal in Northern Ireland, could be sustained.

The county as a whole is, as mentioned above, intensely Nationalist. The areas claimed under heading (2) are not very clearly defined, but certainly contain a Nationalist majority.

Of the areas mentioned under heading (3) the Rural Districts of Derry No. 2 and Strabane No. 2 both have Nationalist majorities. The District Electoral Divisions of Manorcunningham, Convoy and Cliff have Nationalist majorities, leaving Pettigo alone as the only unit mentioned in which, according to the 1911 census, the Unionists had a majority, which was small and has not been maintained.

It is entirely untrue to suggest that a considerable number of Catholic inhabitants of Donegal would vote for inclusion in Northern Ireland.

The economic association of the City of Derry with the County Donegal, referred to in this representation, is well establishd. The people both of Derry and Donegal have suffered much inconvenience from the fact that this City was arbitrarily cut off from the area for which it was the natural port and distributing centre, and also from the fact that Strabane, which is the focus of the Donegal Light Railway system, was cut off from the county which it served as a railway centre. These difficulties can, it is submitted, only be adjusted in accordance with the wishes of the inhabitants by the restoration of Derry City and the town of Strabane and its surrounding area to the jurisdiction of the Free State.

Secretary to the Executive Council,
    President's Office,
        Upper Merrion Street,
            Dublin.

Irish Boundary Commission,
    6, Clements Inn,
        London, W.C.2.
            24th July, 1925.

SIR,

I AM directed by the Irish Boundary Commission to refer to your letter of 11th July in which you transmit copies of a memorandum containing submissions which the Government of the Irish Free State desire to make to the Commission on the points raised in the representations forwarded with my letters of 7th May and 24th June. The Commission notes that the submissions contained in the said memorandum relate (1) to questions as to the interpretation of Article 12 of the Articles of Agreement for a Treaty between Great Britain and Ireland and the principles which should govern the application of that Article, and (2) to questions of the detailed application of the Article and to questions of fact regarding particular areas both in Northern Ireland and in the Irish Free State.

With reference to your statement that Counsel on behalf of the Irish Free State will be prepared to appear before the Commission to supplement the submissions contained in the memorandum, I am directed to state that the Commission is willing to hear Counsel in support of the submissions made by your Government so far as they relate to questions of the interpretation of Article 12 and the principles which should govern its application.

The Commission assumes that it is not contemplated that Counsel appearing on behalf of your Government should deal with questions of the detailed application of Article 12, otherwise than by way of illustration, or with questions of fact regarding particular areas which would involve the examination of evidence already received or the hearing of fresh evidence. The Commission would be glad to know whether this assumption is correct.

I am to suggest Wednesday, 12th August, at 11 a.m. at this address, as a convenient time and place for the hearing of Counsel by the Commission.

I am, Sir,
Your obedient Servant,
(Signed)   F. B. BOURDILLON,
Secretary to the Commission.

Oifig an Runai Do'n Ard Chomhairle
(Office of the Secretary to the Executive Council),
Baile Atha Cliath
(Dublin).
1st August, 1925.

To The Secretary, Irish Boundary Commission,
6, Clement's Inn, London, W.C.2.

SIR,

I HAVE to acknowledge the receipt of your letter of the 24th ultimo, and to state that Counsel for the Irish Free State would find it very inconvenient to appear before the Commission on the 12th instant, and I am accordingly to suggest the 25th instant as an alternative date for the hearing if that date would be suitable to the Commission.

The Commission is correct in assuming that it is not contemplated that Counsel appearing on behalf of my Government should deal with questions of the detailed application of Article 12, otherwise than by way of illustration, or with questions of fact regarding particular areas which would involve the examination of evidence already received, or the hearing of fresh evidence.

I am, Sir,
Your obedient Servant,
(Signed)   DIARMUID O'HEIGCEARTUIGH,
Secretary to the Executive Council.

APPENDIX IV.

HEARING OF COUNSEL

Representing the Government of the Irish Free State*

August 25th, 1925

At 6, Clement's Inn, London, W.C.2

The SITTING opened at 3 p.m.

PRESENT.

THE HON. MR. JUSTICE FEETHAM, C.M.G. (*in the Chair*).

MR. J. R. FISHER.

DR. E. MacNEILL, D.Litt., T.D.

MR. F. B. BOURDILLON (*Secretary of Commission*).

The following were present representing the Government of the Irish Free State:—

THE ATTORNEY-GENERAL OF THE IRISH FREE STATE (MR. JOHN O'BYRNE, K.C.).

MR. PATRICK LYNCH, K.C.

MR. CECIL LAVERY, B.L.

MR. GEORGE MURNAGHAN (*Instructing Solicitor*).

MR. E. M. STEPHENS (*Secretary of the North-Eastern Boundary Bureau*).

The ATTORNEY-GENERAL: On the 7th May Mr. Bourdillon forwarded to the Executive Council a letter in the third paragraph of which he says:—

"With reference to the third paragraph of your letter, in which you inform the Commission that your Government desire an opportunity of examining certain representations made to the Commission in respect of the Belfast Water Supply and similar cases, and also representations made in respect to claims for inclusion in Northern Ireland by persons and associations at present within the jurisdiction of the Irish Free State, I am directed to forward for your Government's information copies of the following. . . ."

Copies of or extracts from Representations lodged with the Commission on behalf of certain local bodies accompanied that letter. These, with the exception of the Representation dealing with the sluice gates at Belleek, fall into two categories. The first class deals with certain

---

* Two copies of the verbatim Report of the Proceedings at the hearing of Counsel on 25th August, 1925, were sent to the Government of the Irish Free State for the purpose of enabling the Attorney-General to make any necessary corrections early in September, and one copy corrected by the Attorney-General was returned on the 25th September. The Report as printed below embodies the corrections made.

waterworks, chiefly the Belfast Waterworks; and the second class deals with applications from persons and bodies at present within the jurisdiction of the Irish Free State to be transferred to Northern Ireland.

On the 11th July the Executive Council replied to that letter and forwarded copies of a memorandum dealing with these various Representations. The memorandum contains the submissions of the Executive Council with reference to these Representations, and it is stated at the end of the letter that Counsel on behalf of the Irish Free State will be prepared to appear before the Commission to supplement by oral exposition the submissions contained in the memorandum. In reply to that letter, the Secretary of the Commission stated: "With reference to your statement that Counsel on behalf of the Irish Free State will be prepared to appear before the Commission to supplement the submissions contained in the memorandum, I am directed to state that the Commission is willing to hear Counsel in support of the submissions made by your Government so far as they relate to questions of the interpretation of Article XII and the principles which should govern its application."

As I stated, the representations, or rather the first lot of these representations, deal with waterworks—the Belfast Waterworks, Bambridge, Kilkeel, &c. The water for the City of Belfast comes from the south portion of the County of Down. The waterworks are situate in that area near the southern extremity of the County of Down. As I understand the representation of the Belfast City and District Water Commissioners, they allege that Belfast City and the consumers of water there would be prejudiced by the inclusion in the jurisdiction of the Irish Free State of these waterworks, and accordingly they ask that the area comprising these waterworks should not be transferred into the area of jurisdiction of the Irish Free State. I do not think I am going too far in saying that their claim is based, and based almost entirely, upon the inconvenience which would be caused to consumers of water in Belfast. That is the basis of their claim. They state in the end of their representation, "The Commissioners object to any change in the boundary of South Down which would have the effect of placing such boundary north of the existing southern boundary (Carlingford Lough) for the following reasons:—

" 1. The Carlingford Lough boundary of South Down is a natural boundary and obviously better than any artificial boundary can be."

So far as that particular ground is concerned, it is not a matter which in any way comes home to the Belfast Water Commissioners. That is, of course, a general matter which the Commission will have to consider and on which, as I understand, the Commission has received evidence during their sittings in Ireland. I am instructed that so far from Carlingford Lough being a boundary it is a means, and a very useful and convenient means, of transit between the counties of Louth and Down. However, as I stated, the question of what constitutes a natural boundary or an artificial boundary is not one in which the Belfast Water Commissioners are particularly interested.

Then they go on to No. 2 and say:—

" 2. Any boundary drawn further to the north but still south of the Commissioners' Mourne Area would expose the Commissioners' Works to easier attack and necessitate continuous protection.

" 3. A boundary drawn north of the Commissioners' Mourne Area would put the Commissioners' Works under a jurisdiction different from that under which the Area served must be; and involve the risk of—

" (a) interference with the undertaking;
" (b) restrictions in the use of the water;
" (c) increased taxation."

The 4th deals with a question of finance, in which South Down is certainly not interested. That is dealt with by a memorandum which has been forwarded by the Executive Council. This memorandum states:—

> " The representation dealing with the waterworks which supply the City of Belfast, submitted to the Boundary Commission by the Belfast City and District Water Commissioners, appears to be based on a misconception of the Boundary Commissions' terms of reference as contained in Article 12 of the Treaty.
>
> " That representation suggests that effect should not be given to the wishes of the inhabitants of the area from which the water supply is derived, on the grounds of possible inconvenience to the consumers of water in Belfast, an area which is not in dispute."

That submission is one, as I would suggest, which is founded on reason and upon the terms of the Treaty. If you look at Article XII, you will find that the work of the Commission is to " determine in accordance with the wishes of the inhabitants, so far as may be compatible with economic and geographic conditions, the boundaries, etc. . . ." The governing factor there is clearly *the wishes of the inhabitants* " Economic and geographic conditions," as I would suggest, are economic and geographic conditions relevant to and affecting the area in which these inhabitants live. It is intended, as a corrective, to prevent absurdities. Take, for instance, the provisions with reference to geographic conditions. There is little doubt as to what that was intended to guard against. At the time this Treaty was being entered into it was well known that there was, to take one instance, an area in the County of Antrim which was strongly in favour of being within the jurisdiction of the Free State. It was surrounded by a district the inhabitants of which did not wish to be in the jurisdiction of the Free State; and accordingly that provision regarding geographic conditions was put in to guard against a situation in which the wishes of the inhabitants, if taken without a corrective, might result in an absurd and totally unworkable position.

The CHAIRMAN : That is an instance; but it is only one instance, and you cannot take it as being exclusive, the sole type of case contemplated.

The ATTORNEY-GENERAL : I do not suggest it as such. I suggest it as an instance that must have been present in the minds of those who entered into the Treaty, because it was a very glaring instance. There may be other instances; I am not suggesting there are not. Take then the question of economic conditions. I put this case : Supposing you have an area—take for simplicity an area adjacent to the present border —a self-contained, self-sufficient area, with the inhabitants by a big majority, or unanimously if you wish, in favour of being placed under the jurisdiction of the Free State; suppose also that their economic interests are in favour of being included in the Free State. Is it to be suggested that that area is not to be transferred because the economic position of some other area that is not about to be transferred, or about which there is no question, would be prejudicially affected by transferring that other area into the jurisdiction of the Free State? Economic conditions, as I suggest, supply a corrective, but I suggest that is the only effect and the only purpose of this provision of the Article.

The CHAIRMAN : But you suggest more than that. Your contention is that the meaning to be given to the term " economic conditions " is to be restricted. I understand you say the same with regard to the term " geographic conditions "—that we are confined by something in this Article. I am dealing with the question of interpretation; I quite understand you have a separate argument on application. I understand you say with regard both to economic conditions and geographic conditions that the only conditions to be looked at are the conditions of the area the wishes of whose inhabitants are being considered.

The ATTORNEY-GENERAL: Yes.

The CHAIRMAN: Of course, economic conditions imply a relation between two persons or two areas—a buyer and a seller. Economic conditions suggest a relation of some kind.

The ATTORNEY-GENERAL: Undoubtedly they suggest that.

The CHAIRMAN: Therefore the position of two areas, A and B, where there is only a one-sided economic interest, so to speak, would be an unusual position. I do not know if we could find an example of it. I understand the real gist of your contention about this question of economic conditions, so far as interpretation is concerned, is that we are to restrict our study of economic conditions in relation to any particular area to the area itself.

The ATTORNEY-GENERAL: I do not quite suggest that, because it might be impossible for you to determine what were the economic conditions in a particular area without considering the conditions of surrounding areas to some extent. A consideration of the economic conditions in any particular area might involve, and probably would involve, to some extent at any rate, the examination of the economic conditions of surrounding areas. To that extent, so far as your examination is concerned, it may have to go outside a particular area. What I suggest is this, that when you apply that provision as a corrective so as to prevent your giving effect to the wishes of the inhabitants considered alone, then you are restricted to the economic conditions affecting that particular area which is the subject of your decision.

The CHAIRMAN: We are to look at economic conditions generally as affecting the relation between the area under consideration and adjoining areas; but where it comes to a question of economic interest, the only interest that is to be protected is that of the area whose inhabitants have expressed a wish that something should be done with them, or not done with them, as the case may be?

The ATTORNEY-GENERAL: Yes.

The CHAIRMAN: It becomes almost a question of application rather than of interpretation. Taking the term " economic conditions " generally, you say we could not consider the economic conditions of a particular area in isolation because its economic conditions would inevitably involve its relations with other areas, so that we cannot restrict our examination of conditions to a particular area.

The ATTORNEY-GENERAL: No.

The CHAIRMAN: You urge that when we come perhaps to a further stage and consider economic interests, the only interests to be protected are the interests of the area the wishes of whose inhabitants we are considering?

The ATTORNEY-GENERAL: Yes, that is my suggestion.

The CHAIRMAN: It comes to this then—if the inhabitants could have been trusted to take a sufficiently enlightened view of their own interests, this reference to economic conditions would have been unnecessary, according to your contention.

The ATTORNEY-GENERAL: I suggest it was put in to prevent absurdities and anomalies.

The CHAIRMAN: To prevent inhabitants voting themselves out and destroying themselves by the process?

The ATTORNEY-GENERAL: Quite so, and I think you cannot lose sight of the fact that in expressing their wishes the inhabitants will have regard, to some extent at any rate, to economic conditions. They are bound to. It may determine their wishes to a greater or lesser extent according to the strength of their political feelings; to some extent it is certain to be taken into account.

The CHAIRMAN: It comes to this, that in this view of the reference to economic conditions the considerations arising from economic conditions are only to be used for the purpose of protecting the inhabitants of a given area from themselves.

The ATTORNEY-GENERAL: I really think it is to prevent absurdities.

The CHAIRMAN: And similarly with geographic conditions, I gather from what you said just now?

The ATTORNEY-GENERAL: Yes, certainly. Of course you might have a situation of this kind arising:—You might proceed to take the wishes of the inhabitants in a certain number of areas and the inhabitants of a particular area might express a wish to be included on one side or the other without knowing what decision has been expressed by the inhabitants of surrounding areas. In that way they might not be in a position when expressing their wish to have before them the economic conditions which would arise by reason of the inhabitants of surrounding areas having expressed their wishes in a particular way. You may bring in the provision in a case of that kind to prevent absurdities.

The CHAIRMAN: You do say, I understand, that even in dealing with geographical conditions the same restriction should operate? That is, the Commission should consider geographic conditions so as not to give effect to the wishes of an area where those wishes may involve its own isolation; but it may give effect to the wishes of an area where its wishes would involve the isolation of another area?

The ATTORNEY-GENERAL: Yes, but the Commission will consider the position of the other area.

The CHAIRMAN: Then you will get this position, that to give effect to the wishes of one area might involve the isolation of another. Are not we to consider both cases; to consider the effect of the wishes of both areas?

The ATTORNEY-GENERAL: Surely you will consider the position in the adjoining area.

The CHAIRMAN: I understand from what you say that we may throw the adjoining area in because it is isolated. Supposing there are two adjoining areas, A and B, which differ in their wishes, and the giving effect to the wishes of A would isolate B, you say that is no argument against giving effect to A's wishes?

The ATTORNEY-GENERAL: I say not.

The CHAIRMAN: But it may be an argument against giving effect to B's wishes.

The ATTORNEY-GENERAL: Yes.

The CHAIRMAN: Then, of course, in such a case it would be a question of whether A and B could not be treated as one unit. That is one of the points that I think has to be taken into account in your argument, that the whole question of units is left open by this clause.

The ATTORNEY-GENERAL: It is, and that is why, when I appeared before this Commission first, I suggested certain units, by reason of their convenience for the purpose of transfer; by reason of the fact that they were, taken as a whole, self-contained.

The CHAIRMAN: Economically?

The ATTORNEY-GENERAL: Economically and geographically.

The CHAIRMAN: That was considering them in relation to one another. You are now really trying to restrict the view which the Commission may take of economic conditions, and that is one of the difficulties I have with regard to it. As you have put the argument now I find difficulty in seeing how it is a question of interpretation. I do not see what there is in the clause itself which suggests this restriction. If there is something which you rely on as suggesting a restriction in the clause, perhaps you will point it out to us.

The ATTORNEY-GENERAL: There is this in it, that the boundary is to be determined " in accordance with the wishes of the inhabitants, so far as may be compatible with economic and geographic conditions." The very manner in which these words " so far as may be compatible with economic and geographic conditions " are used shows that it was intended to be a qualification upon the wishes of the inhabitants taken alone. It is not an unusual clause. You will find the same kind of clause in other documents of a similar nature. I referred last December to various provisions in the Treaty of Versailles, and I should like for a moment to refer to one of the provisions in the Report of the Committee of Experts appointed to determine the frontier to be laid down between Germany and Poland in Upper Silesia. They say : " The allocation of different parts of the territory must be based primarily on the wishes of the inhabitants expressed by communes."

The CHAIRMAN: But what is that to show? How does this Report guide us? I do not know at the moment what clause of the Treaty this particular Commission was talking of. They do not all agree in their terms.

The ATTORNEY-GENERAL: There is not exact agreement, but there is substantial agreement between these various clauses.

The CHAIRMAN: I do not know that you can say that. Is this Upper Silesia?

The ATTORNEY-GENERAL: Yes. The provision is: " Regard will be had to the wishes of the inhabitants as shown by the vote and the geographic and economic conditions of the locality." It is not as strong as it is in the Treaty, because they say regard is to be had to economic conditions "; in the Treaty the provision is that the boundary is to be determined " in accordance with the wishes of the inhabitants." That is the governing factor, " so far as may be compatible with economic and geographic conditions."

The CHAIRMAN: You come back now to the governing factor. They use the word " primarily," I think, in the quotation you read just now. You read a quotation to us in which they referred to the wishes of the inhabitants as being the *primary* factor.

The ATTORNEY-GENERAL: That is in the Report, not in the Treaty. The provision in the Treaty is " On the conclusion of the voting . . . ." (see Annex V to Article 88, p. 107. " In this recommendation regard will be paid to the wishes of the inhabitants as shown by the vote, and to the geographical and economic conditions of the locality." That is the provision in the Treaty. What this Committee of Experts said when they reported was " The allocation of the different parts of the territory must be based primarily on the wishes of the inhabitants expressed by communes." That was their interpretation of this provision.

The CHAIRMAN: I want to point out to you one distinction which I think may be drawn between this provision and the provision of Article XII. Perhaps there are two distinctions that suggest themselves to my mind: (1) that Article XII does not, as this Article and the Annex do, provide for a plebiscite; which is a point to be borne in mind. The beginning of Article 88 is: " In the portion of Upper Silesia included within the boundaries described below, the inhabitants will be called upon to indicate by a vote whether they wish to be attached to Germany or

Poland." The predominating object of the Article is to provide for the vote. We have not got that here, but we have got the wishes of the inhabitants. When you come to the relation between the wishes of the inhabitants and geographic and economic conditions, there is this to be remarked: that in Article XII the expression used is, "determine in accordance with the wishes of the inhabitants, so far as may be compatible with economic and geographic conditions"; while in Section 5 of the Annex which you have quoted it says, "regard will be paid to the wishes of the inhabitants as shown by the vote, and to the geographical and economic conditions of the locality." The two things are grouped together by an *and* in the Annex, but in Article XII regard is to be paid to the wishes of the inhabitants only "so far as may be compatible with economic and geographic conditions." Though the wishes of the inhabitants are put first, I am not sure that they can rightly be described as the governing factor. Some of those who have come before us have referred to that as the paramount factor. Of course they are not paramount, where the result they indicate is not compatible with economic and geographic conditions. They seem to be the first thing to look at, but I doubt whether, as Article XII stands, you can correctly say it makes the wishes the governing factor because it puts in another factor which may over-ride them.

The ATTORNEY-GENERAL. I would suggest from the way the words are put in that they are the first and principal thing to be looked at. The other provision, "so far as may be compatible . . . ," is put in to prevent, possibly, in all cases the wishes of the inhabitants having their ordinary effect. But if you take the case of an area where the inhabitants have expressed a wish in one direction and there are no economic or geographic conditions affecting that area which would tend to make it unreasonable that effect should be given to the wishes of the inhabitants of that area, why should that area not be transferred?

The CHAIRMAN: You say "economic conditions affecting that area." Really, you want to go further than that. You say "economic interests of the persons in that area." The economic conditions of another area which has an interest in the area you are dealing with affect the area; but you say the interests of the inhabitants of other areas are not to be considered.

The ATTORNEY-GENERAL: They are not to be considered in considering whether or not you will transfer the area.

The CHAIRMAN: That is what I find it very difficult to see in the clause. That is a suggestion which you ask us to adopt in applying the clause, I understand, but where it is a question of interpretation I find it difficult to see how the words of the clause can assist you. From the point of view of reasonableness, is not this clause an invitation to the Commission to look at the problem as a whole, not to look at one area in isolation from another, and not to do more harm than good by trying to do good to one area and doing serious harm to another? The parties could have used words which would restrict this to the economic interests of the inhabitants who had expressed a wish, "so far as is compatible with the interests of those inhabitants." They have not said that, but "in accordance with the wishes of the inhabitants, so far as may be compatible with economic and geographic conditions."

The ATTORNEY-GENERAL: Is not that a reasonable construction of the words "in accordance with the wishes of the inhabitants"? "Inhabitants" implies a certain area. I think I am entitled to substitute for "inhabitants" the words "persons living in an area." Reading it in that way, the words "economic and geographic conditions" would mean the economic and geographic conditions affecting the area. The word "inhabitants" implies an area. In so far as it implies an area, I suggest the grammatical construction of those words "economic and geographic conditions" would be such as to restrict them to that area.

Dr. MacNEILL: You distinguish between two classes of economic conditions and economic interests—those which belong to and are beneficial to the area, and may be beneficial to other areas adjoining or outside of it; and external economic interests.

The ATTORNEY-GENERAL: Interests which other people might have in the area.

DR. MacNEILL: If you take into account the external conditions. how far can you go in that direction? Could you consider the interests of Manchester, for example, or some other area affected ?

The ATTORNEY-GENERAL: I would suggest not, and I would suggest that when you come to apply this provision so as to prevent you from giving effect to the wishes of the inhabitants, you must apply it in a very restricted and special way. If you have an area whose inhabitants are in favour of being on one side or the other and there is nothing economic- ally affecting that area which would render it improper or unreasonable to give effect to their wishes, then I suggest that the Commission is bound to give effect to the wishes of the area. I could have understood a repre- sentation being made by, say, the people of South Down to the effect that by reason of these waterworks being situated in South Down employment was given there, and that it would prejudice the area if a boundary were drawn north of it. I could understand that kind of representation, but when you have the wishes of the inhabitants and the economic conditions affecting the particular area both in favour of inclusion in the Free State, then I suggest that no other consideration should be applied.

The CHAIRMAN: Supposing the waterworks were something that could be taken away, and supposing the presence of the waterworks was, from the point of view of the inhabitants of the area in which they were situate, desirable for the purpose of providing employment and so on, then you say the Commission, if they thought the giving effect to the wishes of the inhabitants of the area by including the area in the Free State might imperil the continued existence of the waterworks in the area, would be justified in principle in saying, " In the interests of the inhabitants of the area itself we cannot give effect to your wishes, because we think your wishes are inconsistent with your interests." If the Commission took the view that the waterworks were there for good or evil, and that it was a question of the security of those works, from the point of view of Belfast, or the jurisdiction and maintenance of the Northern Ireland jurisdiction over those works in connection with future development or protection of those works, then you say the Commission would not be justified, owing to the interests of the inhabitants of Belfast, in refusing to give effect to the wishes of the inhabitants of the area in which the works are situate?

The ATTORNEY-GENERAL: I do say so, and I say further that the Commission would not be entitled to take such consideration into account at all as affecting their determination.

The CHAIRMAN: You say " would not be entitled." Again, is that in the terms of the Article, or is it some principle which you ask us to bring in in exercising whatever discretion is given to the Commission under the Article? Here you have an economic condition affecting both areas. Belfast has invested large sums of money in this area for the purpose of providing something that is essential to its life. The investment of this sum of money has affected the economic conditions of the area and the continued investment of that money and the expansion of the works will also affect economic conditions. There is an economic interest both ways. One may be more or less secure than another, but there is an economic interest in both areas owing to the relation between them. The fact of these two areas being linked in this way is an economic condition which the Commission is entitled to look at under this phrase " so far as may be compatible with economic and geographic conditions." But you say in looking at it we are to shut our eyes, when it is a question of what is to be done with this portion of South Down, to the fact that the interests of Belfast may suffer. I am not dealing for the moment with the question of whether they will suffer or not. I cannot see how, having agreed that " economic conditions " means conditions generally, you can ask us on the interpretation of the Article to close our eyes to the interests of the more distant area in the area which is nearer the border.

The ATTORNEY-GENERAL: I have already stated that I consider it is in the Article, and I have stated why. The word " inhabitants " implies an area.

The CHAIRMAN: It implies many areas, because you say we are to deal with the country in areas. It implies the inhabitants of Northern Ireland ascertained by areas—that is the view you put forward? You cannot restrict the clause or read in " in a particular area " into this clause, because it is a general clause directing what is to be done with the entire country which, as you say, we are to deal with in areas. I do not see how that helps you in this question of interpretation.

The ATTORNEY-GENERAL: I think it does, because you ascertain the wishes according to areas. When you are considering what effect you should give to those wishes you must then consider in connection with that economic and geographic conditions for the purpose of ascertaining whether or not these conditions are consistent with giving due effect to the wishes of the inhabitants. If the other construction is adopted, I fail to see where it will lead you. Supposing it was suggested that Belfast was at the present time the seat of a Parliament and Government, that it was benefited by that, and that any diminution of the area of jurisdiction of that Parliament and Government would prejudicially affect Belfast, is that a circumstance to be taken into consideration in determining whether or not you are to give effect to the wishes of the inhabitants of, say, South Down or South Armagh?

The CHAIRMAN: The Article has very wisely left the Commission a good deal of discretion in interpreting and applying its reference to economic conditions. The fact that the phrase is wide does not mean to say that every conceivable application by which you can twist some economic condition out of a set of circumstances gives you the right to do so.

The ATTORNEY-GENERAL: I am not suggesting that is not so wide.

The CHAIRMAN: You asked me a question and I am putting the answer which suggests itself. " Economic conditions " is a very wide phrase. You say that if you look at the conditions of this other area, then we are prompted to go to extravagant lengths. What I put to you is that the phrase is wide; that means that there is a certain discretion with regard to its application, because particular conditions are not specified, and the Commission is to be guided by the light of reason and common sense. But nobody can question that the supply of water to a great centre is a very vital thing affecting its economic life.

The ATTORNEY-GENERAL: It is a very vital thing to that area, undoubtedly, a very vital thing. I do not for a moment wish to minimise that, but I suggest that the Article is not so wide as that and that you are not entitled to enquire into these economic conditions in that very very wide sense as affecting perhaps Belfast, perhaps Liverpool, perhaps Manchester, but you are to give effect to the wishes of the inhabitants.

The CHAIRMAN: Do you see that in travelling to Liverpool and Manchester you are travelling beyond the limits of Ireland? I am not quite sure that I follow this. According to your view, Northern Ireland is the area to which the Commission is restricted. The place whose economic interests we are asked to consider is a place in Northern Ireland. You may say the term " economic and geographic conditions " applies to the economic and geographic conditions of the country to be dealt with, whether that is the whole of Ireland, or Northern Ireland, or Northern Ireland and the Free State; but it seems to me that by stretching your horizon so as to include Liverpool and Manchester you are bringing in quite a new consideration.

The ATTORNEY-GENERAL: I merely suggest it for the purpose of showing the absurdity of giving the words an absolutely unlimited meaning: you must qualify them.

The CHAIRMAN: Would it not be time to deal with that when somebody suggested that you ought to over-ride the wishes of the inhabitants in Northern Ireland owing to the interests of Liverpool; that is, when they ask you to look outside that country with which admittedly we have to deal? Then you would have another line of argument open to you, which is not open to you in the case of Belfast. It does seem to me that we are invited to follow a false scent if we treat this as an economic interest of Manchester or Liverpool—some place outside Ireland. You see the reason why I have put the point? It seems to lead you to a different line of argument. Fortunately, you have not to deal with any such case at present.

The ATTORNEY-GENERAL: Admittedly there must be some qualification on the words. You cannot take them in the broad sense without any limitation. I suggest again that the proper limitation is to limit these conditions to the particular area whose fate is being determined by the Commission, the particular area whose transfer or whose inclusion in one State or the other is being determined. I do not think I have anything else to say on that question of construction, but I should like to refer to one other matter in that Representation, and that is the suggestion that there is a real danger of these waterworks being interfered with in the event of the area being included in the jurisdiction of the Free State—a real danger and a danger that is likely to continue. We have had some troublous times in Ireland during the past few years, but fortunately we are at the end of that. I should be very sorry to think that there is likely in future to be any danger to any works or property in the Free State simply because they belong to Belfast or to any Corporation or person in Northern Ireland. There is at the present time very great peace and very great harmony between Northern Ireland and the Free State, between the Governments of the two areas; and I hope that that condition of things will continue. I do not think it helps the situation even to suggest that there is a danger of these works being interfered with merely by reason of the fact that they belong to Northern Ireland. So far as the other representations dealing with waterworks are concerned, there is no necessity for me to refer to them in particular, because the same considerations apply and I would suggest that the same principles of construction should be applied in considering these various representations.

Mr. FISHER: There is one point mentioned in the evidence. The contention was that assuming you had your source of supply and your reservoirs under one jurisdiction and your place of use under another jurisdiction, if it was found necessary to expand their source of supply the suggestion was that there might be inconvenience in having to go to a foreign and external legislature for that. I do not know if you would care to refer to that.

The ATTORNEY-GENERAL: Surely that is the position with every person or Corporation wishing for powers of this kind. They must go to the Parliament of the territory in which they are operating. If a Corporation in Belfast wished for compulsory powers to acquire land in the Free State, surely it is not unreasonable that they, like any other corporation or body requiring similar powers, should go to the Parliament of the Free State for the purpose of getting the necessary Bill through.

The CHAIRMAN: Obviously they would have to if the area concerned was on the Free State side of the border. They do not question the reasonableness of having to go to the Parliament of the country in which the area is situated; what they say is: " Do not put us in a position in which we have to go to the Parliament of another country which may or may not be prepared to consider us favourably, but which is not in any way subject to our direct influence. This region is at present inside our country, and if we require further powers we can go to our own Parliament. Do not put us in a position in which we shall have the difficulty of having to go to two Parliaments—to our own Parliament for authority to raise funds and so on, to another Parliament for authority to carry out the works and acquire the land."

The ATTORNEY-GENERAL: Really is that a serious reason against giving effect to the wishes of the inhabitants.

The CHAIRMAN: Undoubtedly it is a complication.

The ATTORNEY-GENERAL: It is a complication for this particular Corporation, and will be for every person and Corporation requiring to operate on both sides of the border.

The CHAIRMAN: The question is whether from the economic point of view such a complication should be created in respect of an existing undertaking.

The ATTORNEY-GENERAL: That complication is not confined, unfortunately, to the Belfast Water Supply. It affects a great many other undertakings—railways, and other things.

The CHAIRMAN: They exist on both sides of the border, but here is an undertaking which serves Belfast, its people and its industries. One of their objections, they say, is that they will be faced with a new set of difficulties if they cannot get powers to expand their undertaking from their own Parliament.

The ATTORNEY-GENERAL: Belfast gets its water supply from an area which, I would suggest according to the wishes of the inhabitants ought to be included in the Free State. That being so, I admit it would be an added inconvenience to the Belfast Water Commissioners in operating, but I suggest it is not an unreasonable thing. They would merely be placed in the same position as any other person or Corporation who, unfortunately, had to carry on a big undertaking of this kind on both sides of the border.

Dr. MacNEILL: They get a great benefit from this area, and you suggest that the fact that they derive this benefit from this area should not disenfranchise the people of this area?

The ATTORNEY-GENERAL: Yes. The existence of a boundary at all will cause inconvenience to a great many people. That is the unfortunate position that has been created by reason of the Parliament of Northern Ireland having taken a certain course.

The CHAIRMAN: There is one other point which perhaps it is right to mention to you. With regard to this question of risk, apart from people wanting to injure these works owing to some feeling against Northern Ireland—apart from the reality of any such risk as that—they put the argument also in this way: They say, " The fact that this is outside our border will lead to a feeling of insecurity and a condition of public anxiety, which we ought to avoid if possible. It may be that such things will not happen, but we know that such things have happened in the past and people have not yet forgotten them and there will be this feeling of insecurity. That, in itself, will be a serious thing even if nothing happens. It may hamper us economically, because if this water supply is not safe the industry of Belfast is not safe. The people of Belfast will be satisfied as to the security of these works if they are under the control of their own Government, but nervous about them if they are not. Apart from the question of whether any damage is going to be done to these works or not, the mere existence of this feeling of insecurity is a serious thing, and is a thing of which account ought to be taken."

The ATTORNEY-GENERAL: In so far as it exists it is disappearing, and disappearing rapidly. Things have happened in the past when the country was in a state of civil war, but that has come to an end and at the present time I think I might suggest there is as much security for property in the area of jurisdiction of the Free State as there is in any other country. If the Belfast Water Commissioners have to go into the Irish Free State to get their water supply and to get property for the purpose of that water supply, they will to that extent be citizens of the Free State; they will be paying rates, and I think they can rely upon getting all the protection that the Free State can afford. There may be a little insecurity. I do not want to minimise that, but it is not a thing that is likely to last very long.

The remaining representations all deal with areas, most of them very small areas, on the Free State side of the existing border which it is suggested should be transferred to Northern Ireland. It would not be in accordance with the letters which have passed between the Commission and my Government that I should go into any question of the evidence which has been brought forward in support of these various representations. When I last appeared before this Commission I contended that the Commission had no jurisdiction to consider the wishes of the inhabitants in any area outside the six counties of Northern Ireland. I spent some time over that proposition. I do not intend to repeat what I said before, but perhaps I may be permitted to recapitulate as shortly as possible some of the considerations which I put before the Commission in December last. I suggested that on the face of the Treaty itself there were indications that the work of the Commission was to be restricted to Northern Ireland. I pointed out that this particular provision setting up this Commission is contained in an Article dealing with Northern Ireland and is inserted, as I suggested, as a qualification upon the right of Northern Ireland to opt out of the system of the Free State. I put before the Commission another reason. The Treaty contains two alternative methods of dealing with Northern Ireland. One is contained in Article XII; the other is contained in Article XIV. Article XIV provides for the contingency of Northern Ireland electing to remain within the jurisdiction of the Free State, and it is immediately followed by another Article which provides for certain things which are to happen in that event. One of the things that was to be provided for was the safeguarding of minorities in Northern Ireland, so that you have recognised upon the face of the Treaty itself the fact that there are in Northern Ireland minorities requiring to be safeguarded. There is no suggestion of that kind with reference to the remaining 26 counties, so that I am certainly justified in saying this: that the Treaty itself recognised in Northern Ireland and nowhere else a population that was not homogeneous. Now that course contemplated by Article XIV was not adopted. Northern Ireland elected to adopt the provision made by Article XII, under which, should the Houses of Parliament of Northern Ireland present a petition to that effect, they go out of the system of the Irish Free State, but they do so subject to a qualification. The qualification is this Commission, which is to determine what area in the future is to be under the jurisdiction of the Parliament and Government of Northern Ireland. That is a qualification upon the right of Northern Ireland to go out. It implies that they go out, not with the entire of the territory which was provided for them by the Act of 1920, but with so much of that territory as this Commission should determine to contain a homogeneous population desiring to be under the control of the Parliament and Government of Northern Ireland. So much, I would suggest, is to be found in the Treaty itself, on the face of it; but when considering a document of this kind and the effect that is to be given to it, I would suggest, as I submitted before, that the Commission is not confined to the words of the Treaty—they are not blindfolded, they are entitled to look outside the Treaty, to consider the events that led up to it and to consider what was the difficulty which this provision in Article XII was intended to solve. The Act of 1920 was passed under rather peculiar circumstances. It was passed while a body was meeting in Ireland.

The CHAIRMAN: We have got the full report of the previous proceedings in which you dealt with this. I quite understand that in putting forward any other arguments in relation to these representations you do not abandon your main contention. I do not want you to feel that it is necessary to develop that contention at length to us, because we have among our records a full report of your argument.

The ATTORNEY-GENERAL: I think there is little which I can usefully add to what I said before, but I do submit that the Commission should consider carefully the events which led up to the Treaty, and should consider carefully why this Proviso is contained in Article XII. I think if they consider it in that way they will be satisfied that it was put there for the purpose of dealing with this great difficulty which existed in Northern Ireland where you had in 1921 a Parliament from which 12 members abstained as not recognising the jurisdiction of that Parliament. I suggest that this Proviso is confined to Northern Ireland, that the work of the Commission is confined to Northern Ireland, and that their only function is to determine how much of these six counties is entitled to go permanently out of the system of the Free State.

Mr. PATRICK LYNCH, K.C.: Perhaps the Commission would be kind enough to allow me to supplement what has been so fully dealt with by my colleague. I do not think I can occupy usefully the time of the Commission at any length, and I do not propose to do so. If I say anything which is a repetition of what has been so forcibly and clearly urged by my learned friend the Attorney-General it will be by inadvertence, and I certainly will not occupy the time of the Commission uselessly. I respectfully submit to the Commission that in interpreting the language of the Treaty the Commission should endeavour to ascertain what was the intention of the parties at the time they made the Agreement for the Treaty. I do not propose to do more than to emphasise what has already been urged upon the Commission as to the principle of law which is applicable to the interpretation of the language of a Treaty such as this. In order to interpret the Treaty the first work, if I might respectfully press it upon the Commission, might be to endeavour to ascertain what the parties intended who signed the Treaty. For the purpose of arriving at a conclusion upon the portion of the matter for consideration might I briefly call the attention of the Commission to a few facts?—No one representing Northern Ireland has ever claimed an inch of Ireland outside the Six Counties.

The CHAIRMAN: You would agree, would you not, that if it is our business to ascertain the intention of the parties, for the purpose of ascertaining that intention, the first thing we have to do is to look at the language of the Treaty?

Mr. LYNCH: The language of the Treaty, having regard to the facts.

The CHAIRMAN: Our business is to look at the Treaty, and then if we find difficulties or ambiguities or have trouble in identifying the subjects dealt with we are entitled to look outside to clear up those difficulties. But our first business is to look at the language of the Treaty and where such language does not admit of doubt other extraneous facts will not assist us. It is only when we are in difficulties about the language that we ought to look at extraneous facts. You would agree to that, would you not?

Mr. LYNCH: Yes, subject to this qualification, which I respectfully press upon the Commission, that you must interpret the language as you find it having regard to the facts that you have ascertained and the parties you were dealing with at the time you signed the contract. You find what the position of the parties entering into the contract was. You find them signing a contract. Surely it is an essential matter to find what was the *status quo ante* before signing the contract if there is anything that is doubtful to be interpreted in the document that is signed, before you would essay categorically to answer the question. You were good enough to put the question to me—I always invite questions suggesting difficulties to be dealt with—and I was going to elaborate very briefly some matters on that question.

The CHAIRMAN: The reason I interrupted you was because I wanted to know if that was your view of the points you wished to make to us.

Mr. LYNCH: No; I was going to lead up to that. I started with one historical fact—the Act of 1920. You find that in the Act of 1920 a line is drawn around the Six Counties which is the determining boundary between those two areas of what was originally one country. You find that done by the Act of 1920. What is the next act you find? I deal with this Treaty as ratified by legislation. The next act you find is that the two contracting parties to this Treaty signed this Agreement for a Treaty; and what else was done? An Act of Parliament was passed which gave the Free State jurisdiction over the whole of Ireland, but it does this: It suspended the operation of the Legislature of the Free State over the Six Counties which were determined as forming the territory of Northern Ireland. It suspended the operation of that Legislature until the happening of a certain event. That certain event has not happened, namely, the Parliament of Northern Ireland did not decide to "come in," if I may use the expression, under the powers of that Legislature that was to be established, and the suspended operation of the powers of the Legislature of the Irish Free State never came into operation. But what occurred? This occurred. The Commission before which I have the privilege to appear now was appointed. Something else occurred and continues. Although there is a Parliament of Northern Ireland and a Parliament of the Irish Free State, you will see if you look into the legislation that follows the Treaty that there is what is called an Irish Council which is to operate as regards certain matters that are allocated to that Council, and that is the creation of the legislation which follows this Treaty and of the Treaty itself—an Irish Council, which is to have effect in both areas, although the operation of the Legislature in the Free State has no effect and the powers of the Parliament of Northern Ireland continue to be limited, as I respectfully say with all respect to them. The reason why I stress these matters is for the purpose of dealing with the language of Article XII. I respectfully press upon this Commission that if it was within the contemplation of the parties to this Treaty that there should be, if I might use the ordinary expression, an exchange of territory or a changing of the territory by transfer to the jurisdiction of the Parliament of Northern Ireland by this Commission, we might reasonably expect to find some language to that effect in the Article. But what do we find? We find this: This area of Northern Ireland is defined by the Act of 1920; you have a Treaty entered into, and what is the interpretation to be put having regard to those facts which I take the liberty of pressing upon the Commission? You find this language in the Article, and what is the interpretation to be put upon it in the light of those facts? Might I respectfully read the words of it?

The Commission "shall determine in accordance with the wishes of the inhabitants, so far as may be compatible with economic and geographic conditions, the boundaries between Northern Ireland and the rest of Ireland."

Now if this Commission took away a part, or was to take away a part, in the area under the jurisdiction of the Parliament of the Free State, what is there in that Article No. XII that gives the Parliament of Northern Ireland powers over an inch of the ground that is now under the jurisdiction of the Irish Free State? I submit there is nothing.

The CHAIRMAN: You say there is nothing?

Mr. LYNCH: I submit there is nothing. That is the reason why I pressed upon the Commission a moment ago that legislation merely suspended the operation of the enactments to be passed by the Parliament of the Irish Free State until the happening of a certain event. That event did not happen. Therefore their operations within the area limited by the boundary of Northern Ireland never took place or had effect there. Their operations were confined and the effect of their legislation was confined to what was within the area of the twenty-six counties. The Northern Parliament had jurisdiction to legislate according to the powers vested in them for the area within their own territory. They still have that power to legislate for every portion of it that remains, but if this Commission transfers any portion of the territory of the Irish Free State, I respectfully submit that there is no power in the Northern Parliament under Article XII to legislate for that. I am putting that respectfully before you, as a lawyer, and head of this Commission, as the view that I respectfully put upon even the most strict interpretation that can be put on the language of this Treaty. But I go further and submit this. I hope I shall not unnecessarily infringe upon the indulgence granted me by representing anything already stated upon it, but I do respectfully submit that in interpreting this clause the Commission cannot shut out from its consideration those facts which have been so repeatedly urged upon them—the antecedent facts, the facts at the time the parties were contracting; and I respectfully submit they will have to ascertain the intention of the parties to this contract when they signed this Treaty. They must find that both the parties to this Treaty agreed that the Commission that was to be set up could not order an exchange of territory or a changing of territory which would result in a transfer of part of the area of Southern Ireland to the jurisdiction of the Northern Ireland Parliament.

The CHAIRMAN: I think I ought to interrupt you at this stage. That is a point that has been made before, but as you are dealing with it I want to put a point to you that I think you should deal with in order to assist us. You say there are no words in Article XII which give the Government and Parliament of Northern Ireland jurisdiction over any area which might be transferred to them by the Commission under Article XII.

Mr. LYNCH: I do say that.

The CHAIRMAN: Assume for the moment that the power to determine boundaries gives the Commission power in itself to shift the boundary either way. Then take the last words of the Proviso:—
" . . . for the purposes of the Government of Ireland Act, 1920, and of this instrument, the boundary of Northern Ireland shall be such as may be determined by such Commission." You say those words give back to the Irish Free State the territory of Northern Ireland where the boundary is shifted so as to reduce that territory?

Mr. LYNCH: The jurisdiction automatically operates upon that portion of the territory. There is no corresponding legislation which gives the Northern Parliament power to have jurisdiction.

The CHAIRMAN: The boundary of Northern Ireland for the purpose of the Government of Ireland Act is surely the boundary of the area in which the Government and Parliament of Northern Ireland exercise jurisdiction, and the boundary which the Commission fix is made by this clause the boundary of Northern Ireland for the purposes of the Government of Ireland Act and for the purposes of the Treaty. Why therefore do you say there is nothing in the clause to enable the Northern Parliament to exercise jurisdiction over any portion of the Free State which might be included in Northern Ireland as a result of the Commission's determination of the boundary?

Mr. LYNCH: To give that effect you look for something in this Article which is not there. If both parties intended such a state of things to be brought about it is a curious thing that there is a complete absence of language to that effect in the Article.

The CHAIRMAN: Why are not the words I have quoted wide enough to have the effect suggested?

Mr. LYNCH: They are to be taken in connection with the previous words of the Article. Read in conjunction with those previous words that, I submit, is the boundary or limited area.

The CHAIRMAN: It is a limited area in any case. We were assuming for the moment that that power to determine the boundary in itself would give power to shift the boundary either way. You said if that was so there was no provision in this clause which would give the Government and Parliament of Northern Ireland jurisdiction over added territory, and I asked you "why is it that these words are not wide enough to give them such jurisdiction"?

Mr LYNCH: Because they do not say so.

The CHAIRMAN: But they do say what I have just said.

Mr. LYNCH: If that was the intention of the parties the words of the Article would have pointed out that the Government and Parliament of Northern Ireland would have jurisdiction over the transferred area or any portion of the transferred area of the Free State, but it does not.

The CHAIRMAN: The effect must be to give that Government jurisdiction over the territory included in its boundary.

Mr. LYNCH: You have to bear in mind that the Parliament of Northern Ireland is one which has a limited jurisdiction. Serjeant Hanna dealt with that as distinct from the jurisdiction of the Free State.

The CHAIRMAN: So far as I recall, he dealt with that in more than one connection, but it was pointed out that there were certain powers which the Government of Northern Ireland did not possess—which the British Government possessed—so that bringing an area of Northern Ireland under the provisions of the Government of Ireland Act, 1920, affected not only the Government and Parliament of Northern Ireland but also the Government and Parliament of the United Kingdom. The words are wide enough, because they say "for the purposes of the Government of Ireland Act," which deals with the powers of both Parliaments and Governments.

Mr. LYNCH: Under the Government of Ireland Act, 1920, the Parliament of Northern Ireland had jurisdiction of a limited character, as was pointed out by Serjeant Hanna. Under this Treaty the people of the Free State and the legislature of the Free State, which represents the people of the Free State, have a greater measure of freedom, if I may say so, from external control. They are not subject to any control in their legislation. The Parliament of Northern Ireland is. If Article XII contemplated cutting down the liberties—I might say the legislative powers—of a portion of the people in the Free State and substituting for that power a limited power, namely, that which electors in Northern Ireland would have, surely it would be done by language precise and specific, and would say so.

The CHAIRMAN: But this language is precise and comprehensive, is it not?

Mr. LYNCH: It is a matter for the interpretation of the tribunal. I do not wish to be taken as declining to deal with it.

The CHAIRMAN: I interrupted the thread of your argument, and I want you to resume it when you wish.

Mr. LYNCH: I put it to the Commission that the legislative powers of the two tribunals are entirely distinct and different. One has a limited legislative power—the Parliament of Northern Ireland. The Parliament of the Free State has powers of legislation of an entirely different character. That Parliament represents the people of the Free State. If the liberties and powers of legislation of any portion of the Free State were to be taken away, I would respectfully submit that that would be expressed in this Article. I therefore respectfully press the view that the intention, having regard to the words of this Article, of the parties, so far as was expressed, was an intention to limit the area of Northern Ireland if this Commission thought that within that area there were units or areas whose inhabitants expressed their wishes in a particular way, having regard to the considerations expressed in the Article. I do not know that I would be justified in occupying the time of the Commission further, except with this. Suppose the Commission were to consider for a moment that they ought to ascertain, or endeavour to ascertain, the views of people, bodies or inhabitants outside the boundary of the Northern area and go into the Free State to ascertain the wishes of sections of the inhabitants there. What is the limit to which they could go? How far could they go in order to ascertain those wishes? Is not the reasonable construction to be put upon it this: The Commission has heard evidence and has studied statistics, I have no doubt, as regards the result of the census for a number of years. Now I respectfully press upon the Commission that what was operating upon the minds of the contracting parties at the time this contract or Treaty was entered into was this·—If you find as a fact, as a result of your investigations, that there are large areas—take counties, even counties—the population of which you have ascertained as a fact, the inhabitants of which you have ascertained as a fact, desiring to be under the jurisdiction of the Free State; suppose you ascertain that, suppose you ascertain that that applies to one county or two counties—I put a hypothetical case—suppose you ascertain in the case of one or two counties that the census discloses a particular result, say, for 40 or 50 years down to the last census, is it not far more likely that what the contracting parties were at when signing this Treaty? The Northern area is now defined as being six counties, but if these six counties do not wish to come under the jurisdiction of the Free State and if these six counties wish to remain out and have a Parliament of their own, " Well, we will set up a Commission and get them to ascertain if there are large units of the population within that area who express their wishes contrary to the position existing now, having regard of course to the other matters—geographic and economic conditions." But if you find this, and I respectfully press it upon the Commission, that there are large areas—take counties, take cities—which you come to a conclusion about at the present time which for 40 or 50 years have expressed their intention, so far as they could express it, in a particular way, I would ask you to come to the conclusion that what the parties were at when they signed this agreement was that there may be such districts and that the Commission should deal with them lest any injustice be done. I adopt the argument which you were kind enough to suggest a moment ago might be applied to these matters—reasonableness, " sweet reasonableness." What pressed upon people in various parts of the Six Counties—I suppose I may have permission to say it; it is a matter of history—was that they did not want to be forced under a Legislature they did not wish to be under. They were excluded by the Act of 1920. The Treaty came in December, 1921. Apparently that was the attitude of the contracting parties, subject to this: "We would not force any of those people to come in if they do not want to, but if there are people within this area who wish to have the suspended powers come into operation, we will allow them to express it and appoint a Commission to ascertain if there are such people or not." That is what I respectfully submit was in the minds of the parties when they signed this Treaty, and that is the interpretation that ought to be put upon it by the Commission. The matter of geographic and economic conditions has been fully dealt with by the learned Attorney-General. Of course we adopt what has been said by you, or members of the Commission, that economic considerations are relative. Economy is a thing that depends upon the interests of a number of people, demand and supply, and market facilities and things of that sort. We must recognise that. What is the reasonable interpretation, again applying that method of dealing with this portion of the Article? What is the reasonable interpretation to be put upon the expression "so far as may be compatible with economic and geographic conditions." The Commission, no doubt, has come across districts, or units—call them whatever you like, poor-law areas or any other areas—where you found them, so far as you could ascertain, expressing their wishes in a particular way. The Commission might possibly think, "Well, this construction suggested by the Free State rather suggests that those people would, against their own interests, in a foolish way say 'We desire to vote ourselves out of the jurisdiction of Northern Ireland' —foolishly and disregarding their own interests." That is a very delicate matter, and an extremely difficult matter to deal with. But what we respectfully submit is that economic considerations and geographic considerations that affect these inhabitants are rare—because sometimes, of course, legislation deals with people in a way they do not wish themselves. You may think, although the people, of a district say, "We prefer to be under the Free State; we prefer not to be under the jurisdiction of Northern Ireland," still the economic and geographic considerations which we respectfully press upon you are to influence you on the economic and geographic conditions of the inhabitants themselves. Nothing I could say further would be of use to the Commission having regard to the full discussion of the various matters that have been under your consideration, and I do not propose further to occupy your time. If I have done anything by way of infringement on the promise I made not to deal with matters dealt with before, I am very sorry.

The CHAIRMAN: We have no fault to find with you so far as that is concerned. (*To the Attorney-General*). Is that all you propose to say to us to-day, Mr. Attorney-General?

The ATTORNEY-GENERAL: I do not think there is anything else arising out of this correspondence on which I can address the Commission. If there is any other point which the Commission would like me to discuss, I would be very glad to do so. I think I have covered the points dealt with in the correspondence.

The CHAIRMAN: We are much obliged to you. I do not think there are any other points we will ask you to deal with to-day.

(*The Hearing then terminated.*)

DRAFT.

APPENDIX V.

AWARD OF IRISH BOUNDARY COMMISSION.

WHEREAS it is provided by Article 12 of the Articles of Agreement for a Treaty between Great Britain and Ireland, dated the sixth day of December, Nineteen hundred and twenty-one, that, in the event of such an address as is in the said Article mentioned being presented to His Majesty by both Houses of Parliament of Northern Ireland within the time mentioned in the said Article, a Commission consisting of three persons, one to be appointed by the Government of the Irish Free State, one to be appointed by the Government of Northern Ireland, and one who shall be Chairman to be appointed by the British Government, shall determine in accordance with the wishes of the inhabitants, so far as may be compatible with economic and geographic conditions, the boundaries between Northern Ireland and the rest of Ireland, and that for the purposes of the Government of Ireland Act 1920 and of the said Articles, the boundary of Northern Ireland shall be such as may be determined by such Commission : *10 & 11 Geo. V, Ch. 67.*

AND WHEREAS the said Articles of Agreement for a Treaty have been duly ratified by legislation, namely, by the Irish Free State Agreement Act 1922 and by the Irish Free State Constitution Act 1922 (Session 2) (enacted by the Parliament of the United Kingdom of Great Britain and Ireland) and by the Constitution of the Irish Free State (Saorstát Eireann) Act 1922 (enacted by the House of the Parliament constituted pursuant to the Irish Free State Agreement Act 1922 (Dail Eireann) sitting as a Constituent Assembly) : *12 Geo. V, Ch. 4. 13 Geo. V, Ch. 1.*

AND WHEREAS such an address as is mentioned in the said Article 12 was duly presented to His Majesty within the time mentioned in the said Article :

AND WHEREAS by an Agreement dated the Fourth day of August 1924 supplementing the said Article 12 of the said Articles of Agreement for a Treaty it is provided that, if the Government of Northern Ireland does not before the date therein mentioned appoint the Commissioner to be appointed under the said Article 12 by that Government, the power of the Government of Northern Ireland to appoint such Commissioner shall thereupon be transferred to and exercised by the British Government, and that for the purposes of the said Article any Commissioner so appointed by the British Government shall be deemed to be a Commissioner appointed by the Government of Northern Ireland :

AND WHEREAS the said supplementing Agreement was duly confirmed by the Irish Free State (Confirmation of Agreement) Act 1924 (enacted by the Parliament of the United Kingdom of Great Britain and Ireland) and by the Treaty (Confirmation of *14 & 15 Geo. V, Ch. 41.*

[13849A]

No. 51 of
1924. Supplemental Agreement) Act 1924 (enacted by the Oireachtas of Saorstát Eireann) :

AND WHEREAS the Commission provided for by the said Article 12 as supplemented by the said supplementing Agreement was duly constituted as follows :—

The Honourable Mr. Justice Feetham, Commissioner appointed by the British Government (Chairman) :

Professor Eoin MacNeill, Commissioner appointed by the Government of the Irish Free State :

Joseph R. Fisher, Esquire, Commissioner appointed by the British Government to be the Commissioner deemed to be a Commissioner appointed by the Government of Northern Ireland for the purposes of the said Article 12 :

AND WHEREAS the said three Commissioners have duly undertaken and entered upon the work of determining the boundaries between Northern Ireland and the rest of Ireland with which the Commission is charged under the terms of the said Article 12, and have examined and enquired into all matters relating thereto, and have duly weighed and considered all evidence and arguments heard by them or submitted to them in writing :

NOW THEREFORE WE the undersigned Commissioners DO HEREBY under and by virtue of the powers vested in us as constituting a majority of such Commission finally determine the boundaries between Northern Ireland and the rest of Ireland to be the boundaries constituted by the Boundary Line described in the following Description and further shown on the Admiralty Charts, Ordnance Survey Sheets and Plans specified in the Schedule to the said Description and signed by us :

PROVIDED ALWAYS that if there should be found to be an inconsistency in any respect between the boundary line as described in the said Description and the Boundary Line as shown on the said Charts, Sheets and Plans the Description shall in such respect prevail :

DESCRIPTION OF THE BOUNDARY LINE.

This Description is subject to the Rules of Interpretation which appear at the end thereof.

NOTE.—The Sheets referred to in this Description are the NORTH OF IRELAND BOUNDARY SHEETS, consisting of Admiralty Charts, Ordnance Survey Sheets and Plans, on which the Boundary Line and necessary details are shown, lettered "N.I.B.S." and numbered consecutively from 1 to 68, signed by Major R. A. Boger, R.E., Chief Technical Assistant, on the 4th day of December, 1925.

From point (1), where a line bearing 61° true from DUNAGREE POINT EAST LIGHTHOUSE intersects an arc of a circle drawn

at a radius of 3 nautical miles from Low Water Mark at
INISHOWEN HEAD,

to point (2), situated at 5 cables, 96° true from DUNAGREE
POINT EAST LIGHTHOUSE,
>   the Boundary Line is a straight line running in the direction
>   235° true;

thence to point (2a), 7.5 cables, 136° true from MOVILLE SCOTCH
CHURCH, as shown on Sheet 1 :—
>   the median line of the North Channel, then the median line
>   of the entrance channel (between MOVILLE BANK and
>   McKENNY'S BANK), all as shown on Sheet 1;

thence to point (3), 3.4 cables, 135° true from CARRICKARORY
PIER HEAD :—
>   a straight line;

thence North-Westward to point (4), 1 cable, 135° true from
CARRICKARORY PIER HEAD :—
>   a straight line;

thence to point (5), a perch situated at approximately 19.6 cables,
98° true from the CONDUM ROCKS, Trigonometrical Station
(477) :—
>   a straight line;

thence to point (6), a perch situated at approximately 13.2 cables
165° true from the above Trigonometrical Station :—
>   a straight line;

thence to point (7), a perch situated at approximately 24.2 cables
135° true from CLOGHGLASS Trigonometrical Station (1302) :—
>   the line following the shortest possible distance between
>   points (6) and (7) consistently with including in NORTHERN
>   IRELAND the whole dredged channel, as shown on
>   Sheet 1;

thence to point (8), formed by the intersection of the prolongation
South-Westward of a straight line drawn between points (6) and (7)
with the prolongation South-Eastward of a line drawn between
points "X" and "Y" (as shown on Sheet 2) on the boundary
between the townlands of ARDMORE and DRUMSKELLAN, both
in the County of Donegal :—
>   a straight line;

thence to point (9), the point of junction of the boundary between
the townlands of ARDMORE and DRUMSKELLAN with the High
Water of ordinary tides :—
>   a straight line;

thence Westward to point (10), (about 500 yards North-East of
THOMPSON'S TOWN BRIDGE) on the boundary between the

[13849A]

townlands of CARNAMOYLE and MUFF where this boundary turns Southward :—

in succession the boundaries between the townland of ARDMORE (NORTHERN IRELAND) and the townlands of DRUMSKELLAN and ESKAHEEN (IRISH FREE STATE), then the boundary between the townlands of ARDMORE and CARNAMOYLE, then a portion of the boundary between the townlands of MUFF and CARNAMOYLE;

thence to point (11), (about 550 yards South-West of THOMPSON'S TOWN BRIDGE), where the Western end of the dividing line of parcels "A" and "B," shown on Sheet 2, meets the SOPPOG–CARNAMOYLE townland boundary :—

the line including in NORTHERN IRELAND parcels "A" of the townland of CARNAMOYLE, and including in the IRISH FREE STATE parcels "B" of the same townland, as well as the GORTCORMACAN–THOMPSON'S TOWN BRIDGE ROAD and ROAD JUNCTION, all as shown on Sheet 2;

thence to point (12), (about 280 yards South-East of BALLYLENA LOWER ROAD JUNCTION), where the Eastern end of the dividing line of parcels "C" and "D," as shown on Sheet 2, meets the GORTNASKEA–GORTCORMACAN townland boundary :—

a portion of the SOPPOG–CARNAMOYLE townland boundary, then in succession the boundaries between the townland of DRUMHAGGART (NORTHERN IRELAND), and the townlands of CARNAMOYLE and GORTCORMACAN (IRISH FREE STATE), then a portion of the GORTNASKEA–GORTCORMACAN townland boundary;

thence to point (13), (about 150 yards South-West of BALLYLENA LOWER ROAD JUNCTION), forming the Easternmost point of the BIRDSTOWN DEMESNE townland, as shown on Sheet 3 :—

the line dividing parcels "C" (NORTHERN IRELAND) of the townland of GORTNASKEA from parcels "D" (IRISH FREE STATE) of the same townland, all as shown on Sheets 2 and 3;

thence to point (14), (about 200 yards South of the Westernmost point of the BIRDSTOWN DEMESNE townland), where the Eastern end of the dividing line of parcels "E" and "F" meets the BIRDSTOWN DEMESNE–GARVARY townland boundary, as shown on Sheet 3 :—

a portion of the BIRDSTOWN DEMESNE–GORTNASKEA townland boundary, then a portion of the BIRDSTOWN DEMESNE–GARVARY townland boundary;

thence to point (15), (about 500 yards West of GLEN BRIDGE), where the Southern end of the dividing line of parcels "E" and

"F," as shown on Sheet 3, meets the BALLYEDEROWEN–GARVARY townland boundary :—

the line including in NORTHERN IRELAND the parcels "E" of the townland of GARVARY and including in the IRISH FREE STATE the parcels "F" of the same townland, as well as a portion of the GLEN BRIDGE–GLACK ROAD lying between two of the parcels "E" and "F," as shown on Sheet 3;

thence to point (16), the point of junction of the townlands of BALLYEDEROWEN, GARVARY and MONREAGH or BARR OF KILMACKILVENNY :—

a portion of the BALLYEDEROWEN–GARVARY townland boundary;

thence to point (17), the point of junction of the BALLYEDEROWEN, SKEOGE and INCH LEVEL (E.D. BURT) townlands :—

Southward, for a distance of about 100 yards, a straight line as far as the Northern end of the dividing line of parcels "G" and "H," as shown on Sheet 3, then the line which includes in NORTHERN IRELAND the parcels "G" of the townland of BALLYEDEROWEN as well as the road on the West side of the Rectory Grounds and the road fork East of the said grounds, and including in the IRISH FREE STATE the parcels "H" of the townland of BALLYEDEROWEN as well as the road North of the Rectory Grounds, the road junction on the North-West corner of the said grounds, and the portion of the LONDONDERRY AND LOUGH SWILLY RAILWAY which lies between the parcels "G" and "I," all as shown on Sheet 3;

thence to point (18), where the CARROWNAMADDY–INCH LEVEL (E. D. BURT) townland boundary meets the Eastern edge of the drain along the East side of the road running Northward from SPEENOGE POST OFFICE, as shown on Sheet 4 :—

in succession the boundaries between the townlands of SKEEOGE and LISFANNAN (NORTHERN IRELAND) and the townland of INCH LEVEL (E. D. BURT) (IRISH FREE STATE), then a portion of the CARROWNAMADDY–INCH LEVEL townland boundary;

thence to point (19), where the CARROWNAMADDY–SPEENOGE townland boundary crosses the Southern fence of the SPEENOGE–SKEOGE road, as shown on Sheet 4 :—

a line following the Eastern edge of the last-mentioned drain, then across the SPEENOGE–SKEOGE road, then the Southern fence of the SPEENOGE–SKEOGE ROAD, (the last-mentioned drain and fence, and the road junction of the last-mentioned roads being included in the IRISH FREE STATE);

thence to point (20), (about 520 yards North-East of the centre of GREENAN FORT), where the CARROWREAGH–SPEENOGE townland boundary meets the South-West corner of parcel "K," as shown on Sheet 4 :—

a portion of the CARROWNAMADDY–SPEENOGE townland boundary, then a portion of the CARROWREAGH–SPEENOGE townland boundary;

thence to point (21), (about 180 yards South-East of the centre of GREENAN FORT), where the CARROWREAGH–TOULETT townland boundary turns from a South-Easterly to a South-Westerly direction, as shown on Sheet 4 :—

a straight line joining point (20) with the intersection of parcels "L," "M" and "N," then in a South-Westerly direction the line dividing parcels "M" (NORTHERN IRELAND) of the townland of CARROWREAGH from the portion of parcel "L" (IRISH FREE STATE) of the same townland, all as shown on sheet 4 ;

thence to point (22), (about 500 yards N.E. by E. from B.M. 115.0, KESHENDS UPPER), where the GORTLUSH–BOHULLION LOWER townland boundary first strikes the KESHENDS UPPER –PORTLOUGH UPPER ROAD, as shown on Sheet 4 :—

a portion of the CARROWREAGH–TOULETT townland boundary, then in succession the boundaries between the townlands of GORTINLIEVE, BOGAY GLEBE and PORTLOUGH (NORTHERN IRELAND) and the townlands of TOULETT and BOHULLION UPPER (IRISH FREE STATE), then the GORTLUSH–BOHULLION UPPER townland boundary, then a portion of the GORTLUSH-BOHULLION LOWER townland boundary;

thence to point (23), the point of junction of the townlands of ROOSKY, CASTLEFORWARD DEMESNE and KESHENDS :—

a line crossing the KESHENDS UPPER–PORTLOUGH UPPER ROAD at right angles, then a line including in NORTHERN IRELAND the parcels "O" of the townlands of GORTLUSH, KESHENDS and ROOSKY, as well as the road leading to KESHENDS farm, and including in the IRISH FREE STATE the parcels "P" of the townlands of BOHULLION LOWER, DEER PARK WEST and KESHENDS, as well as the portion of the road South of KESHENDS UPPER which lies between the said parcels "O" and "P," all as shown on Sheet 4 ;

thence to point (24), where the DOOISH–GORTREE townland boundary strikes the Eastern boundary of the LONDONDERRY and LOUGH SWILLY RAILWAY (LETTERKENNY BRANCH) :—

in succession the boundaries between the townlands of ROOSKY (E. D. CASTLEFORWARD), DRUMMAY and TULLY-ANNAN (NORTHERN IRELAND) and the townlands of CASTLEFORWARD DEMESNE, BALLYHASKY, PLASTER and GORTREE (IRISH FREE STATE), then a portion of the DOOISH–GORTREE townland boundary;

thence Southward to point (25), where the RYELANDS–GALDONAGH townland boundary cuts the Eastern boundary of the last mentioned railway :—
the Eastern boundary of the railway;

thence to point (26), where the ARDAGH–DRUMATOLAND townland boundary strikes the Western side of the HEATHERY HILL–ARDAGH LOWER ROAD :—
a portion of the RYELANDS–GALDONAGH townland boundary, then in succession the boundaries between the townlands of LISMOGHRY and ARDAGH (NORTHERN IRELAND) and the townlands of GALDONAGH, GALDONAGH GLEBE and CASTLEDOWEY (IRISH FREE STATE), then a portion of the ARDAGH–DRUMATOLAND townland boundary;

thence to point (27), the point of junction of the townlands of BROCKAGH, MOMEEN and DRUMATOLAND :—
the line including in NORTHERN IRELAND the parcels "Q" of the townlands of DRUMATOLAND and BROCKAGH, as well as the portion of the HEATHERY HILL–ARDAGH LOWER ROAD between two of the parcels "Q" and "R," and including in the IRISH FREE STATE parcels "R" of the townland of DRUMATOLAND, all as shown on Sheet 7;

thence Southward to point (28), (about 380 yards North-West of WREN'S NEST), where the Northern end of the line dividing parcels "S" from parcels "T" meets the WOODLANDS–CARRICKADAWSON townland boundary, as shown on Sheet 7 :—
the MOMEEN–DRUMATOLAND townland boundary, then the MOMEEN–CARRICKADAWSON townland boundary, then a portion of the WOODLANDS–CARRICKADAWSON townland boundary;

thence to point (29), (about 500 yards to the South of WREN'S NEST), where the Southern end of the line dividing parcels "S" from parcels "T" meets the WOODLANDS–CARNSHANNAGH townland boundary, as shown on Sheet 7 :—
the line including in NORTHERN IRELAND parcels "S" of the townlands of CARRICKADAWSON and CARNSHANNAGH, and including in the IRISH FREE STATE the parcels "T" of the said townlands, as well as the portion of the CARNSHANNAGH–RUSHYMULLAN ROAD, West of the parcels "S," all as shown on Sheet 7;

thence in a general Easterly direction to point (30), (about 470 yards to the North of the BALLYLENNAN ROAD JUNCTION), where the Western end of the dividing line of parcels "V" and

" W " meets the LETTERGULL–BALLYLENNAN townland
boundary :—
> a portion of the WOODLANDS–CARNSHANNAGH townland
> boundary, then in succession the boundaries between the
> townlands of WOODLANDS and LETTERGULL
> (NORTHERN IRELAND) and the townland of DRUM-
> MUCKLAGH (IRISH FREE STATE), then a portion of the
> LETTERGULL–BALLYLENNAN townland boundary;

thence to point (31), the point of junction of the townlands of
RATTEEN, CAVANACAW and CREATLAND :—
> the line dividing the parcels " V " (NORTHERN IRELAND)
> of the townlands of BALLYLENNAN, BALLYBOE (E. D.
> FEDDYGLASS), CREAGHADOOS, CAVANACAW and
> CREATLAND from the parcels " W " (IRISH FREE
> STATE) of the townlands of BALLYLENNAN,
> LISTANNAGH, CREAGHADOOS and CAVANACAW, as
> shown on Sheet 7;

thence to point (32), the point of junction of the CUTTYMANHILL–
CARRICKMORE townland boundary with the High Water Mark
along the West bank of the RIVER FOYLE, as shown on
Sheet 8 :—
> in succession the boundaries between the townlands of
> CREATLAND, WHITEHILL and CUTTYMANHILL
> (NORTHERN IRELAND), and the townlands of RATTEEN,
> DRUMEARN and CARRICKMORE (IRISH FREE STATE);

thence to point (33), (about 150 yards East of point (32)), where a
line drawn due East from point (32) intersects the County and
Barony boundary up the RIVER FOYLE as represented on
Sheets 8 and 9 :—
> a straight line;

thence Southward to point (34), (South of the town of LIFFORD),
where the last-mentioned County and Barony boundary meets the
TOWN PARKS–CONEYBURROW townland boundary :—
> portions of the County and Barony boundary up the RIVERS
> FOYLE and FINN, as represented on Sheets 8 and 9;

thence to point (35), (about 500 yards South of CLADY BRIDGE),
where the County, Barony and townland boundary leaves the
RIVER FINN, going Southward :—
> the last-mentioned County, Barony and Townland boundary;

thence to point (36), where the TYRONE–DONEGAL County
boundary meets the FEARN–TULLYARD townland boundary :
> the last-mentioned County boundary;

thence Westward to point (37), where the FEARN–SKELPY
townland boundary cuts the East side of the CASTLEDERG-
STRABANE ROAD :—
> the FEARN–TULLYARD townland boundary, then a portion
> of the FEARN–SKELPY townland boundary;

thence to point (38), (about 630 yards West of B.M. 590.8), where the line dividing the portion "B.1" of the parcel "B" from the parcels "A" meets the FEARN–DRUMDOIT townland boundary, as shown on Sheet 11 :—

the East side of the CASTLEDERG–STRABANE road, then the line dividing the portion "B.1" (NORTHERN IRELAND) of the parcel "B" of the townland of FEARN from the parcels "A" and the portions "B.2" and "B.3" (IRISH FREE STATE) of the parcel "B" of the same townland, all as represented on Sheet 11;

thence Southward to point (39), where the FEARN–DRUMDOIT townland boundary meets the TYRONE–DONEGAL County boundary :—
a portion of the FEARN–DRUMDOIT townland boundary :

thence to point (40), where the CARNOUGHTER–GARVAGH townland boundary meets the TYRONE–DONEGAL County Boundary :—
a portion of the TYRONE–DONEGAL County boundary;

thence to point (41), (about 800 yards South-West of AGHAMORE BRIDGE), where the AGHAMORE–SEEGRONAN townland boundary meets the North end of the dividing line of parcels "C" and "D," as shown on Sheet 14 :—

in succession the boundaries between the townlands of CARNOUGHTER, DREENAN, LISNACLOON, LISLAIRD, CREEDUFF, LEITRIM and SCRALEA (NORTHERN IRELAND), and the townlands of GARVAGH, LEGATON-EGAN, MAGHERANAGEERAGH, WOODSIDE, GLEBE (E. D. KILLETER), WOODSIDE, CRILLY'S HILL and SEEGRONAN (IRISH FREE STATE), then a portion of the AGHAMORE–SEEGRONAN townland boundary;

thence to point (42), the point of junction of the townlands of AGHAMORE, CARRICKAHOLTEN and SEEGRONAN :—
the line dividing the portion "C.1" (NORTHERN IRELAND) of parcel "C" of the townland of AGHAMORE from the parcels "D" and the portion "C.2" (IRISH FREE STATE) of parcel "C" of the same townland, all as shown on Sheet 14;

thence to point (43), the point of junction of the CARRICKA-HOLTEN–SEEGRONAN townland boundary with the TYRONE-DONEGAL County boundary :—
the CARRICKAHOLTEN–SEEGRONAN townland boundary;

thence to point (44), where the TIEVEMORE–CROCKNACUNNY townland boundary meets the TYRONE–DONEGAL County boundary :—
a portion of the last-mentioned County boundary;

thence to point (45), (about 375 yards West of the point of junction of the CARN, BALLYMACAVANY and TAWLAGHT townlands), where the Northern end of the line dividing parcels " E " from parcels " F " meets the CARN–BALLYMACAVANY townland boundary, as shown on Sheet 16 :—

> in succession the boundaries between the townlands of TIEVE-MORE, CULLION, SESSIAGHKEELTA (NORTHERN IRELAND), and the townlands of CROCKNACUNNY and TAWLAGHT (IRISH FREE STATE), then the boundary between the townlands of CARN and TAWLAGHT, then a portion of the boundary between the townlands of CARN and BALLYMACAVANY;

thence in a South-Westerly direction to point (46), (about 450 yards North-West of SPA WELL), where the Southern end of the dividing line between parcels " E " and " F " meets the CROAGH–BOEESHILL townland boundary, as shown on Sheet 17 :—

> the line dividing parcels " E " (NORTHERN IRELAND) of the townlands of CARN and CROAGH from parcels " F " (IRISH FREE STATE) of the same townlands, all as shown on Sheets 16 and 17;

thence Southward to point (47), (about 180 yards North-West of the point of junction of the townlands of DRUMGUN, CARRICK-RORY and KIMMID), where the Eastern end of the dividing line of parcels " G " and " H " meets the KIMMID–CARRICKRORY townland boundary, as shown on Sheet 17 :—

> a portion of the CROAGH–BOEESHILL townland boundary, then in succession the boundaries between the townlands of AGHALOUGH and DRUMNASKEA (NORTHERN IRELAND) and the townlands of BOEESHILL and CORLEA (E.D. PETTIGOE) (IRISH FREE STATE), then the DRUMNASKEA–CARRICKRORY townland boundary, then a portion of the KIMMID–CARRICKRORY townland boundary;

thence to point (48), the point of junction of the townlands of DRUMGUN, FINCASHEL and CARRICKRORY :—

> the line dividing parcels " G " (NORTHERN IRELAND) of the townland of CARRICKRORY from the parcels " H " (IRISH FREE STATE) of the same townland, then in a Southerly direction a straight line about 150 yards long through DRUMGUN LOUGH, all as shown on Sheet 17;

thence to point (49), (about 750 yards South of point (48)), where the Eastern end of the dividing line of parcels " K " and " L " meets the DRUMGUN–FINCASHEL townland boundary :—

> a portion of the last-mentioned townland boundary;

thence to point (50), the point of junction of the townlands of MULNAGOAD, BANNUS and CARNTRESSY :—

> the line dividing the parcels " K " (NORTHERN IRELAND) of the townland of FINCASHEL from the parcels " L "

(IRISH FREE STATE) of the same townland, then a straight line about 260 yards long across the CARNTRESSY SCHOOL–PETTIGOE ROAD, the intervening parcel and the Northern portion of BANNUS LOUGH, all as shown on Sheet 17;

thence to point (51), where the BANNUS–CARNTRESSY townland boundary meets the FERMANAGH–DONEGAL County boundary :—
the last-mentioned townland boundary;

thence to point (52), the point of junction of the TULLYCHURRY–TULLYVOGY townland boundary with the FERMANAGH–DONEGAL County boundary :—
a portion of the last-mentioned County boundary;

thence to point (53), Trigonometrical Point 476 on BLACK HILL, shown on Sheet 18 :—
a straight line;

thence to point (54), the point of junction of the TULLYNA-BOHOGE, DERRYCHULLOO and TULLYVOGY townlands :—
a straight line;

thence to point (55), (near B.M. 272.3 on the TAWNAGHGORM–DERRYCHULLOO townland boundary), where this townland boundary meets the North end of the dividing line between parcels " M " and " N," as shown on Sheet 18 :—
in succession the boundaries between the townlands of TULLYNABOHOGE and ROSSHARBOUR (NORTHERN IRELAND) and the townland of DERRYCHULLOO (IRISH FREE STATE), then a portion of the TAWNAGH-GORM–DERRYCHULLOO townland boundary;

thence to point (56), (about 110 yards East of GARVARY LODGE), where the TAWNAGHGORM–GARVARY townland boundary leaves, going in a Southerly direction, the Southern side of the GARVARY LODGE–TAWNAGHGORM SCHOOL LANE, as shown on Sheet 18 :—
the line dividing parcels " M " (NORTHERN IRELAND) of the townland of TAWNAGHGORM from parcels " N " (IRISH FREE STATE) of the townlands of TAWNAGHGORM and GARVARY, as shown on Sheet 18;

thence to point (57), (about 210 yards South-East of the disused iron shaft), where the TAWNYNORAN–BALLAGHGEE townland boundary meets the South-Eastern end of the dividing line of parcels " P " and " Q," as shown on Sheet 20 :—
a portion of the TAWNAGHGORM–GARVARY townland boundary, then in succession the boundaries between the townlands of BALLYMAGAGHRAN, TIRIGANNON, TAWNYNORAN (NORTHERN IRELAND) and the town-

lands of GARVARY, DERRYRONA GLEBE and
DERRYNACRANNOG (IRISH FREE STATE), then a
portion of the TAWNYNORAN–BALLAGHGEE townland
boundary;

thence to point (58), on the TIEVEALOUGH–GADALOUGH
townland boundary, situated at a distance of 100-ft. measured in
a straight line Westward from the point of junction of the
TIEVEALOUGH – GADALOUGH – BALLAGHGEE townland
boundary, as shown on Sheet 20 :—

    the dividing line of parcel " P " (NORTHERN IRELAND) of
    the townland of BALLAGHGEE from parcels " Q " (IRISH
    FREE STATE) of the same townland, then a straight line
    about 215 yards long, all as shown on Sheet 20 ;

thence to point (59), the point of junction of the KEENAGHAN–
GADALOUGH townland boundary with the FERMANAGH–
DONEGAL County boundary :—

    a portion of the TIEVEALOUGH–GADALOUGH townland
    boundary, then the KEENAGHAN–GADALOUGH townland
    boundary;

thence to point (60), the point of junction of the KEENAGHAN–
COMMONS townland boundary with the FERMANAGH–
DONEGAL County boundary :—

    a portion of the last-mentioned County boundary;

thence to point (61), (about 500 yards to the West of the point of
junction of the GRAFFY, RATHMORE and COMMONS townlands), forming the Westernmost point of the townland of
GRAFFY :—

    in succession the boundaries between the townlands of
    KEENAGHAN, DRUMINILLAR and GRAFFY
    (NORTHERN IRELAND) and the townlands of COMMONS,
    BELLANADOHY and COMMONS (IRISH FREE STATE),
    then a portion of the GRAFFY–RATHMORE townland
    boundary;

thence to point (62), where the line dividing parcels " R " (areas
1.708 and 1.519) from parcels " S " (areas .815 and 1.579) as shown
on Sheets 21 and 24 meets the Eastern bank of the MILL RACE :—

    the line dividing parcels " R " (NORTHERN IRELAND) of the
    townland of RATHMORE from parcels " S " (IRISH FREE
    STATE) of the same townland, as shown on Sheets 20, 21
    and 24 ;

thence to point (63), the point of junction of parcel " V " (area .257),
parcel " W " (area 1.890) and parcel " X " (area 3.750) :—

    a straight line as shown on Sheet 21 ;

thence to point (64), the Easternmost corner of parcel " Y "
(area .190), which is situated immediately East of the lock gates :—

    a straight line as shown on Sheet 21 ;

thence to point (65), formed by the intersection of the dividing line between parcel " G " (area 2.217) and parcel " H " (area .919) with the bank of the RIVER ERNE :—

in succession the Eastern limit of parcel " Y," then the Northern limit of parcel " Y," then a straight line across the RIVER ERNE, then the Southern limit of parcel " A " (area .833), Sheet 23, then the Eastern limit of parcel " B " (area .307), then the Eastern limit of parcel " C " (area .436) as far as the road leading to BELLEEK ISLAND, then a straight line across this road, then the Eastern limit of parcel " D " (area .272), then the South-Eastern limit of parcel " E " (area 1.216), then the Eastern limit of parcel " F " (area .948) on Sheet 21, then the Northern limit of parcel " G " (area 2.217), the whole of these parcels " A " to " G " of the townlands of CLOGHOGE and CORRY, exclusive of the bridge to BELLEEK ISLAND being included in the IRISH FREE STATE ;

thence to point (66), (about 200 yards East of the point of junction of the townlands of ROSSCOR, CARRAN BEG and MAGHERAMENAGH), where the Northern end of the dividing line of parcels " T " and " U " meets the South bank of the RIVER ERNE, as shown on Sheet 25 :—

Eastward, a line following the South bank of the RIVER ERNE, provided always that where the bank of the RIVER ERNE is referred to in this description, the same shall be held to be the Northern limit of the parcels shown on Sheets 21, 24 and 25, to be immediately contiguous to the South bank of the River between the last two described points, and the line shall be so drawn as to include in the IRISH FREE STATE the whole of the area of the said parcels as shown on the said Sheets and to include in NORTHERN IRELAND the whole of the River up to the Northern limit of the said parcels ;

thence Southward to point (67), (immediately West of the point of junction of the townlands of ROSSCOR, CARRIGOLAGH and CALLAGHEEN), where the Southern end of the line dividing parcels " T " from parcels " U " meets the ROSSCOR–CALLAGHEEN townland boundary, as shown on Sheet 20 :—

the line dividing parcels " T " (NORTHERN IRELAND) of the townland of ROSSCOR from parcels " U " (IRISH FREE STATE) of the same townland and leaving in the IRISH FREE STATE the road lying between the said parcels, all as shown on Sheet 20 ;

thence to point (68), (about 450 yards West of CALLAGHEEN HOUSE), where the Northern end of the line dividing parcels " V " from parcels " W " meets the CARRIGOLAGH–CALLAGHEEN townland boundary, as shown on Sheet 20 ;

a portion of the ROSSCOR–CALLAGHEEN townland boundary, then a portion of the CARRIGOLAGH–CALLAGHEEN townland boundary ;

thence to point (69), the point of junction of the townlands of
ARDGART, ARDEES UPPER and CALLAGHEEN :—

> the line dividing the parcels " V " (NORTHERN IRELAND) of
> the townland of CALLAGHEEN from the parcels " W "
> (IRISH FREE STATE) of the same townland as shown on
> Sheet 20 ;

thence to point (70), the South-Eastern corner of the townland of
ARDGART :—

> a portion of the ARDGART–ARDEES UPPER townland
> boundary ;

thence to point (71), the point of junction of the townlands of
TIRANAGHER MORE, BARR OF DRUMBADMEEN and
ARDEES UPPER :—

> a straight line, as shown on Sheet 20 ;

thence to point (72), in LOUGH NAVAR, the South-Easterly point
of the townland of BARR OF DRUMBADMEEN :—

> in succession the boundaries between the townlands of
> TIRANAGHER MORE, BARR OF BOLUSTY MORE,
> LOUGHACHORK (NORTHERN IRELAND) and the town-
> land of BARR OF DRUMBADMEEN (IRISH FREE
> STATE), then a portion of the BRAADE–BARR OF
> DRUMBADMEEN townland boundary ;

thence due South (for a distance of about 380 yards) to point (73),
on the BRAADE–GLENNASHEEVAR townland boundary :—

> a straight line, as shown on Sheet 27 ;

thence to point (74), the point of junction of the townlands of
DERRYVAHON, CONAGHER, GLENNASHEEVAR :—

> a portion of the BRAADE–GLENNASHEEVAR townland
> boundary, then the DERRYVAHON (NORTHERN
> IRELAND)–GLENNASHEEVAR (IRISH FREE STATE)
> townland boundary ;

thence to point (75), (about 450 yards North of DOAGH SCHOOL),
where the Northern end of the dividing line of parcels " X " and
" Y " meets the STRATONAGHER–CONAGHER townland
boundary, as shown on Sheet 27 :—

> a straight line, as shown on Sheet 27 ;

thence to point (76), (about 150 yards East of DOAGH SCHOOL),
where the Southern end of the dividing line of parcels " X " and
" Y " meets the road :—

> the line dividing parcels " X " (NORTHERN IRELAND) of
> the townland of STRATONAGHER from parcels " Y "
> (IRISH FREE STATE) of the same townland, as shown
> on Sheet 27 ;

thence to point (77), (about 700 yards to the West of WHITE-
HOUSE CAVE), where the Northern end of the dividing line of

parcels "A" and "B" meets the ROSSINURE MORE–ROSSINURE BEG townland boundary, as shown on Sheet 27 :—
    a straight line;

thence to point (78), (about 300 yards South of Trigonometrical Point 1100), where the Southern end of the dividing line of parcels "A" and "B" meets the KNOCK BEG–ROSSINURE MORE townland boundary, as shown on Sheet 27 :—
    the line dividing parcels "A" (NORTHERN IRELAND) of the townland of ROSSINURE MORE from parcels "B" (IRISH FREE STATE) of the same townland, as shown on Sheet 27 ;

thence to point (79), (about 700 yards North of B.M. 971.5 CARRICKAPHREGHAUN), where the Northern end of the dividing line of parcels "C" and "D" meets the TULLYNASRAHAN–LEGLAND townland boundary, as shown on Sheet 28 :—
    a straight line, as shown on Sheets 27 and 28 ;

thence to point (80), (about 220 yards East of B.M. 895.4), the confluent of the two streams shown on Sheet 28 :—
    a straight line;

thence to point (81), where the MULLYCOVET–CREENAGHO townland boundary cuts the South side of the road running along the Northern boundary of the townland of CREENAGHO :—
    a portion of the GLENKEEL–TULLYNASRAHAN townland boundary, then in succession the boundaries between the townlands of GLENKEEL, REYFAD, LEGNAGAY BEG, AGHANAGLACK, DOOLETTER, CAVANTREEDUFF, CLEGGAN, MULLYCOVET (NORTHERN IRELAND), and the townlands of TULLINWONNY, CARRIGAN (E. D. GLENKEEL), CLOGHERBOG, SLAPRAGH, BALLINTEMPO, KILLYCREEN WEST, KILLYCREEN EAST, ORA BEG, MULLYLUSTY, GARDEN HILL, DRUMMAN, CROTTAN, KEELAGHO (IRISH FREE STATE), then a portion of the MULLYCOVET–CREENAGHO townland boundary;

thence to point (82), (immediately South of the North-West corner of the CREENAGHO townland), where the CREENAGHO–DRUMMAN townland boundary cuts the Southern side of the road on the North side of CREENAGHO townland, as shown on Sheet 29 :—
    the South side of the last-mentioned road;

thence to point (83), (on the shore of LOUGH MACNEAN LOWER), forming the Southern end of the DRUMAWILLIN–DORNOGAGH townland boundary, as shown on Sheet 30 :—
    a portion of the CREENAGHO–DRUMMAN townland boundary, then the CREENAGHO–CARRONTREE MALL townland

boundary, then the CREENAGHO–KILTYFELAN townland boundary, then in succession the boundaries between the townlands of DRUMAWILLIN (NORTHERN IRELAND) and KILTYFELAN and DORNOGAGH (IRISH FREE STATE);

thence to point (84), formed by the intersection of a line drawn between point (83) and the Northern end of the boundary between the townlands of GORTATOLE (E.D. KILLESHER) and, ROSSAA, and a line drawn between Trigonometrical Point 213 on CUSHRUSH ISLAND and the point in LOUGH MACNEAN LOWER, where the FERMANAGH–CAVAN boundary turns from a North and South to an East and West direction :—
a straight line, as shown on Sheets 29 and 30;

thence to point (85), the last-mentioned point on the FERMANAGH–CAVAN County boundary :—
a straight line, as shown on Sheet 29;

thence to point (86), formed by the intersection of the AGHATIROURKE–BEIHY townland boundary with the FERMANAGH–CAVAN County boundary :—
a portion of the last-mentioned County boundary;

thence to point (87), (about 100 yards South of the point of junction of the townlands of DRUMROOSK, CLONTURKLE and GLASDRUMMAN), where the Northern end of the line dividing parcels "E" from parcels "F" meets the CLONTURKLE–GLASDRUMMAN townland boundary, as shown on Sheet 35 :—
in succession the boundaries between the townlands of AGHATIROURKE, LEGNAVEA, DOOHATTY GLEBE, COOLINFIN GLEBE, TIRAVREE GLEBE, KILGARROW GLEBE, CORAGH (CRAWFORD), DRUMBINNIS, SHANRAA, TIROOGAN, LISMONAGHAN, KINAWLEY, STRAGOWNA, DRUMROOSK (NORTHERN IRELAND) and the townlands of BEIHY, GORTALUGHANY (E.D. DERRYLESTER), LARGANACARRAN, TEESNAGHTAN, CULLATAGH, KEENAGHAN, DRUMHARRIFF (E.D. KINAWLEY), CORNASKEOGE, SHANVALLY, MOHER (E.D. KINAWLEY), CORRAMEEN, CORRARDREEN, GLASDRUMMAN (IRISH FREE STATE), then a portion of the CLONTURKLE–GLASDRUMMAN townland boundary;

thence to point (88), (about 840 yards West of Trigonometrical Point 710 in the townland of BARR OR RAMOAN), where the Southern end of the dividing line of parcels "E" and "F" meets the CARN–CLONTURKLE townland boundary, as shown on Sheet 35 :—
the line dividing parcel "E" (NORTHERN IRELAND) of the townland of CLONTURKLE from parcels "F" (IRISH FREE STATE) of the same townland, as shown on Sheet 35;

thence to point (89), where the canalised portion of the water-course which forms the DRUMANY MORE–DERRINTONY townland boundary leaves the said boundary going Southward, as shown on Sheet 35 :—

a portion of the CARN–CLONTURKLE townland boundary, then in succession the boundaries between the townlands of CARN, BARR OR RAMOAN, MULLYNAHERB, MULLYNEENY, DERRYGURDRY, CALLOWHILL, CARROWCARLAN, MILLTOWN, CULLEEN, DRUM-LUGHT, DRUMANY MORE (NORTHERN IRELAND), and the townlands of MOLLY, TONYNELT, DRUMDONEY, GORTEEN, CAMLETTER, GREAGHMORE, DERRYLEA, CORRATRASNA, DRUMSHIMUCK (IRISH FREE STATE), then a portion of the DRUMANY MORE–DERRINTONY townland boundary;

thence to point (90), the point of junction of the townlands of DERRYLANEY, MULLAN and DERRYHOOLY :—

the canalised portion of the last-mentioned watercourse (thus including in NORTHERN IRELAND the townlands of DERRYART and DERRYLANEY, exclusive of parcels "H," and including in the IRISH FREE STATE the townlands of DERRINTONY and GARVARY, exclusive of the parcels "G"), then the DERRYLANEY–DERRY-HOOLY townland boundary;

thence to point (91), the point of junction of the CORRY–DERRYHOOLY townland boundary with the FERMANAGH–CAVAN County boundary :—

in succession the boundaries between the townlands of MULLAN and CORRY (NORTHERN IRELAND), and the townland of DERRYHOOLY (IRISH FREE STATE);

thence to point (92), the point of junction of the CORRY–DRUMETTAGH townland boundary with the FERMANAGH–CAVAN County boundary :—

a portion of the last-mentioned County boundary;

thence to point (93), (about 250 yards to the North of the point of junction of the townlands of KILLYCLOGHAN, AGHALANE and KILLYCRAMPH), where the Western end of the dividing line of parcels "I" and "K" meets the KILLYCLOGHAN–KILLYCRAMPH townland boundary, as shown on Sheet 37 :—

in succession the boundaries between the townlands of CORRY and KILLYMACKAN (NORTHERN IRELAND) and the townlands of DRUMETTAGH, TONYMORE (E.D. CRUM) and KILLYCRAMPH (IRISH FREE STATE), then a portion of the KILLYCLOGHAN–KILLYCRAMPH townland boundary;

thence to point (94), (about 500 yards measured in a straight line North-East of point (93)), where the Northern end of the dividing

[13849A]

line of parcels "I" and "K" meets the KILLYNICK–KILLYCLOGHAN townland boundary, as shown on Sheet 37 :—
the line including in NORTHERN IRELAND the parcels "I" of the townland of KILLYCLOGHAN as well as the portions of road lying between the parcels "I" and the parcels "K," and including in the IRISH FREE STATE the parcels "K" of the same townland, all as shown on Sheet 37 ;

thence to point (95), where the KILLYNICK–KILLYCLOGHAN townland boundary meets the FERMANAGH–CAVAN County boundary :—
a portion of the last-mentioned townland boundary ;

thence North-Eastward to point (96) in UPPER LOUGH ERNE (East of MULLYNACOAGH WOOD), where the FERMANAGH–CAVAN County boundary turns from a North-Easterly to a South-Easterly direction, as shown on Sheet 37 :—
a portion of the last-mentioned County boundary ;

thence to point (97) in LOUGH ERNE (about 100 yards North of GAD ISLAND), where the Barony boundary shown on Sheet 38 turns through an angle of about 80° :
a straight line ;

thence to point (98) (about 70 yards South-West of the Southern end of the DOOHAT–AGHADRUM townland boundary), where the Union and R.D. boundary forms a right angle :—
Eastward for about 1,200 yards the Barony boundary South of CRUM OLD CASTLE, then Northward the last-mentioned Union and R.D. boundary ;

thence to point (99), formed by the intersection of the median line drawn through the channel indicated on Sheet 38 with a line drawn due West from the median point of the mouth of the stream which forms the ASKILL–DERRYKENY townland boundary :—
the median line of the channel lying North and East of the townlands of GUBB, KILLYNUBBER and KILLYRAW ;

thence to point (100), the median point of the mouth of the last-mentioned stream :—
a straight line ;

thence to point (101), the South-Western end of the ASKILL–DERRYKENY townland boundary :—
the median line of the last-mentioned stream ;

thence to point (102), (about 300 yards South-West of the point of junction of the townlands of CULLION, SANDHOLES and LANDBROCK), where the Northern end of the dividing line of parcels "L" and "M" meets the CULLION–LANDBROCK townland boundary, as shown on Sheet 39 :—
in succession the boundaries between the townlands of ASKILL and CULLION (NORTHERN IRELAND) and the townland

of DERRYKENY (IRISH FREE STATE), then a portion
of the CULLION–LANDBROCK townland boundary;

thence South-eastward to point (103), the point of junction of the
townlands of FARM, STARRAGHAN and LANDBROCK :—
  the line dividing parcels "L" (NORTHERN IRELAND) of
  the townland of LANDBROCK from parcels "M" (IRISH
  FREE STATE) of the same townland, then a straight line
  to the point indicated, all as on Sheet 39;

thence in a general Easterly direction to point (104), formed by
the junction of the LEITRIM–CAVANAGH townland boundary
with the FERMANAGH–MONAGHAN County boundary :—
  in succession the boundaries between the townlands of FARM,
  MULLAGHGARE, CROCKERAHOAS, PARSON'S GREEN
  GLEBE, KILLYCARNAN, LEITRIM (NORTHERN
  IRELAND) and the townlands of STARRAGHAN,
  KILGARROW, CLONNAROO, KILTOBER, CLONKEE,
  CAVANAGH (IRISH FREE STATE);

thence to point (105), (about 10 yards East of the intersection of
the East side of the road running North and South over LEITRIM
BRIDGE with the FERMANAGH–MONAGHAN County boundary),
where this boundary turns Northward :—
  a portion of the last-mentioned County boundary;

thence (for a distance of about 120 yards), to point (106)
formed by the intersection of parcels "N" and "O" with the
CORYAGHAN–CLONOULA townland boundary, as shown on
Sheet 41 :—
  the line dividing parcel "N" (NORTHERN IRELAND) of the
  townland of CLONOULA from parcel "O" (IRISH FREE
  STATE) of the same townland, as shown on Sheet 41;

thence to point (107), the point of junction of the COLEMAN–
DERRYBEG townland boundary with the FERMANAGH–
MONAGHAN County boundary :—
  a portion of the CORVAGHAN–CLONOULA townland boundary,
  then in succession the boundaries between the townlands of
  CORVAGHAN and COLEMAN (NORTHERN IRELAND)
  and the townlands of CLONKEELAN and DERRYBEG
  (IRISH FREE STATE);

thence to point (108), (about 80 yards North-West of the North
corner of the townland of DERRYGOAS), where the Southern end
of the dividing line of parcels "P" and "Q" meets the
FERMANAGH–MONAGHAN County boundary, as shown on
Sheet 39 :—
  a portion of the last-mentioned County boundary;

thence Northward to point (109), (about 130 yards South-West of
the point of junction of the townlands of CLONMAULIN,

[13849A]

CLONTIVRIN and CLONAGUN), where the Northern end of the dividing line of parcels " P " and " Q " meets the CLONAGUN–CLONMAULIN townland boundary, as shown on Sheet 39 :—

the line including in Northern Ireland the parcels " P " of the townland of CLONAGUN and including in the IRISH FREE STATE the parcels " Q " of the same townland, as well as the road lying between the said parcels " P " and " Q," all as shown on Sheet 39 ;

thence to point (110), where the LISLEA, MULLYNAVANNOGE townland boundary meets the FERMANAGH–MONAGHAN County boundary :—

a portion of the CLONAGUN–CLONMAULIN townland boundary, then in succession the boundaries between the townlands of KILTURK SOUTH, CLONUMPHRY, BELLMOUNT, CONCKERA, LISLEA (NORTHERN IRELAND), and the townlands of CLONMAULIN, CLONTIVRIN and MULLYNAVANNOGE (IRISH FREE STATE) ;

thence to point (111), (in DUMMY'S LOUGH), the Southern point of junction of the DRUMRAINY–KILROOSKY townland boundary with the FERMANAGH–MONAGHAN County boundary :—

a portion of the last-mentioned County boundary ;

thence to point (112), (in SUMMERHILL LOUGH), the northern point of junction of the townland boundary of DRUMRAINY and KILROOSKY with the FERMANAGH–MONAGHAN County boundary :—

the DRUMRAINY–KILROOSKY townland boundary ;

thence North-Eastward (for a distance of about 400 yards) to point (113), where the line dividing parcels " R " from parcels " S " meets the FERMANAGH–MONAGHAN County boundary, as shown on Sheet 42 :—

a portion of the last-mentioned County boundary ;

thence Westward (for a distance of about 360 yards) to point (114), where the Western end of the dividing line of parcels " R " and " S " meets the East side of the road which runs South-West from LACKY BRIDGE, as shown on Sheet 43 :—

the line dividing parcels " R " (NORTHERN IRELAND) of the townland of DRUMARD from parcels " S " (IRISH FREE STATE) of the same townland, as shown on Sheets 42 and 43 ;

thence Northward to point (115), on the East side of the last-mentioned road and at a distance of 180-ft. measured in a straight line from point (114) :—

the East side of the last-mentioned road ;

thence across the last-mentioned road to point (116), on the FERMANAGH–MONAGHAN County boundary where this boundary turns from a North-Easterly to a Westerly direction :—
> a line across the road leading South-West from LACKY BRIDGE and following the shortest distance between the two last-mentioned points consistent with leaving the junction of the carriageway, leading to SUMMERHILL HOUSE, with the last-mentioned road entirely in NORTHERN IRELAND, as shown on Sheet 43 ;

thence to point (117), (about 130 yards North-East of LACKY BRIDGE), where the Southern end of the dividing line of parcels " T " and " U " meets the FERMANAGH–MONAGHAN County boundary, as shown on Sheet 39 :—
> a portion of the last-mentioned County boundary ;

thence Northward to point (118), where the Northern end of the dividing line of parcels " T " and " U " strikes the Southern side of the road separating the townlands of SHANNOCK and SHANNOCK GREEN :—
> the line dividing parcels " T " (NORTHERN IRELAND) of the townland of SHANNOCK GREEN from parcels " U " (IRISH FREE STATE) of the same townland, as shown on Sheet 39 ;

thence to point (119), where the TATTYMORRIS–SHANNOCK GREEN townland boundary cuts the South side of the road running South-east of SHANNOCK townland :—
> the Southern side of the last-mentioned road ;

thence to point (120), the point of junction of the TATTYMORRIS–SHANNOCK GREEN townland boundary with the FERMANAGH–MONAGHAN County boundary :—
> a portion of the last-mentioned townland boundary ;

thence to point (121), the point of junction of the ANNACHULLION GLEBE–MULLANAHINCH townland boundary with the FERMANAGH–MONAGHAN County boundary :—
> a portion of the last-mentioned County boundary ;

thence to point (122), (about 120 yards North of the point of junction of the townlands of ANNAGOLGAN, LISKILLY and MULLAGHGLASS), where the Southern end of the dividing line of parcels " V " and " W " meets the ANNAGOLGAN–LISKILLY townland boundary, as shown on Sheet 44 :—
> in succession the boundaries between the townlands of ANNACHULLION GLEBE, ANNAHONE, INVER, LISNAVOE, MULLAGHGLASS (NORTHERN IRELAND) and the townlands of MULLANAHINCH, COOLNALONG, LISKILLY (IRISH FREE STATE), then a portion of the ANNAGOLGAN–LISKILLY townland boundary ;

thence in a general North-Westerly direction to point (123), (at a distance of about 470 yards measured in a straight line from point (122)), situated on the prolongation of the line dividing arable area " X " from arable area " Y," as represented on Sheet 44, and at a distance of 300-ft. from the point where this dividing line meets the South side of the road bordering these two last-mentioned areas on the South-West :—

the line dividing parcels " V " (NORTHERN IRELAND) of the townland of ANNAGOLGAN from parcels " W " (IRISH FREE STATE) of the same townland, then a straight line about 140 yards long, as shown on Sheet 44 ;

thence Westward to point (124), (about 340 yards North of the point of junction of the townlands of MULLAGHGLASS, DRESTERNAN and ANNAGOLGAN), where the Western end of the line dividing parcels " A " from parcels " B " meets the DRESTERNAN–ANNAGOLGAN townland boundary :—

a straight line 300-ft. long, then a line dividing parcels " A " (NORTHERN IRELAND) of the townland of ANNAGOLGAN from parcels " B " (IRISH FREE STATE) of the same townland, all as shown on Sheet 44 ;

thence to point (125), (about 420 yards West of the point of junction of the townlands of CARNMORE, ERVEY and BUNNABLANEY-BANE), where the Southern end of the dividing line of parcels " C " and " D " meets the ERVEY–CARNMORE townland boundary, as shown on Sheet 45 :—

a portion of the DRESTERNAN–ANNAGOLGAN townland boundary, then in succession the boundaries between the townlands of DRESTERNAN, CORTRASNA, DRUMBRUGHAS, DERRYNACLOY, CORTAHER, FOLLUM LITTLE, CROCKAWADDY GLEBE, GREAGHACHOLEA, ERRASALLAGH, CARNMORE (NORTHERN IRELAND), and the townlands of FEAGH, DRUMERWINTER, TONYDRUMMALLARD, GREAGHA-CAPPLE, FOLLUM BIG, BUNNABLANEYBANE (IRISH FREE STATE), then a portion of the CARNMORE–ERVEY townland boundary ;

thence to point (126), (about 800 yards North-West of the point of junction of the townlands of BUNMICHAEL, ESHEKERIN and BUNLOUGHER), where the Northern end of the line dividing parcels " C " and " D " meets the ESHEKERIN–BUNLOUGHER townland boundary, as shown on Sheet 46 :—

the line dividing parcels " C " (NORTHERN IRELAND) of the townlands of ERVEY and ESHEKERIN from parcels " D " (IRISH FREE STATE) of the same townland, as shown on Sheets 45 and 46 ;

thence (for a distance of about 150 yards) to point (127), where the BUNLOUGHER–ESHEKERIN townland boundary turns from a Northerly to a North-Westerly direction, as shown on Sheet 46 :—

a portion of the last-mentioned townland boundary ;

thence to point (128), (about 200 yards South-West of B.M. 793.7, The LODGE), where the ESHNADARRAGH–BUNLOUGHER townland boundary forms a salient towards the South, as shown on Sheet 46 :—

    the line dividing parcels " E " (NORTHERN IRELAND) of the townland of BUNLOUGHER from parcels " F " (IRISH FREE STATE) of the same townland, as shown on Sheet 46 ;

thence Northward (for a distance of about 200 yards) to point (129), where the Western end of the line dividing parcels " G " from parcels " H " meets the BUNLOUGHER–ESHNADARRAGH townland boundary, as shown on Sheet 46 :—

    a portion of the last-mentioned townland boundary ;

thence to point (130), (about 400 yards North-East of Trigonometrical Point 862–ESHNADARRAGH), where the Northern end of the line dividing parcels " G " and " H " meets the ESHNADARRAGH–CORRALEEK townland boundary, as shown on Sheet 46 :—

    the line dividing parcels " G " (NORTHERN IRELAND) of the townland of ESHNADARRAGH from the parcels " H " (IRISH FREE STATE) of the same townland, as shown on Sheet 46 ;

thence to point (131), the point of junction of the MULLAGHFAD–CORRAGUNT townland boundary with the FERMANAGH–MONAGHAN County boundary :—

    a portion of the ESHNADARRAGH–CORRALEEK townland boundary, then in succession the boundaries between the townland of MULLAGHFAD (NORTHERN IRELAND) and the townlands of CORRALEEK and CORRAGUNT (IRISH FREE STATE) ;

thence to point (132), the point of junction of the Counties of FERMANAGH, TYRONE and MONAGHAN :—

    a portion of the FERMANAGH–MONAGHAN County boundary ;

thence to point (133), the point of junction of the TYRONE–ARMAGH–MONAGHAN Counties :—

    the TYRONE–MONAGHAN County boundary ;

thence to point (134), where the boundary between the townland of TULLYBRICK ETRA or BONDVILLE, and the townland of TULLYBRICK (HAMILTON) meets the ARMAGH–MONAGHAN County boundary :—

    a portion of the last-mentioned County boundary ;

thence to point (135), (about 100 yards South-East of the point of junction of the townlands of ISLAND SPA, MULLAN and TULLYGLUSH (NEVIN), where the Northern end of the dividing line of parcels " I " and " K " meets the MULLAN–

TULLYGLUSH (NEVIN) townland boundary, as shown on Sheet 55 :—

In succession the boundaries between the townlands of TULLYBRICK ETRA or BONDVILLE and COOLKILL (NORTHERN IRELAND) and the townland of TULLY-BRICK (HAMILTON) (IRISH FREE STATE), then the COOLKILL–TULLYGLUSH (NEVIN) townland boundary, then the ISLAND SPA–TULLYGLUSH (NEVIN) townland boundary, then a portion of the MULLAN–TULLYGLUSH (NEVIN) townland boundary ;

thence to point (136), (about 280 yards South-West of the point of junction of the townlands of MULLAN, KILTUBBRID and TULLYGLUSH (NEVIN), where the prolongation of the boundary between the Eastern two of the parcels " I " and " K " meets the KILTUBBRID–TULLYGLUSH (NEVIN) townland boundary, as shown on Sheet 55 :—

the line dividing parcels " I " (NORTHERN IRELAND) of the townland of TULLYGLUSH (NEVIN) from parcels " K " (IRISH FREE STATE) of the same townland, then a straight line about 80 yards long, all as shown on Sheet 55 ;

thence to point (137), (about 300 yards North-West of GUN BRIDGE), where the Northern end of the dividing line of parcels " L " and " M " meets the LISSLANLY–HANSLOUGH townland boundary, as shown on Sheet 55 :—

a portion of the KILTUBBRID–TULLYGLUSH (NEVIN) townland boundary, then in succession the boundaries between the townlands of KILTUBBRID and DOOGARY (NORTHERN IRELAND) and the townlands of CAVAN-DOOGAN and MULLANARY (IRISH FREE STATE), then the DOOGARY–HANSLOUGH townland boundary, then a portion of the LISSLANLY–HANSLOUGH townland boundary ;

thence to point (138), (about 400 yards East of HANSLOUGH HOUSE) where the Southern end of the dividing line of parcels " L " and " M " meets the CREEVEKEERAN–HANSLOUGH townland boundary, as shown on Sheet 55 :—

the line including in NORTHERN IRELAND the parcels " L " of the townland of HANSLOUGH and in the IRISH FREE STATE parcels " M " of the same townland, as well as that portion of the road running South-Westward from GUN BRIDGE, which lies between the parcels " L " and " M," all as shown on Sheet 55 ;

thence to point (139), the point of junction of the townlands of HANSLOUGH–CREEVEKEERAN and CARRICKLANE :—

a portion of the CREEVEKEERAN–HANSLOUGH townland boundary ;

thence to point (140), (about 250 yards South-West of the point of junction of the townlands of DRUMHILLARY, RAWES and CARRICKLANE), where the Southern end of the dividing line of parcels " N " and " O " meets the RAWES–CARRICKLANE townland boundary, as shown on Sheet 56 :—

a straight line about 100 yards long through HANSLOUGH LOUGH, then the line dividing parcels " N " (NORTHERN IRELAND) of the townland of CARRICKLANE from parcels " O " (IRISH FREE STATE) of the same townland, as shown on Sheets 55 and 56;

thence South-Westward (for a distance of about 300 yards in a straight line) to point (141), where the Northern end of the dividing line of parcels " P " and " Q " meets the RAWES–CARRICKLANE townland boundary, as shown on Sheet 56 :—

a portion of the last-mentioned townland boundary;

thence to point (142), (about 360 yards West of the point of junction of the townlands of LISLEA, TIVNACREE and RAWES), where the Southern end of the line dividing parcels " P " and " Q " meets the TIVNACREE–RAWES townland boundary, as shown on Sheet 56 :—

the line dividing parcels " P " (NORTHERN IRELAND) of the townland of RAWES from parcels " Q " (IRISH FREE STATE) of the same townland, as shown on Sheet 56;

then South-Westward (for a distance of about 300 yards measured in a straight line) to point (143), where the Northern end of the line dividing parcels " R " from parcels " S " meets the TIVNACREE–RAWES townland boundary, as shown on Sheet 56 :—

a portion of the last-mentioned townland boundary;

thence to point (144), the point of junction of the townlands of CARGALISGORRAN, DRUMMELAND and TIVNACREE :—

the line dividing parcels " R " (NORTHERN IRELAND) of the townlands of TIVNACREE and CARGALISGORRAN from parcels " S " (IRISH FREE STATE) of the townland of TIVNACREE, as shown on Sheet 56;

thence South-Eastward (for a distance of about 650 yards measured in a straight line) to point (145), where the Northern end of the line dividing parcels " T " and " U " meets the South side of the road running along the Northern boundary of the townland of CROSSNAMOYLE :—

a portion of the CARGALISGORRAN–DRUMMELAND townland boundary, then along the North side of the road coincident with this boundary, then across the road, all as shown on Sheet 56;

thence to point (146), the point of junction of the townlands of CROSSNAMOYLE, CARRICKABOLIE and MULLYARD :—

the line dividing parcels "T" (NORTHERN IRELAND) of the townland of CROSSNAMOYLE from parcels "U" (IRISH FREE STATE) of the same townland, and including in the IRISH FREE STATE for a distance in each case of about 150 yards the roads running North-Eastward from B.M. 562.8, all as shown on Sheet 56;

thence Southward (for a distance of about 160 yards measured in a straight line) to point (147), where the Northern end of the line dividing parcels "V" and "W" meets the CROSSNAMOYLE-CARRICKABOLIE townland boundary, as shown on Sheet 56 :—
a portion of the last-mentioned townland boundary;

thence to point (148), (about 560 yards West of the point of junction of the townlands of KILCAM, DRUMNAHAVIL, BRACKLY), where the Southern end of the dividing line of parcels "V" and "W" meets the CARRICKABOLIE-DRUMNAHAVIL townland boundary, as shown on Sheet 56 :—
the line including in NORTHERN IRELAND the parcels "V" of the townland of CARRICKABOLIE, as well as the road lying between parcels "V" and "W," and including in the IRISH FREE STATE the parcels "W" of the same townland, all as shown on Sheet 56;

thence Westward (for a distance of about 50 yards) to point (149), where the Northern end of the dividing line of parcels "X" and "Y" meets the DRUMNAHAVIL-CARRICKABOLIE townland boundary :—
a portion of the last-mentioned townland boundary;

thence to point (150), (about 260 yards South-West of the point where the CROSSNENAGH-DRUMNAHAVIL townland boundary cuts the West side of the MIDDLETOWN-CASTLEBLANEY road, as shown on Sheet 57 :—
the line dividing the parcels "X" (NORTHERN IRELAND) of the townland of DRUMNAHAVIL from parcels "Y" (IRISH FREE STATE) of the same townland;

thence Southward (for a distance of about 420 yards measured in a straight line) to point (151), where the Northern end of the dividing line of parcels "A" and "B" meets the CROSSNENAGH-DRUMNAHAVIL townland boundary, as shown on Sheet 57 :—
a portion of the last-mentioned townland boundary;

thence Southward (for a distance of about 350 yards measured in a straight line) to point (152), where the Southern end of the dividing line of parcels "A" and "B" meets the CROSSNENAGH-DRUMHERNEY townland boundary, as shown on Sheet 57 :—
the line dividing parcels "A" (NORTHERN IRELAND) of the townland of CROSSNENAGH from the parcels "B" (IRISH FREE STATE) of the same townland as shown on Sheet 57;

thence to point (153), the point of junction of the CARRICKDUFF–DRUMHERNEY townland boundary with the ARMAGH–MONAGHAN County boundary :—
> a portion of the CROSSNENAGH–DRUMHERNEY townland boundary, then the CARRICKDUFF–DRUMHERNEY townland boundary;

thence to point (154), (about 130 yards East of the point of junction of the TULLYNAGROW–LURGANBOY townland boundary with the ARMAGH–MONAGHAN County boundary), where the Northern end of the dividing line of parcels "C" and "D" meets the ARMAGH–MONAGHAN County boundary, as shown on Sheet 58 :—
> a portion of the last-mentioned County boundary;

thence to point (155), (about 120 yards North of the point of junction of the townlands of DROLLAGH, TULLYCAGHNY and TULLINEARLY), where the Southern end of the dividing line of parcels "C" and "D" meets the DROLLAGH–TULLINEARLY townland boundary, as shown on Sheet 59 :—
> the line dividing parcels "C" (NORTHERN IRELAND) of the townlands of LURGANBOY and TULLINEARLY from parcels "D" (IRISH FREE STATE) of the same townlands, as shown on Sheets 58 and 59;

thence to point (156), (about 280 yards South-East of the point of junction of the townlands of FORMIL (E.D. CHURCH HILL), DRUMAGELVIN and LISDONNY), where the Western end of the line dividing parcels "E" and "F" meets the DRUMAGELVIN–LISDONNY townland boundary :—
> a portion of the DROLLAGH–TULLINEARLY townland boundary, then in succession the boundaries between the townlands of TULLYCAGHNY, LISEENAN, FORMIL (E.D. CHURCH HILL) (NORTHERN IRELAND), and the townlands of TULLYNAMALRA, ORAM, LISDONNY (IRISH FREE STATE), then a portion of the DRUMA-GELVIN–LISDONNY townland boundary;

thence to point (157), (about 410 yards to the West of the point of junction of the townlands of DRUMACRIB, DRUMAGELVIN and FORMIL), where the Eastern end of the dividing line of parcels "E" and "F" meets the FORMIL–DRUMAGELVIN townland boundary, as shown on Sheet 59 :—
> the line dividing parcels "E" (NORTHERN IRELAND) of the townland of DRUMAGELVIN from parcels "F" (IRISH FREE STATE) of the same townland, as shown on Sheet 59;

thence Eastward (for a distance of about 410 yards, measured in a straight line), to point (158), the point of junction of the townlands of DRUMACRIB, DRUMAGELVIN and FORMIL :—
> a portion of the boundary between the townlands of FORMIL and DRUMAGELVIN;

thence to point (159), (about 10 yards North of the point of junction of the townlands of TULLYVANUS, TULLINTLISNY and TULLYCOORA), where the Eastern end of the line dividing parcels "G" and "H" meets the TULLINTLISNY–TULLYCOORA townland boundary :—

> Northward (for a distance of about 30 yards), a portion of the FORMIL–DRUMACRIB townland boundary, then the line dividing parcels "G" (NORTHERN IRELAND) of the townlands of DRUMACRIB and TULLYCOORA from parcels "H" (IRISH FREE STATE) of the same townlands;

thence to point (160), (about 700 yards West of TRAYNORS BRIDGE), where the Northern end of the dividing line of parcels "I" and "K" meets the TULLYVANUS–TULLINTLISNY townland boundary :—

> a portion of the TULLYVANUS–TULLYCOORA townland boundary, then a portion of the TULLYVANUS–TULLINTLISNY townland boundary;

thence to point (161), (about 610 yards South-West of TRAYNORS BRIDGE), where the Southern end of the dividing line of parcels "I" and "K" meets the ARMAGH–MONAGHAN County boundary :—

> the line dividing parcels "I" (NORTHERN IRELAND) of the townland of TULLINTLISNY from parcels "K" (IRISH FREE STATE) of the same townland, as shown on Sheet 59;

thence Northward to point (162), the point of junction of the ALTNAMACKAN–BALLYNAREA townland boundary with the ARMAGH–MONAGHAN County boundary, as shown on Sheet 60 :—

> a portion of the last-mentioned County boundary;

thence to point (163), (South-West of HARRY MOUNT) where the TULLYVALLAN–CULLYHANNA BIG townland boundary going Eastward leaves the TULLYVALLAN RIVER, as shown on Sheet 61 :—

> the boundary between the townland of ALTNAMACKAN and TULLYVALLAN (NORTHERN IRELAND) and the townlands of BALLYNAREA, and SKERRIFF (TICHBURN) and SKERRIFF (TRUEMAN), (IRISH FREE STATE), then the TULLYVALLAN–SKERRIFF (TRUEMAN) townland boundary, then a portion of the TULLYVALLAN–CULLYHANNA BIG townland boundary;

thence North-Eastward to point (164), where the TULLYVALLAN RIVER reaches the Northern boundary of the TULLYVALLAN (HAMILTON) WEST townland :—

> the median line of the channel of the last-mentioned river, as shown on Sheets 60 and 61;

thence to point (165), (situated at a distance of about 550 yards East of point (164)), where the Western end of the dividing line of parcels "L" and "M" meets the TULLYVALLAN–TULLY-VALLAN (HAMILTON) WEST townland boundary, as shown on Sheet 61 :—
   a portion of the last-mentioned townland boundary;

thence Eastward (for a distance of about 530 yards) to point (166), where the Eastern end of the line dividing parcels "L" and "M" meets the TULLYVALLAN–TULLYVALLAN (HAMILTON) EAST townland boundary, as shown on Sheet 60 :—
   the line dividing parcels "L" (NORTHERN IRELAND) of the townland of TULLYVALLAN from parcels "M" (IRISH FREE STATE) of the same townland, as shown on Sheets 60 and 61 ;

thence Northward (for a distance of about 170 yards) to point (167), where the Western end of the line dividing parcels "O" from parcels "P" meets the TULLYVALLAN–TULLYVALLAN (HAMILTON) EAST townland boundary, as shown on Sheet 60 :—
   a portion of the last-mentioned townland boundary;

thence to point (168), where the TULLYVALLAN (HAMILTON) EAST–CAMLY (BALL) townland boundary intersects the East side of the road about 250 yards South of LAKE VIEW COTTAGE :—
   the line dividing parcels "O" (NORTHERN IRELAND) of the townland of TULLYVALLAN (HAMILTON) EAST from parcels "P" (IRISH FREE STATE) of the same townland, then across the road, all as shown on Sheets 60 and 62 ;

thence Eastward to point (169), (about 400 yards South-West of BLACK BRIDGE), where the Western end of the dividing line of parcels "Q" and "R" meets the CAMLY (MACULLAGH)–DORSY (MACDONALD) or CARRICKROVADDY townland boundary :—
   a portion of the TULLYVALLAN (HAMILTON) EAST-CAMLY (BALL) townland boundary, then the CAMLY (MACULLAGH)–CAMLY (BALL) townland boundary, then a portion of the CAMLY (MACULLAGH)–DORSY (MAC-DONALD) townland boundary;

thence to point (170), (about 350 yards Northward from the Northernmost point of the townland of DORSY (HEARTY)), where the Eastern end of the dividing line of parcels "Q" and "R" meets the TULLYOGALLAGHAN–DORSY (MACDONALD) or CARRICKROVADDY townland boundary, as shown on Sheet 62 :—
   the line dividing parcels "Q" (NORTHERN IRELAND) of the townland of DORSY (MACDONALD) or CARRICK-ROVADDY from parcels "R" (IRISH FREE STATE) of the same townland, and including in the IRISH FREE STATE the intervening road junction, all as shown on Sheet 62 ;

thence to point (171), the point of junction of the townlands of TULLYOGALLAGHAN, DORSY (HEARTY) and DORSY (MAC-DONALD) :—

    a portion of the TULLYOGALLAGHAN–DORSY (MAC-DONALD) or CARRICKROVADDY townland boundary;

thence to point (172), (about 180 yards South-West of the point of junction of the townlands of CARROWMANNAN–AUGHANDUFF and TULLYOGALLAGHAN), where the Eastern end of the dividing line of parcels " S " and " T " meets the TULLYOGALLAGHAN–AUGHANDUFF townland boundary, as shown on Sheet 62 :—

    the line dividing parcels " S " (NORTHERN IRELAND) of the townland of TULLYOGALLAGHAN from parcels " T " (IRISH FREE STATE) of the same townland;

thence Eastward (for a distance of about 620 yards) to point (173), where the Western end of the line dividing parcels " U " from parcels " V " meets the CARROWMANNAN–CARRICKNAGAVNA townland boundary, as shown on Sheet 62 :—

    a portion of the TULLYOGALLAGHAN–AUGHANDUFF townland boundary, then the CARROWMANNAN–AUGHANDUFF townland boundary, then a portion of the CARROWMANNAN – CARRICKNAGAVNA townland boundary;

thence Eastward (for a distance of about 630 yards) to point (174), where the Eastern end of the dividing line of parcels " U " and " V " meets the CARROWMANNAN–CARNACALLY townland boundary, as shown on Sheet 62 :—

    the line dividing parcels " U " (NORTHERN IRELAND) of the townland of CARROWMANNAN from parcels " V " (IRISH FREE STATE) of the same townland, as shown on Sheet 62;

thence North-Eastward to point (175), (about 1,050 yards South of the Southernmost point of DEER PARK), where the Western end of the dividing line of parcels " W " and " X " meets the BELLEEK–TULLYAH townland boundary, as shown on Sheet 62 :—

    a portion of the CARROWMANNAN–CARNACALLY townland boundary, then in succession the boundaries between the townland of BELLEEK (NORTHERN IRELAND) and the townlands of CARNACALLY and ANNACLOGHMULLIN (IRISH FREE STATE), then a portion of the BELLEEK–TULLYAH townland boundary;

thence South-Eastward (for a distance of about 200 yards) to point (176), where the Eastern end of the dividing line of parcels " W " and " X " meets the TULLYAH–DRUMILLY townland boundary, as shown on Sheet 62 :—

    the line dividing parcel " W " (NORTHERN IRELAND) of the townland of TULLYAH from parcels " X " (IRISH FREE STATE) of the same townland, as shown on Sheet 62;

thence North-Eastward to point (177), (about 1,110 yards South of the Southernmost point of DEER PARK), where the Western end of the line dividing parcels " Y " and " Z " meets the TULLYAH-DRUMILLY townland boundary, as shown on Sheet 62 :—
    a portion of the last-mentioned townland boundary ;

thence Eastward (for a distance of about 230 yards, measured in a straight line) to point (178), where the Eastern end of the dividing line of parcels " Y " and " Z " meets the DRUMILLY–DUBURREN townland boundary, as shown on Sheet 62 :—
    the line dividing parcels " Y " (NORTHERN IRELAND) of the townland of DRUMILLY from parcels " Z " (IRISH FREE STATE) of the same townland ;

thence to point (179), (about 700 yards South-East of MOUNTAIN HOUSE INN), where the Western end of the line dividing parcels " A " and " B " meets the DRUMILLY–DUBURREN townland boundary :—
    a portion of the last-mentioned townland boundary ;

thence Eastward to point (180), (about 350 yards South-West of MOUNTAIN LODGE), where the Eastern end of the dividing line of parcels " A " and " B " meets the DUBURREN–STURGAN townland boundary :—
    the line dividing parcels " A " (NORTHERN IRELAND) of the townland of DUBURREN from parcels " B " (IRISH FREE STATE) of the same townland ;

thence Southward to point (181), (about 300 yards South-West of Trigonometrical Point 1159 (BALLINTEMPLE), where the Western end of the line dividing parcels " C " and " D " meets the BALLINTEMPLE–BALLARD townland boundary, as shown on Sheet 64 :—
    a portion of the STURGAN–DUBURREN townland boundary, then the AGHMAKANE–DUBURREN townland boundary, then the boundary between the townland of AGHMAKANE (NORTHERN IRELAND) and the townlands of LISLEA and BALLARD (IRISH FREE STATE), then a portion of the BALLINTEMPLE–BALLARD townland boundary ;

thence Eastward to point (182), (about 550 yards South-West of the Road Crossing West of BALLINLISS SCHOOLS), where the Eastern end of the dividing line of parcels " C " and " D " meets the BALLINTEMPLE–CLONLUM townland boundary, as shown on Sheet 64 :—
    the line dividing parcels " C " (NORTHERN IRELAND) of the townland of BALLINTEMPLE from parcels " D " (IRISH FREE STATE) of the same townland, as shown on Sheet 64 ;

thence Eastward to point (183), (about 250 yards South-East of the point of junction of the townlands of BALLINLISS, SEAFIN and

CLONLUM), where the Western end of the dividing line of parcels "E" and "F" meets the SEAFIN–CLONLUM townland boundary :—

> a portion of the BALLINTEMPLE–CLONLUM townland boundary, then the BALLINLISS–CLONLUM townland boundary, then a portion of the SEAFIN–CLONLUM townland boundary;

thence Eastward (for a distance of about 970 yards) to point (184), where the Eastern end of the dividing line of parcels "E" and "F" meets the SEAFIN–AGHAYALLOGE townland boundary, as shown on Sheet 64 :—

> the line dividing parcels "E" (NORTHERN IRELAND) of the townland of SEAFIN from parcels "F" (IRISH FREE STATE) of the same townland;

thence to point (185), (about 300 yards South of the South-West corner of HEATH HALL DEMESNE), where the Western end of the line dividing parcels "G" and "H" meets the East side of the road running Northward to the South-West corner of HEATH HALL DEMESNE :—

> a portion of the SEAFIN–AGHAYALLOGE townland boundary, then a portion of the BALLYMACDERMOT–AGHA-YALLOGE townland boundary, then Southward along the East side of the last-mentioned road;

thence Eastward to point (186), (about 300 yards South of the South-East corner of HEATH HALL DEMESNE), where the Eastern end of the line dividing parcels "G" and "H" meets the NEWTOWN–BALLYMACDERMOT townland boundary, as shown on Sheet 64 :—

> the line dividing parcels "G" (NORTHERN IRELAND) of the townland of BALLYMACDERMOT from parcels "H" (IRISH FREE STATE) of the same townland;

thence Southward (for a distance of about 250 yards) to point (187), where the Western end of the dividing line of parcels "I" and "K" meets the NEWTOWN–BALLYMACDERMOT townland boundary, as shown on Sheet 64 :—

> a portion of the last-mentioned townland boundary;

thence Eastward to point (188), (about 830 yards South-East of the South-East corner of HEATH HALL DEMESNE), where the Eastern end of the dividing line of parcels "I" and "K" meets the ELLISHOLDING–NEWTOWN townland boundary, as shown on Sheet 64 :—

> the line dividing parcels "I" (NORTHERN IRELAND) of the townland of NEWTOWN from parcels "K" (IRISH FREE STATE) of the same townland;

thence Northward to point (189), (about 300 yards South-East of the point of junction of the townlands of CARRIVEMACLONE, ELLIS-HOLDING and NEWTOWN), where the Western end of the dividing line of parcels "L" and "M" meets the ELLIS-HOLDING–NEWTOWN townland boundary, as shown on Sheet 64 :—

a portion of the last-mentioned townland boundary;

thence Eastward to point (190), (about 1,100 yards South of the B.M. on DUBLIN ROAD BRIDGE), where the Eastern end of the dividing line of parcels "L" and "M" meets the ELLIS-HOLDING–CLOGHOGE townland boundary, as shown on Sheet 64 :—

the line dividing parcels "L" (NORTHERN IRELAND) of the townland of ELLISHOLDING from parcels "M" (IRISH FREE STATE) of the same townland;

thence Southward, (for a distance of about 50 yards), to point (191), where the Western end of parcels "O" and "P" meets the GLOGHOGE–ELLISHOLDING townland boundary, as shown on Sheet 64 :—

a portion of the last-mentioned townland boundary;

thence Eastward, (for a distance of about 210 yards), to point (192), where a prolongation of the line dividing parcels "O" and "P" meets the Eastern boundary of the GREAT NORTHERN RAILWAY, as shown on Sheet 64 :—

the line dividing parcels "O" (NORTHERN IRELAND) of the townland of CLOGHOGE from parcels "P" of the same townland, then a line crossing the railway, all as shown on Sheet 64;

thence Southward to point (193), (about 330 yards North of ROGER'S BRIDGE), where the Western end of the line dividing parcels "Q" and "R" meets the Eastern boundary of the GREAT NORTHERN RAILWAY, as shown on Sheet 64 :—

a portion of the Eastern boundary of the last-mentioned railway;

thence North-Eastward to point (194), (about 300 yards South-West of the bridge over the railway South of FATHOM PARK), where the line dividing parcels "Q" and "R" meets the line dividing parcels "S" and "T," as shown on Sheet 64 :—

the line dividing parcels "Q" (NORTHERN IRELAND) of the townland of FATHOM LOWER from parcels "R" (IRISH FREE STATE) of the same townland, and including in NORTHERN IRELAND the portion of the road leading South-Westward from the above-mentioned bridge, which lies between the parcels "Q" and "R," all as shown on Sheet 64;

thence Southward to point (195), (about 1,030 yards South-East of Trigonometrical Point 819, FATHOM MOUNTAIN), where the Southern end of the line dividing parcels "S" and "T" meets

[13849A]

the road running parallel to the NEWRY CANAL at about 300 yards from its bank, as shown on Sheet 64 :—

> the line dividing parcels "S" (NORTHERN IRELAND) of the townland of FATHOM LOWER and FATHOM UPPER from parcels "T" (IRISH FREE STATE) of the same townlands ;

thence Southward to point (196), (about 600 yards South-West of the North gate of the Lock leading into NEWRY CANAL), where an arc of a circle drawn at a radius of 1,150 feet from Trigonometrical Point 801 (FATHOM UPPER) cuts the East side of the last-mentioned road :—

> the East side of the last-mentioned road ;

thence to point (197), on the Eastern boundary of the DUNDALK, NEWRY and GREENORE BRANCH RAILWAY, and at a distance measured in a straight line of 1,050 feet from B. M. 26.0 by NEWRY CANAL lock gate :—

> a straight line ;

thence to point (198), where the High Water mark intersects the ARMAGH–LOUTH County boundary :—

> the last-mentioned High Water Mark, as shown on Sheet 64 ;

thence to point (199), the point of junction of the Counties of ARMAGH, LOUTH and DOWN :—

> a portion of the ARMAGH–LOUTH County boundary ;

thence to point (200), the point of junction of the Counties of DOWN and LOUTH with CARLINGFORD LOUGH, as shown on Sheet 66 :—

> the DOWN–LOUTH County boundary ;

thence to point (201), 6.8 cables 114° true from HAULBOWLINE ROCKS LIGHT (that is with HAULBOWLINE ROCKS LIGHT in line with GREENORE LIGHT) :—

> the median line of the deep water channel from NEWRY RIVER to the entrance of CARLINGFORD LOUGH, as shown on Sheet 67 ;

thence to point (202), the intersection of an arc 3 nautical miles in radius drawn from the Low Water Mark South-Eastward of CRANFIELD POINT with that of a similar arc drawn from the Low Water Mark South-Eastward of BALLAGAN POINT :—

> a straight line, as shown on Sheet 68.

RULES OF INTERPRETATION.

1. The following Rules of Interpretation shall apply to the foregoing Description, unless the context otherwise requires.

2. Where reference is made to the points of the compass, the direction given is to be taken as approximate only, unless the word due (in the case of cardinal points) or true (in the case of degrees) is added.

The words, "Northward," "Southward," "Eastward," "Westward," "Northeastward" and the like, shall respectively be understood to denote only the general direction in which the Boundary Line proceeds from the point last described, and not that such Boundary shall continue to proceed throughout in the same direction to the point next described.

3. Where the Boundary Line is described as following the boundaries of minor territorial units (Counties, Baronies or Townlands), the boundaries of these minor territorial units shall be held to be the boundaries represented on the Ordnance Survey Sheets and Plans specified in Schedule 1. In those cases where the same area of ground is shown on Ordnance Survey Sheets and Plans, specified in the said Schedule, prepared to different scales, the boundaries of the territorial units shall be deemed to be the boundaries represented on the Ordnance Survey Plans prepared to the largest of these scales.

4. In those cases where the boundaries between two adjoining territorial units, forming a portion of the Line, are constituted by a watercourse, the Line shall follow in the future the same rules as to alteration with the watercourse as, according to existing law and usage, are followed by the existing boundaries between the said territorial units.

5. In those cases where the Boundary Line is constituted by a watercourse, which is not already used as a boundary between existing territorial units, the Boundary shall, save as otherwise provided, follow the median line of the principal channel of the said watercourse, as the median line is shown on the Ordnance Survey Sheets and Plans referred to in the Schedule. In the event of changes having taken place, or in the event of changes taking place in the future, in the bed of the watercourse, the Boundary Line shall continue to follow the median line if the change be natural and gradual, but shall remain in its original place if the change be sudden, such as that caused by the cutting off of a meander by flood or by artificial means.

6. Whenever a line is said to be drawn from, to, or through an object, such line shall, in the absence of any direction to the contrary, be understood to be drawn from, to or through the centre of such object, as nearly as the centre thereof can be ascertained.

7. In those cases where the Boundary Line is described as following the side of a road, the road shall, save as otherwise provided, be deemed to include in addition to the carriageway, any footpath or ditch appurtenant to the road.

8. The term "fence" includes walls, hedges, banks, palings, or any structure erected for the purpose of dividing two parcels of land, whether of the same or different ownership, or for the purpose of separating a road from adjoining land.

9. Schedule I specifies and identifies by numbers the Admiralty Charts and the Ordnance Survey Sheets and Plans which are utilised as North of Ireland Boundary Sheets and referred to in this Description as "Sheets" and identified by the Schedule numbers.

SCHEDULE I.

Referred to in para. 9 of the Rules of Interpretation,
attached to the Description of the Boundary Line.

N.I.B.S. Sheet No.	Description of Chart, Sheet or Plan.	Admiralty or Ordnance No.	Date.	—
1	Admiralty Chart Lough Foyle ..	2499	New Edition, 1912	
2	Ordnance Sheets 6" Donegal	39 and 39A	2nd Ed., 1904 ..	Reprinted 1925.
3	Do.	38	Do. 1905 ..	Do. 1925.
4	Do. ..	47	Do. 1905 ..	Do. 1925.
5	Do.	55	Do. 1905 ..	Do. 1925.
6	Do.	54	Do. 1905 ..	Do. 1921.
7	Do.	62	Do. 1906 ..	Do. 1920.
8	Do. . ..	63	Do. 1906 ..	Do. 1920.
9	Do.	71 and 71A	Do. 1906 .	Do. 1925.
10	Do.	79	Do. 1906 ..	Do. 1921.
11	Do. ..	88	Do. 1906 ..	Do. 1920.
12	Do.	87 and 87A	Do. 1906 .	Do. 1924.
13	Tyrone	15 and 15A	Edition 1907 ..	Revised 1904–5.
14	Do. ..	23	Do. 1907 ..	Reprinted 1919.
15	Donegal	102 and 102A	2nd Ed , 1906 ..	Do. 1919.
16	Do.	101	Do. 1906 ..	Do. 1919.
17	Do. ..	105	Do. 1906 ..	Do. 1920.
18	Fermanagh . ..	4	Edition 1908 ..	Do. 1918.
19	Do. ..	3	Do. 1908 ..	Do. 1920.
20	Do.	8	Do. 1908 ..	Do. 1921.
21	Ordnance Plan 25" Fermanagh	VIII–5	Surveyed 1905 ..	Do. 1916.
22	Ordnance Sheet 6" Donegal	108	2nd Ed., 1907 ..	Do. 1922.
23	Ordnance Plans 25" .. Donegal ..	CVIII–13, 14	Surveyed 1905 ..	Do. 1925.
24	Fermanagh	VIII–6	Do. 1905 ..	Published 1907.
25	Do.	VIII–7	Surveyed 1905 .	Do. 1907.
26	Ordnance Sheets 6" Fermanagh . ..	9	Edition 1908 ..	Reprinted 1919.
27	Do.	14	Do. 1908 ..	Do. 1918.
28	Do.	20	Do. 1908 ..	Do. 1917.
29	Do	25	Do. 1908 ..	Do. 1918.
30	Do.	26	Do. 1908 ..	Do. 1920.
31	Do.	31	Do. 1908 ..	Do. 1920.
32	Do.	37 and 37A	Do. 1909 ..	Do. 1920.
33	Do.	32	Do. 1909 ..	Do. 1920.
34	Do.	33	Do. 1909 ..	Do. 1920.
35	Do.	38	Do. 1909 ..	Do. 1919.
6	Do.	41	Do. 1909 ..	Do. 1921.
37	Do.	42	Do. 1909 .	Do. 1920.
38	Do.	39	Do. 1909 ..	Do. 1920.
39	Do.	40	Do. 1909 ..	Do. 1921.
40	Do.	43	Do. 1909 ..	Do. 1919.
41	Monaghan	16	Do. 1910 ..	Do. 1925.
42	Do.	11	Do. 1909 ..	Do. 1923.
43	Ordnance Plan 25" Monaghan	XI–3 and 4	Surveyed 1907 ...	Published 1909.
44	Ordnance Sheets 6" Fermanagh	36	Edition 1909 ..	Reprinted 1919.
45	Do.	35	Do. 1909 ..	Do. 1921.
46	Do.	29	Do. 1908 ..	Do. 1920.
47	Do.	30 and 30A	Do. 1909 ..	Do. 1920.
48	Tyrone	68	Do. 1909 .	Do. 1919.
49	Do.	65 and 69	Do. 1909 ..	Do. 1917.

N.I.B.S. Sheet No.	Description of Chart, Sheet or Plan.	Admiralty or Ordnance No.	Date.	—
50	Tyrone	59	Edition 1909 ..	Reprinted 1920.
51	Do.	60	Do. 1910 ..	Do. 1924.
52	Do.	66	Do. 1910 ..	Revised 1907.
53	Do.	67, 70 and 71	Do. 1910 ..	Do. 1907.
54	Armagh	11	Do. 1908 ..	Reprinted 1921.
55	Do.	15	Do. 1908 ..	Do. 1920.
56	Do.	19	Do. 1908 ..	Do. 1920.
57	Do.	23	Do. 1908 ..	Do. 1921.
58	Monaghan	15	Do. 1910 ..	Do. 1920.
59	Do.	20	Do. 1910 ..	Do. 1925.
60	Armagh	24	Do. 1908 ..	Do. 1921.
61	Do.	27	Do. 1909 ..	Do. 1920.
62	Do.	25	Do. 1909 ..	Do. 1921.
63	Do.	28	Do. 1909 ..	Do. 1920.
64	Do.	29	Do. 1909 ..	Do. 1921.
65	Co. Down	51	2nd Ed., 1905 ..	Do. 1921.
66	Do. ..	54	Do. 1904 ..	Do. 1920
	Admiralty Chart			
67	Lough Carlingford ..	2800	Pubd. 1874 ..	Corrected 1925.
68	Skerries Island to Lough Carlingford	44	Do. 1883	Do. 1925.

AND WE DO FURTHER hereby declare that the Boundary Line so determined by us and described and shown as aforesaid is for the purposes of the Government of Ireland Act 1920 and of the said Articles of Agreement for a Treaty the Boundary of Northern Ireland.

Executed and published in triplicate by us in London this day of , A.D. 1925.

(Signed) ....,

Chairman.

............................,

Commissioner.

(Signed) ....,

Secretary.